Graduate Mathematics

for Business, Economics and Finance

Eivind Eriksen

Graduate Mathematics

for Business, Economics and Finance

CAPPELEN DAMM AKADEMISK

© CAPPELEN DAMM AS, 2021

ISBN 978-82-02-57639-4

1. edition, 1. printing 2021

This publication and its content are protected by and subject to the provisions of the Norwegian CopyrightAct. No part of this publication may be reproduced or disseminated further in any form or by any means whatsoever without the express prior written permission of the publisher, Cappelen Damm AS, in accordance with the law, or according to the terms of an agreement with the Norwegian reprographic rights organization, Kopinor.

Cover design: Kristin Berg Johnsen
Typesetting: Vegard Brekke / Gamma grafisk AS
Printing and binding: Livonia Print SIA, Latvia

The author of this book has received financial support from Norsk faglitterær forfatter- og oversetterforening

www.cda.no
e-mail: akademisk@cappelendamm.no

Preface

This book is intended as a textbook for a mathematics course at the graduate level, and it is well suited for master students in business, economics and finance. I wrote this book while I was teaching the course GRA6035 Mathematics at BI Norwegian Business School, a core course taught in the first semester of the Master of Science programs in Business, Finance and Applied Economics.

Mathematics is the language used to analyse problems in economics and finance, and the mathematical requirements for graduate studies go far beyond material taught in undergraduate courses of mathematics in business schools. This textbook covers the relevant mathematical models, theories, and methods.

I have tried to make this book as self-contained as possible, and assumptions of previous knowledge in mathematics have been kept at a minimum. Although most students at this level have completed an elementary mathematics course and know calculus reasonably well, it is my experience that most to a lesser extent have studied linear algebra, and many are not fluent in basic integration techniques. I have therefore chosen to treat linear algebra starting from scratch, and to include a review of important integration techniques in an appendix.

The presentation is centered around many worked examples, written out in full, to make it easier for the reader to understand the mathematical theory and grasp the abstract notions introduced in this book. My intention has been to develop a deep conceptual understanding and fluency with the computational techniques, and I often use a geometric point of view. In cases where a proof can facilitate understanding of the theory, I have included reasonably complete but non-formal proofs. These are clearly marked, and can be skipped in a first reading. I have also included a number of relevant applications.

Preface

The main topics covered are i) linear algebra, matrices and vectors, ii) optimization in several real variables, iii) differential and difference equations, and systems of differential and difference equations. An appendix provides a short introduction to complex numbers and trigonometric functions. In addition to the many worked examples, each chapter comes with many problems and exercises.

The cover shows a *hypocycloid with four cusps*, an algebraic curve described by a point on a smaller circle as it rolls around a larger circle, when the radius of the smaller circle is 1/4 of the radius of the larger circle.

Oslo, June 1st 2021

Eivind Eriksen

Contents

Preface 5

1 Linear systems and Gaussian elimination 11
1.1 Linear system 11
1.2 Geometry of linear systems 13
1.3 Solving linear systems 16
1.4 Gaussian elimination 18
1.5 Free variables and parameterizations 26
1.6 Rank of a matrix 27
Problems 31

2 Vectors and vector spaces 35
2.1 Introduction to vectors 35
2.2 Vectors and coordinates 37
2.3 Parametric description of lines and planes 41
2.4 Inner products 43
2.5 Projections and the Cauchy-Schwarz inequality 45
2.6 Span and linear independence 47
2.7 Vector spaces 51
Problems 57

3 Matrices and determinants 61
3.1 Matrices and matrix algebra 61
3.2 Determinants 69
3.3 Determinants and Gaussian elimination 71
3.4 Minors, rank and linear systems 75
Problems 80

4 Eigenvectors and eigenvalues 83
- 4.1 Introduction to eigenvectors and eigenvalues 83
- 4.2 The characteristic polynomial 87
- 4.3 Diagonalization 92
- 4.4 Nonnegative matrices and Markov chain 96
- 4.5 Spectral theory of symmetric matrices 101
- 4.6 Definiteness of quadratic forms 106
- Problems 117

5 Unconstrained optimization 121
- 5.1 Functions in several variables 121
- 5.2 Partial derivatives 124
- 5.3 The Hessian matrix 128
- 5.4 Unconstrained optimization 129
- 5.5 Convex and concave functions 133
- 5.6 Quadratic functions 136
- 5.7 Envelope theorem 138
- Problems 143

6 Constrained optimization 145
- 6.1 Constrained optimization problem 145
- 6.2 The Extreme Value Theorem 146
- 6.3 Introduction to the method of Lagrange multipliers 148
- 6.4 Lagrange problems 150
- 6.5 Kuhn-Tucker problems 157
- 6.6 Envelope theorem 165
- 6.7 Minimum variance portfolios 169
- Problems 175

7 Differential equations 177
- 7.1 Introduction to differential equations 177
- 7.2 Modeling change using differential equations 179
- 7.3 First order differential equations 182
- 7.4 Separable differential equations 183
- 7.5 Linear first order differential equation 185
- 7.6 Superposition principle 188

7.7	Exact differential equations.	191
7.8	Equilibrium states and stability	194
7.9	Second order differential equations	197
7.10	Linear second order differential equations	198
Problems.		204

8	Difference equations.	207
8.1	Introduction to difference equations	207
8.2	Linear first order difference equations	209
8.3	Equilibrium states and stability	210
8.4	Linear second order difference equations	211
Problems.		215

9	Systems of differential and difference equations	217
9.1	Introduction to systems of differential equations	217
9.2	Linear systems of differential equations	219
9.3	Equilibrium states of systems of differential equations	223
9.4	Linear systems of difference equations	225
9.5	Equilibrium states of systems of difference equations	228
Problems.		229

A	Complex numbers and trigonometric functions	231
A.1	Complex numbers	231
A.2	Conjugation and complex roots	235
A.3	Polar coordinates and de Moivre's formula	238
A.4	Angles in radians	241
A.5	Trigonometric functions.	242
Problems.		246

B	Indefinite integrals	247
B.1	The indefinite integral.	247
B.2	Computing indefinite integrals	248
B.3	Integration by parts	250
B.4	Integration by substitution	251
B.5	Integration of rational functions	252
Problems.		257

CHAPTER 1

Linear systems and Gaussian elimination

1.1 Linear systems

A *linear system*, or a linear system of equations, consists of several linear equations in a given set of v//tgcqzariables. This is an example of a linear system:

$$2x + 3y - z = 7$$
$$-x + y + 2z = 2$$
$$5x - 4y - 5z = 1$$

It is called a 3×3 linear system, since it consists of 3 linear equations in the 3 variables x, y, z.

A *solution* of a linear system is a value for each of the variables such that all equations in the system are satisfied. For example, $x = 3$, $y = 1$, and $z = 2$ is a solution of the linear system above since these values satisfy all three equations. We write this solution as $(x, y, z) = (3, 1, 2)$.

Often, the linear systems that we face in applications have many equations and many variables. In this chapter, we consider linear systems of any size, and describe how to solve these linear systems in a systematic way using *Gaussian elimination*.

When we have many variables, we will name them in a systematic way such as $x_1, x_2, \ldots, x_n$. We define a *linear equation* in these variables to be an equation that can be written in the form

$$a_1 x_1 + a_2 x_2 + \ldots + a_n x_n = b$$

for given numbers $a_1, a_2, \ldots, a_n$ and b. It may happen that we need to rearrange a linear equation to get it in the general form given above. Any equation that cannot be written in this form, such as $x_1^2 + 2x_2 = 3$ or $x_1 x_2 = 4$, is not linear. Another (equivalent) way to define a linear equation is to say that a linear equation is a polynomial equation of degree at most one. In fact, a linear equation has degree one in all cases except when $a_1 = a_2 = \ldots = a_n = 0$, which we call the degenerate case.

An $m \times n$ linear system in the variables $x_1, x_2, \ldots, x_n$ is a system of m linear equations in these n variables. It is called *quadratic* if $m = n$, or the number of equations equals the number of variables. Any $m \times n$ linear system can be written in the general form

$$\begin{aligned} a_{11}x_1 + a_{12}x_2 + \ldots + a_{1n}x_n &= b_1 \\ a_{21}x_1 + a_{22}x_2 + \ldots + a_{2n}x_n &= b_2 \\ \vdots \qquad \vdots \qquad \qquad \vdots \qquad &\;\; \vdots \\ a_{m1}x_1 + a_{m2}x_2 + \ldots + a_{mn}x_n &= b_m \end{aligned} \qquad (1.1)$$

where $a_{11}, \ldots, a_{mn}, b_1, \ldots, b_m$ are given numbers. Note the use of indices: We write a_{ij} for the coefficient of x_j in equation i, and b_i for the constant term in equation i.

A *solution* of the $m \times n$ linear system (1.1) is an n-tuple $(s_1, s_2, \ldots, s_n)$ of numbers such that the substitutions $x_1 = s_1, x_2 = s_2, \ldots, x_n = s_n$ satisfy all m equations in the system simultaneously. We write $(x_1, x_2, \ldots, x_n) = (s_1, s_2, \ldots, s_n)$ for this solution.

It is useful to use *matrices* to write the general $m \times n$ linear system (1.1). An $m \times n$ matrix is a rectangular array of numbers, with m rows and n columns, and we usually use capital letters to refer to matrices. We define the *coefficient matrix* of the linear system (1.1) to be the matrix

$$A = \begin{pmatrix} a_{11} & a_{12} & a_{13} & \ldots & a_{1n} \\ a_{21} & a_{22} & a_{23} & \ldots & a_{2n} \\ a_{31} & a_{32} & a_{33} & \ldots & a_{3n} \\ \vdots & \vdots & \vdots & \ddots & \vdots \\ a_{m1} & a_{m2} & a_{m3} & \ldots & a_{mn} \end{pmatrix}$$

It consists of the coefficients a_{ij} in the linear system. To describe the linear system completely, we must also account for the constants b_i.

We define the *augmented matrix* of the linear system (1.1) to be the matrix

$$(A|\mathbf{b}) = \left(\begin{array}{ccccc|c} a_{11} & a_{12} & a_{13} & \ldots & a_{1n} & b_1 \\ a_{21} & a_{22} & a_{23} & \ldots & a_{2n} & b_2 \\ a_{31} & a_{32} & a_{33} & \ldots & a_{3n} & b_3 \\ \vdots & \vdots & \vdots & \ddots & \vdots & \vdots \\ a_{m1} & a_{m2} & a_{m3} & \ldots & a_{mn} & b_m \end{array} \right)$$

It is called augmented since we have extended the coefficient matrix with an extra column (to augment means to increase). The vertical line is included to separate the coefficients a_{ij} from the constants b_i. We call the first n columns *variable columns* since they correspond to the variables $x_1, x_2, \ldots, x_n$ of the system.

As an example, we write down the coefficient matrix A and the augmented matrix $(A|\mathbf{b})$ of the 3×3 linear system mentioned in the start of this section:

$$\begin{array}{r} 2x + 3y - z = 7 \\ -x + y + 2z = 2 \\ 5x - 4y - 5z = 1 \end{array} \Rightarrow A = \begin{pmatrix} 2 & 3 & -1 \\ -1 & 1 & 2 \\ 5 & -4 & -5 \end{pmatrix}, (A|\mathbf{b}) = \begin{pmatrix} 2 & 3 & -1 & 7 \\ -1 & 1 & 2 & 2 \\ 5 & -4 & -5 & 1 \end{pmatrix}$$

When the augmented matrix $(A|\mathbf{b})$ is given, we can write down the corresponding linear system if we know the variable names x, y and z and their order.

1.2 Geometry of linear systems

We can think of a solution $(x_1, x_2, \ldots, x_n) = (s_1, s_2, \ldots, s_n)$ of an $m \times n$ linear system as a point in an n-dimensional coordinate system. The set of all solutions of a linear system is therefore a geometric figure in n-dimensional space $\mathbb{R}^n$, and it is very useful to study these geometric figures.

Let us first consider the case $n = 2$, corresponding to a system of linear equations in two variables. We shall call the variables x and y instead of x_1 and x_2 in this case. The general form of a single linear equation in x and y is $ax + by = c$ and this is the equation of a straight line in the two-dimensional coordinate system $\mathbb{R}^2$ (unless $a = b = 0$). In fact, if $b \neq 0$, then we can rewrite the equation as

$$ax + by = c \quad \Rightarrow \quad by = c - ax \quad \Rightarrow \quad y = \frac{c}{b} - \frac{a}{b} \cdot x$$

This is the equation of a straight line with slope $-a/b$ and y-intercept c/b. If $b = 0$, but $a \neq 0$, then the linear equation $ax + by = c$ becomes $ax = c$, or $x = c/a$. This is the equation of a vertical line.

For example, the linear equation $x - y = 2$ can be written $y = x - 2$, and it is therefore the equation of a straight line with slope 1 and y-intercept -2, and the linear equation $2x = -6$ can be written $x = -3$, and it is therefore the equation of a vertical line. These lines are shown in the figure below:

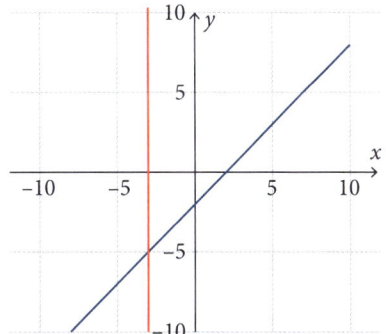

Let us consider an $m \times n$ linear system in $n = 2$ variables. Each of the m equations is the equation of a straight line in the two-dimensional coordinate system $\mathbb{R}^2$, and a solution of the linear system is a point (x, y) that lies on all m lines. In other words, the solutions of the linear system is the intersection of all m lines.

The possible solutions of $m \times 2$ linear systems are therefore given by how straight lines can meet in $\mathbb{R}^2$. By thinking geometrically about m lines, we can say something about the solutions of the system. In fact, if there are $m = 2$ equations, there are just three possibilities, shown in Figure 1.1 and Figure 1.2.

It is not difficult to see how this continues if $m > 2$. The first two lines meet in a point, in a line, or not at all. When we introduce additional lines, we get either the intersection of a point and a line, the intersection of two lines, or the intersection of an empty set with a line. This will give a point, a line, or an empty set.

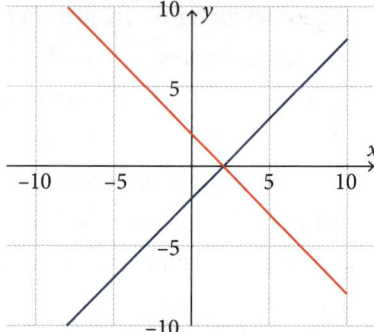

Figure 1.1 The intersection of two non-parallel lines is a point

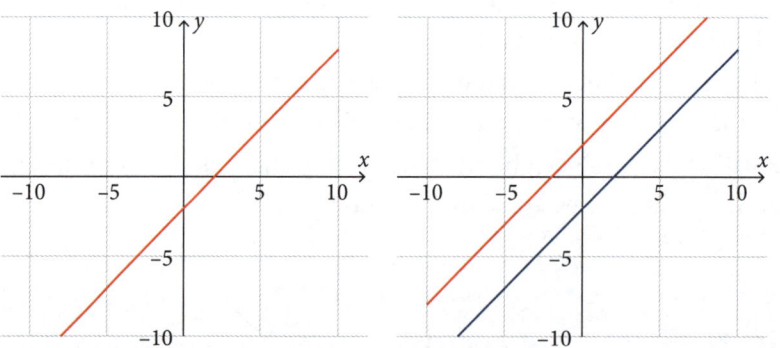

Figure 1.2 The intersection of two parallel lines is either a line or empty (no intersection points)

Proposition 1.1. A linear system in two variables has either one solution, infinitely many solutions, or no solutions.

Proof. This follows from the geometric arguments given above. In these arguments, we have not considered what happens in the degenerate case
$$0 \cdot x + 0 \cdot y = b$$
This is not the equation of a straight line. If $b \neq 0$, the equation has no solutions, and if $b = 0$, the equation has all of $\mathbb{R}^2$ as solutions. To include the degenerate case in the geometric argument, we must allow one (or more) of the m lines to be either an empty set or all of $\mathbb{R}^2$. This means that there could be infinitely many solutions in two different ways: The solutions could correspond to a straight line, which is one-dimensional, or all of the two-dimensional coordinate system $\mathbb{R}^2$, which is two-dimensional. □

Let us also consider the case $n = 3$, corresponding to a system of linear equations in three variables. The general form of a single linear equation in three variables is $ax + by + cz = d$, and this is the equation of a *plane* in the three-dimensional coordinate system $\mathbb{R}^3$ (unless $a = b = c = 0$). When $n \geq 4$, it is more difficult to imagine what the geometric picture looks like. In general, the solutions of a linear equation
$$a_1 x_1 + a_2 x_2 + \ldots + a_n x_n = b$$
in n variables form a geometric figure called a *hyperplane* in the n-dimensional space $\mathbb{R}^n$ (unless $a_1 = a_2 = \ldots = a_n = 0$). Lines and planes are special cases of hyperplanes.

Lemma 1.2. Let H be a hyperplane in $\mathbb{R}^n$. If P and Q are two different points in H, then the line through P and Q lies in H.

Proof. The hyperplane H is the solutions of an equation $a_1 x_1 + a_2 x_2 + \ldots + a_n x_n = b$ that is nondegenerate, and the points P and Q are given by $P = (p_1, p_2, \ldots, p_n)$ and $Q = (q_1, q_2, \ldots, q_n)$. Since P and Q lie in the hyperplane, their coordinates must satisfy the linear equation of H:
$$a_1 p_1 + a_2 p_2 + \ldots + a_n p_n = b$$
$$a_1 q_1 + a_2 q_2 + \ldots + a_n q_n = b$$
We will show that any point on the straight line l through P and Q also satisfies the linear equation of H. We use a parametric description of l; it can be obtained using vectors, and we will explain this in detail in Section 2.3: The points on l are the

points with coordinates $(tq_1 + (1-t)p_1, tq_2 + (1-t)p_2, \ldots, tq_n + (1-t)p_n)$ for any number t. To check that these points satisfy the equation of H, we compute the left-hand side (LHS) of the equation of the hyperplane:

$$\text{LHS} = a_1(tq_1 + (1-t)p_1) + a_2(tq_2 + (1-t)p_2) + \ldots + a_n(tq_n + (1-t)p_n)$$
$$= t(a_1q_1 + \ldots + a_nq_n) + (1-t)(a_1p_1 + \ldots + a_np_n)$$
$$= t(b) + (1-t)b = tb + b - tb = b$$

Since $\text{LHS} = b$ for any t, all points on the line l satisfy the equation of the hyperplane H, and this proves that l lies in the hyperplane. □

The property of the lemma is called the *linear property* and it holds for any hyperplane in $\mathbb{R}^n$. In particular, a line in $\mathbb{R}^2$ and a plane in $\mathbb{R}^3$ has the linear property. This means that any hyperplane is *linear* in the sense that it does not curve, and this is why the equations defining hyperplanes are called *linear* equations.

Theorem 1.3. Any linear system has either one solution, infinitely many solutions, or no solutions.

Proof. Assume that the $m \times n$ linear system has at least two solutions $P \neq Q$ in $\mathbb{R}^n$. This means that P and Q lie in all m hyperplanes defined by the m equations in the system, and the straight line through P and Q also lies on all m hyperplanes by the linear property. Since a line contains infinitely many points, any linear system with two different solutions must have infinitely many solutions. □

1.3 Solving linear systems

In this section, we look at different methods for solving linear systems. We start with *substitution methods*, which are usually the first methods we learn in school. These methods are useful for solving simple systems, such as the 2×2 linear system

$$x + 3y = 13$$
$$5x - 4y = 8$$

We start by solving the first equation for x, and get $x = 13 - 3y$. Next, we substitute x with the expression $13 - 3y$ in the second equation. This gives an equation in only one variable

$$5(13 - 3y) - 4y = 8 \quad \Rightarrow \quad 65 - 15y - 4y = 8$$

We solve this equation for y, and get $19y = 57$, or $y = 3$. Finally, we substitute $y = 3$ into the expression for x, and get $x = 13 - 3 \cdot 3 = 4$. The linear system therefore has one solution $(x, y) = (4, 3)$.

There are many different ways of using substitution to solve linear systems. For example, we could have started by solving the first equation for y instead of x, or started by solving the second equation for x or y.

We can also use *elimination methods* to solve linear systems. These methods work by eliminating some variables from certain equations in the linear system. We illustrate the process by solving the linear system

$$x + y = 4$$
$$x - y = 2$$

We first add the two equations, since this will cancel or *eliminate* the y-terms from the resulting equation. We obtain the equation $2x = 6$, which gives $x = 3$. Finally, we substitute $x = 3$ into the first equation $x + y = 4$, and get $3 + y = 4$, or $y = 1$. Hence this linear system has one solution $(x, y) = (3, 1)$.

There are many different ways of using elimination to solve linear systems. For example, we could have solved the system above by subtracting the two equations to eliminate x, instead of adding them to eliminate y.

Both substitution methods and elimination methods can be used to solve more complicated linear systems. To do this, we will have to find a systematic way to substitute or eliminate variables, and it turns out that it is more convenient to use elimination methods. One reason for this preference is that it is easy to express the steps in an elimination process using the augmented matrix of the linear system. For example, the steps in the example above could be written

$$\begin{pmatrix} 1 & 1 & | & 4 \\ 1 & -1 & | & 2 \end{pmatrix} \rightarrow \begin{pmatrix} 1 & 1 & | & 4 \\ 2 & 0 & | & 6 \end{pmatrix}$$

or

$$\begin{pmatrix} 1 & 1 & | & 4 \\ 1 & -1 & | & 2 \end{pmatrix} \rightarrow \begin{pmatrix} 1 & 1 & | & 4 \\ 0 & -2 & | & -2 \end{pmatrix}$$

The first matrix is the augmented matrix of the original linear system. The step we use is to keep the first row of the matrix, but replace the second row with the sum $R_2 + R_1$ or the difference $R_2 - R_1$ of the two rows R_1 and R_2.

Note that a row in the augmented matrix corresponds to an equation, so adding R_1 to R_2 or subtracting R_1 from R_2 means adding or subtracting the two equations. The matrices we obtain correspond to new linear systems, which are simpler than the original system since the presence of zeros means that one of the variables has been eliminated from the second equation. Still, the new linear systems have the same solutions as the original system since the operations that we have used do not change the solutions of the system.

1.4 Gaussian elimination

In this section, we shall explain *Gaussian elimination*, an elimination method for solving linear systems. It is *general*, as it can be used to solve any linear system. It is also *instructive*, in the sense that when we learn to solve relatively small linear systems by hand using Gaussian elimination we understand better how the process works in general. This will be useful later, when we use computers to solve large linear systems in applications. Under the hood, a computer is likely to use Gaussian elimination because it is a *fast* method for solving large linear systems.

The starting point for Gaussian elimination is an $m \times n$ linear system, and the main steps of the method are outlined in the box below. We have explained the first step. Next, we explain the remaining steps in detail.

Gaussian elimination
a) Write down the *augmented matrix* of the linear system.
b) Use *elementary row operations* on the matrix until it is in *echelon form*.
c) Write down the linear system that the echelon form corresponds to.
d) Solve the new linear system by *back substitution*.

Elementary row operations. The rows of the augmented matrix correspond to the equations of the linear system, and to perform row operations on the matrix corresponds to performing operations on the equations of the system. The following row operations are called *elementary row operations*:

a) to interchange (or switch) two rows of the matrix
b) to multiply a row (that is, each element in a row) by a nonzero number
c) to change a row by adding to it a multiple of another row

Note that these operations preserve the solutions of the linear system. This means that the linear system of the new matrix has the same solutions as the linear system of the original matrix. It is not difficult to see that when we interchange two equations, multiply one equation with a nonzero number, or add a multiple of one equation to another equation this will not change the solutions of the system.

For example, in the last example in the previous section, we eliminated y from the last equation by adding the two equations, and we could have eliminated x by subtracting them instead. When we write matrices instead of linear systems, these operations are both elementary row operations. We can write them in the following way if we want to show which elementary row operation we are using:

$$\begin{pmatrix} 1 & 1 & | & 4 \\ 1 & -1 & | & 2 \end{pmatrix} \begin{matrix} \cdot 1 \\ + \end{matrix} \rightarrow \begin{pmatrix} 1 & 1 & | & 4 \\ 2 & 0 & | & 6 \end{pmatrix}$$

or

$$\begin{pmatrix} 1 & 1 & | & 4 \\ 1 & -1 & | & 2 \end{pmatrix} \begin{matrix} \cdot -1 \\ + \end{matrix} \rightarrow \begin{pmatrix} 1 & 1 & | & 4 \\ 0 & -2 & | & -2 \end{pmatrix}$$

We take the first row, multiply it by 1 or by -1 and add the result to the second row. This means that the second row is replaced with the sum $R_2 + R_1$ or the difference $R_2 - R_1$ of the two rows R_1 and R_2.

Let us consider a different example with slightly more complicated computations. We write down the linear system, its augmented matrix, and an elementary row operation to simplify the augmented matrix:

$$\begin{matrix} 3x + 4y = 15 \\ 5x + 7y = 12 \end{matrix} \Rightarrow \begin{pmatrix} 3 & 4 & | & 15 \\ 5 & 7 & | & 12 \end{pmatrix} \begin{matrix} \cdot -5/3 \\ + \end{matrix} \rightarrow \begin{pmatrix} 3 & 4 & | & 15 \\ 0 & 1/3 & | & -13 \end{pmatrix}$$

We want to use the coefficient 3 in the first row to eliminate the 5 from the second row. In other words, we want to use the term $3x$ in the first equation to eliminate x from the second equation. To eliminate 5, we have to add -5, and $3 \cdot (-5/3) = -5$. Therefore, we multiply the first row with $-5/3$ and add the result to the second row. If we want to avoid fractions, we could have started by multiplying the first row by 5 and the second row by 3, and then subtracting the resulting rows:

$$\begin{pmatrix} 3 & 4 & | & 15 \\ 5 & 7 & | & 12 \end{pmatrix} \begin{matrix} \cdot 5 \\ \cdot 3 \end{matrix} \rightarrow \begin{pmatrix} 15 & 20 & | & 75 \\ 15 & 21 & | & 36 \end{pmatrix} \begin{matrix} \cdot -1 \\ + \end{matrix} \rightarrow \begin{pmatrix} 15 & 20 & | & 75 \\ 0 & 1 & | & -39 \end{pmatrix}$$

When we use Gaussian elimination, we perform a sequence of elementary row operations to obtain a new matrix, or linear system, that is easy to solve. This is called the Gaussian process. To know when we can stop the Gaussian process (that is, when the matrix is simple enough), we need the definition of an echelon form.

Echelon form. A row in a matrix is called a *zero row* if it is a row of only zeros, and a nonzero row otherwise. For each nonzero row, we define the leading coefficient or *pivot* to be the first nonzero entry (starting from the left-hand side of the matrix). We define an *echelon form* to be a matrix that satisfies the following properties:

a) all nonzero rows are above zero rows
b) all entries under a pivot are zero

It is called a *reduced echelon form* if, in addition, the following conditions hold:

c) all pivots are equal to 1

d) all entries over a pivot are zero

When we use Gaussian elimination, we continue with the Gaussian process until we obtain an echelon form. There is also a version of the method, called *Gauss-Jordan elimination*, where we continue the Gaussian process until we have a reduced echelon form.

When we want to figure out if a matrix is in (reduced) echelon form, it is a good idea to mark the pivots. For example, among the matrices

$$A = \begin{pmatrix} \underline{1} & 1 & 1 & 3 \\ 1 & 2 & 4 & 7 \\ 1 & 3 & 9 & 13 \end{pmatrix} \quad B = \begin{pmatrix} \underline{1} & 1 & 1 & 3 \\ 0 & \underline{1} & 3 & 4 \\ 0 & 0 & \underline{2} & 2 \end{pmatrix} \quad C = \begin{pmatrix} \underline{1} & 2 & 0 & 3 & 10 \\ 0 & 0 & \underline{1} & 4 & 5 \\ 0 & 0 & 0 & 0 & 0 \end{pmatrix}$$

we see that A is not an echelon form, B is an echelon form but not a reduced echelon form, and C is a reduced echelon form. The pivots are marked in blue.

How to obtain an echelon form. Any matrix can be transformed into an echelon form by a Gaussian process. It is possible to do this in many different ways, but there is a standard algorithm that can always be used:

> **Algorithm: How to obtain an echelon form**
>
> a) Set the current position to the position in the upper left corner.
>
> b) If the entry in the current position is nonzero: It is a pivot, and we mark it. Adding multiples of the row of the current position to the rows below, we obtain zero entries under the pivot. Finally, we delete the row and column of the current position, and repeat steps a) - d) for the matrix that remains.
>
> c) If the entry in the current position is zero, but another entry below it is nonzero: We interchange the two rows so that we get a pivot in the current position and mark it. Adding multiples of the row of the current position to the rows below, we obtain zero entries under the pivot. Finally, we delete the row and column of the current position, and repeat steps a) - d) for the matrix that remains.
>
> d) If the entry in the current position and all entries below it are zero: We have no pivot in the column of the current position. We delete this column, and repeat steps a) - d) for the matrix that remains.

1.4 Gaussian elimination

One of the conditions in b) - d) will always be satisfied, and each time, we repeat steps a) - d) with a smaller matrix, since we delete a row and a column or just a column. Therefore, an empty matrix (a matrix with no rows or columns) will remain after a finite number of steps. When this happens, the algorithm terminates.

Note that each step in the algorithm involves elementary row operations, and that when the algorithm terminates, we have an echelon form. We will show how the algorithm works in an example to illustrate this. We start with the following 3×3 linear system and its augmented matrix:

$$\begin{aligned} x + y + z &= 3 \\ x + 2y + 4z &= 7 \\ x + 3y + 9z &= 13 \end{aligned} \quad \Rightarrow \quad \begin{pmatrix} 1 & 1 & 1 & 3 \\ 1 & 2 & 4 & 7 \\ 1 & 3 & 9 & 13 \end{pmatrix}$$

The upper left corner is nonzero and therefore a pivot, so we mark it. Then we add multiples of the first row to the last two rows to obtain two zeros under the first pivot:

$$\begin{pmatrix} \underline{1} & 1 & 1 & 3 \\ 1 & 2 & 4 & 7 \\ 1 & 3 & 9 & 13 \end{pmatrix} \to \begin{pmatrix} \underline{1} & 1 & 1 & 3 \\ 0 & 1 & 3 & 4 \\ 1 & 3 & 9 & 13 \end{pmatrix} \to \begin{pmatrix} \underline{1} & 1 & 1 & 3 \\ 0 & 1 & 3 & 4 \\ 0 & 2 & 8 & 10 \end{pmatrix}$$

Then we delete the first row and the first column, and work with the matrix that remains. The current position is now in row 2 and column 2, and we mark it since it is nonzero and therefore the second pivot. Finally, we add multiples of the second row to the last row to obtain a zero under the second pivot:

$$\begin{pmatrix} \underline{1} & 1 & 1 & 3 \\ 0 & \underline{1} & 3 & 4 \\ 0 & 2 & 8 & 10 \end{pmatrix} \to \begin{pmatrix} \underline{1} & 1 & 1 & 3 \\ 0 & \underline{1} & 3 & 4 \\ 0 & 0 & 2 & 2 \end{pmatrix}$$

Next, we delete the second row and the second column, and work with the matrix that remains. The current position is now in row 3 and column 3, and we mark it since it is nonzero and is therefore the third pivot:

$$\begin{pmatrix} \underline{1} & 1 & 1 & 3 \\ 0 & \underline{1} & 3 & 4 \\ 0 & 0 & \underline{2} & 2 \end{pmatrix}$$

There are no entries under the third pivot. Finally, we delete the third row and the third column. There are no rows left, hence the algorithm terminates and the matrix that we have obtained is an echelon form.

We say that two matrices are *row equivalent* if you can get from one to the other using a sequence of elementary row operations. The existence of the algorithm we have described means that we can always obtain an echelon form using a Gaussian process. In other words, any matrix is row equivalent to an echelon form.

1 • Linear systems and Gaussian elimination

We will show another example of a Gaussian process. This time we start from the following 3×3 linear system and its augmented matrix:

$$\begin{array}{l} 2x + 3y - z = 7 \\ -x - y + 2z = 2 \\ 5x - 4y - 5z = 1 \end{array} \Rightarrow \begin{pmatrix} 2 & 3 & -1 & | & 7 \\ -1 & -1 & 2 & | & 2 \\ 5 & -4 & -5 & | & 1 \end{pmatrix}$$

In this case, we choose to start by switching the first two rows. The reason is that with 2 as the first pivot, the algorithm gives fractions, but when the pivot is -1, we avoid this:

$$\begin{pmatrix} 2 & 3 & -1 & | & 7 \\ -1 & -1 & 2 & | & 2 \\ 5 & -4 & -5 & | & 1 \end{pmatrix} \rightarrow \begin{pmatrix} -1 & -1 & 2 & | & 2 \\ 2 & 3 & -1 & | & 7 \\ 5 & -4 & -5 & | & 1 \end{pmatrix}$$

Next, we mark the first pivot, and add multiples of the first row to the last two rows to obtain two zeros under the first pivot:

$$\begin{pmatrix} \underline{-1} & -1 & 2 & | & 2 \\ 2 & 3 & -1 & | & 7 \\ 5 & -4 & -5 & | & 1 \end{pmatrix} \rightarrow \begin{pmatrix} \underline{-1} & -1 & 2 & | & 2 \\ 0 & 1 & 3 & | & 11 \\ 5 & -4 & -5 & | & 1 \end{pmatrix} \rightarrow \begin{pmatrix} \underline{-1} & -1 & 2 & | & 2 \\ 0 & 1 & 3 & | & 11 \\ 0 & -9 & 5 & | & 11 \end{pmatrix}$$

Next, we mark the second pivot and use it to obtain a zero under it. Finally, we mark the third pivot:

$$\begin{pmatrix} \underline{-1} & -1 & 2 & | & 2 \\ 0 & \underline{1} & 3 & | & 11 \\ 0 & -9 & 5 & | & 11 \end{pmatrix} \rightarrow \begin{pmatrix} \underline{-1} & -1 & 2 & | & 2 \\ 0 & \underline{1} & 3 & | & 11 \\ 0 & 0 & \underline{32} & | & 110 \end{pmatrix}$$

We have obtained an echelon form using a sequence of elementary row operations. But we have not followed the algorithm described above exactly. If we had used the algorithm, we would have obtained an echelon form with fractions. It is a useful exercise to do the computations yourself, and we will just write down the result:

$$\begin{pmatrix} 2 & 3 & -1 & | & 7 \\ -1 & -1 & 2 & | & 2 \\ 5 & -4 & -5 & | & 1 \end{pmatrix} \rightarrow \cdots\cdots\cdots \rightarrow \begin{pmatrix} \underline{2} & 3 & -1 & | & 7 \\ 0 & \underline{1/2} & 3/2 & | & 11/2 \\ 0 & 0 & \underline{32} & | & 110 \end{pmatrix}$$

Note that starting from the same matrix, we have found different echelon forms by using different Gaussian processes. Even though the coefficients in the two echelon forms are not the same, the positions of their pivots are. In fact, the *pivot positions* of both matrices are $(1, 1)$, $(2, 2)$ and $(3, 3)$. Note that we write (i, j) for the position in row i and column j.

Back substitution. When we have an echelon form, the next step is to write down the linear system that it corresponds to. This will be a system that is easy to solve and we do it by a process called *back substitution*: We start with the last equation and solve it for the variable corresponding to the pivot. Next, we solve the equations above it in reverse order, each time solving for the variable that corresponds to the pivot. The variables we solve for are called *basic variables*, and if they appear in subsequent equations, we substitute them with the expressions we have found.

Let us show back substitution in an example where we already carried out the Gaussian process. We consider the following augmented matrix in echelon form, with pivots marked in blue, and the linear system it corresponds to:

$$\begin{pmatrix} \underline{1} & 1 & 1 & | & 3 \\ 0 & \underline{1} & 3 & | & 4 \\ 0 & 0 & \underline{2} & | & 2 \end{pmatrix} \quad \Rightarrow \quad \begin{array}{r} \underline{x} + y + z = 3 \\ \underline{y} + 3z = 4 \\ 2\underline{z} = 2 \end{array}$$

Using back substitution, we first solve the last equation for z, and get $z = 1$. Next, we solve the middle equation for y, substituting $z = 1$, and get $y = 4 - 3z = 1$. Finally, we solve the first equation for x, substituting $y = 1$ and $z = 1$, and get $x = 3 - y - z = 1$. We conclude that this linear system has one solution $(x, y, z) = (1, 1, 1)$. Note that all variables are basic in this case. As we shall see later, this is not always the case.

For some linear systems, we get an echelon form that contains zero rows or rows with pivots in the last column.

These types of rows correspond to degenerate linear equations

$$(0 \quad 0 \quad \ldots \quad 0 \, | \, b) \quad \Rightarrow \quad 0 \cdot x_1 + 0 \cdot x_2 + \ldots + 0 \cdot x_n = b$$

with $b = 0$ or $b \neq 0$. In either of these cases we cannot solve for any of the variables. In the case $b = 0$ or a zero row, we get the equation $0 = 0$, which is satisfied for all values of $(x_1, \ldots, x_n)$. Such equations we will simply ignore; they contain no information. In the case $b \neq 0$, we get the equation $0 = b$, which has no solutions. This means that if there is a pivot position in the last column, then the linear system has no solutions. We say that it is *inconsistent*.

When the echelon form does not have a pivot in the last column, all pivots are in the variable columns. We call the linear system *consistent* in this case, and there are two possibilities: Either there is a pivot in each of the variable columns, or there is at least one of these columns without a pivot position. In the first case, all variables are basic, and we can solve for all of them. Therefore, the system has one solution. In the second case, there are variables that are not basic (that is, there is no pivot in the corresponding column). Variables that are not basic are called *free variables*.

1 • Linear systems and Gaussian elimination

A consistent linear system with at least one free variable has infinitely many solutions. We illustrate this fact with an example:

$$\begin{aligned} x + 2y + z + 3w &= 10 \\ 2x + 4y + z + 10w &= 25 \\ 3x + 6y + z + 13w &= 36 \end{aligned} \quad \Rightarrow \quad \begin{pmatrix} 1 & 2 & 1 & 3 & | & 10 \\ 2 & 4 & 1 & 10 & | & 25 \\ 3 & 6 & 1 & 13 & | & 36 \end{pmatrix}$$

The Gaussian process leads to an echelon form:

$$\begin{pmatrix} 1 & 2 & 1 & 3 & | & 10 \\ 2 & 4 & 1 & 10 & | & 25 \\ 3 & 6 & 1 & 13 & | & 36 \end{pmatrix} \rightarrow \begin{pmatrix} \underline{1} & 2 & 1 & 3 & | & 10 \\ 0 & 0 & -1 & 4 & | & 5 \\ 0 & 0 & -2 & 4 & | & 6 \end{pmatrix} \rightarrow \begin{pmatrix} \underline{1} & 2 & 1 & 3 & | & 10 \\ 0 & 0 & \underline{-1} & 4 & | & 5 \\ 0 & 0 & 0 & \underline{-4} & | & -4 \end{pmatrix}$$

We notice that there are no pivots in the last column or in the y-column, but pivots in the x-, z- and w-column. This means that the system is consistent, that x, z and w are basic variables, and that y is a free variable. We write down the linear system and solve for the basic variables using back substitution:

$$\begin{pmatrix} \underline{1} & 2 & 1 & 3 & | & 10 \\ 0 & 0 & \underline{-1} & 4 & | & 5 \\ 0 & 0 & 0 & \underline{-4} & | & -4 \end{pmatrix} \Rightarrow \begin{aligned} \underline{x} + 2y + z + 3w &= 10 \\ -\underline{z} + 4w &= 5 \\ -4\underline{w} &= -4 \end{aligned}$$

We solve for w in the last equation, and get $w = 1$. Then we solve for z in the middle equation, substituting $w = 1$, and get $z = 4w - 5 = 4 \cdot 1 - 5 = -1$. Finally, we solve for x in the first equation, substituting $z = -1$ and $w = 1$, and get that $x = 10 - 2y - z - 3w = 10 - 2y - (-1) - 3 \cdot 1 = 8 - 2y$. The result is that the basic variables x, z and w are given by expressions in the free variable y:

$$x = 8 - 2y, \quad z = -1, \quad w = 1$$

The fact that y is free means that any choice of a value for y gives a solution of the system. In other words, y can be chosen freely. When a value for y is given, then the basic variables x, z and w are determined by the expressions above. We can write the solutions as

$$(x, y, z, w) = (8 - 2y, y, -1, 1) \quad \text{where } y \text{ is a free variable}$$

When there are free variables, there are infinitely many solutions, since there is at least one variable with an infinite number of possible values.

A consequence of the discussion above is that the pivot positions in the echelon form determine what kind of solutions we have. If there is a pivot in the last column, then the system is inconsistent and this means there are no solutions. If all pivots are in the variable columns, then the system is consistent, and there is either one solution (if all variable columns have pivots, which means that all variables are basic) or there are infinitely many solutions (if there is at least one variable column without a pivot, which means that there is at least one free variable).

Uniqueness. Depending on the choice of Gaussian process, a given linear system can lead to different echelon forms. In other words, an echelon form is not unique. In fact, starting from the same augmented matrix, we can find echelon forms that are quite different from each other. These different echelon forms must give the same solutions since they originate from the same linear system. In particular, they must have the same pivot positions. We shall show why this is the case.

Theorem 1.4. *Any matrix is row equivalent to a unique reduced echelon form.*

Proof. We have seen that any matrix can be transformed into an echelon form using a Gaussian process. It is not difficult to see that it can be transformed into a reduced echelon form by using further elementary row operations: For each pivot $c \neq 0$, we multiply the corresponding row with $1/c$ to make the pivot equal to 1. If there are nonzero entries over some of the pivots, we use the pivot in the same column to eliminate these entries, starting with the last pivot and working backwards. Therefore, any matrix is row equivalent with a reduced echelon form. We must prove that the reduced echelon form is unique: Assume that $U \neq V$ are two reduced echelon forms that are row equivalent. Then we pick the first column where U and V are different, and all pivot columns further to the left, and form new matrices U' and V'. For example, if U and V are the reduced echelon forms below, we get

$$U = \begin{pmatrix} 1 & 7 & 0 & 4 \\ 0 & 0 & 1 & 2 \end{pmatrix}, \quad V = \begin{pmatrix} 1 & 7 & 0 & 5 \\ 0 & 0 & 1 & 7 \end{pmatrix}$$

$$\Downarrow$$

$$U' = \begin{pmatrix} 1 & 0 & 4 \\ 0 & 1 & 2 \end{pmatrix}, \quad V' = \begin{pmatrix} 1 & 0 & 5 \\ 0 & 1 & 7 \end{pmatrix}$$

In general, U' and V' will be row equivalent reduced echelon forms (we have just deleted certain columns from the row equivalent matrices U and V). If we interpret U' and V' as augmented matrices of linear systems, these linear systems should have the same solutions by row equivalence. This leads to a contradiction, since U' and V' are reduced echelon forms where only the last columns are different. Since the assumption $U \neq V$ leads to a contradiction, it follows that $U = V$, and therefore the reduced echelon form is unique. □

In practice, we do not use Gauss-Jordan elimination and the reduced echelon form so often since Gauss elimination is usually quicker, and can always be used. However, the uniqueness of the reduced echelon form has an important consequence that is very useful: Since there is a Gaussian process from an echelon form to a reduced echelon form that does not change the position of the pivots, any echelon form of a given matrix will have the same pivot positions as its reduced echelon form. This proves the following result:

Corollary 1.5. Any matrix is row equivalent to an echelon form. In general, this echelon form is not unique. However, if a matrix is row equivalent to two different echelon forms $E \neq E'$, then E and E' have the same pivot positions.

A consequence of the corollary is that when we start with an augmented matrix $(A|\mathbf{b})$ we can obtain many different echelon forms by making different choices in the Gaussian process, but all these echelon forms have the same pivot positions. We define the *pivot positions* of $(A|\mathbf{b})$ to be the pivot position of one of its echelon forms.

1.5 Free variables and parameterizations

Consider a simple linear system, consisting of a single linear equation $4x - 2y = 12$. To find all solutions of this equation, we can assign any value to x and solve for y. Alternatively, we can assign any value to y and solve for x. Using these approaches, we obtain

$$x = t, \quad y = 2t - 6 \quad \text{or} \quad y = t, \quad x = t/2 + 3$$

We can write the solutions as either $(x, y) = (t, 2t - 6)$, or as $(x, y) = (t/2 + 3, t)$. In this way, we obtain two different *parameterizations* or *parametric descriptions* of the solutions, which are illustrated in Figure 1.3. The set of all solutions is a line, and the two parameterizations give all the points on this line in two different ways. For example, the point $(x, y) = (4, 2)$ is the point with $t = 4$ in the first parameterization, and with $t = 2$ in the second parameterization.

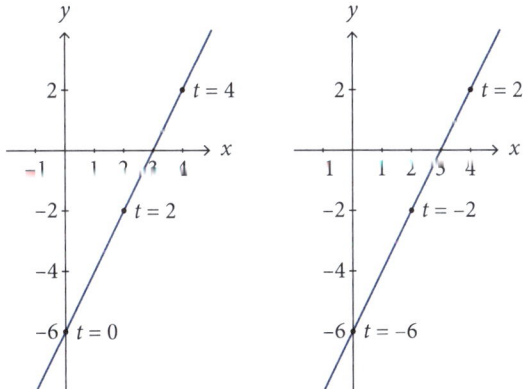

Figure 1.3 The line $4x - 2y = 12$ with parameterizations $(x, y) = (t, 2t - 6)$ and $(x, y) = (t/2 + 3, t)$

It is usual to use the symbol t for the parameter. We sometimes think of t as time and of the parameterization as a way to move along the line as time passes.

When we use Gaussian elimination, we define a free variable to be a variable without a pivot in the corresponding variable column. When we solve $4x - 2y = 12$ using Gaussian elimination, it is natural to say that x is basic and y is free, since the coefficient 4 of the x-term is the pivot. This corresponds to the parameterization $(x, y) = (t/2 + 3, t)$.

But there is also a parameterization $(x, y) = (t, 2t - 6)$ with $x = t$ as a parameter. This means that x can be considered as a free variable. If we change the order of the variables to obtain the equation $-2y + 4x = 12$, then Gaussian elimination gives solutions in this form: Since -2 is the pivot, y is basic and x is free with this ordering.

1.6 Rank of a matrix

Let A be any $m \times n$ matrix. We define the *rank* of A to be the number of pivot positions in A. We know from the previous section that there is a Gaussian process leading to an echelon form E:

$$A \to \cdots \cdots \to E$$

To compute the rank of A, we find such an echelon form E and count the number of pivots in E. According to Corollary 1.5, the result is independent of which Gaussian process we use. Note that this definition makes sense whether A is a coefficient matrix or an augmented matrix of a linear system, or a matrix obtained in some other way.

1 • Linear systems and Gaussian elimination

We write rk(A) for the rank of an $m \times n$ matrix A. Notice that rk$(A) = 0$ if and only if A is a zero matrix

$$\mathbf{0} = \begin{pmatrix} 0 & 0 & \cdots & 0 \\ 0 & 0 & \cdots & 0 \\ \vdots & \vdots & \ddots & \vdots \\ 0 & 0 & \cdots & 0 \end{pmatrix}$$

since the zero matrix is the only matrix without any pivot positions. In all other cases, rk(A) is a positive integer. We have that rk$(A) \leq m$ and that rk$(A) \leq n$, since there cannot be more than one pivot in each row or column.

As an example, we compute the rank of the coefficient matrix A and the augmented matrix $(A|\mathbf{b})$ of the linear system

$$\begin{array}{l} x + y + z = 3 \\ x + 2y + 4z = 7 \\ x + 3y + 9z = 13 \end{array} \Rightarrow A = \begin{pmatrix} 1 & 1 & 1 \\ 1 & 2 & 4 \\ 1 & 3 & 9 \end{pmatrix}, \ (A|\mathbf{b}) = \begin{pmatrix} 1 & 1 & 1 & 3 \\ 1 & 2 & 4 & 7 \\ 1 & 3 & 9 & 13 \end{pmatrix}$$

The rank of a matrix is equal to the number of pivot positions in an echelon form, so we find an echelon form of $(A|\mathbf{b})$ and count the pivot positions to find rk$(A|\mathbf{b})$:

$$\begin{pmatrix} \underline{1} & 1 & 1 & 3 \\ 1 & 2 & 4 & 7 \\ 1 & 3 & 9 & 13 \end{pmatrix} \to \begin{pmatrix} \underline{1} & 1 & 1 & 3 \\ 0 & 1 & 3 & 4 \\ 1 & 3 & 9 & 13 \end{pmatrix} \to \begin{pmatrix} \underline{1} & 1 & 1 & 3 \\ 0 & \underline{1} & 3 & 4 \\ 0 & 2 & 8 & 10 \end{pmatrix} \to \begin{pmatrix} \underline{1} & 1 & 1 & 3 \\ 0 & \underline{1} & 3 & 4 \\ 0 & 0 & \underline{2} & 2 \end{pmatrix}$$

Since there are three pivot positions, we have rk$(A|\mathbf{b}) = 3$. To compute the rank of A we do not have to go though the Gaussian process again: We just look at the first three columns in the Gaussian process above. Since there are three pivots in the first three columns of the echelon form, we have that rk$(A) = 3$ as well.

Theorem 1.6. We consider an $m \times n$ linear system with coefficient matrix A and augmented matrix $(A|\mathbf{b})$. Then we have:

a) The linear system is consistent if rk$(A) = $ rk$(A|\mathbf{b})$, and inconsistent otherwise.
b) If the linear system is consistent, then it has a unique solution if rk$(A) = n$, and infinitely many solutions if rk$(A) < n$.

Proof. This theorem is a summary of what we learned in the previous section about the relationship between the number of solutions and the pivot positions, expressed using rank. The linear system is inconsistent (that is there are no solutions) if and only if there is a pivot position in the last column, and this can be expressed as $\mathrm{rk}(A|\mathbf{b}) = \mathrm{rk}(A) + 1$. On the other hand, if there are no pivot positions in the last column, then we have that $\mathrm{rk}(A|\mathbf{b}) = \mathrm{rk}(A)$. The number of basic variables is $\mathrm{rk}(A)$ in this case, since there is one basic variable for each pivot position and the total number of variables is n. Hence, the number of free variables is equal to $n - \mathrm{rk}(A)$. If $\mathrm{rk}(A) = n$, there are no free variables and the system has one solution. If $\mathrm{rk}(A) < n$, there is at least one free variable and the system has infinitely many solutions. □

When a linear system has infinitely many solutions, we define the number of *degrees of freedom* to be the number of free variables. It follows from the theorem that the number of degrees of freedom is given by $n - \mathrm{rk}(A)$.

Let V be the geometric figure in n-dimensional space $\mathbb{R}^n$ formed by the solutions of the linear system. Then we can interpret the number of degrees of freedom as the dimension of V, and write $\dim V = n - \mathrm{rk}(A)$. For example, we solved the following linear system in the previous section:

$$x + 2y + z + 3w = 10$$
$$2x + 4y + z + 10w = 25$$
$$3x + 6y + z + 13w = 36$$

We found that there were infinitely many solutions and one free variable, and that the set of solutions was given by

$$V = \{(x, y, z) = (8 - 2y, y, -1, 1) : y \text{ is free }\}$$

Since there is one free variable in this case, V is a one-dimensional geometric figure, and it is linear (not curved) by the linear property in Lemma 1.2. Hence the set V of solutions of the linear system is a straight line in four-dimensional space $\mathbb{R}^4$.

Homogeneous linear systems. A *homogeneous* linear system is a linear system where all the constant terms are zero, which can be written in the general form

$$a_{11}x_1 + a_{12}x_2 + \ldots + a_{1n}x_n = 0$$
$$a_{21}x_1 + a_{22}x_2 + \ldots + a_{2n}x_n = 0$$
$$\vdots \qquad \vdots \qquad \qquad \vdots \quad \vdots$$
$$a_{m1}x_1 + a_{m2}x_2 + \ldots + a_{mn}x_n = 0$$

It is the special case where $b_1 = b_2 = \ldots = b_m = 0$. If we write down the augmented matrix of a homogeneous linear system, the last column consists of zeros, and it is easy to see that this will not change in a Gaussian process. Therefore, there is never a pivot position in the last column of a homogeneous linear system, and this means that it is always consistent. In fact, the last column is often omitted when solving homogeneous systems.

Note that $(x_1, x_2, \ldots, x_n) = (0, 0, \ldots, 0)$ is a solution of any homogeneous linear system. It is called the *trivial solution*. There are only two possibilities: Either the trivial solution is the only solution, or there are other solutions, called *nontrivial solutions*, in addition to the trivial one. In the first case, the system has one solution, and in the second case, the system must have infinitely many solutions. It follows from Theorem 1.6 that we can find the number of solutions using rank:

Proposition 1.7. *An $m \times n$ homogeneous linear system with coefficient matrix A has only the trivial solution if $\mathrm{rk}(A) = n$, and it has nontrivial solutions if $\mathrm{rk}(A) < n$.*

Problems

Problem 1.1 Write down the coefficient matrix and the augmented matrix of the following linear systems:

a) $7x + 2y = 4$
$4x - 4y = 7$

b) $y - z + w = 1$
$x + y + z - 2w = 3$
$x - 4y + 7z + 3w = 14$

Problem 1.2 Write down linear systems with the following augmented matrices:

a) $\begin{pmatrix} 2 & 1 & 0 & | & 7 \\ 1 & 3 & 4 & | & 5 \\ 5 & -4 & 2 & | & 13 \end{pmatrix}$

b) $\begin{pmatrix} 1 & 1 & 1 & | & 7 \\ 1 & 2 & 4 & | & 12 \\ 1 & 3 & 9 & | & 19 \end{pmatrix}$

c) $\begin{pmatrix} 1 & 1 & -1 & 1 & | & 12 \\ 2 & -3 & 4 & 7 & | & 10 \end{pmatrix}$

Problem 1.3 Use substitution to solve the following linear system, and then solve the same linear system using Gaussian elimination:

$$x + y + z = 7$$
$$x + 2y + 4z = 12$$
$$x + 3y + 9z = 19$$

Problem 1.4 Solve the following linear systems by Gaussian elimination. Use the pivot positions to determine the number of solutions:

a) $-4x + 6y + 4z = 4$
$2x - y + z = 1$

b) $6x + y = 7$
$3x + y = 4$
$-6x - 2y = 1$

Problem 1.5 Solve the following linear system, and give a geometric description of its solutions:

a) $3x - 4y = 6$

b) $x + y + z = 4$
$2x - y + 3z = 3$
$3x + 4z = 7$

c) $2x + y - 4z = 3$
$3x - 2y + z = 1$

Problem 1.6 Determine all values of h such that the following linear system has solutions, and describe the solutions geometrically in these cases:

a) $hx - hy = 3$

b) $x + 2y = h$
$3x + 6y = 12$

c) $x + y + z = 1$
$2x - y + 3z = 4$
$x + 7y - z = h$

1 • Linear systems and Gaussian elimination

Problem 1.7 Find the reduced echelon form of the following augmented matrix:
$$\begin{pmatrix} 1 & 1 & 1 & 3 \\ 1 & 2 & 4 & 7 \\ 1 & 3 & 9 & 13 \end{pmatrix}$$

Problem 1.8 Solve the following linear system by Gaussian elimination, and mark the pivot positions:
$$\begin{aligned} x + y + z + w &= 5 \\ 2x - y + 2z - w &= 11 \\ x + 4y + z + 5w &= 7 \end{aligned}$$

Problem 1.9 We consider the following 4×4 linear system, where the last equation is nondegenerate. Note that the first three equations are the same as the equations in the previous problem:
$$\begin{aligned} x + y + z + w &= 5 \\ 2x - y + 2z - w &= 11 \\ x + 4y + z + 5w &= 7 \\ ax + by + cz + dw &= e \end{aligned}$$

If possible, find a nondegenerate equation $ax + by + cz + dw = e$ such that this linear system has

a) one solution

b) infinitely many solutions with one degree of freedom

c) no solutions

d) infinitely many solutions with two degrees of freedom

Problem 1.10 Determine whether the matrices A and B are row equivalent:

a) $A = \begin{pmatrix} 1 & 3 \\ 0 & 5 \end{pmatrix}$, $B = \begin{pmatrix} 1 & 1 \\ 3 & 0 \end{pmatrix}$

b) $A = \begin{pmatrix} 1 & 3 \\ 4 & 5 \end{pmatrix}$, $B = \begin{pmatrix} 1 & 2 \\ 3 & 6 \end{pmatrix}$

c) $A = \begin{pmatrix} 1 & 3 & 2 \\ 0 & 0 & 1 \end{pmatrix}$, $B = \begin{pmatrix} 2 & 5 & 6 \\ 0 & 4 & 0 \end{pmatrix}$

d) $A = \begin{pmatrix} 1 & 3 & 2 \\ 0 & 0 & 1 \end{pmatrix}$, $B = \begin{pmatrix} 2 & 5 & 6 \\ 0 & 0 & 4 \end{pmatrix}$

Problem 1.11 Determine the number of solutions of the following linear system for all values of the parameters a and b:
$$\begin{aligned} x + y + z &= 3 \\ 2x + 3y + az &= b \\ x + ay + z &= 7 \end{aligned}$$

Problem 1.12 Show that the following linear system has infinitely many solutions. Find free variables and express the basic variables in terms of the free ones:
$$\begin{aligned} x + 7y - 7z + 3w &= 1 \\ x + 6y - 6z + 4w &= 2 \end{aligned}$$

Problem 1.13 Consider a 3×4 homogeneous linear system. Prove that it has nontrivial solutions.

Problem 1.14 Determine the rank of the matrix A for all values of the parameters p and q:
$$A = \begin{pmatrix} 1 & 1 & 1 \\ 1 & p & p^2 \\ 1 & q & q^2 \end{pmatrix}$$

Problem 1.15 Compute the rank of the following matrices:

a) $\begin{pmatrix} 2 & 5 & -3 & -4 & 8 \\ 4 & 7 & -4 & -3 & 9 \\ 6 & 9 & -5 & -2 & 4 \end{pmatrix}$ b) $\begin{pmatrix} 2 & 10 & 6 & 8 \\ 1 & 5 & 4 & 11 \\ 3 & 15 & 7 & -2 \end{pmatrix}$

c) $\begin{pmatrix} 1 & 2 & -5 & 0 & -1 \\ 2 & 5 & -8 & 4 & 3 \\ -3 & -9 & 9 & -7 & -2 \\ 3 & 10 & -7 & 11 & 7 \end{pmatrix}$

Problem 1.16 Determine the rank of the following matrices for all values of the parameter t:

a) $\begin{pmatrix} 1 & 1 & t \\ 1 & t & 1 \\ t & 1 & 1 \end{pmatrix}$ b) $\begin{pmatrix} 1 & 3 & -1 & 4 \\ 2 & 4 & 0 & 6 \\ t & -1 & 5 & 3 \end{pmatrix}$

c) $\begin{pmatrix} 1 & 2 & 3 & 2 \\ 2 & -1 & 1 & -3 \\ 1 & t & t+1 & 9 \end{pmatrix}$

Problem 1.17 Is it true that two $m \times n$ matrices with the same pivot positions are row equivalent? Explain why/why not.

CHAPTER 2

Vectors and vector spaces

2.1 Introduction to vectors

A *vector* is a quantity that has a magnitude and a direction. We represent a vector geometrically as an *arrow*, or a directed line segment, so that the length of the arrow represents the magnitude of the vector. The figure below shows examples of vectors:

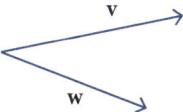

We shall use boldface letters to denote vectors and recall that we use upper case letters to denote matrices. These conventions are useful; it means that $A\mathbf{v}$ is the product of a matrix and a vector and that $r\mathbf{v}$ is the product of a number and a vector. To denote the length of the vector $\mathbf{v}$, we shall write $\|\mathbf{v}\|$.

Vectors originate from physics, where many quantities such as force, velocity and acceleration are vector quantities. This means that these quantities cannot be described by their magnitude alone; they also have a direction. In order to compute the combined effect of two forces, we must take into account their directions and add them as vectors.

We can add two vectors $\mathbf{v}$ and $\mathbf{w}$ by constructing a parallelogram in the way shown in Figure 2.1. We make a new copy of the vector $\mathbf{v}$ so that its starting point is the endpoint of $\mathbf{w}$, and vice versa. The vector sum is the diagonal in the parallelogram shown in the figure.

Note that the dashed copy of $\mathbf{v}$ in Figure 2.1 has the same length and direction as the original vector $\mathbf{v}$. When we keep the length and direction of a vector, but

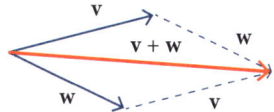

Figure 2.1 Addition of vectors by completing their parallelogram

35

move its starting point, we say that we *translate* the vector. Any translation of a vector is considered as the same vector, since it has the same length and direction.

We can multiply a vector **v** with a positive number $r > 0$. The result is a new vector $r\mathbf{v}$ with the same direction as **v** and a length that is multiplied with a factor r. The number r is often called a *scalar* when used together with vectors, since its effect is to scale vectors.

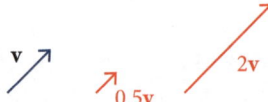

We write $-\mathbf{v}$ for the vector that has the same length but the opposite direction of **v**. It is sometimes called the opposite vector. Using opposite vectors, we can define multiplication of a vector with a negative number $r < 0$ as $r\mathbf{v} = |r| \cdot (-\mathbf{v})$. The result is a vector with the opposite direction of **v** and a length that is multiplied with the factor $|r|$, the absolute value of r.

We can define subtraction of vectors as $\mathbf{v} - \mathbf{w} = \mathbf{v} + (-\mathbf{w})$ using opposite vectors. This can be illustrated geometrically by the parallelogram in Figure 2.2.

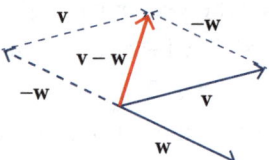

Figure 2.2 Subtraction $\mathbf{v} - \mathbf{w}$ of vectors by completing the parallelogram of **v** and $-\mathbf{w}$

There is a unique vector of length 0, which we call the *zero vector* and write as **0**. It has no natural direction and is therefore said to have the same direction as any other vector. We define that $0 \cdot \mathbf{v} = \mathbf{0}$ for any vector **v**.

To summarize, we have defined vector addition $\mathbf{v} + \mathbf{w}$ and vector subtraction $\mathbf{v} - \mathbf{w}$ of any two vectors, and scalar multiplication $r\mathbf{v}$ of any number (scalar) and any vector. Note that the definitions are given geometrically. Even though the illustrations in this section are two-dimensional, the geometric construction would work equally well in three-dimensional space (or in n-dimensional space, even though that is more difficult to imagine).

Even though vectors originate from physics, they are useful in a wide range of other situations as well, and we shall give some examples in this book. For many of the applications, it is useful to use coordinates to describe vectors.

2.2 Vectors and coordinates

Let us consider a plane with a two-dimensional coordinate system. We use the two coordinates, which we call x and y, to describe points in the plane, and we usually write (x, y) for the point with coordinates x and y. For example, we write $(4, 2)$ for the point with coordinates $x = 4$ and $y = 2$.

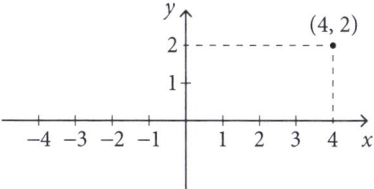

We can describe a vector **v** by specifying the coordinates (x_1, y_1) of its starting point and (x_2, y_2) of its endpoint. For instance, the vector with starting point $(1, 1)$ and endpoint $(4, 2)$ is shown in Figure 2.3. We think of the vector **v** as a *displacement*, where we move $\Delta x = x_2 - x_1$ units along the x-axis, and $\Delta y = y_2 - y_1$ units along the y-axis, with $\Delta x = 3$ and $\Delta y = 1$ in the example.

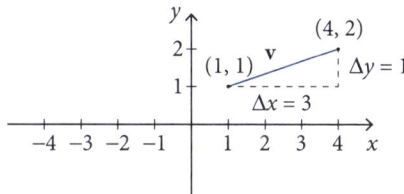

Figure 2.3 The vector with starting point (1, 1) and endpoint (4, 2)

In a two-dimensional coordinate system, we use the notation $\mathbf{v} = (v_x, v_y)$ for a vector, where $v_x = \Delta x$ and $v_y = \Delta y$, and call v_x and v_y the *components* of the vector **v**. For instance, we would write $\mathbf{v} = (3, 1)$ for the vector in the example above. Note that the components of a vector give the changes in coordinates relative to the starting point. This means that if we translate a vector, it would still have the same components. In Figure 2.4 we show two vectors obtained by translating the vector with starting point $(1, 1)$ and endpoint $(4, 2)$. All three vectors are the same and they are all written $\mathbf{v} = (3, 1)$. We often think of the vector $\mathbf{v} = (v_x, v_y)$ with components v_x and v_y as the vector with starting point $(0, 0)$ and endpoint (v_x, v_y).

2 • Vectors and vector spaces

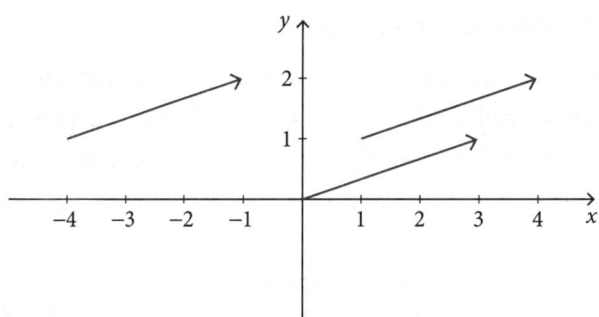

Figure 2.4 Three geometric representations of the vector $\mathbf{v} = (3, 1)$

Vectors in three-dimensional space can be thought of in a similar way, using a three-dimensional coordinate system. In this case, we call the coordinates x, y and z, and we write $\mathbf{v} = (v_x, v_y, v_z)$ for the vector with components v_x, v_y and v_z along the three axes. We can think of $\mathbf{v}$ as the vector with starting point $(0, 0, 0)$ and endpoint (v_x, v_y, v_z).

The n-dimensional space is far less familiar and far more difficult to imagine geometrically when $n > 3$. For any positive integer n, we define n-dimensional space to be the set of all ordered n-tuples of numbers $(a_1, a_2, a_3, \ldots, a_n)$, and write $\mathbb{R}^n$ for this space. Note that $\mathbb{R}^n$ comes equipped with an n-dimensional coordinate system and we shall call the coordinates $x_1, x_2, \ldots, x_n$. The element $(a_1, a_2, a_3, \ldots, a_n)$ in $\mathbb{R}^n$ is the point with coordinates $x_1 = a_1$, $x_2 = a_2$, $x_3 = a_3, \ldots, x_n = a_n$.

A vector in $\mathbb{R}^n$ has a starting point $(a_1, a_2, \ldots, a_n)$ and an endpoint $(b_1, b_2, \ldots, b_n)$. We shall write $\mathbf{v} = (v_1, v_2, \ldots, v_n)$ for this vector, with components given by

$$v_1 = \Delta x_1 = b_1 - a_1, v_2 = \Delta x_2 = b_2 - a_2, \ldots, v_n = \Delta x_n = b_n - a_n$$

For example, the vector $\mathbf{v} = (3, -1, 4, 2, 1)$ is a vector in $\mathbb{R}^5$, or five-dimensional space. It is easy to define this vector, but difficult to imagine it what it looks like geometrically; we may think of it as the vector with starting point $(0, 0, 0, 0, 0)$ and endpoint $(3, -1, 4, 2, 1)$.

Note that the way we described vectors in n-dimensional space in terms of its components is very similar to how we did it in the plane $\mathbb{R}^2$. In fact, vectors in two-dimensional space $\mathbb{R}^2$ or three-dimensional space $\mathbb{R}^3$ can be thought of as special cases of vectors in n-dimensional space $\mathbb{R}^n$.

We remark that even though it can be mind-boggling to think geometrically about vectors in higher-dimensional spaces, it is natural to consider datasets with n variables where $n > 3$, and these give rise to vectors in $\mathbb{R}^n$. When we think of vectors in this way, n-dimensional vectors for very large values of n are natural.

2.2 Vectors and coordinates

Vector operations in n-dimensional space. In Section 2.1, we described vector operations geometrically. We shall now explain how to compute vector sums, vector differences, and scalar multiplications of vectors in n-dimensional space $\mathbb{R}^n$.

We used the notation $\mathbf{v} = (v_1, v_2, \ldots, v_n)$ earlier in this section. Sometimes we also write vectors as *column vectors*, that is, as a special case of matrices that consist of a single column. As a column vector, we would write $\mathbf{v} = (v_1, v_2, \ldots, v_n)$ as

$$\mathbf{v} = \begin{pmatrix} v_1 \\ v_2 \\ \vdots \\ v_n \end{pmatrix}$$

Clearly, the notation $\mathbf{v} = (v_1, v_2, \ldots, v_n)$ is easier to use in running text and takes less space. On the other hand, the column vector representation is very useful when we compute with vectors and matrices.

Let $\mathbf{v} = (v_1, v_2, \ldots, v_n)$ and $\mathbf{w} = (w_1, w_2, \ldots, w_n)$ be two vectors in $\mathbb{R}^n$ and let r be a number. We define the vector sum $\mathbf{v} + \mathbf{w}$, difference $\mathbf{v} - \mathbf{w}$, and scalar product $r \cdot \mathbf{v}$ in $\mathbb{R}^n$ to be given by the following formulas:

Vector sum, difference and scalar multiplication using components:

$$(v_1, v_2, \ldots, v_n) + (w_1, w_2, \ldots, w_n) = (v_1 + w_1, v_2 + w_2, \ldots, v_n + w_n)$$
$$(v_1, v_2, \ldots, v_n) - (w_1, w_2, \ldots, w_n) = (v_1 - w_1, v_2 - w_2, \ldots, v_n - w_n)$$
$$r \cdot (v_1, v_2, \ldots, v_n) = (rv_1, rv_2, \ldots, rv_n)$$

It is not difficult to see that for $n = 2$ and $n = 3$, these definitions give the same result as the geometric constructions in the previous section. The zero vector is written $\mathbf{0} = (0, 0, \ldots, 0)$ using components, and the opposite vector $-\mathbf{v}$ is written as $-(v_1, v_2, \ldots, v_n) = (-v_1, -v_2, \ldots, -v_n)$.

2 • Vectors and vector spaces

Proposition 2.1. For any vectors **u**, **v**, **w** and any numbers r, s, we have:

a) $\mathbf{u} + \mathbf{v} = \mathbf{v} + \mathbf{u}$
b) $(\mathbf{u} + \mathbf{v}) + \mathbf{w} = \mathbf{u} + (\mathbf{v} + \mathbf{w})$
c) $\mathbf{v} + \mathbf{0} = \mathbf{0} + \mathbf{v} = \mathbf{v}$
d) $\mathbf{u} + (-\mathbf{u}) = \mathbf{0}$
e) $r(s\mathbf{u}) = (rs)\mathbf{u}$
f) $r(\mathbf{u} + \mathbf{v}) = r\mathbf{u} + r\mathbf{v}$
g) $(r + s)\mathbf{u} = r\mathbf{u} + s\mathbf{u}$
h) $1 \cdot \mathbf{u} = \mathbf{u}$

Proof. To prove each result, we can use the formulas (2.1) - (2.1) to compute the left-hand side and right-hand side and compare the results. It is also possible to give geometric proofs based on the constructions in the previous section. □

The length of a vector $\mathbf{v} = (v_1, v_2)$ in $\mathbb{R}^2$ is given by Pythagoras' Theorem; see Figure 2.5. This gives the formula

$$\|\mathbf{v}\| = \sqrt{v_1^2 + v_2^2}$$

The formula can be extended to vectors in $\mathbb{R}^n$. The length of a vector $\mathbf{v} = (v_1, v_2, \ldots, v_n)$ is defined to be

$$\|\mathbf{v}\| = \sqrt{v_1^2 + v_2^2 + \ldots + v_n^2}$$

By using Pythagoras' Theorem several times, one can show that this formula gives the actual length of the vectors **v** also when $n = 3$. For $n > 3$, we can take this formula as the definition of the length of **v**.

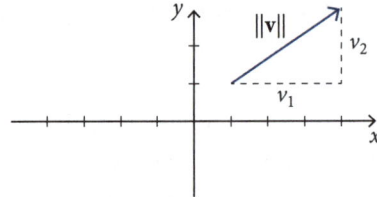

Figure 2.5 The length of the vector $\mathbf{v} = (v_1, v_2)$ is given by Pythagoras' Theorem

Proposition 2.2. For any vector **v** in $\mathbb{R}^n$, we have that $\|\mathbf{v}\| \geq 0$, and $\|\mathbf{v}\| = 0$ if and only if $\mathbf{v} = \mathbf{0}$.

Proof. We have that $\|\mathbf{v}\| \geq 0$ for all vectors $\mathbf{v} = (v_1, v_2, \ldots, v_n)$, since

$$\|\mathbf{v}\| = \sqrt{v_1^2 + v_2^2 + \ldots + v_n^2} \geq 0$$

and $\|\mathbf{v}\| = 0$ if and only if $\|\mathbf{v}\|^2 = v_1^2 + v_2^2 + \ldots + v_n^2 = 0$, and this only holds if $v_1 = v_2 = \ldots = v_n = 0$. □

We can use this to find a formula for the distance between two points in $\mathbb{R}^n$: For any points $A = (a_1, a_2, \ldots, a_n)$ and $B = (b_1, b_2, \ldots, b_n)$, we can form the vector $\mathbf{v}$ with starting point A and endpoint B, and the distance $d(A, B)$ between A and B is simply the length $\|\mathbf{v}\|$ of this vector. Since $\mathbf{v} = (b_1 - a_1, b_2 - a_2, \ldots, b_n - a_n)$, we find the formula

$$d(A, B) = \sqrt{(b_1 - a_1)^2 + (b_2 - a_2)^2 + \ldots + (b_n - a_n)^2}$$

As we shall see later, this is a very useful formula. For example, the distance between the point $A = (1, -1, 3)$ and $B = (3, 0, 2)$ in $\mathbb{R}^3$ is given by

$$d(A, B) = \|\mathbf{v}\| = \sqrt{2^2 + 1^2 + (-1)^2} = \sqrt{6}$$

since $\mathbf{v} = (3 - 1, 0 - (-1), 2 - 3) = (2, 1, -1)$ is the vector with starting point A and endpoint B.

2.3 Parametric description of lines and planes

Let us start with a simple example, the line l through the two points $A = (1, 3)$ and $B = (3, 2)$ in two-dimensional space $\mathbb{R}^2$, shown in Figure 2.6. It has the equation $y = -x/2 + 7/2$, since its slope is $-1/2$ and its y-intercept is $7/2$. We shall consider an alternative way to describe the line l, called a *parametric description*.

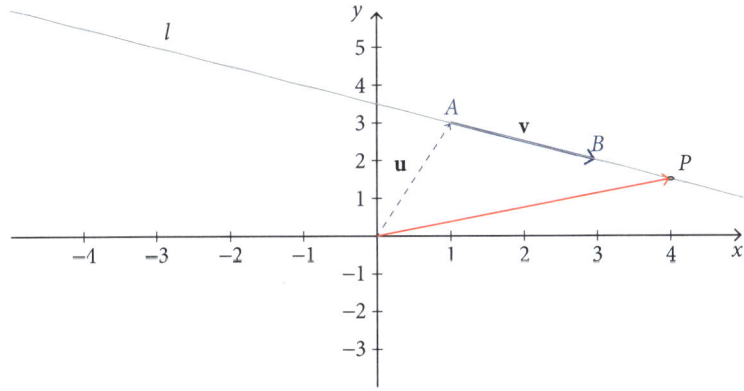

Figure 2.6 Parametric description of the line *l* through two points A and B

Let $\mathbf{v} = (2, -1)$ be the blue vector $\overrightarrow{AB}$ with starting point A and endpoint B, and let $\mathbf{u} = (1, 3)$ be the vector with starting point at the origin and with endpoint A. For any point P on the line l, we have that

$$\overrightarrow{AP} = t \cdot \overrightarrow{AB} = t \cdot \mathbf{v}$$

for a real number t (the point P shown in the figure corresponds to $t = 1.5$).

2 • Vectors and vector spaces

When we write O for the origin, this means that

$$\overrightarrow{OP} = \overrightarrow{OA} + \overrightarrow{AP} = \mathbf{u} + t \cdot \mathbf{v} = (1, 3) + t \cdot (2, -1) = (1 + 2t, 3 - t)$$

When we identify the components of this vector with the coordinates of P, we find that any point P on the line l has coordinates given by

$$(x, y) = (1, 3) + t \cdot (2, -1) = (1 + 2t, 3 - t)$$

This is called a *parametric description* of the line l. When t varies among all real numbers, the point (x, y) will run through all points on the line l. We can think of t as time, with $t = 0$ corresponding to the starting point A. The vector $\mathbf{v}$ is *velocity*, or the movement along the line during one unit of time.

We remark that any given line has many different parameterizations. In fact, any choice of two different points on a line will give rise to a different parameterization. The construction can easily be extended to parametric descriptions of lines in $\mathbb{R}^n$:

Proposition 2.3. Let $A = (a_1, a_2, \ldots, a_n)$ and $B = (b_1, b_2, \ldots, b_n)$ be two distinct points in $\mathbb{R}^n$, and let l be the straight line through A and B. Then any point P on l has coordinates

$$\begin{aligned}(x_1, x_2, \ldots, x_n) &= (a_1, a_2, \ldots, a_n) + t \cdot (b_1 - a_1, b_2 - a_2, \ldots, b_n - a_n) \\ &= (1 - t) \cdot (a_1, a_2, \ldots, a_n) + t \cdot (b_1, b_2, \ldots, b_n)\end{aligned}$$

where t is any real number.

We say that three points are *collinear* if there is a straight line going through all three points. For any three points A, B and C that are not collinear, there is a unique plane passing through all three points. We shall find a parametric description of this plane.

Let us first consider the example given by the points $A = (1, 0, 1)$, $B = (-3, 1, 0)$ and $C = (0, 2, 2)$. We consider the two vectors with starting point A and endpoints B and C, given by

$$\mathbf{v} = \overrightarrow{AB} = (-4, 1, -1), \quad \mathbf{w} = \overrightarrow{AC} = (-1, 2, 1)$$

We notice that none of these vectors are scalar multiples of the other, and this means that the points A, B and C are not collinear. By definition, a point P is in the plane π going through A, B and C if there are real numbers s and t, such that

$$\overrightarrow{AP} = s \cdot \overrightarrow{AB} + t \cdot \overrightarrow{AC} = s \cdot \mathbf{v} + t \cdot \mathbf{w} = s(-4, 1, -1) + t(-1, 2, 1)$$

This means that
$$\overrightarrow{OP} = \overrightarrow{OA} + \overrightarrow{AP} = (1, 0, 1) + s(-4, 1, -1) + t(-1, 2, 1)$$
When we identify the components of this vector with the coordinates of P, we find that any point P on the line l has coordinates given by
$$\begin{aligned}(x, y) &= (1, 0, 1) + s(-4, 1, -1) + t(-1, 2, 1) \\ &= (1 - 4s - t, s + 2t, 1 - s + t)\end{aligned}$$
This is called a *parametric description* of the plane π.

2.4 Inner products

Let $\mathbf{v} = (v_1, v_2, \ldots, v_n)$ and $\mathbf{w} = (w_1, w_2, \ldots, w_n)$ be two vectors in $\mathbb{R}^n$. We define the *inner product* of $\mathbf{v}$ and $\mathbf{w}$ to be
$$\langle \mathbf{v}, \mathbf{w} \rangle = v_1 w_1 + v_2 w_2 + \ldots + v_n w_n$$
We sometimes write $\mathbf{v} \cdot \mathbf{w}$ for the inner product and call it the *dot product* of $\mathbf{v}$ and $\mathbf{w}$. We notice that the inner product $\mathbf{v} \cdot \mathbf{w}$ is a real number and if $\mathbf{v} = \mathbf{w}$, then
$$\mathbf{v} \cdot \mathbf{v} = v_1^2 + v_2^2 + \ldots + v_n^2 \geq 0$$
In fact, comparing the expression above with the formula for the length of $\mathbf{v}$, we see that $\mathbf{v} \cdot \mathbf{v} = \|\mathbf{v}\|^2$ for any vector $\mathbf{v}$ in $\mathbb{R}^n$.

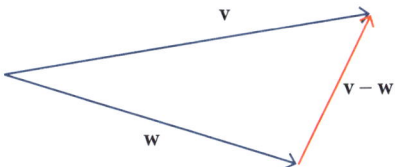

Let $\mathbf{v}, \mathbf{w}$ be nonzero vectors in $\mathbb{R}^2$. Then we can make the triangle above by translating the two vectors to start at the same point and the vector $\mathbf{v} - \mathbf{w}$ will make up the third side of the triangle. Since $\mathbf{v} - \mathbf{w} = (v_1 - w_1, v_2 - w_2)$, we have that
$$\begin{aligned}\|\mathbf{v} - \mathbf{w}\|^2 &= (v_1 - w_1)^2 + (v_2 - w_2)^2 \\ &= v_1^2 - 2v_1 w_1 + w_1^2 + v_2^2 - 2v_2 w_2 + w_2^2 \\ &= (v_1^2 + v_2^2) + (w_1^2 + w_2^2) - 2(v_1 w_1 + v_2 w_2) \\ &= \|\mathbf{v}\|^2 + \|\mathbf{w}\|^2 - 2(\mathbf{v} \cdot \mathbf{w})\end{aligned}$$
This means that
$$\mathbf{v} \cdot \mathbf{w} = \frac{1}{2}\left(\|\mathbf{v}\|^2 + \|\mathbf{w}\|^2 - \|\mathbf{v} - \mathbf{w}\|^2\right) \tag{2.1}$$

Using Pythagoras' Theorem, we see that the parenthesis is zero if and only if the angle between $\mathbf{v}$ and $\mathbf{w}$ is a straight angle. Therefore, we have that $\mathbf{v} \cdot \mathbf{w} = 0$ if and only if the angle between $\mathbf{v}$ and $\mathbf{w}$ is a straight angle.

The angle between $\mathbf{v}$ and $\mathbf{w}$ is called an *acute* angle if it is smaller than a straight angle and an *obtuse* angle if it is greater than a straight angle. From Equation (2.1), we see that $\mathbf{v} \cdot \mathbf{w} > 0$ implies that $\|\mathbf{v}\|^2 + \|\mathbf{w}\|^2 > \|\mathbf{v} - \mathbf{w}\|^2$, and $\mathbf{v} \cdot \mathbf{w} < 0$ implies that $\|\mathbf{v}\|^2 + \|\mathbf{w}\|^2 < \|\mathbf{v} - \mathbf{w}\|^2$. Hence $\mathbf{v} \cdot \mathbf{w} > 0$ corresponds to an acute angle between $\mathbf{v}$ and $\mathbf{w}$, and $\mathbf{v} \cdot \mathbf{w} < 0$ corresponds to an obtuse angle between $\mathbf{v}$ and $\mathbf{w}$.

Let us try to generalize this and consider two nonzero vectors $\mathbf{v}, \mathbf{w}$ in $\mathbb{R}^n$. We can make a similar construction and see that Equation (2.1) still holds. We say that the angle between $\mathbf{v}$ and $\mathbf{w}$ is

- a straight angle if $\mathbf{v} \cdot \mathbf{w} = 0$
- an acute angle if $\mathbf{v} \cdot \mathbf{w} > 0$
- an obtuse angle if $\mathbf{v} \cdot \mathbf{w} < 0$

When $n = 2$ or $n = 3$, this definition of the angle between $\mathbf{v}$ and $\mathbf{w}$ coincides with the angle we can picture geometrically. When $n > 3$, it is difficult to picture the angle between $\mathbf{v}$ and $\mathbf{w}$, and we must take the above statement as a definition. In general, we say that the vectors $\mathbf{v}$ and $\mathbf{w}$ are *orthogonal* (or perpendicular) if the angle between them is a straight angle, and write $\mathbf{v} \perp \mathbf{w}$ if this is the case.

Orthogonal vectors.

For any vectors $\mathbf{v}, \mathbf{w}$ in $\mathbb{R}^n$, we have that $\mathbf{v} \perp \mathbf{w}$ if and only if $\mathbf{v} \cdot \mathbf{w} = 0$.

Proposition 2.4. Let $\mathbf{u}, \mathbf{v}, \mathbf{w}$ be vectors in $\mathbb{R}^n$ and let r, s be scalars in $\mathbb{R}$. Then we have:

a) $\mathbf{v} \cdot \mathbf{w} = \mathbf{w} \cdot \mathbf{v}$
b) $\mathbf{u} \cdot (r\mathbf{v} + s\mathbf{w}) = r\mathbf{u} \cdot \mathbf{v} + s\mathbf{u} \cdot \mathbf{w}$
c) $\mathbf{v} \cdot \mathbf{v} \geq 0$, and $\mathbf{v} \cdot \mathbf{v} = 0$ only if $\mathbf{v} = \mathbf{0}$

Proof. A straightforward computation will prove each statement. For instance, we prove the last statement by computing $\mathbf{v} \cdot \mathbf{v}$ for an arbitrary vector $\mathbf{v} = (v_1, v_2, \ldots, v_n)$ in $\mathbb{R}^n$:

$$\mathbf{v} \cdot \mathbf{v} = v_1^2 + v_2^2 + \ldots + v_n^2$$

We see that $\mathbf{v} \cdot \mathbf{v} \geq 0$ since it is a sum of squares, and if $\mathbf{v} \cdot \mathbf{v} = 0$, then we must have $v_1 = v_2 = \ldots = v_n = 0$ since each square must be zero. □

2.5 Projections and the Cauchy-Schwarz inequality

The above result gives some useful rules for computing dot products. The first two properties are called the symmetric and bilinear property. An important consequence of these properties is that we can compute inner products in the familiar way we multiply parentheses. For example, we have

$$(\mathbf{v}_1 + 2\mathbf{v}_2) \cdot (\mathbf{v}_1 - \mathbf{v}_2) = \mathbf{v}_1 \cdot \mathbf{v}_1 + 2\mathbf{v}_2 \cdot \mathbf{v}_1 - \mathbf{v}_1 \cdot \mathbf{v}_2 - 2\mathbf{v}_2 \cdot \mathbf{v}_2$$
$$= \mathbf{v}_1 \cdot \mathbf{v}_1 + \mathbf{v}_1 \cdot \mathbf{v}_2 - 2\mathbf{v}_2 \cdot \mathbf{v}_2$$

for any vectors $\mathbf{v}_1, \mathbf{v}_2$.

2.5 Projections and the Cauchy-Schwarz inequality

Let $\mathbf{v}, \mathbf{w}$ be vectors in $\mathbb{R}^n$ with $\mathbf{w} \neq \mathbf{0}$. Let us try to decompose $\mathbf{v}$ into a component along the vector $\mathbf{w}$ and a component orthogonal to $\mathbf{w}$, such that $\mathbf{v} = r\mathbf{w} + \mathbf{u}$ for a scalar r and a vector $\mathbf{u}$ with $\mathbf{u} \perp \mathbf{w}$. This is illustrated in the figure below. The component $r\mathbf{w}$ in the direction of $\mathbf{w}$ is called the *orthogonal projection* of $\mathbf{v}$ onto $\mathbf{w}$, and it is written $\text{Proj}_\mathbf{w}(\mathbf{v})$.

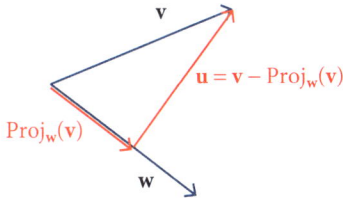

The orthogonality $\mathbf{u} \perp \mathbf{w}$ means that $\mathbf{u} \cdot \mathbf{w} = 0$, and when we solve $\mathbf{v} = r\mathbf{w} + \mathbf{u}$ for $\mathbf{u}$, we get $\mathbf{u} = \mathbf{v} - r\mathbf{w}$. Putting this together, we get $(\mathbf{v} - r\mathbf{w}) \cdot \mathbf{w} = \mathbf{v} \cdot \mathbf{w} - r(\mathbf{w} \cdot \mathbf{w}) = 0$. If $\mathbf{w} \neq \mathbf{0}$, there is a unique solution $r = (\mathbf{v} \cdot \mathbf{w})/(\mathbf{w} \cdot \mathbf{w})$.

> **Orthogonal projection.**
> When $\mathbf{v}, \mathbf{w}$ are vectors in $\mathbb{R}^n$ with $\mathbf{w} \neq \mathbf{0}$, the orthogonal projection of $\mathbf{v}$ onto $\mathbf{w}$ is given by
> $$\text{Proj}_\mathbf{w}(\mathbf{v}) = \frac{\mathbf{v} \cdot \mathbf{w}}{\mathbf{w} \cdot \mathbf{w}} \cdot \mathbf{w}$$

Theorem 2.5 (Cauchy-Schwarz inequality). Let $\mathbf{v}, \mathbf{w}$ be vectors in $\mathbb{R}^n$. Then we have that
$$(\mathbf{v} \cdot \mathbf{w})^2 \leq \|\mathbf{v}\|^2 \cdot \|\mathbf{w}\|^2$$
Moreover, equality holds if and only if one of the vectors $\mathbf{v}, \mathbf{w}$ is a scalar multiple of the other vector.

2 • Vectors and vector spaces

Proof. If $\mathbf{w} = \mathbf{0}$, then both sides of the inequality are zero and the theorem holds. We may therefore assume that $\mathbf{w} \neq \mathbf{0}$ and this means that $\mathbf{w} \cdot \mathbf{w} > 0$. Let us consider the vector

$$\mathbf{u} = \mathbf{v} - \text{Proj}_\mathbf{w}(\mathbf{v}) = \mathbf{v} - \frac{\mathbf{v} \cdot \mathbf{w}}{\mathbf{w} \cdot \mathbf{w}} \cdot \mathbf{w} = \mathbf{v} - r\mathbf{w}, \quad \text{with } r = \frac{\mathbf{v} \cdot \mathbf{w}}{\mathbf{w} \cdot \mathbf{w}}$$

Then we have that $\mathbf{u} \cdot \mathbf{w} = \mathbf{v} \cdot \mathbf{w} - (r\mathbf{w}) \cdot \mathbf{w} = \mathbf{v} \cdot \mathbf{w} - \mathbf{v} \cdot \mathbf{w} = 0$, hence $\mathbf{u} \perp \mathbf{w}$. This means that we can write $\mathbf{v} = \mathbf{u} + r\mathbf{w}$ as a sum of orthogonal vectors. We have that

$$\mathbf{v} \cdot \mathbf{v} = (\mathbf{u} + r\mathbf{w}) \cdot (\mathbf{u} + r\mathbf{w}) = \mathbf{u} \cdot \mathbf{u} + 2r(\mathbf{u} \cdot \mathbf{w}) + r^2(\mathbf{w} \cdot \mathbf{w})$$

$$= \mathbf{u} \cdot \mathbf{u} + r^2 \mathbf{w} \cdot \mathbf{w} \geq r^2(\mathbf{w} \cdot \mathbf{w}) = \frac{(\mathbf{v} \cdot \mathbf{w})^2}{\mathbf{w} \cdot \mathbf{w}}$$

since $\mathbf{u} \cdot \mathbf{w} = 0$ and $\mathbf{u} \cdot \mathbf{u} \geq 0$. Multiplying both sides with $\mathbf{w} \cdot \mathbf{w}$, we get the Cauchy-Schwarz inequality:

$$(\mathbf{v} \cdot \mathbf{v}) \cdot (\mathbf{w} \cdot \mathbf{w}) = \|\mathbf{v}\|^2 \cdot \|\mathbf{w}\|^2 \geq (\mathbf{v} \cdot \mathbf{w})^2$$

Finally, we see that equality holds if and only if $\mathbf{u} \cdot \mathbf{u} = 0$, which means that $\mathbf{u} = \mathbf{0}$, or that $\mathbf{v} = r\mathbf{w}$. □

Corollary 2.6. Let $\mathbf{v}, \mathbf{w}$ be nonzero vectors in $\mathbb{R}^n$. Then we have that

$$-1 \leq \frac{\mathbf{v} \cdot \mathbf{w}}{\|\mathbf{v}\| \cdot \|\mathbf{w}\|} \leq 1$$

Proof. The Cauchy-Schwarz inequality can be written $|\mathbf{v} \cdot \mathbf{w}| \leq \|\mathbf{v}\| \cdot \|\mathbf{w}\|$. This gives

$$\frac{|\mathbf{v} \cdot \mathbf{w}|}{\|\mathbf{v}\| \cdot \|\mathbf{w}\|} \leq 1 \quad \Rightarrow \quad -1 \leq \frac{\mathbf{v} \cdot \mathbf{w}}{\|\mathbf{v}\| \cdot \|\mathbf{w}\|} \leq 1$$

□

2.6 Span and linear independence

Let $\{\mathbf{v}_1, \mathbf{v}_2, \ldots, \mathbf{v}_r\}$ be a collection of vectors in $\mathbb{R}^n$. We define a *linear combination* of these vectors to be a vector of the form

$$\mathbf{v} = c_1 \mathbf{v}_1 + c_2 \mathbf{v}_2 + \ldots + c_r \mathbf{v}_r$$

where $c_1, c_2, \ldots, c_r$ are scalars. We write $V = \text{Span}(v_1, v_2, \ldots, v_r)$ for the collection of all such linear combinations, and call it the *span* of the vectors $\{\mathbf{v}_1, \mathbf{v}_2, \ldots, \mathbf{v}_r\}$. In other words,

$$V = \text{Span}(v_1, v_2, \ldots, v_r) = \{c_1 \mathbf{v}_1 + c_2 \mathbf{v}_2 + \ldots + c_r \mathbf{v}_r : c_1, c_2, \ldots, c_r \in \mathbb{R}\}$$

We call the subset V of $\mathbb{R}^n$ a *linear subspace* when V is the span of a collection of vectors in $\mathbb{R}^n$.

Let us consider some examples. First, consider the vector $\mathbf{v} = (2, 1)$ in $\mathbb{R}^2$. Then $V = \text{Span}(\mathbf{v}) = \{c\mathbf{v}_1 : c \in \mathbb{R}\}$ is the line spanned by the vector $\mathbf{v}$ shown in the figure below.

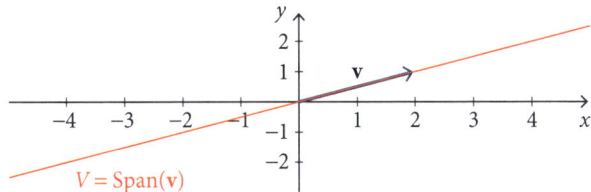

In fact, it is not difficult to see that the span of a single nonzero vector $\mathbf{v}$ in $\mathbb{R}^n$ is always the line spanned by $\mathbf{v}$. When $\mathbf{v} = (v_1, v_2, \ldots, v_n) \neq \mathbf{0}$, the line $V = \text{Span}(\mathbf{v})$ consists of all points of the form

$$(x_1, x_2, \ldots, x_n) = t(v_1, v_2, \ldots, v_n) = (tv_1, tv_2, \ldots, tv_n)$$

for some scalar t. In other words, when we write a line as $V = \text{Span}(\mathbf{v})$, we obtain a parametric description of the line V.

Next, we consider an example of linear subspace spanned by two vectors, the two vectors $\mathbf{v}_1 = (3, 1)$ and $\mathbf{v}_2 = (2, -3)$ in $\mathbb{R}^2$. In this case, the span is given by

$$V = \text{Span}(\mathbf{v}_1, \mathbf{v}_2) = \{s\mathbf{v}_1 + t\mathbf{v}_2 : s, t \in \mathbb{R}\}$$

We show this linear subspace in the figure below, and we see that it is a two-dimensional plane.

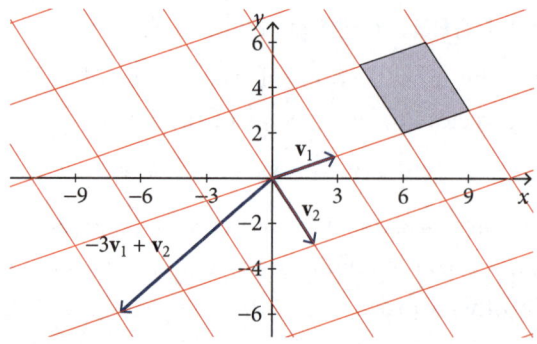

All intersections in the grid correspond to vectors of the form $\mathbf{v} = c_1\mathbf{v}_1 + c_2\mathbf{v}_2$ where c_1, c_2 are integers. For instance, the vector $-3\mathbf{v}_1 + \mathbf{v}_2$ is shown in the figure above. Vectors inside a parallelogram in the grid correspond to values of c_1 and c_2 between two consecutive integers. For example, the one marked in blue corresponds to vectors $\mathbf{v} = c_1\mathbf{v}_1 + c_2\mathbf{v}_2$ with $2 \leq c_1 \leq 3$ and $-1 \leq c_2 \leq 0$. This means that $V = \mathbb{R}^2$ since this span fills up the two-dimensional coordinate system.

For another example, let us consider the span of the vectors $\mathbf{v}_1 = (6, -2)$ and $\mathbf{v}_2 = (-3, 1)$. In this case, we have $\mathbf{v}_1 = -2\mathbf{v}_2$, hence the two vectors lie along the same line. This means that the linear subspace $V = \text{Span}(\mathbf{v}_1, \mathbf{v}_2)$ is a line.

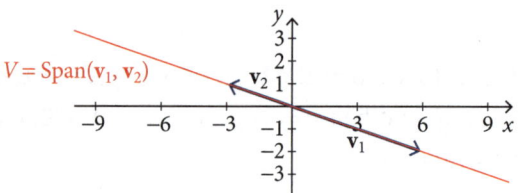

In fact, we have $c_1\mathbf{v}_1 + c_2\mathbf{v}_2 = c_1(-2\mathbf{v}_2) + c_2\mathbf{v}_2 = (c_2 - 2c_1)\mathbf{v}_2$ for any vector in $V = \text{Span}(\mathbf{v}_1, \mathbf{v}_2)$ and this means that $V = \text{Span}(\mathbf{v}_1, \mathbf{v}_2) = \text{Span}(\mathbf{v}_2)$. We could also have expressed $\mathbf{v}_2$ as $\mathbf{v}_2 = -0.5\mathbf{v}_1$, and written $V = \text{Span}(\mathbf{v}_1, \mathbf{v}_2) = \text{Span}(\mathbf{v}_1)$.

The above examples show us that the span of two vectors can be a plane or a line (that is, either two-dimensional or one-dimensional). Next, we shall see how to determine the dimension of $V = \text{Span}(\mathbf{v}_1, \mathbf{v}_2, \ldots, \mathbf{v}_r)$.

Let $\{\mathbf{v}_1, \mathbf{v}_2, \ldots, \mathbf{v}_r\}$ be a collection of vectors in $\mathbb{R}^n$. We say that the collection is *linearly dependent* if at least one of the vectors can be written as a linear combination of the others, and *linearly independent* otherwise.

2.6 Span and linear independence

For example, two nonzero vectors are linearly dependent if they span the same line, and linearly independent otherwise. Hence $\mathbf{v}_1 = (6, -2)$ and $\mathbf{v}_2 = (-3, 1)$ are linearly dependent since $\mathbf{v}_1 = -2\mathbf{v}_2$ (or because $\mathbf{v}_2 = -0.5\mathbf{v}_1$). On the other hand, the vectors $\mathbf{v}_1 = (3, 1)$ and $\mathbf{v}_2 = (2, -3)$ are linearly independent. We can see this from the figure in this simple case. But in more complicated cases, the following result is useful:

Lemma 2.7. Let $\{\mathbf{v}_1, \mathbf{v}_2, \ldots, \mathbf{v}_r\}$ be a collection of vectors in $\mathbb{R}^n$. The vectors are linearly independent if the vector equation

$$x_1\mathbf{v}_1 + x_2\mathbf{v}_2 + \ldots + x_r\mathbf{x}_r = \mathbf{0}$$

has only the trivial solution $(x_1, x_2, \ldots, x_r) = (0, 0, \ldots, 0)$, and linearly dependent if there are nontrivial solutions.

Proof. Assume that the vectors are linearly dependent, so that one of the vectors is a linear combination of the others, and let us say that $\mathbf{v}_1$ is a linear combination

$$\mathbf{v}_1 = c_2\mathbf{v}_2 + c_3\mathbf{v}_3 + \ldots + c_r\mathbf{v}_r$$

This can be written $\mathbf{0} = -1 \cdot \mathbf{v}_1 + c_2\mathbf{v}_2 + c_3\mathbf{v}_3 + \ldots + c_r\mathbf{v}_r$, which means that $(x_1, x_2, \ldots, x_r) = (-1, c_2, \ldots, c_r)$ is a solution to the vector equation. We see that this solution is nontrivial since $x_1 = -1 \neq 0$. If $\mathbf{v}_i$ for $i > 1$ is a linear combination of the other vectors, we can use a similar argument and get a nontrivial solution with $x_i = -1 \neq 0$. This proves that if the vectors are linearly dependent, then there are nontrivial solutions of the vector equation. Conversely, let us assume that the vector equation has a nontrivial solution $(x_1, x_2, \ldots, x_n) \neq (0, 0, \ldots, 0)$. Then at least one $x_i \neq 0$, and let us say that $x_1 \neq 0$. This means that

$$\mathbf{0} = x_1\mathbf{v}_1 + x_2\mathbf{v}_2 + \ldots + x_r\mathbf{x}_r$$
$$-x_1\mathbf{v}_1 = x_2\mathbf{v}_2 + x_3\mathbf{v}_3 + \ldots + x_r\mathbf{x}_r$$
$$\mathbf{v}_1 = -\frac{x_2}{x_1}\mathbf{v}_2 - \frac{x_3}{x_1}\mathbf{v}_3 - \ldots - \frac{x_r}{x_1}\mathbf{x}_r$$

Hence $\mathbf{v}_1$ is a linear combination of the other vectors, and the vectors are linearly dependent. If instead $x_i \neq 0$ for $i > 1$, we can use a similar argument to write $\mathbf{v}_i$ as a linear combination of the other vectors. This proves that if there are nontrivial solutions, then the vectors are linearly dependent. □

As an example, we consider the following three vectors in $\mathbb{R}^3$, and we will try to determine if they are linearly dependent:

$$\mathbf{v}_1 = \begin{pmatrix} 2 \\ 1 \\ 4 \end{pmatrix}, \quad \mathbf{v}_2 = \begin{pmatrix} 3 \\ 5 \\ -1 \end{pmatrix}, \quad \mathbf{v}_3 = \begin{pmatrix} 5 \\ -1 \\ 17 \end{pmatrix}$$

We use Lemma 2.7 and consider the vector equation $x_1\mathbf{v}_1 + x_2\mathbf{v}_2 + x_3\mathbf{v}_3 = \mathbf{0}$. This gives

$$x_1 \begin{pmatrix} 2 \\ 1 \\ 4 \end{pmatrix} + x_2 \begin{pmatrix} 3 \\ 5 \\ -1 \end{pmatrix} + x_3 \begin{pmatrix} 5 \\ -1 \\ 17 \end{pmatrix} = \begin{pmatrix} 0 \\ 0 \\ 0 \end{pmatrix}$$

which is a homogeneous linear system, with the following augmented matrix:

$$\begin{array}{r} 2x_1 + 3x_2 + 5x_3 = 0 \\ x_1 + 5x_2 - x_3 = 0 \\ 4x_1 - x_2 + 17x_3 = 0 \end{array} \quad \Rightarrow \quad \begin{pmatrix} 2 & 3 & 5 & | & 0 \\ 1 & 5 & -1 & | & 0 \\ 4 & -1 & 17 & | & 0 \end{pmatrix}$$

We notice that the coefficient matrix of this homogeneous linear system has the vectors $\mathbf{v}_1, \mathbf{v}_2, \mathbf{v}_3$ as its column vectors. To see if the system has nontrivial solutions, we solve it using Gaussian elimination. We start by switching the first two rows to get simpler computations:

$$\begin{pmatrix} 1 & 5 & -1 & | & 0 \\ 2 & 3 & 5 & | & 0 \\ 4 & -1 & 17 & | & 0 \end{pmatrix} \rightarrow \begin{pmatrix} 1 & 5 & -1 & | & 0 \\ 0 & -7 & 7 & | & 0 \\ 0 & -21 & 21 & | & 0 \end{pmatrix} \rightarrow \begin{pmatrix} 1 & 5 & -1 & | & 0 \\ 0 & -7 & 7 & | & 0 \\ 0 & 0 & 0 & | & 0 \end{pmatrix}$$

We see that the system has one free variable x_3, and this means that there are nontrivial solutions: We can choose any value for x_3, hence there are solutions with $x_3 \neq 0$. We could also find the nontrivial solutions explicitly: Back substitution gives $-7x_2 + 7x_3 = 0$, or $x_2 = x_3$, and $x_1 + 5x_2 - x_3 = 0$, or $x_1 = -5x_2 + x_3 = -4x_3$. With $x_3 = t$, we can write the solutions as $(x_1, x_2, x_3) = (-4t, t, t)$. With $t \neq 0$, we find the nontrivial solution $(-4t, t, t)$. This corresponds to

$$-4t\mathbf{v}_1 + t\mathbf{v}_2 + t\mathbf{v}_3 = \mathbf{0} \quad \Rightarrow \quad -4\mathbf{v}_1 + \mathbf{v}_2 + \mathbf{v}_3 = \mathbf{0} \quad \Rightarrow \quad \mathbf{v}_3 = 4\mathbf{v}_1 - \mathbf{v}_2$$

Note that by solving the linear system explicitly, we discover not only that the vectors are linear dependent (which we can see from the echelon form), but we also find a linear dependency relation $\mathbf{v}_3 = 4\mathbf{v}_1 - \mathbf{v}_2$.

2.7 Vector spaces

We define a *vector space* to be a set V of vectors, with defined operations of vector addition and scalar multiplication satisfying the properties of Proposition 2.1. The zero vector $\mathbf{0}$ and the opposite vector $-\mathbf{v}$ of any vector $\mathbf{v}$ are needed to write down the properties of Proposition 2.1, and it is part of the definition of a vector space that these vectors exist.

The set $V = \mathbb{R}^n$ is a vector space, since the vector addition and scalar multiplication that we have defined earlier in this chapter satisfy Proposition 2.1. The idea is to call any other space of vectors with similar properties a vector space as well. Hence $V = \mathbb{R}^n$ is a model for all vector spaces. It is called the *Euclidean n-space*.

To find other examples of vector spaces, we may consider subsets of $\mathbb{R}^n$. Let us start with a simple example: Let V be the set of all solutions of the linear equation $x + 2y = 0$, which we can write as $V = \{(x, y) : x + 2y = 0\}$. This is a subset of $\mathbb{R}^2$, since any solution can be viewed as a vector $\mathbf{v} = (x, y)$. If we solve the equation as a linear system, we get that $x = -2y$ with y free, so the solutions can be written

$$(x, y) = (-2t, t) = t \cdot (-2, 1) \quad \Rightarrow \quad V = \text{Span}(\mathbf{v}) \text{ with } \mathbf{v} = (-2, 1)$$

We show the subset V of $\mathbb{R}^2$ and the vector $\mathbf{v}$ that spans V in the figure below.

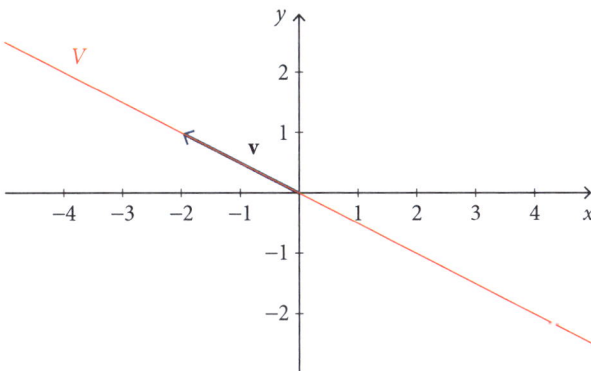

In general, a subset V of $\mathbb{R}^n$ is a vector space if the following conditions are satisfied:

a) The vector $\mathbf{0}$ is in V
b) For any vectors $\mathbf{v}, \mathbf{w}$ in V, the vector sum $\mathbf{v} + \mathbf{w}$ is in V
c) For any vector $\mathbf{v}$ in V and any scalar r, the scalar product $r\mathbf{v}$ is in V

If this is the case, we say that V is closed under vector addition and scalar multiplication. Hence there are defined operations of vector addition and scalar multiplication internally in V, and they will, of course, satisfy all the properties of Proposition 2.1.

Returning to our example $V = \{(x, y) : x + 2y = 0\}$, it is not difficult to see that V is closed under vector addition and scalar multiplication: First notice that $\mathbf{0} = (0, 0)$ is in V. Since any vectors $\mathbf{v}_1$ and $\mathbf{v}_2$ in V must be of the form $\mathbf{v}_1 = t_1(2, -1)$ and $\mathbf{v}_2 = t_2(2, -1)$, we have that

$$\mathbf{v}_1 + \mathbf{v}_2 = (t_1 + t_2) \cdot (2, -1), \quad r\mathbf{v}_1 = (rt_1) \cdot (2, -1)$$

These are vectors in V, and therefore V is closed under vector addition and scalar multiplication. This means that the line V is a vector space.

Vector subspaces.
Let V be any subset of $\mathbb{R}^n$. It is a vector space if it is closed under vector addition and scalar multiplication and contains the zero vector $\mathbf{0}$. In this case, V is called a *vector subspace* of $\mathbb{R}^n$.

A vector subspace V of $\mathbb{R}^n$ is called a *concrete vector space* since all vectors in V are n-vectors $\mathbf{v} = (v_1, v_2, \ldots, v_n)$. It is also possible to consider *abstract vector spaces*, where the vectors can be of more general types (for instance functions), but we shall not consider these kinds of vector spaces in this chapter.

Lemma 2.8. Let $V = \mathrm{Span}(\mathbf{v}_1, \mathbf{v}_2, \ldots, \mathbf{v}_r)$ be the span of r vectors $\{\mathbf{v}_1, \mathbf{v}_2, \ldots, \mathbf{v}_r\}$ in $\mathbb{R}^n$. Then V is a vector subspace of $\mathbb{R}^n$.

Proof. Let $\mathbf{v} = c_1 \mathbf{v}_1 + \ldots + c_r \mathbf{v}_r$ and $\mathbf{w} = d_1 \mathbf{v}_1 + \ldots + d_r \mathbf{v}_r$ be vectors in V, and let s be a scalar. Then we have that

$$\mathbf{v} + \mathbf{w} = (c_1 + d_1)\mathbf{v}_1 + \ldots + (c_r + d_r)\mathbf{v}_r$$
$$s\mathbf{v} = (sc_1)\mathbf{v}_1 + \ldots + (sc_r)\mathbf{v}_r$$

Since these vectors are in V, it follows that V is closed under vector addition and scalar multiplication. Clearly $\mathbf{0}$ is in V, hence V is a vector subspace of $\mathbb{R}^n$. □

The set of solutions of a nonhomogeneous linear equation is not a vector subspace since $\mathbf{0}$ is not included among the solutions. For instance, the solutions of $x + 2y = 1$ is not a vector subspace of $\mathbb{R}^2$ since $(x, y) = (0, 0)$ is not a solution.

2.7 Vector spaces

Bases and dimension. Let V be a vector space. A set $B = \{\mathbf{v}_1, \mathbf{v}_2, \ldots, \mathbf{v}_d\}$ of vectors in V is called a *base* for V if the following conditions hold:

a) $V = \text{Span}(\mathbf{v}_1, \mathbf{v}_2, \ldots, \mathbf{v}_d)$
b) B is a linearly independent set of vectors

If V has a base that consists of d vectors, then we say that V has dimension d, and write $\dim V = d$. We will not prove it in this chapter, but it is a fact that if B and B' are two different bases of V, then they contain the same number of vectors. The dimension of a vector subspace of $\mathbb{R}^n$ is therefore well-defined.

As a simple example, let us consider the Euclidean space $\mathbb{R}^2$. It is clearly spanned by the vectors $\mathbf{e}_1 = (1, 0)$ and $\mathbf{e}_2 = (0, 1)$, since we have

$$(v_1, v_2) = v_1 \cdot (1, 0) + v_2 \cdot (0, 1) = v_1 \mathbf{e}_1 + v_2 \mathbf{e}_2$$

for any vector $\mathbf{v} = (v_1, v_2)$ in $\mathbb{R}^2$. We can write this as $\mathbb{R}^2 = \text{Span}(\mathbf{e}_1, \mathbf{e}_2)$. It is not difficult to see that the vectors $\{\mathbf{e}_1, \mathbf{e}_2\}$ are linearly independent. Together, the two requirements for a base mean that any vector $\mathbf{v} = (v_1, v_2)$ in $\mathbb{R}^2$ can be expressed as a linear combination of $\mathbf{e}_1$ and $\mathbf{e}_2$ in a unique way. We conclude that $B = \{\mathbf{e}_1, \mathbf{e}_2\}$ is a base for $\mathbb{R}^2$, and that $\dim \mathbb{R}^2 = 2$. Note that the two vectors are the unit vectors (that is, vectors of length one) along the two coordinate axes.

In a similar way, we get a base for the Euclidean n-space $V = \mathbb{R}^n$ by considering the set $B = \{\mathbf{e}_1, \mathbf{e}_2, \ldots, \mathbf{e}_n\}$ of unit vectors along the n coordinate axes, given by

$$\mathbf{e}_1 = (1, 0, 0, \ldots, 0), \quad \mathbf{e}_2 = (0, 1, 0, \ldots, 0), \quad \ldots \quad \mathbf{e}_n = (0, 0, 0, \ldots, 1)$$

In fact, we have that any vector $\mathbf{v} = (v_1, v_2, \ldots, v_n)$ in $\mathbb{R}^n$ can be written

$$(v_1, v_2, \ldots, v_n) = v_1 \cdot (1, 0, \ldots, 0) + v_2 \cdot (0, 1, \ldots, 0) + \ldots + v_n \cdot (0, 0, \ldots, 1)$$

in a unique way. This means that B is a base for $\mathbb{R}^n$, and that $\dim \mathbb{R}^n = n$.

Column space of a matrix. Let A be any $n \times r$ matrix. Then the column vectors of A are r vectors in $\mathbb{R}^n$ that we may call $\mathbf{v}_1, \mathbf{v}_2, \ldots, \mathbf{v}_r$. The *column space* of the matrix A is written $\text{Col}(A)$, and it is defined to be the span $\text{Col}(A) = \text{Span}(\mathbf{v}_1, \mathbf{v}_2, \ldots, \mathbf{v}_r)$ of the column vectors of A.

Let us consider a simple example. We let $V = \text{Col}(A)$, where A is the 3×4 matrix given by

$$A = \begin{pmatrix} 1 & 2 & -1 & 3 \\ 2 & 5 & 0 & 2 \\ 3 & 6 & 4 & 2 \end{pmatrix}$$

and we let $\mathbf{v}_1, \mathbf{v}_2, \mathbf{v}_3, \mathbf{v}_4$ be its columns. By definition, $V = \text{Span}(\mathbf{v}_1, \mathbf{v}_2, \mathbf{v}_3, \mathbf{v}_4)$, so the four column vectors span V. To find out if the vectors are linearly independent, we consider the vector equation $x_1 \mathbf{v}_1 + x_2 \mathbf{v}_2 + x_3 \mathbf{v}_3 + x_4 \mathbf{v}_4 = \mathbf{0}$, which is a homogeneous linear system with coefficient matrix A. We use Gaussian elimination to find the pivot positions, marked in blue:

$$A = \begin{pmatrix} 1 & 2 & -1 & 3 \\ 2 & 5 & 0 & 2 \\ 3 & 6 & 4 & 2 \end{pmatrix} \rightarrow \begin{pmatrix} \underline{1} & 2 & -1 & 3 \\ 0 & \underline{1} & 2 & -4 \\ 0 & 0 & \underline{7} & -7 \end{pmatrix}$$

We see that there is one free variable x_4, and therefore infinitely many solutions. This means that the vectors are linearly dependent. We find nontrivial solutions by back substitution, and get $x_4 = t$, $7x_3 - 7x_4 = 0$ or $x_3 = t$, $x_2 + 2x_3 - 4x_4 = 0$ or $x_2 = -2t + 4t = 2t$, and $x_1 + 2x_2 - x_3 + 3x_4 = 0$ or $x_1 = -2(2t) + t - 3t = -6t$. We choose $t = 1$ to find one nontrivial solution $(x_1, x_2, x_3, x_4) = (-6, 2, 1, 1)$. This means that

$$-6\mathbf{v}_1 + 2\mathbf{v}_2 + \mathbf{v}_3 + \mathbf{v}_4 = \mathbf{0} \quad \Rightarrow \quad \mathbf{v}_4 = 6\mathbf{v}_1 - 2\mathbf{v}_2 - \mathbf{v}_3$$

We have that $V = \text{Span}(\mathbf{v}_1, \mathbf{v}_2, \mathbf{v}_3)$ since $\mathbf{v}_4 = 6\mathbf{v}_1 - 2\mathbf{v}_2 - \mathbf{v}_3$ is in this span. Moreover, the first three vectors are linearly independent: Had we carried out the computations above with only the three first columns or vectors, we would have obtained a pivot in every column. We conclude that $B = \{\mathbf{v}_1, \mathbf{v}_2, \mathbf{v}_3\}$ is a base for $V = \text{Col}(A)$, and that $\mathbf{v}_4 = 6\mathbf{v}_1 - 2\mathbf{v}_2 - \mathbf{v}_3$. Note that the three vectors in the base correspond to variable columns with pivots (or basic variables) and the other vectors correspond to variables without pivots (free variables).

Proposition 2.9. Let A be any $n \times r$ matrix, and let $V = \text{Col}(A)$ be its column space. Then the set B consisting of those column vectors corresponding to pivot columns is a base for V. In particular, $\dim V = \text{rk } A$.

Proof. We can reduce the matrix A to an echelon form E, and choose B to be the set of column vectors in A which correspond to a pivot in E. It is clear that the vectors in B are linearly independent: If we carried out the Gaussian process on the matrix with only these columns, there would be a pivot in every column of the echelon form. Moreover, all column vectors not in B must be a linear combination of the vectors in B: To see this, put the free variable corresponding to this column equal to 1, and all other free variables (if any) equal to 0. Therefore, the vectors in B span V, and form a base of V. □

2.7 Vector spaces

Note that any vector subspace in $\mathbb{R}^n$ of the form $V = \text{Span}(\mathbf{v}_1, \mathbf{v}_2, \ldots, \mathbf{v}_r)$ for some vectors $\mathbf{v}_1, \mathbf{v}_2, \ldots, \mathbf{v}_r$ is a column space. In fact, $V = \text{Col}(A)$ for the matrix A with the vectors $\mathbf{v}_1, \mathbf{v}_2, \ldots, \mathbf{v}_r$ as columns. Therefore, the method shown above is a quite general method for finding the base and the dimension of a vector subspace.

Proposition 2.10. Let V be a vector subspace of $\mathbb{R}^n$. Then V has a base B, and $\dim V \leq n$.

Proof. If $V = 0$ then the empty set is a base for V and $\dim V = 0$. Otherwise, we may pick a nonzero vector $\mathbf{v}_1$ in V. If $V = \text{Span}(\mathbf{v}_1)$, then $B = \{\mathbf{v}_1\}$ is a base of V and $\dim V = 1$. Otherwise, there is another nonzero vector $\mathbf{v}_2$ in V that is not in $\text{Span}(\mathbf{v}_1)$, and this implies that $\{\mathbf{v}_1, \mathbf{v}_2\}$ is a set of linearly independent vectors in V. We can continue in this way until we find a linearly independent set $B = \{\mathbf{v}_1, \mathbf{v}_2, \ldots, \mathbf{v}_r\}$ of vectors in V such that $V = \text{Span}(\mathbf{v}_1, \mathbf{v}_2, \ldots, \mathbf{v}_r)$. In fact, the process will stop for some $r \leq n$, otherwise we would obtain a set of $n+1$ linearly independent vectors in $\mathbb{R}^n$, and this is impossible according to Proposition 2.9. This also implies that $\dim V \leq n$. □

The null space of a matrix. Let A be any $m \times n$ matrix, and consider the homogeneous linear system with coefficient matrix A. We call the set V of all solutions $\mathbf{x} = (x_1, x_2, \ldots, x_n)$ in $\mathbb{R}^n$ of this linear system the *null space* of A, and write $V = \text{Null}(A)$.

Let us consider a simple example. We let $V = \text{Null}(A)$, where A is the 3×5 matrix given by

$$A = \begin{pmatrix} 1 & 2 & -1 & 3 & 1 \\ 2 & 5 & 0 & 2 & 3 \\ 3 & 6 & 4 & 2 & 3 \end{pmatrix}$$

This means that V is the set of all solutions $\mathbf{x} = (x_1, x_2, x_3, x_4, x_5)$ of the homogenous linear system with coefficient matrix A. We solve this system by Gaussian elimination, and find the echelon form

$$A = \begin{pmatrix} 1 & 2 & -1 & 3 & 1 \\ 2 & 5 & 0 & 2 & 3 \\ 3 & 6 & 4 & 2 & 3 \end{pmatrix} \rightarrow \begin{pmatrix} \underline{1} & 2 & -1 & 3 & 1 \\ 0 & \underline{1} & 2 & -4 & 1 \\ 0 & 0 & \underline{7} & -7 & 0 \end{pmatrix}$$

We see that there are two free variables x_4 and x_5, and infinitely many solutions. We find the solutions by back substitution, using $x_4 = s$ and $x_5 = t$ for the free variables. This gives $7x_3 - 7x_4 = 0$ or $x_3 = s$ from the last equation, $x_2 + 2x_3 - 4x_4 + x_5 = 0$ or $x_2 = -2s + 4s - t = 2s - t$ from the middle equation,

55

and $x_1 + 2x_2 - x_3 + 3x_4 + x_5 = 0$ or $x_1 = -2(2s - t) + s - 3s - t = -6s + t$ from the first equation. This gives the general solution of the form

$$\mathbf{x} = (-6s + t, 2s - t, s, s, t) = s \cdot (-6, 2, 1, 1, 0) + t \cdot (1, -1, 0, 0, 1)$$

where s and t are free variables or parameters. In other words, we can write the set of all solutions of the homogeneous linear system as

$$V = \text{Null}(A) = \text{Span}(\mathbf{w}_1, \mathbf{w}_2) \quad \text{with} \quad \mathbf{w}_1 = (-6, 2, 1, 1, 0), \; \mathbf{w}_2 = (1, -1, 0, 0, 1)$$

It is easy to see that $B = \{\mathbf{w}_1, \mathbf{w}_2\}$ is a set of linearly independent vectors, and is therefore a base for $V = \text{Null}(A)$. It follows that $\dim V = 2$. Note that there is one vector in the base B for each free variable in the linear system.

Proposition 2.11. Let A be an $m \times n$ matrix, and let $V = \text{Null}(A)$ be its null space. Then $\dim V = n - \text{rk } A$.

Proof. The number of degrees of freedom in the homogeneous linear system with coefficient matrix A is given by $n - \text{rk}(A)$, and if we solve the linear system using Gaussian elimination, we can always write the solutions in the form

$$\mathbf{x} = t_1 \cdot \mathbf{w}_1 + t_2 \cdot \mathbf{w}_2 + \ldots + t_s \cdot \mathbf{w}_s$$

where $s = n - \text{rk } A$ is the number of free variables, and $t_1, t_2, \ldots, t_s$ are the free variables or parameters. In other words, $B = \{\mathbf{w}_1, \mathbf{w}_2, \ldots, \mathbf{w}_s\}$ spans $V = \text{Null}(A)$, and it is a consequence of the Gaussian elimination method that the vectors in B are linearly independent. □

Problems

Problem 2.1 Show the vector $\mathbf{u} = (1, 3)$, $\mathbf{v} = (4, -1)$, and $\mathbf{w} = (-2, 2)$ in a figure, and use the geometric construction to find $\mathbf{u} + \mathbf{v}$, $\mathbf{u} - \mathbf{w}$, and $-2\mathbf{w}$. Then compute these vectors using coordinates.

Problem 2.2 Let $\mathbf{u} = (1, 3)$, $\mathbf{v} = (4, -1)$, and $\mathbf{w} = (-2, 2)$. Compute the following:

a) $\|\mathbf{u}\|$ b) $\|\mathbf{v}\|$ c) $\|\mathbf{w}\|$
d) $\mathbf{u} \cdot \mathbf{v}$ e) $\mathbf{u} \cdot \mathbf{w}$ f) $\mathbf{v} \cdot \mathbf{w}$

Problem 2.3 Let $\mathbf{u} = (1, 3)$, $\mathbf{v} = (4, -1)$, and $\mathbf{w} = (-2, 2)$. Compute the following:

a) $\text{Proj}_\mathbf{u}(\mathbf{v})$ b) $\text{Proj}_\mathbf{u}(\mathbf{w})$ c) $\text{Proj}_\mathbf{v}(\mathbf{w})$ d) $\text{Proj}_\mathbf{v}(\mathbf{u})$

Problem 2.4 Express the vector $\mathbf{w} = (8, 9)$ as a linear combination of $\mathbf{v}_1 = (2, 5)$ and $\mathbf{v}_2 = (-1, 3)$, if possible.

Problem 2.5 Find a parametric description of the following lines and planes:

a) The line through $(4, 1)$ and $(1, -3)$ in $\mathbb{R}^2$
b) The line in $\mathbb{R}^2$ with equation $2x + 3y = 1$
c) The line through $(1, 1, -1)$ and $(2, 0, 3)$ in $\mathbb{R}^3$
d) The plane through $(1, 1, -1)$, $(0, 3, 1)$ and $(2, 0, 3)$ in $\mathbb{R}^3$
e) The plane in $\mathbb{R}^3$ with equation $x + 2y + 3z = 6$

Problem 2.6 What is the distance from the origin to a point in $\mathbb{R}^3$ satisfying the equation $x^2 + y^2 + z^2 = 16$?

Problem 2.7 Let $\mathbf{u}$, $\mathbf{v}$, and $\mathbf{w}$ be vectors of length $\|\mathbf{u}\| = \|\mathbf{v}\| = \|\mathbf{w}\| = 2$ with
$$\mathbf{u} \cdot \mathbf{v} = 1, \quad \mathbf{u} \cdot \mathbf{w} = -2, \quad \mathbf{v} \cdot \mathbf{w} = 3$$
What is the length of the vector $\mathbf{u} - \mathbf{v} + 2\mathbf{w}$?

Problem 2.8 Determine whether the following pairs of vectors are linearly independent:

a) $\mathbf{v} = (-1, 2)$, $\mathbf{w} = (3, -6)$ b) $\mathbf{v} = (2, -1)$, $\mathbf{w} = (3, 4)$

2 • Vectors and vector spaces

Problem 2.9 Show that the following vectors are linearly dependent and find a linear dependency relation:
$$\mathbf{v}_1 = (1, 1, 1), \quad \mathbf{v}_2 = (2, 1, 0), \quad \mathbf{v}_3 = (3, 1, 4), \quad \mathbf{v}_4 = (1, 2, -2)$$

Problem 2.10 Assume that $\{\mathbf{u}, \mathbf{v}, \mathbf{w}\}$ are linearly independent vectors.

a) Show that the vectors $\{\mathbf{u} + \mathbf{v}, \mathbf{v} + \mathbf{w}, \mathbf{u} + \mathbf{w}\}$ are linearly independent

b) Are the vectors $\{\mathbf{u} - \mathbf{v}, \mathbf{v} + \mathbf{w}, \mathbf{u} + \mathbf{w}\}$ linearly independent?

Problem 2.11 Let $\{\mathbf{v}_1, \mathbf{v}_2, \ldots, \mathbf{v}_r\}$ be a set of r vectors in $\mathbb{R}^n$. Explain why the set of vectors must be linearly dependent if $r > n$.

Problem 2.12 Determine the values of a such that the following vectors are linearly independent:

a) $\mathbf{v}_1 = (1, 0, 1), \quad \mathbf{v}_2 = (2, 1, 0), \quad \mathbf{v}_3 = (a, 1, 1)$

b) $\mathbf{v}_1 = (2, 1, 4), \quad \mathbf{v}_2 = (-1, 2, 0), \quad \mathbf{v}_3 = (1, a, 4)$

Problem 2.13 We consider the column vectors $\mathbf{v}_1, \mathbf{v}_2, \mathbf{v}_3$ of the matrix
$$A = \begin{pmatrix} 1 & 2 & 4 \\ 3 & 7 & 0 \\ 5 & 11 & 8 \end{pmatrix}$$

a) Show that the vectors $\{\mathbf{v}_1, \mathbf{v}_2, \mathbf{v}_3\}$ are linearly dependent.

b) Find a nontrivial solution of $x_1 \mathbf{v}_1 + x_2 \mathbf{v}_2 + x_3 \mathbf{v}_3 = \mathbf{0}$, and use this solution to express one of the three vectors as a linear combination of the two others.

Problem 2.14 Let $\mathbf{v} = c_1 \mathbf{v}_1 + c_2 \mathbf{v}_2 + \ldots + c_r \mathbf{v}_r$. Show that the vectors $\{\mathbf{v}_1, \mathbf{v}_2, \ldots, \mathbf{v}_r\}$ are linearly independent if and only if
$$\mathbf{v} = c_1 \mathbf{v}_1 + c_2 \mathbf{v}_2 + \ldots + c_r \mathbf{v}_r$$
is the only way to express $\mathbf{v}$ as a linear combination of these vectors.

Problem 2.15 We consider the column vectors v_1, v_2, v_3, v_4 of the matrix
$$A = \begin{pmatrix} 1 & 2 & 4 & -1 \\ 3 & 7 & 0 & 4 \\ 5 & 11 & 8 & 2 \\ -2 & -5 & 4 & 5 \end{pmatrix}$$

a) Show that the vectors $\{v_1, v_2, v_3, v_4\}$ are linearly dependent and find a linear dependency relation.

b) Find a base of the vector space $V = \text{Col}(A)$ and determine its dimension

c) Find a base of the vector space $W = \text{Null}(A)$ and determine its dimension

Problem 2.16 Let $V = \text{Span}(v_1, v_2, \ldots, v_r)$ for a set $\{v_1, v_2, \ldots, v_r\}$ of vectors in $\mathbb{R}^n$, and let A be the matrix with the vectors $v_1, v_2, \ldots, v_r$ as columns.

a) Explain how to find a base of V among the vectors in the set $\{v_1, v_2, \ldots, v_r\}$

b) Show that $\dim V = \text{rk}(A)$

CHAPTER 3

Matrices and determinants

3.1 Matrices and matrix algebra

We define an $m \times n$ matrix A to be a rectangular array of numbers with m rows and n columns

$$A = \begin{pmatrix} a_{11} & a_{12} & a_{13} & \cdots & a_{1n} \\ a_{21} & a_{22} & a_{23} & \cdots & a_{2n} \\ a_{31} & a_{32} & a_{33} & \cdots & a_{3n} \\ \vdots & \vdots & \vdots & \ddots & \vdots \\ a_{m1} & a_{m2} & a_{m3} & \cdots & a_{mn} \end{pmatrix}$$

We shall use uppercase letters such as A as symbols for matrices, and we write a_{ij} for the entry in position (i, j) of the matrix A. That is, a_{ij} is the entry in row i and column j of the matrix.

To specify a matrix A, we have to specify its size $m \times n$, and to specify all the entries a_{ij} in the matrix for $1 \leq i \leq m$ and $1 \leq j \leq n$. A more compact way of writing the matrix is $A = (a_{ij})$.

Matrices are used in many different contexts. Any set of data in tabular form (that is, a two-dimensional array of numbers) can be represented by a matrix. Matrices are therefore frequently used in data analysis. In this book, we have already seen that matrices can be used to represent linear systems in Chapter 1. Later in the book, we will use matrices to analyze functions in several variables and systems of differential equations.

In what follows, we shall describe the most common and useful operations that we perform on matrices, and the formal rules that hold for these operations. Many of these *algebraic laws* for matrices (but not all) are similar to the laws we use when we compute with numbers.

Addition and subtraction of matrices. We say that two matrices A and B have the same size if they have the same number of rows and the same number of columns. If this is the case, we can add or subtract the matrices position by position:

$$A + B = (a_{ij}) + (b_{ij}) = (a_{ij} + b_{ij})$$
$$A - B = (a_{ij}) - (b_{ij}) = (a_{ij} - b_{ij})$$

This means that the entry in position (i, j) of the matrix $A + B$ is given by $a_{ij} + b_{ij}$, and that the entry in position (i, j) of the matrix $A - B$ is given by $a_{ij} - b_{ij}$. For example, we have that

$$\begin{pmatrix} 1 & 0 & 7 \\ 2 & -1 & 2 \end{pmatrix} + \begin{pmatrix} 4 & 1 & -3 \\ 0 & 4 & -3 \end{pmatrix} = \begin{pmatrix} 5 & 1 & 4 \\ 2 & 3 & -1 \end{pmatrix}$$

$$\begin{pmatrix} 1 & 0 & 7 \\ 2 & -1 & 2 \end{pmatrix} - \begin{pmatrix} 4 & 1 & -3 \\ 0 & 4 & -3 \end{pmatrix} = \begin{pmatrix} -3 & -1 & 10 \\ 2 & -5 & 5 \end{pmatrix}$$

If the matrices A and B do not have the same size, then the addition $A + B$ and subtraction $A - B$ are not defined.

Scalar multiplication of matrices. The multiplication of a matrix with a number is called scalar multiplication of matrices, since numbers are called *scalars* when used together with matrices. Given any matrix A and any number r, we can multiply r with the matrix A position by position:

$$r \cdot A = r \cdot (a_{ij}) = (r \cdot a_{ij})$$

This means that the entry in position (i, j) of the matrix $r \cdot A$ is given by $r \cdot a_{ij}$. For example, we have that

$$2 \cdot \begin{pmatrix} 1 & 0 & 7 \\ 2 & -1 & 2 \end{pmatrix} = \begin{pmatrix} 2 & 0 & 14 \\ 4 & -2 & 4 \end{pmatrix}$$

When we multiply a matrix with a number r, the matrix is scaled up by a factor of r, and this is the reason for the name scalar. We define the scalar multiplication $A \cdot r$ of a matrix by a scalar similarly, so that $A \cdot r = r \cdot A$. The matrix $-1 \cdot A$ is usually written $-A$. The matrix $0 \cdot A = 0$ is called the *zero matrix* since all its entries are zero.

Vectors as column vectors. A matrix that consists of a single column is called a *column vector*, and we have seen in Chapter 2 that any vector $\mathbf{v} = (v_1, v_2, \ldots, v_n)$ in $\mathbb{R}^n$ can be thought of as a column vector

$$\mathbf{v} = \begin{pmatrix} v_1 \\ v_2 \\ \vdots \\ v_n \end{pmatrix}$$

When we consider vectors as column vectors, we can think of vector addition and scalar multiplication of vectors as special cases of the corresponding operations for matrices. It is often useful to consider vectors as column vectors when we compute with both vectors and matrices.

We shall use boldface letters as symbols for column vectors, just as we did for vectors in Chapter 2. The convention that uppercase letters are used for matrices, lowercase letters are used for scalars (numbers), and boldface letters are used for vectors is very useful.

Matrix multiplication. The matrix multiplication $A \cdot B$ is defined when the number of columns in A equals the number of rows in B. If $A = (a_{ij})$ is an $m \times n$ matrix and $B = (b_{ij})$ is an $n \times p$ matrix, then $A \cdot B$ is the $m \times p$ matrix (c_{ij}) where

$$c_{ij} = a_{i1}b_{1j} + a_{i2}b_{2j} + \ldots + a_{in}b_{nj}$$

This means that the entry in position (i, j) of the product $A \cdot B$ is determined by inner product or dot product of the i'th row of A and the j'th column of B, considered as vectors, for $1 \leq i \leq m$ and $1 \leq j \leq p$. For example, we have that

$$\begin{pmatrix} 1 & 3 \\ 2 & -1 \end{pmatrix} \cdot \begin{pmatrix} 1 & 0 & 1 \\ 2 & -1 & 2 \end{pmatrix} = \begin{pmatrix} 7 & -3 & 7 \\ 0 & 1 & 0 \end{pmatrix}$$

In this example, we show the entry in position $(1, 3)$ of the product AB in blue, and show the first row of the first factor A and the third column of the second factor B in blue. The formula $c_{13} = a_{11}b_{13} + a_{12}b_{23}$ gives $c_{13} = 1 \cdot 1 + 3 \cdot 2 = 7$. The computation is similar for the other positions of the product.

We notice that matrix multiplication is not symmetric; the product BA will therefore not equal AB. In the example above, the product BA is not even defined, since B is a 2×3 matrix and A is a 2×2 matrix. This is an example of two matrices A and B, where both AB and BA are defined, but $AB \neq BA$:

$$AB = \begin{pmatrix} 0 & 1 \\ 0 & 0 \end{pmatrix} \cdot \begin{pmatrix} 0 & 0 \\ 0 & 1 \end{pmatrix} = \begin{pmatrix} 0 & 1 \\ 0 & 0 \end{pmatrix},$$

$$BA = \begin{pmatrix} 0 & 0 \\ 0 & 1 \end{pmatrix} \cdot \begin{pmatrix} 0 & 1 \\ 0 & 0 \end{pmatrix} = \begin{pmatrix} 0 & 0 \\ 0 & 0 \end{pmatrix}$$

We say that matrix multiplication is *noncommutative* since $AB \neq BA$ for general matrices A and B. There are special cases of matrices A and B such that $AB = BA$, and such matrices are called commuting matrices.

Proposition 3.1 (Distributive and associative laws). For all matrices A, B, C such that the following operations are defined, we have that:

a) $A(B + C) = AB + AC$
b) $(A + B)C = AC + BC$
c) $A(BC) = (AB)C$

Proof. We prove the first distributive law $A(B + C) = AB + AC$. The proofs of the remaining matrix laws are similar: Let A be an $m \times n$ matrix $A = (a_{ij})$ and let B and C be $n \times p$ matrices with $B + C = (b_{ij} + c_{ij})$. Then all operations are defined, and it follows from the definition of matrix multiplication that the entry in position (i, j) in the product $A(B + C)$ is given by

$$(A(B+C))_{ij} = a_{i1}(b_{1j} + c_{1j}) + a_{i2}(b_{2j} + c_{2j}) + \ldots + a_{in}(b_{nj} + c_{nj})$$
$$= (a_{i1}b_{1j} + a_{i2}b_{2j} + \ldots + a_{in}b_{nj}) + (a_{i1}c_{1j} + a_{i2}c_{2j} + \ldots + a_{in}c_{nj})$$
$$= (AB + AC)_{ij}$$

It equals the entry in position (i, j) of the matrix $AB + AC$ for all i, j, and therefore $A(B + C) = AB + AC$. $\square$

Matrix form of linear systems. We consider an $m \times n$ linear system, which can be written on the form

$$a_{11}x_1 + a_{12}x_2 + \ldots + a_{1n}x_n = b_1$$
$$a_{21}x_1 + a_{22}x_2 + \ldots + a_{2n}x_n = b_2$$
$$\vdots \qquad \vdots \qquad \vdots \qquad \vdots$$
$$a_{m1}x_1 + a_{m2}x_2 + \ldots + a_{mn}x_n = b_m$$

Let us write $A = (a_{ij})$ for its coefficient matrix, and consider $\mathbf{x} = (x_1, x_2, \ldots, x_n)$ and $\mathbf{b} = (b_1, b_2, \ldots, b_m)$ as column vectors. Then the linear system can be written as a matrix equation $A\mathbf{x} = \mathbf{b}$, or

$$\begin{pmatrix} a_{11} & a_{12} & \ldots & a_{1n} \\ a_{21} & a_{22} & \ldots & a_{2n} \\ \vdots & \vdots & \ddots & \vdots \\ a_{m1} & a_{m2} & \ldots & a_{mn} \end{pmatrix} \cdot \begin{pmatrix} x_1 \\ x_2 \\ \vdots \\ x_n \end{pmatrix} = \begin{pmatrix} b_1 \\ b_2 \\ \vdots \\ b_m \end{pmatrix}$$

This is called the *matrix form* of the linear system.

Powers of matrices. An $m \times n$ matrix A is called *square* if $m = n$, or the number of rows equals the number of columns. For square matrices, we can define the powers A^k for all positive integers $k \geq 1$ by matrix multiplication:

$$A^1 = A, \quad A^2 = A \cdot A, \quad A^3 = A \cdot A \cdot A, \quad \ldots$$

More formally, we can define these powers inductively by $A^k = A^{k-1} \cdot A$ for $k \geq 2$. It is clear that if A is an $n \times n$ matrix, then A^k is an $n \times n$ matrix for $k \geq 2$. For example, we have

$$A = \begin{pmatrix} 1 & 3 \\ 2 & -1 \end{pmatrix} \Rightarrow A^2 = \begin{pmatrix} 1 & 3 \\ 2 & -1 \end{pmatrix} \cdot \begin{pmatrix} 1 & 3 \\ 2 & -1 \end{pmatrix} = \begin{pmatrix} 7 & 0 \\ 0 & 7 \end{pmatrix}$$

We can also compute higher powers of the matrix in this example, for instance $A^3 = A \cdot A^2$ and $A^4 = A^2 \cdot A^2$:

$$A^3 = \begin{pmatrix} 1 & 3 \\ 2 & -1 \end{pmatrix} \cdot \begin{pmatrix} 7 & 0 \\ 0 & 7 \end{pmatrix} = \begin{pmatrix} 7 & 21 \\ 14 & -7 \end{pmatrix},$$

$$A^4 = \begin{pmatrix} 7 & 0 \\ 0 & 7 \end{pmatrix} \cdot \begin{pmatrix} 7 & 0 \\ 0 & 7 \end{pmatrix} = \begin{pmatrix} 49 & 0 \\ 0 & 49 \end{pmatrix}$$

Note that it is hard to compute A^k directly when k is a large integer.

Special matrices. The *diagonal* of an $n \times n$ matrix A consists of the entries $a_{11}, a_{22}, \ldots, a_{nn}$ on the main diagonal. We say that A is a *diagonal matrix* if $a_{ij} = 0$ when $i \neq j$. This means that all entries that are not on the diagonal are zero. These are examples of diagonal 3×3 matrices:

$$\begin{pmatrix} 1 & 0 & 0 \\ 0 & 4 & 0 \\ 0 & 0 & 7 \end{pmatrix}, \quad \begin{pmatrix} 2 & 0 & 0 \\ 0 & -1 & 0 \\ 0 & 0 & 0 \end{pmatrix}$$

An $n \times n$ matrix A is called *upper triangular* if $a_{ij} = 0$ when $i > j$. This means that all entries under the diagonal are zero. Another way to say this is that the positions where we allow nonzero entries form a triangle, consisting of the diagonal and the entries over the diagonal. These are examples of upper triangular matrices:

$$\begin{pmatrix} 1 & 5 \\ 0 & 4 \end{pmatrix}, \quad \begin{pmatrix} 2 & 0 & 1 \\ 0 & 3 & 4 \\ 0 & 0 & 7 \end{pmatrix}, \quad \begin{pmatrix} 3 & 0 & 0 \\ 0 & 2 & 0 \\ 0 & 0 & 7 \end{pmatrix}$$

Note that if a square matrix is in echelon form, then it is upper triangular. We also notice that it is especially easy to multiply diagonal matrices. We have, for instance,

$$\begin{pmatrix} 1 & 0 \\ 0 & 4 \end{pmatrix} \cdot \begin{pmatrix} 6 & 0 \\ 0 & -2 \end{pmatrix} = \begin{pmatrix} 1 \cdot 6 & 0 \\ 0 & 4 \cdot (-2) \end{pmatrix} = \begin{pmatrix} 6 & 0 \\ 0 & -8 \end{pmatrix}$$

It follows that it is easy to compute powers of diagonal matrices. For any diagonal $n \times n$ matrix D and any integer $k \geq 2$, we have that

$$D^k = \begin{pmatrix} d_1 & 0 & \cdots & 0 \\ 0 & d_2 & \cdots & 0 \\ \vdots & \vdots & \ddots & \vdots \\ 0 & 0 & \cdots & d_n \end{pmatrix}^k = \begin{pmatrix} d_1^k & 0 & \cdots & 0 \\ 0 & d_2^k & \cdots & 0 \\ \vdots & \vdots & \ddots & \vdots \\ 0 & 0 & \cdots & d_n^k \end{pmatrix}$$

The reason is that when we multiply diagonal matrices, the multiplication is carried out position by position; there are no cross-terms.

Identity matrix. The diagonal $n \times n$ matrix, where all diagonal entries are equal to 1, is called the *identity matrix*, and it is written I or I_n. This is the 3×3 identity matrix:

$$I = \begin{pmatrix} 1 & 0 & 0 \\ 0 & 1 & 0 \\ 0 & 0 & 1 \end{pmatrix}$$

The identity matrix I has the property that $I \cdot A = A$ and $A \cdot I = A$ for any $m \times n$ matrix A, and it is the only matrix with this property. We could also write this as $I_m \cdot A = A$ and $A \cdot I_n = A$. It is not difficult to check that the identity matrix has this property. For instance, we have that

$$\begin{pmatrix} 1 & 0 \\ 0 & 1 \end{pmatrix} \cdot \begin{pmatrix} 1 & 3 & 5 \\ 2 & -1 & 4 \end{pmatrix} = \begin{pmatrix} 1 & 3 & 5 \\ 2 & -1 & 4 \end{pmatrix}$$

and

$$\begin{pmatrix} 1 & 3 & 5 \\ 2 & -1 & 4 \end{pmatrix} \begin{pmatrix} 1 & 0 & 0 \\ 0 & 1 & 0 \\ 0 & 0 & 1 \end{pmatrix} = \begin{pmatrix} 1 & 3 & 5 \\ 2 & -1 & 4 \end{pmatrix}$$

This means that the identity matrix I plays the same role for matrices as 1 plays for numbers. That is, I is the *multiplicative identity* for matrices; this is the reason for the name identity matrix. By convention, we set $A^0 = I$ for any square matrix A.

Transpose of a matrix. Let A be an $m \times n$ matrix $A = (a_{ij})$. We define the *transpose* of an $m \times n$ matrix $A = (a_{ij})$ to be the $n \times m$ matrix $A^T = (a_{ji})$. This means that the entry in position (i, j) in A is the entry in position (j, i) in A^T. For example, we have that

$$A = \begin{pmatrix} 3 & 7 & 1 \\ 4 & 2 & 1 \end{pmatrix} \quad \Rightarrow \quad A^T = \begin{pmatrix} 3 & 4 \\ 7 & 2 \\ 1 & 1 \end{pmatrix}$$

We see that the transposed matrix A^T is the reflection of A across the diagonal when A is a square matrix. For instance, we have

$$A = \begin{pmatrix} 3 & 7 \\ 4 & 1 \end{pmatrix} \quad \Rightarrow \quad A^T = \begin{pmatrix} 3 & 4 \\ 7 & 1 \end{pmatrix}$$

We say that a matrix is *symmetric* if $A^T = A$. It follows from the comments above that a matrix $A = (a_{ij})$ is symmetric if and only if it is square and $a_{ij} = a_{ji}$ for all pairs of indices (i, j) with $i \neq j$. This is an example of a symmetric matrix:

$$A = \begin{pmatrix} 3 & 4 & 1 \\ 4 & 2 & 5 \\ 1 & 5 & 7 \end{pmatrix}$$

Proposition 3.2 (Properties of the transpose). For all numbers r and all matrices A, B such that the following operations are defined, we have that:

a) $(A + B)^T = A^T + B^T$
b) $(rA)^T = rA^T$
c) $(AB)^T = B^T A^T$

Proof. We prove the last statement $(AB)^T = B^T A^T$. The proofs of the remaining laws are similar (and straightforward): Let A be an $m \times n$ matrix $A = (a_{ij})$ and let $B = (b_{ij})$ be an $n \times p$ matrix with (b_{ij}). Then all operations are defined, and it follows from the definition of the transpose that the entry in position (i, j) in $(AB)^T$ is given by

$$((AB)^T)_{ij} = (AB)_{ji} = a_{j1}b_{1i} + a_{j2}b_{2i} + \ldots + a_{jn}b_{ni}$$
$$= b_{1i}a_{j1} + b_{2i}a_{j2} + \ldots + b_{ni}a_{jn}$$

and this equals the entry in position (i, j) of the matrix $B^T A^T$ for all indices i, j.
□

Inverse matrices. Let A be an $m \times n$ matrix. An *inverse matrix* of A is a matrix B such that $A \cdot B = I$ and $B \cdot A = I$. It is not difficult to see that if an inverse matrix exists, then it is unique, and we write A^{-1} for the inverse matrix of A. In fact, if B and C are two matrices that are inverses of A, then we have

$$B = B \cdot I = B(AC) = (BA)C = IC = C$$

by the properties of an inverse matrix.

We shall explain several general methods for computing inverse matrices later in this chapter, but this is a simple example:

$$A = \begin{pmatrix} 3 & 5 \\ 1 & 2 \end{pmatrix} \quad \Rightarrow \quad A^{-1} = \begin{pmatrix} 2 & -5 \\ -1 & 3 \end{pmatrix}$$

3 • Matrices and determinants

To check this, we compute AA^{-1} and $A^{-1}A$, and see that both matrix products equal the identity matrix I.

Not all matrices have an inverse matrix. We say that A is *invertible* if A^{-1} exists, and *non-invertible* otherwise. This is an example of a matrix that is not invertible:

$$A = \begin{pmatrix} 1 & 1 & 1 \\ 1 & 2 & 4 \\ 2 & 3 & 5 \end{pmatrix}$$

It turns out that only square matrices can be invertible, and that they are invertible if and only if they have maximal rank.

Proposition 3.3. Let A be an $m \times n$ matrix. Then A is invertible if and only if $m = n$ and $\text{rk}(A) = n$.

Proof. Let us first assume that A is invertible. This means that the linear system $A\mathbf{x} = \mathbf{b}$ has a unique solution $\mathbf{x}$ for every vector $\mathbf{b}$, since

$$A\mathbf{x} = \mathbf{b} \quad \Rightarrow \quad \mathbf{x} = A^{-1}\mathbf{b}$$

by left multiplication by A^{-1}. This means that the augmented matrix $(A|\mathbf{b})$ of the linear system has a pivot position in each variable column, but not in the last column. Hence $\text{rk}\,A = n$ and $m = n$. Conversely, assume that $m = n$ and $\text{rk}\,A = n$. By the argument above, this means that $A\mathbf{x} = \mathbf{b}$ has a unique solution for any vector $\mathbf{b}$. Taking $\mathbf{b}$ to be each of the columns in I_n, we see that there is a unique $n \times n$ matrix X such that $AX = I$. We claim that X is an inverse matrix of A. In fact, we have that

$$AX = I \quad \Rightarrow \quad AXA = A \quad \Rightarrow \quad AXA - A = 0 \quad \Rightarrow \quad A(XA - I) = 0$$

Since $A\mathbf{0} = \mathbf{0}$ and $A\mathbf{x} = \mathbf{b}$ has a unique solution for each vector $\mathbf{b}$, it follows that $XA - I = 0$, or $XA = I$. This proves that $X = A^{-1}$, hence A is invertible. □

Let $A\mathbf{x} = \mathbf{b}$ be a quadratic linear system in matrix form. If A is invertible, then we have that

$$A\mathbf{x} = \mathbf{b} \quad \Rightarrow \quad A^{-1} \cdot (A\mathbf{x}) = A^{-1} \cdot \mathbf{b} \quad \Rightarrow \quad \mathbf{x} = A^{-1}\mathbf{b}$$

In particular, the linear system has a unique solution. This is in agreement with the proposition above, since $\text{rk}\,A = n$ means that all variables are basic, hence the system has a unique solution. Moreover, we know that the system does not have a unique solution if A is non-invertible, since $\text{rk}\,A < n$ means that there are free variables or that the system is inconsistent.

Proposition 3.4 (Properties of the inverse). For all numbers $r \neq 0$ and all matrices A, B such that the following operations are defined, we have that:

a) $(rA)^{-1} = r^{-1}A^{-1}$
b) $(AB)^{-1} = B^{-1}A^{-1}$
c) $(A^T)^{-1} = (A^{-1})^T$

Proof. We prove the second statement. The proofs of the remaining ones are similar: We have $(AB) \cdot B^{-1}A^{-1} = A(BB^{-1})A^{-1} = I$ and $B^{-1}A^{-1} \cdot (AB) = B^{-1}(A^{-1}A)B = I$. By definition, this means that $(AB)^{-1} = B^{-1}A^{-1}$. □

Let us end this section by describing a general method for finding A^{-1}, if it exists. Let A be an $n \times n$ matrix, and consider the matrix equation $AX = I$. By the proof of Proposition 3.3, we know that if this equation has a solution X, then $A^{-1} = X$. To solve this matrix equation means to solve n linear systems $A\mathbf{x} = \mathbf{b}$ at the same time (with $\mathbf{b}$ equal to each of the columns of I). We can solve them all simultaneously using Gaussian elimination: We consider the matrix $(A|I)$ and find its reduced echelon form $(B|C)$. If $B = I$, then $A^{-1} = C$ since $X = C$ is the solution to the matrix equation $AX = I$. If $B \neq I$, then $\text{rk } A < n$ and this means that A is not invertible.

> **Method for finding the inverse matrix.**
> For any square matrix A, we consider the matrix $(A|I)$ and find its reduced echelon form $(B|C)$.
> a) If $B = I$, then $A^{-1} = C$.
> b) If $B \neq I$, then A is not invertible.

3.2 Determinants

Let $A = (a_{ij})$ be an $n \times n$ matrix. In this section, we define the *determinant* of A, which is a function of the entries in A. Its value is a number, and we write $\det(A)$ or $|A|$ for the determinant of A. When $n = 2$, it is given by the simple formula

$$A = \begin{pmatrix} a & b \\ c & d \end{pmatrix} \quad \Rightarrow \quad \det(A) = ad - bc$$

When $n > 2$, the determinant of A is given by a much more complicated formula. It is possible to write the formula in several different ways, and we shall use *cofactor expansion*.

3 • Matrices and determinants

For $1 \leq i, j \leq n$, the cofactor C_{ij} in position (i, j) of A is defined by the formula $C_{ij} = (-1)^{i+j} M_{ij}$, where M_{ij} is the determinant of the submatrix of A that we obtain when we delete row i and column j from A. The determinant of a submatrix is in general called a *minor*, and this is why we use the notation M_{ij}. As an example, let us compute all the cofactors of the matrix A given by

$$A = \begin{pmatrix} 1 & 1 & 1 \\ 1 & 2 & 4 \\ 1 & 3 & 9 \end{pmatrix}$$

We start by computing the cofactors in the first row:

$$C_{11} = (-1)^{1+1} \begin{vmatrix} 2 & 4 \\ 3 & 9 \end{vmatrix} = +(2 \cdot 9 - 4 \cdot 3) = 6$$

$$C_{12} = (-1)^{1+2} \begin{vmatrix} 1 & 4 \\ 1 & 9 \end{vmatrix} = -(1 \cdot 9 - 4 \cdot 1) = -5$$

$$C_{13} = (-1)^{1+3} \begin{vmatrix} 1 & 2 \\ 1 & 3 \end{vmatrix} = +(1 \cdot 3 - 2 \cdot 1) = 1$$

We can continue and compute the cofactors in the other rows in the same way, and we get

$$C = \begin{pmatrix} C_{11} & C_{12} & C_{13} \\ C_{21} & C_{22} & C_{23} \\ C_{31} & C_{32} & C_{33} \end{pmatrix} = \begin{pmatrix} 6 & -5 & 1 \\ -6 & 8 & -2 \\ 2 & -3 & 1 \end{pmatrix}$$

The matrix $C = (C_{ij})$ is called the *cofactor matrix* of A. Note that the signs of the cofactors form an alternating pattern, with a positive sign in the upper left corner, and that the minors M_{ij} are determinants of 2×2 matrices when A is a 3×3 matrix.

For an $n \times n$ matrix $A = (a_{ij})$, we call $a_{i1}C_{i1} + a_{i2}C_{i2} + \ldots + a_{in}C_{in}$ the cofactor expansion along row i, and $a_{1j}C_{1j} + a_{2j}C_{2j} + \ldots + a_{nj}C_{nj}$ the cofactor expansion along column j. We define the determinant of A to be the cofactor expansion along the first row, and write

$$\det(A) = a_{11}C_{11} + a_{12}C_{12} + \ldots + a_{1n}C_{1n}$$

In the example above, this gives $\det(A) = 1 \cdot 6 + 1 \cdot (-5) + 1 \cdot 1 = 2$, since

$$A = \begin{pmatrix} 1 & 1 & 1 \\ 1 & 2 & 4 \\ 1 & 3 & 9 \end{pmatrix}, \quad C = \begin{pmatrix} 6 & -5 & 1 \\ -6 & 8 & -2 \\ 2 & -3 & 1 \end{pmatrix}$$

We might as well have defined the determinant to be the cofactor expansion along any row or column, since we have the following result:

Lemma 3.5. *Let A be a square matrix. Then the cofactor expansion along any row or column will give the same result, the determinant $\det(A)$.*

3.3 Determinants and Gaussian elimination

If we multiply row i with $c \neq 0$, and use cofactor expansion along row i to compute $|A|$ and $|B|$, it is clear that $|B| = c|A|$, since the entries in row i are multiplied by c and the cofactors are the same.

If we add c times row i to row j and use cofactor expansion along row j to compute $|A|$ and $|B|$, then $|A| = |B|$. In fact, let $\mathbf{a}_i$ and $\mathbf{a}_j$ denote row i and row j in A, let $\mathbf{a}_j + c \cdot \mathbf{a}_i$ denote row j in B, and let $\mathbf{c}_j$ denote row j of the cofactor matrix of A and B, which are the same since the other rows are unchanged. By the definition of cofactor expansions expressed using dot products, we have

$$|B| = (\mathbf{a}_j + c\mathbf{a}_i) \cdot \mathbf{c}_j = \mathbf{a}_j \cdot \mathbf{c}_j + c\mathbf{a}_i \cdot \mathbf{c}_j = \mathbf{a}_j \cdot \mathbf{c}_j = |A|$$

Note that $\mathbf{a}_i \cdot \mathbf{c}_j = 0$ when $i \neq j$. This dot product is the determinant of a matrix containing two rows equal to $\mathbf{a}_i$, which is zero by Lemma 3.6. $\square$

Let us compute the determinant of the 3×3 matrix A using Gaussian elimination. We first reduce A to an echelon form:

$$A = \begin{pmatrix} 1 & 1 & 1 \\ 1 & 2 & 4 \\ 1 & 3 & 9 \end{pmatrix} \rightarrow \begin{pmatrix} 1 & 1 & 1 \\ 0 & 1 & 3 \\ 0 & 2 & 8 \end{pmatrix} \rightarrow \begin{pmatrix} 1 & 1 & 1 \\ 0 & 1 & 3 \\ 0 & 0 & 2 \end{pmatrix} = E$$

Then we note that $|E| = 1 \cdot 1 \cdot 2 = 2$, and $|A| = |E|$, since the only type of elementary row operations that we used was to add a multiple of one row to another row. We can therefore conclude that $|A| = 2$. Notice that we used cofactor expansion to compute the determinant of the same matrix earlier in this section, with the same result.

Proposition 3.9. Let A be an $n \times n$ matrix. Then $\mathrm{rk}(A) = n$ if and only if $|A| \neq 0$.

Proof. We reduce A to a square echelon form E using elementary row operations $A \rightarrow \ldots \rightarrow E$, and note that $\det(A) \neq 0$ if and only if $\det(E) \neq 0$ by Lemma 3.8. Since $\det(E) = e_{11} \cdots e_{nn}$ is the product of the diagonal entries, we see that $|E| \neq 0$ if and only if $e_{11}, \ldots, e_{nn} \neq 0$ are pivots. This means that $|E| \neq 0$ if and only if $\mathrm{rk}(A) = n$. $\square$

> **Determinant and rank**
>
> Let A be an $n \times n$ matrix, and let $\mathbf{v}_1, \ldots, \mathbf{v}_n$ be the column vectors of A. Then the following conditions are equivalent:
>
> a) The vectors $\mathbf{v}_1, \ldots, \mathbf{v}_n$ are linearly independent
> b) $\mathrm{rk}(A) = n$
> c) $\det(A) \neq 0$
> d) A is invertible
> e) The linear system $A\mathbf{x} = \mathbf{b}$ has a unique solution for any vector $\mathbf{b}$

The above summary gives an overview of the main results obtained for square matrices so far. The equivalence of a), b) and e) are established in Chapter 1 and Chapter 2, and the equivalence of b), c) and d) follows from Proposition 3.3 and Proposition 3.9. In fact, if $|A| \neq 0$, there is also the following formula for the inverse matrix:

$$A^{-1} = \frac{1}{|A|} C^T = \frac{1}{|A|} \begin{pmatrix} C_{11} & C_{12} & \cdots & C_{1n} \\ C_{21} & C_{22} & \cdots & C_{2n} \\ \vdots & \vdots & \ddots & \vdots \\ C_{n1} & C_{n2} & \cdots & C_{nn} \end{pmatrix}^T = \frac{1}{|A|} \mathrm{Adj}(A)$$

The transpose of the cofactor matrix C is called the *adjungated matrix* of A, and it is written $\mathrm{Adj}(A)$. We end this section with some useful properties of the determinant:

Proposition 3.10 (Properties of the determinant). For all numbers r and all $n \times n$ matrices A, B such that the following operations are defined, we have that:

a) $|AB| = |A| \cdot |B|$
b) $|rA| = r^n \cdot |A|$
c) $|A^T| = |A|$
d) $|A^{-1}| = 1/|A|$

3.4 Minors, rank and linear systems

Let A be an $m \times n$ matrix. We define an *r-minor* of A to be the determinant of an $r \times r$ submatrix of A. Any choice of r rows and r columns from A gives rise to an r-minor. For example, when A is the 3×4 matrix

$$A = \begin{pmatrix} 1 & 2 & 1 & 4 \\ 3 & -1 & 0 & 1 \\ 4 & 1 & 1 & 6 \end{pmatrix}$$

then this is an example of a 3-minor of A:

$$M_{123,123} = |A_{123,123}| = \begin{vmatrix} 1 & 2 & 1 \\ 3 & -1 & 0 \\ 4 & 1 & 1 \end{vmatrix} = 1(3+4) + 1(-1-6) = 0$$

We have named this minor $M_{I,J} = M_{123,123}$, since it is the determinant of the submatrix $A_{I,J} = A_{123,123}$ of A consisting of rows $I = \{1,2,3\}$ and columns $J = \{1,2,3\}$. There are three other 3-minors of A, which we write $M_{123,124}$, $M_{123,134}$ and $M_{123,234}$. Each of the 3-minors is obtained by deleting one of the columns of A. Since the maximal size of a square submatrix of A is 3×3, we call the 3-minors of A the *maximal minors*. Let us compute one more maximal minor as another example:

$$M_{123,124} = \begin{vmatrix} 1 & 2 & 4 \\ 3 & -1 & 4 \\ 4 & 1 & 6 \end{vmatrix} = 1(-6-4) - 2(18-16) + 4(3+4) = 14$$

We know from the previous section that an $r \times r$ submatrix A_{IJ} has a nonzero determinant $M_{I,J} = |A_{I,J}| \neq 0$ if and only if the rank $\text{rk}(A_{I,J}) = r$ or equivalently, the submatrix $A_{I,J}$ has pivot positions in all of its columns.

Proposition 3.11. For any $m \times n$ matrix A, the rank $\text{rk}(A)$ is the maximal integer r such that there is a nonzero r-minor in A.

Proof. Let $r = \text{rk}\, A$ be the number of pivot positions in A, and write I for the rows and J for the columns of the pivot positions. Then $A_{I,J}$ is an $r \times r$ submatrix with $\text{rk}(A_{I,J}) = r$, and its determinant is $M_{I,J} \neq 0$ by Proposition 3.9. Moreover, any minor of order $s > r$ must be zero. Otherwise, there would exist a submatrix of A with s pivot positions, and this is a contradiction since $s > \text{rk}\, A$. Hence $r = \text{rk}(A)$ is the maximal order of a nonzero minor in A. $\square$

In the 3×4 matrix A in the example above, the maximal minors are 3-minors. If any of the four 3-minor are nonzero, then $\operatorname{rk} A = 3$. Since $M_{123,123} = 0$ and $M_{123,124} = 14 \neq 0$, it follows that $\operatorname{rk} A = 3$. If all four 3-minors had been zero, then $\operatorname{rk} A < 3$, and it would be necessary to check 2-minors to determine the rank of A.

> **Minors and rank**
> Let A be an $m \times n$ matrix, and let r be an integer. Then $\operatorname{rk} A < r$ if and only if all r-minors are zero.

The above restatement of Proposition 3.11 can be turned into a procedure for finding the rank of a matrix, and it is particularly useful in those cases where the matrix has parameters. We consider the example

$$A = \begin{pmatrix} a & b & c \\ c & a & b \end{pmatrix}$$

where a, b, c are parameters. The 2-minors are the maximal minors, and we compute all of them:

$$M_{12,12} = a^2 - bc, \quad M_{12,23} = b^2 - ac, \quad M_{12,13} = ab - c^2$$

We have that $\operatorname{rk}(A) < 2$ if and only if $a^2 - bc = b^2 - ac = ab - c^2 = 0$. Let us solve these equations: If $a, b, c \neq 0$, we get

$$a^2 = bc \;\Rightarrow\; a^3 = abc, \quad b^2 = ac \;\Rightarrow\; b^3 = abc, \quad c^2 = ab \;\Rightarrow\; c^3 = abc$$

Hence $a^3 = b^3 = c^3$, and this gives $a = b = c$. If one of the parameters is zero, we see from the equations that all parameters must be zero, and this gives $a = b = c = 0$. In either case, we get $a = b = c$, and we see that the matrix

$$A = \begin{pmatrix} a & a & a \\ a & a & a \end{pmatrix}$$

has rank one if $a \neq 0$, and rank zero if $a = 0$. Therefore, we get the result

$$\operatorname{rk} \begin{pmatrix} a & b & c \\ c & a & b \end{pmatrix} = \begin{cases} 0, & a = b = c = 0 \\ 1, & a = b = c \neq 0 \\ 2, & \text{otherwise} \end{cases}$$

It would have been complicated to find the rank using Gaussian elimination.

3.4 Minors, rank and linear systems

Minors and linear systems. We can use minors to solve linear systems. The idea is that minors can be used to identify pivot positions, which in turn determine the solutions. As an example, let us consider the linear system $A\mathbf{x} = \mathbf{b}$ with the following equations:

$$\begin{aligned} x + y + 2z + w &= 5 \\ x - 2y - z + 5w &= 2 \\ 5x - y + 4z + 11w &= 7 \end{aligned}$$

We start by computing the maximal minor $M_{123,\,123}$ of the coefficient matrix A:

$$M_{123,\,123} = \begin{vmatrix} 1 & 1 & 2 \\ 1 & -2 & -1 \\ 5 & -1 & 4 \end{vmatrix} = 1(-8-1) - 1(4+5) + 2(-1+10) = 0$$

Since the minor is zero, the positions $(1, 1)$, $(2, 2)$, $(3, 3)$ are not all pivot positions. However, $(1, 1)$ and $(2, 2)$ are pivot positions since the 2-minor $M_{12,\,12} = -3 \neq 0$. It is still possible that A can have rank three, with a pivot position at $(3, 4)$, and we compute $M_{123,\,124}$ to check whether this is the case:

$$M_{123,\,124} = \begin{vmatrix} 1 & 1 & 1 \\ 1 & -2 & 5 \\ 5 & -1 & 11 \end{vmatrix}$$
$$= 1(-22+5) - 1(11-25) + 1(-1+10) = 6 \neq 0$$

The fact that the maximal minor $M_{123,\,124} \neq 0$ means that $\text{rk}(A) = 3$ and that $(1, 1)$, $(2, 2)$ and $(3, 4)$ are the pivot positions of A. We write down the augmented matrix of the system with the pivot positions marked in blue. Clearly, there cannot be any pivots in the $\mathbf{b}$-column.

$$(A|\mathbf{b}) = \begin{pmatrix} \underline{1} & 1 & 2 & 1 & | & 5 \\ 1 & \underline{-2} & -1 & 5 & | & 2 \\ 5 & -1 & 4 & \underline{11} & | & 7 \end{pmatrix}$$

Hence the system has one free variable z, and infinitely many solutions. To solve the system, we move the terms with the free variable z to the other side:

$$\begin{aligned} x + y + w &= 5 - 2z \\ x - 2y + 5w &= 2 + z \\ 5x - y + 11w &= 7 - 4z \end{aligned} \quad \text{or} \quad \begin{pmatrix} 1 & 1 & 1 \\ 1 & -2 & 5 \\ 5 & -1 & 11 \end{pmatrix} \cdot \begin{pmatrix} x \\ y \\ w \end{pmatrix} = \begin{pmatrix} 5 - 2z \\ 2 + z \\ 7 - 4z \end{pmatrix}$$

Notice that the coefficient matrix of this linear system is exactly $A_{123,124}$, the submatrix whose determinant was the maximal nonzero minor $M_{123,124}$. Therefore, this matrix is invertible, and the solutions of the linear system are given by

$$\begin{pmatrix} x \\ y \\ w \end{pmatrix} = \begin{pmatrix} 1 & 1 & 1 \\ 1 & -2 & 5 \\ 5 & -1 & 11 \end{pmatrix}^{-1} \begin{pmatrix} 5-2z \\ 2+z \\ 7-4z \end{pmatrix}$$

$$= \frac{1}{6} \begin{pmatrix} -17 & -12 & 7 \\ 14 & 6 & -4 \\ 9 & 6 & -3 \end{pmatrix} \begin{pmatrix} 5-2z \\ 2+z \\ 7-4z \end{pmatrix} = \begin{pmatrix} -10-z \\ 9-z \\ 6 \end{pmatrix}$$

This gives $(x, y, z, w) = (-10 - z, 9 - z, z, 6)$ with z free. It is useful to check the result using Gaussian elimination. Elementary row operations give an echelon form

$$(A|\mathbf{b}) = \begin{pmatrix} \underline{1} & 1 & 2 & 1 & 5 \\ 1 & \underline{-2} & -1 & 5 & 2 \\ 5 & -1 & 4 & \underline{11} & 7 \end{pmatrix} \to \ldots \to \begin{pmatrix} \underline{1} & 1 & 2 & 1 & 5 \\ 0 & \underline{-3} & -3 & 4 & -3 \\ 0 & 0 & 0 & \underline{-2} & -12 \end{pmatrix}$$

and back substitution gives $(x, y, z, w) = (-10 - z, 9 - z, z, 6)$ with z free.

Minors and linear systems

Let $A\mathbf{x} = \mathbf{b}$ be an $m \times n$ linear system, and let $M_{I,J} \neq 0$ be any nonzero r-minor with $r = \text{rk}(A)$. If the linear system is consistent, then it can be solved in the following way:

a) We keep equation i if $i \in I$ and discard the remaining $m - r$ equations. The r variables $\{x_j : j \in J\}$ are basic, and the remaining $n - r$ variables are free. We move the terms with free variables to the right-hand side in each of the r remaining equations.

b) We obtain an $r \times r$ linear system that can be solved by multiplying with $A_{I,J}^{-1}$ from the left since $M_{I,J} = |A_{I,J}| \neq 0$.

3.4 Minors, rank and linear systems

If we use any r-minor $M_{I,J} \neq 0$ with $r = \operatorname{rk} A = \operatorname{rk}(A|\mathbf{b})$, the procedure above would work. To get the same free variables as in Gaussian elimination, we would have to choose a nonzero r-minor with the indices in J minimal. This corresponds to solving for variables as far to the left as possible, which is exactly what we do in a Gaussian elimination.

In the example above, we could also compute the remaining 3-minors $M_{123,134}$ and $M_{123,234}$. We get

$$M_{123,134} = \begin{vmatrix} 1 & 2 & 1 \\ 1 & -1 & 5 \\ 5 & 4 & 11 \end{vmatrix} = 6 \neq 0, \quad M_{123,234} = \begin{vmatrix} 1 & 2 & 1 \\ -2 & -1 & 5 \\ 1 & 4 & 11 \end{vmatrix} = 16 \neq 0$$

This means that it is possible to choose $\{x, z, w\}$ as basic and y as free, or to choose $\{y, z, w\}$ as basic and x as free, since $M_{123,134} \neq 0$ and $M_{123,234} \neq 0$. But it is not possible to choose $\{x, y, z\}$ as basic and w as free, since $M_{123,123} = 0$. The choice of $\{x, y, w\}$ as basic and z as free is the one used in Gaussian elimination.

Problems

Problem 3.1 Let A, B, and C be the 3×3 matrices

$$A = \begin{pmatrix} 1 & 1 & 1 \\ 1 & 2 & 4 \\ 1 & -1 & 1 \end{pmatrix}, \quad B = \begin{pmatrix} 0 & 1 & 1 \\ 1 & 0 & 1 \\ 1 & 1 & 0 \end{pmatrix}, \quad C = \begin{pmatrix} 1 & 1 & 1 \\ 0 & -1 & 1 \\ 0 & 0 & 2 \end{pmatrix}$$

Compute the following matrix expressions:

a) AB b) BA c) A^2

d) B^2 e) $(A+B)^2$ f) ABC

Problem 3.2 Give an example of a symmetric and a nonsymmetric 4×4 matrix.

Problem 3.3 Let A, B, and C be any $n \times n$ matrices. Simplify the following matrix expressions:

a) $AB(BC - CB) + (CA - AB)BC + CA(A - B)C$

b) $(A - B)(C - A) + (C - B)(A - C) + (C - A)^2$

Problem 3.4 We consider a linear system $A\mathbf{x} = \mathbf{b}$, where

$$A = \begin{pmatrix} 3 & 1 & 5 \\ 5 & -3 & 2 \\ 4 & -3 & -1 \end{pmatrix}, \quad \mathbf{x} = \begin{pmatrix} x_1 \\ x_2 \\ x_3 \end{pmatrix}, \quad \mathbf{b} = \begin{pmatrix} 4 \\ -2 \\ -1 \end{pmatrix}$$

a) Write out the linear system of equations.

b) Determine whether A is invertible, and find A^{-1} if it exists.

c) How many solutions does the linear system have?

Problem 3.5 Compute the matrix $A^T A$ when A is the matrix

$$A = \begin{pmatrix} 1 & 2 & 3 & 4 \\ 2 & -1 & 6 & 5 \end{pmatrix}$$

Problem 3.6 Compute $|A|$ using cofactor expansion along the first column, and then along the third row. Compare both the results and the computations.

$$A = \begin{pmatrix} 1 & 2 & 3 \\ 0 & 5 & 6 \\ 1 & 0 & 8 \end{pmatrix}$$

Problem 3.7 Compute the following determinants using elementary row operations:

a) $\begin{vmatrix} 3 & 1 & 5 \\ 9 & 3 & 15 \\ -3 & -1 & -5 \end{vmatrix}$
b) $\begin{vmatrix} 1 & 2 & 2 & 1 \\ 2 & 1 & 1 & 2 \\ 2 & 1 & 1 & 2 \\ 1 & 2 & 2 & 1 \end{vmatrix}$
c) $\begin{vmatrix} 1 & 1 & 1 & -1 \\ 1 & 1 & -1 & 1 \\ 1 & -1 & 1 & 1 \\ -1 & 1 & 1 & 1 \end{vmatrix}$

Problem 3.8 Use determinants and cofactors to determine when A is invertible, and to compute A^{-1} when possible:

a) $A = \begin{pmatrix} 1 & 2 & 3 \\ 0 & 5 & 6 \\ 1 & 0 & 8 \end{pmatrix}$
b) $A = \begin{pmatrix} 1 & 0 & b \\ 0 & 1 & 0 \\ 0 & 0 & 1 \end{pmatrix}$

Problem 3.9 Use determinants to check whether the following vectors are linearly independent:

a) $\mathbf{v}_1 = (3, 5)$, $\mathbf{v}_2 = (7, -1)$

b) $\mathbf{v}_1 = (1, 1, 1)$, $\mathbf{v}_2 = (1, 2, -1)$, $\mathbf{v}_3 = (1, 4, 1)$

c) $\mathbf{v}_1 = (1, 1, 1, 1)$, $\mathbf{v}_2 = (1, 2, -2, -4)$, $\mathbf{v}_3 = (0, 1, 4, 1)$, $\mathbf{v}_4 = (1, 0, 0, -1)$

Problem 3.10 Let A and B be 3×3-matrices with $|A| = 2$ and $|B| = -5$. Find $|AB|$, $|-3A|$, $|A^{-1}|$, and $|-2A^T|$.

Problem 3.11 Compute all 3-minors of A, and use this to find $\mathrm{rk}(A)$. How many 2-minors are there?

$$A = \begin{pmatrix} 1 & 0 & 2 & 1 \\ 0 & 2 & 4 & 2 \\ 1 & -2 & -2 & 1 \end{pmatrix}$$

Problem 3.12 Determine the rank of A for all values of the parameters s and t:

a) $A = \begin{pmatrix} 1 & s & s^2 \\ 1 & 0 & 1 \\ s & -1 & s \end{pmatrix}$
b) $A = \begin{pmatrix} t+6 & 5 & 6 \\ -1 & t & -6 \\ 1 & 1 & t+7 \end{pmatrix}$

Problem 3.13 Let A be any $m \times n$-matrix, and consider the matrix $A^T A$. Show that:

a) $\mathrm{Null}(A^T A) = \mathrm{Null}(A)$
b) $\mathrm{rk}(A^T A) = \mathrm{rk}\, A$

3 • Matrices and determinants

Problem 3.14 Use minors to determine if the systems have solutions. If they do, determine the number of degrees of freedom and find all solutions:

a) $2x_1 - x_2 + 3x_3 = 3$
$4x_1 - 2x_2 + 6x_3 = 1$

b) $x_1 + x_2 + x_3 + 2x_4 = 2$
$2x_1 + 3x_2 - x_3 + 3x_4 = 1$

c) $x_1 - x_2 + 3x_3 + x_4 = 1$
$2x_1 + x_2 + 2x_3 + 3x_4 = 3$
$x_1 + 5x_2 - 7x_3 + x_4 = 1$
$4x_1 + 5x_2 + 7x_4 = 7$

d) $x_1 + x_2 + 2x_3 + x_4 = 5$
$2x_1 + 3x_2 - x_3 - 2x_4 = 2$
$4x_1 + 5x_2 + 3x_3 = 4$

Problem 3.15 Let $A\mathbf{x} = \mathbf{b}$ be a linear system of equations in matrix form. Prove that if $\mathbf{x}_1$ and $\mathbf{x}_2$ are both solutions of the system, then so is $\lambda \mathbf{x}_1 + (1-\lambda)\mathbf{x}_2$ for every number λ. Use this fact to prove that a linear system of equations that is consistent has either one solution or infinitely many solutions. What is the geometric interpretation of the expression $\lambda \mathbf{x}_1 + (1-\lambda)\mathbf{x}_2$?

CHAPTER 4
Eigenvectors and eigenvalues

4.1 Introduction to eigenvectors and eigenvalues

We may think of left multiplication on vectors by an $m \times n$ matrix A as a kind of function T, given by $T(\mathbf{v}) = A \cdot \mathbf{v}$. The inputs are vectors $\mathbf{v}$ in $\mathbb{R}^n$, and the outputs are vectors $\mathbf{w} = A\mathbf{v}$ in $\mathbb{R}^m$. We write $T : \mathbb{R}^n \to \mathbb{R}^m$ for this function, and call it a *linear transformation*. Notice that when $m = n$, the input and output vectors lie in the same n-dimensional vector space $\mathbb{R}^n$.

Let A be an $n \times n$ matrix, and let $T : \mathbb{R}^n \to \mathbb{R}^n$ be the corresponding linear transformation. We define an *eigenvector* of A to be a nonzero vector $\mathbf{v} \neq \mathbf{0}$ such that $A\mathbf{v} = \lambda \mathbf{v}$ for some number λ. More precisely, we call $\mathbf{v}$ an eigenvector of A with *eigenvalue* λ when this is the case. It means that $T(\mathbf{v}) = \lambda \mathbf{v}$ is a scalar multiple of $\mathbf{v}$. For example, the vector $\mathbf{v} = (1, 1, 1)$ is an eigenvector of the matrix

$$A = \begin{pmatrix} 4 & 1 & 1 \\ 1 & 4 & 1 \\ 1 & 1 & 4 \end{pmatrix}$$

with eigenvalue $\lambda = 6$ since $T(\mathbf{v}) = 6\mathbf{v}$:

$$T(\mathbf{v}) = A\mathbf{v} = \begin{pmatrix} 4 & 1 & 1 \\ 1 & 4 & 1 \\ 1 & 1 & 4 \end{pmatrix} \begin{pmatrix} 1 \\ 1 \\ 1 \end{pmatrix} = \begin{pmatrix} 6 \\ 6 \\ 6 \end{pmatrix} = 6 \begin{pmatrix} 1 \\ 1 \\ 1 \end{pmatrix} = 6\mathbf{v}$$

We define an *eigenvalue* of A to be a number λ such that the equation $A\mathbf{v} = \lambda \mathbf{v}$ has nontrivial solutions $\mathbf{v} \neq \mathbf{0}$. The eigenvalues of A are also called *characteristic values*. For an eigenvalue λ, we define the *eigenspace* E_λ to be the set of all solutions $\mathbf{v}$ of the equation $A\mathbf{v} = \lambda \mathbf{v}$.

We notice that the equation $A\mathbf{v} = \lambda \mathbf{v}$ can be written as $A\mathbf{v} = \lambda I \mathbf{v}$, since $\mathbf{v} = I\mathbf{v}$. Hence, we can rewrite the equation $A\mathbf{v} = \lambda \mathbf{v}$ for eigenvectors and eigenvalues as

$$A\mathbf{v} = \lambda I \mathbf{v} \quad \Leftrightarrow \quad A\mathbf{v} - \lambda I \mathbf{v} = \mathbf{0} \quad \Leftrightarrow \quad (A - \lambda I)\mathbf{v} = \mathbf{0}$$

The last equation is the matrix form of an $n \times n$ homogeneous linear system with parameter λ. By Proposition 3.9, this linear system has nontrivial solutions if and only if λ satisfies $|A - \lambda I| = 0$. We call the equation $|A - \lambda I| = 0$ the *characteristic equation* of A.

4 • Eigenvectors and eigenvalues

Proposition 4.1. Let A be an $n \times n$ matrix. We have

a) λ is an eigenvalue of A if and only if $|A - \lambda I| = 0$

b) $E_\lambda = \text{Null}(A - \lambda I)$ for any eigenvalue λ

Proof. The first part is clear from the comments above, and the second part follows from the definition of a null space of a matrix. $\square$

Method for finding eigenvalues and eigenvectors

a) Solve the characteristic equation $|A - \lambda I| = 0$ to find eigenvalues of A

b) Solve the homogeneous linear system $(A - \lambda I)\mathbf{v} = \mathbf{0}$ for each eigenvalue λ to find the eigenspace E_λ of eigenvectors of A with eigenvalue λ

A simple example. Let us consider an example of a matrix A, and compute all eigenvalues and eigenvectors of A using Proposition 4.1. We look at the following 2×2 matrix:

$$A = \begin{pmatrix} 4 & -2 \\ -2 & 1 \end{pmatrix}$$

To find the eigenvalues of A, we write down the characteristic equation $|A - \lambda I| = 0$:

$$\left| \begin{pmatrix} 4 & -2 \\ -2 & 1 \end{pmatrix} - \lambda \begin{pmatrix} 1 & 0 \\ 0 & 1 \end{pmatrix} \right| = \begin{vmatrix} 4 - \lambda & -2 \\ -2 & 1 - \lambda \end{vmatrix} = 0$$

This gives the quadratic equation $(4 - \lambda)(1 - \lambda) - 4 = 0$, or $\lambda^2 - 5\lambda = 0$, and the solutions are $\lambda_1 = 5$ and $\lambda_2 = 0$. These are the eigenvalues of A. To compute eigenvectors, we consider each of the two eigenvalues: For $\lambda_1 = 5$, the eigenspace E_5 is the null space of the matrix

$$A - 5I = \begin{pmatrix} 4 - 5 & -2 \\ -2 & 1 - 5 \end{pmatrix} = \begin{pmatrix} -1 & -2 \\ -2 & -4 \end{pmatrix}$$

We solve the linear system, and see that y is free and that $-x - 2y = 0$, which gives $x = -2y$. We find the solutions

$$\mathbf{v} = \begin{pmatrix} x \\ y \end{pmatrix} = \begin{pmatrix} -2y \\ y \end{pmatrix} = y \cdot \begin{pmatrix} -2 \\ 1 \end{pmatrix} = y \cdot \mathbf{v}_1, \quad \mathbf{v}_1 = \begin{pmatrix} -2 \\ 1 \end{pmatrix}$$

A base of E_5 is therefore given by $B_1 = \{\mathbf{v}_1\}$. For $\lambda_2 = 0$, the eigenspace E_0 is the null space of the matrix

$$A - 0 \cdot I = \begin{pmatrix} 4 - 0 & -2 \\ -2 & 1 - 0 \end{pmatrix} = \begin{pmatrix} 4 & -2 \\ -2 & 1 \end{pmatrix}$$

4.1 Introduction to eigenvectors and eigenvalues

We solve the linear system, and see that x can be free, and that $4x - 2y = 0$, or $y = 2x$. We could also have used y as the free variable, and solved the equation as $x = y/2$. We use the first way of writing the solutions, and find

$$\mathbf{v} = \begin{pmatrix} x \\ y \end{pmatrix} = \begin{pmatrix} x \\ 2x \end{pmatrix} = x \cdot \begin{pmatrix} 1 \\ 2 \end{pmatrix} = x \cdot \mathbf{v}_2, \quad \mathbf{v}_2 = \begin{pmatrix} 1 \\ 2 \end{pmatrix}$$

A base of E_0 is therefore given by $B_2 = \{\mathbf{v}_2\}$. In the figure below, we show the geometric picture. The eigenspaces E_5 and E_0 are shown as red lines. Along E_5, we have $T(\mathbf{v}) = A\mathbf{v} = 5\mathbf{v}$, so A acts by scaling up vectors with a factor 5. Along E_0, we have that $T(\mathbf{v}) = A\mathbf{v} = \mathbf{0}$, so A acts by sending all vectors on E_0 to $\mathbf{0}$.

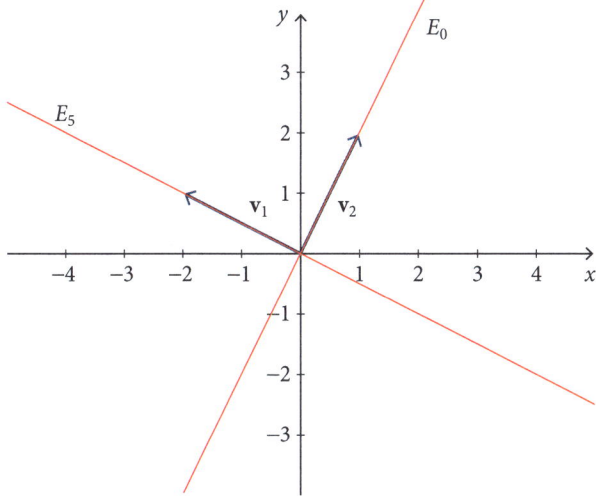

A more complicated example. Let us also consider an example of a 3×3 matrix A, and compute all eigenvalues and eigenvectors of A using Proposition 4.1. We look at the example

$$A = \begin{pmatrix} 4 & 1 & 1 \\ 1 & 4 & 1 \\ 1 & 1 & 4 \end{pmatrix}$$

To find the eigenvalues of A, we write down the characteristic equation $|A - \lambda I| = 0$:

$$\begin{vmatrix} 4-\lambda & 1 & 1 \\ 1 & 4-\lambda & 1 \\ 1 & 1 & 4-\lambda \end{vmatrix} = 0$$

Using cofactor expansion along the first row, the determinant $|A - \lambda I|$ can be written

$$|A - \lambda I| = (4-\lambda)\left[(4-\lambda)^2 - 1\right] - 1[(4-\lambda) - 1] + 1[1 - (4-\lambda)]$$
$$= (4-\lambda)(\lambda^2 - 8\lambda + 15) + 2\lambda - 6$$

4 • Eigenvectors and eigenvalues

We see that this is a cubic equation in λ and it is therefore more difficult to solve. There are two different ways to continue the computation: First, we try to factor the expression above, and get

$$\begin{aligned}|A - \lambda I| &= (4 - \lambda)(\lambda^2 - 8\lambda + 15) + 2\lambda - 6 \\ &= (4 - \lambda)(\lambda - 3)(\lambda - 5) + 2(\lambda - 3) \\ &= (\lambda - 3) \cdot [(4 - \lambda)(\lambda - 5) + 2] \\ &= (\lambda - 3)(-\lambda^2 + 9\lambda - 18) = -(\lambda - 3)(\lambda^2 - 9\lambda + 18) \\ &= -(\lambda - 3)(\lambda - 3)(\lambda - 6) = -(\lambda - 3)^2(\lambda - 6)\end{aligned}$$

Hence the solutions of $|A - \lambda I| = 0$ are $\lambda_1 = \lambda_2 = 3$ and $\lambda_3 = 6$. These are the eigenvalues of A. We say that $\lambda = 3$ has multiplicity two, since $(\lambda - 3)^2$ is a repeated factor, and that $\lambda = 6$ has multiplicity one, since the factor $(\lambda - 6)$ only appears once in the factorization.

Alternatively, we could continue the computation of $|A - \lambda I|$ by expanding and simplifying. This would give

$$\begin{aligned}|A - \lambda I| &= (4 - \lambda)(\lambda^2 - 8\lambda + 15) + 2\lambda - 6 \\ &= -\lambda^3 + 12\lambda^2 - 47\lambda + 60 + 2\lambda - 6 \\ &= -\lambda^3 + 12\lambda^2 - 45\lambda + 54\end{aligned}$$

When the cubic equation is written in the form $-\lambda^3 + 12\lambda^2 - 45\lambda + 54 = 0$, it is more difficult to solve. We could go through the list $\lambda = \pm 1, \pm 2, \pm 3, \pm 6, \ldots$ of integers that divides the constant term 54, and check if any of them are solutions: These are the only possibilities for integer solutions. After trying the first integers on the list, we see that $\lambda = 3$ is a solution. Polynomial division by $\lambda - 3$ gives

$$-\lambda^3 + 12\lambda^2 - 45\lambda + 54 = (\lambda - 3)(-\lambda^2 + 9\lambda - 18) = 0$$

Hence $\lambda = 3$ or $-\lambda^2 + 9\lambda - 18 = 0$, and the quadratic equation gives $\lambda = 3$ and $\lambda = 6$. We find the same eigenvalues $\lambda_1 = \lambda_2 = 3$ and $\lambda_3 = 6$ as before, and also with this method we see that $\lambda = 3$ has multiplicity two since it appears twice.

To compute eigenvectors, we consider each of the eigenvalues in turn: For $\lambda = 3$, the eigenspace E_3 is the null space of the matrix

$$A - 3I = \begin{pmatrix} 4-3 & 1 & 1 \\ 1 & 4-3 & 1 \\ 1 & 1 & 4-3 \end{pmatrix} = \begin{pmatrix} 1 & 1 & 1 \\ 1 & 1 & 1 \\ 1 & 1 & 1 \end{pmatrix}$$

We solve the linear system, and see that y and z are free and that $x + y + z = 0$, which gives $x = -y - z$. We find the solutions

$$\mathbf{v} = \begin{pmatrix} x \\ y \\ z \end{pmatrix} = \begin{pmatrix} -y - z \\ y \\ z \end{pmatrix} = y \cdot \mathbf{v}_1 + z \cdot \mathbf{v}_2, \quad \mathbf{v}_1 = \begin{pmatrix} -1 \\ 1 \\ 0 \end{pmatrix}, \quad \mathbf{v}_2 = \begin{pmatrix} -1 \\ 0 \\ 1 \end{pmatrix}$$

A base of E_3 is therefore given by $B_1 = \{\mathbf{v}_1, \mathbf{v}_2\}$. For $\lambda = 6$, the eigenspace E_6 is the null space of the matrix

$$A - 6I = \begin{pmatrix} 4-6 & 1 & 1 \\ 1 & 4-6 & 1 \\ 1 & 1 & 4-6 \end{pmatrix} = \begin{pmatrix} -2 & 1 & 1 \\ 1 & -2 & 1 \\ 1 & 1 & -2 \end{pmatrix}$$

To solve the linear system, we need to do some elementary row operations:

$$\begin{pmatrix} -2 & 1 & 1 \\ 1 & -2 & 1 \\ 1 & 1 & -2 \end{pmatrix} \to \begin{pmatrix} 1 & -2 & 1 \\ -2 & 1 & 1 \\ 1 & 1 & -2 \end{pmatrix} \to \begin{pmatrix} 1 & -2 & 1 \\ 0 & -3 & 3 \\ 0 & 3 & -3 \end{pmatrix} \to \begin{pmatrix} 1 & -2 & 1 \\ 0 & -3 & 3 \\ 0 & 0 & 0 \end{pmatrix}$$

We see that z is free, that $-3y + 3z = 0$, or $y = z$, and that $x - 2y + z = 0$, or that $x = 2y - z = 2z - z = z$. We find the solutions

$$\mathbf{v} = \begin{pmatrix} x \\ y \\ z \end{pmatrix} = \begin{pmatrix} z \\ z \\ z \end{pmatrix} = z \cdot \mathbf{v}_3, \quad \mathbf{v}_3 = \begin{pmatrix} 1 \\ 1 \\ 1 \end{pmatrix}$$

A base of E_6 is therefore given by $B_2 = \{\mathbf{v}_3\}$. Notice that in general, the dimension $\dim E_\lambda$ is the number of free variables in the linear system $(A - \lambda I)\mathbf{v} = \mathbf{0}$. In this example, we have $\dim E_3 = 2$ and $\dim E_6 = 1$.

4.2 The characteristic polynomial

Let A be an $n \times n$ matrix. We define the *characteristic polynomial* of A to be the polynomial $p(\lambda) = |A - \lambda I|$ of degree n, the left-hand side of the characteristic equation. Let us start by considering the special case $n = 2$. In this case, we have

$$A = \begin{pmatrix} a & b \\ c & d \end{pmatrix} \quad \Rightarrow \quad p(\lambda) = \begin{vmatrix} a - \lambda & b \\ c & d - \lambda \end{vmatrix}$$

This means that $p(\lambda) = (a - \lambda)(d - \lambda) - bc = \lambda^2 - (a + d)\lambda + (ad - bc)$. We define the *trace* of A to be the sum $\mathrm{tr}(A) = a + d$ of the entries on the diagonal of A, and recognize the expression $ad - bc$ as the determinant of A.

Characteristic equation of a 2 × 2 matrix
For a 2 × 2 matrix A, we have $p(\lambda) = \lambda^2 - \mathrm{tr}(A)\lambda + \det(A)$.

For a general $n \times n$ matrix $A = (a_{ij})$, we define the trace of A to be the sum $\operatorname{tr}(A) = a_{11} + a_{22} + \ldots + a_{nn}$ of diagonal entries. We have that

$$p(\lambda) = \begin{vmatrix} a_{11} - \lambda & a_{12} & a_{13} & \ldots & a_{1n} \\ a_{21} & a_{22} - \lambda & a_{33} & \ldots & a_{2n} \\ a_{31} & a_{32} & a_{33} - \lambda & \ldots & a_{3n} \\ \vdots & \vdots & \vdots & \ddots & \vdots \\ a_{n1} & a_{n2} & a_{n3} & \ldots & a_{nn} - \lambda \end{vmatrix}$$

$$= (a_{11} - \lambda)(a_{22} - \lambda) \cdots (a_{nn} - \lambda) + \text{terms of lower degree}$$

$$= (-\lambda)^n + (a_{11} + a_{22} + \ldots + a_{nn})(-\lambda)^{n-1} + \text{terms of lower degree}$$

since the determinant is a sum, where one term is the product of the diagonal entries, and all other terms are products on n entries, among them at least two factors that are non-diagonal entries. Hence $p(\lambda)$ is a polynomial of degree n of the form

$$p(\lambda) = (-\lambda)^n + c_1(-\lambda)^{n-1} + \ldots + c_{n-1}(-\lambda) + c_n$$

where $c_1 = a_{11} + a_{22} + \ldots + a_{nn} = \operatorname{tr}(A)$. We also have that $c_n = p(0) = \det(A)$. We define the *principal minors* of A to be the minors M_{IJ} with $I = J$, and one may show that the coefficient c_i of $(-\lambda)^{n-i}$ in $p(\lambda)$ is the sum of all principal minors of A of order i for $1 \leq i \leq n$. The formulas $c_1 = \operatorname{tr}(A)$ and $c_n = \det(A)$ are special cases.

> **Characteristic polynomial**
> The characteristic polynomial of an $n \times n$ matrix A is given by
> $$p(\lambda) = (-\lambda)^n + \operatorname{tr}(A)(-\lambda)^{n-1} + c_2(-\lambda)^{n-1} \ldots + c_{n-1}(-\lambda) + \det(A)$$
> where c_i is the sum of all principal minors of A of order i.

To solve the characteristic equation is difficult in general. In principle, we have that $p(\lambda^*) = 0$ if and only if $(\lambda - \lambda^*)$ is a factor in $p(\lambda)$, so we could try to factorize $p(\lambda)$, which is equally difficult. In principle, it may happen that there are n linear factors

$$p(\lambda) = (-1)^n (\lambda - \lambda_1)(\lambda - \lambda_2) \cdots (\lambda - \lambda_n)$$

4.2 The characteristic polynomial

In this case, the eigenvalues of A are $\lambda_1, \ldots, \lambda_n$. It may also happen that $p(\lambda)$ has *irreducible quadratic factors*. These are quadratic factors of the form $\lambda^2 + s\lambda + t$ where $s^2 < 4t$ such that there are no real roots. In fact, we have that

$$\lambda^2 + s\lambda + t = 0 \quad \Rightarrow \quad \lambda = \frac{-s \pm \sqrt{s^2 - 4t}}{2}$$

and $s^2 < 4t$ means that $s^2 - 4t < 0$. Each irreducible quadratic factor "uses" two degrees and does not produce any real eigenvalues.

It turns out that $p(\lambda)$ can always be factored into linear factors and irreducible quadratic factors. This follows from Theorem A.4, which is a deep result called the fundamental theorem of algebra. From this, it follows that there is an integer $r \leq n$ and a factorization

$$p(\lambda) = (-1)^n (\lambda - \lambda_1)(\lambda - \lambda_2) \cdots (\lambda - \lambda_r) \cdot q(\lambda)$$

where $q(\lambda)$ is a product of $(n-r)/2$ irreducible quadratic factors. The eigenvalues of A are $\lambda = \lambda_1, \ldots, \lambda_r$ since $q(\lambda) > 0$ for all λ. There may be repeated roots, and we define the *multiplicity* of an eigenvalue λ^* to be the maximal integer m such that $(\lambda - \lambda^*)^m$ is a factor in $p(\lambda)$. The multiplicity m is also called the *algebraic multiplicity* of the eigenvalue λ^*.

If $r = n$, then $p(\lambda) = (-1)^n (\lambda - \lambda_1) \cdots (\lambda - \lambda_n)$, with $q(\lambda) = 1$, and we say that A has n eigenvalues, counted with multiplicity. In both examples in the previous section, this was the case: In the first example, $n = 2$ and the eigenvalues were $\lambda_1 = 5$ and $\lambda_2 = 0$. In the second example, $n = 3$ and the eigenvalues were $\lambda_1 = \lambda_2 = 3$ and $\lambda_3 = 6$. We count $\lambda = 3$ twice since it has multiplicity $m = 2$.

Let us consider an example of an $n \times n$ matrix A with less than n eigenvalues, counted with multiplicity. We look at the following 3×3 matrix A:

$$A = \begin{pmatrix} 2 & 0 & 1 \\ 0 & 2 & 0 \\ -1 & 0 & 2 \end{pmatrix} \quad \Rightarrow \quad p(\lambda) = |A - \lambda I| = \begin{vmatrix} 2-\lambda & 0 & 1 \\ 0 & 2-\lambda & 0 \\ -1 & 0 & 2-\lambda \end{vmatrix}$$

We use cofactor expansion along the middle row, and see that $p(\lambda)$ can be written

$$p(\lambda) = (2-\lambda)((2-\lambda)^2 + 1) = -(\lambda - 2)(\lambda^2 - 4\lambda + 5)$$

Since $\lambda^2 - 4\lambda + 5 = (\lambda - 2)^2 + 1 > 0$ for all λ, the quadratic factor is irreducible. Hence there is just one eigenvalue $\lambda = 2$, counted with multiplicity, and $r = 1$. The "missing" eigenvalues are the roots of the irreducible quadratic factor, given by

$$\lambda = \frac{4 \pm \sqrt{16 - 4(5)}}{2} = \frac{4 \pm \sqrt{-4}}{2} = \frac{4 \pm \sqrt{4}\sqrt{-1}}{2} = 2 \pm \sqrt{-1}$$

Square roots of negative numbers do not exist among real numbers, hence $2 \pm \sqrt{-1}$ are not real numbers.

4 • Eigenvectors and eigenvalues

Proposition 4.2. Let A be an $n \times n$ matrix. If A has n eigenvalues $\lambda_1, \lambda_2, \ldots, \lambda_n$, counted with multiplicity, then we have

a) $\lambda_1 + \lambda_2 + \ldots + \lambda_n = \text{tr}(A)$ \qquad b) $\lambda_1 \cdot \lambda_2 \cdots \lambda_n = |A|$

Proof. Let $p(\lambda)$ be the characteristic polynomial of A. Since $\lambda_1, \lambda_2, \ldots, \lambda_n$ are the eigenvalues of A, we have that

$$p(\lambda) = (-1)^n (\lambda - \lambda_1)(\lambda - \lambda_2) \cdots (\lambda - \lambda_n)$$
$$= (\lambda_1 - \lambda)(\lambda_2 - \lambda) \cdots (\lambda_n - \lambda)$$
$$= (-\lambda)^n + c_1 (-\lambda)^{n-1} + \ldots + c_n$$

where $c_n = \lambda_1 \lambda_2 \cdots \lambda_n$ is the constant term in the polynomial and $c_1 = \lambda_1 + \ldots + \lambda_n$. By definition, we have $p(0) = \det(A - 0 \cdot I) = |A|$, and from the expression above, we have that $p(0) = c_n$. It follows that $\lambda_1 \cdots \lambda_n = |A|$. If we compare the coefficient of $(-\lambda)^{n-1}$ in the expression above and the expression in the beginning of this section, we see that $c_1 = a_{11} + \ldots + a_{nn}$, and it follows that $\lambda_1 + \ldots + \lambda_n = \text{tr}(A)$. $\square$

Let λ^* be an eigenvalue of A of multiplicity m. The dimension $\dim E_{\lambda^*}$ of the eigenspace E_{λ^*} is the number of free variables in the linear system $(A - \lambda^* I)\mathbf{v} = \mathbf{0}$, and we know that $\dim E_{\lambda^*} \geq 1$: There must be nontrivial solutions of the linear system since $|A - \lambda^* I| = 0$. We call $\dim E_{\lambda^*}$ the *geometric multiplicity* of the eigenvalue λ^*. We are going to show that the geometric multiplicity is at most equal to the algebraic multiplicity m. To this end, we use the following construction:

Let us write $s = \dim E_{\lambda^*}$ for the geometric multiplicity of the eigenvalue λ^*. By definition, this means that there is a base $\{\mathbf{v}_1, \ldots, \mathbf{v}_s\}$ of the eigenspace E_{λ^*}. Hence there are s free variables $t_1, \ldots, t_s$ such that all solutions of the linear system $(A - \lambda^* I)\mathbf{v} = \mathbf{0}$ are linear combinations of the form

$$t_1 \mathbf{v}_1 + t_2 \mathbf{v}_2 + \ldots + t_s \mathbf{v}_s$$

where the vectors $\{\mathbf{v}_1, \ldots, \mathbf{v}_s\}$ are linearly independent. Since $\mathbf{v}_1, \ldots, \mathbf{v}_s$ are vectors in $\mathbb{R}^n$, we have that $s \leq n$. We claim that if $s < n$, then it is possible to find vectors $\mathbf{v}_{s+1}, \ldots, \mathbf{v}_n$ in $\mathbb{R}^n$ such that $\{\mathbf{v}_1, \mathbf{v}_2, \ldots, \mathbf{v}_n\}$ is a base of $\mathbb{R}^n$: If $s < n$, then there is a vector $\mathbf{v}_{s+1}$ in $\mathbb{R}^n$ which is not in E_{λ^*}, and this means that $\{\mathbf{v}_1, \ldots, \mathbf{v}_{s+1}\}$ are linearly independent since $\mathbf{v}_{s+1}$ is not a linear combination $t_1 \mathbf{v}_1 + t_2 \mathbf{v}_2 + \ldots + t_s \mathbf{v}_s$. We may continue in this way until we have n linearly independent vectors $\{\mathbf{v}_1, \ldots, \mathbf{v}_n\}$, which will form a base of $\mathbb{R}^n$.

4.2 The characteristic polynomial

Proposition 4.3. Let A be an $n \times n$ matrix, and let λ be an eigenvalue of A. If λ has multiplicity m, then $1 \leq \dim E_\lambda \leq m$.

Proof. Let λ^* be an eigenvalue of A with geometric multiplicity s and algebraic multiplicity m. Using the construction above, we construct a base $\{\mathbf{v}_1, \ldots, \mathbf{v}_n\}$ of $\mathbb{R}^n$ such that $\mathbf{v}_1, \ldots, \mathbf{v}_s$ are eigenvectors of A with eigenvalue λ^*, and let P be the matrix with these vectors as columns. Then P is an invertible matrix since the column vectors of P are linearly independent. We have that

$$AP = A \cdot \left(\mathbf{v}_1 \mid \ldots \mid \mathbf{v}_s \mid \mathbf{v}_{s+1} \mid \ldots \mid \mathbf{v}_n \right) = \left(A\mathbf{v}_1 \mid \ldots \mid A\mathbf{v}_s \mid A\mathbf{v}_{s+1} \mid \ldots \mid A\mathbf{v}_n \right)$$

$$= \left(\lambda^* \mathbf{v}_1 \mid \ldots \mid \lambda^* \mathbf{v}_s \mid \mathbf{w}_{s+1} \mid \ldots \mid \mathbf{w}_n \right)$$

with $\mathbf{w}_i = A\mathbf{v}_i$ for $i > s$, which means that there are matrices B and C such that

$$AP = \left(\mathbf{v}_1 \mid \ldots \mid \mathbf{v}_s \mid \mathbf{v}_{s+1} \mid \ldots \mid \mathbf{v}_n \right) \cdot \left(\begin{array}{c|c} \lambda^* I_s & B \\ \hline 0 & C \end{array} \right) = PQ$$

The last $n - s$ columns of AP are $\mathbf{w}_{s+1}, \ldots, \mathbf{w}_n$, and each of these vectors in $\mathbb{R}^n$ can be written as a linear combination of $\mathbf{v}_1, \ldots, \mathbf{v}_n$ in a unique way, since $\{\mathbf{v}_1, \ldots, \mathbf{v}_n\}$ is a base of $\mathbb{R}^n$. We use the coefficients to define the matrices B and C in Q. We claim that A and Q have the same characteristic equation: In fact, $AP = PQ$ gives $P^{-1}AP = Q$, and we get $P^{-1}(A - \lambda I)P = P^{-1}AP - \lambda P^{-1}P = Q - \lambda I$, and therefore that

$$|Q - \lambda I| = |P^{-1}(A - \lambda I)P| = |P^{-1}| \cdot |A - \lambda I| \cdot |P| = |A - \lambda I|$$

Finally, using cofactor expansion along the first column and repeating this s times, we see that

$$|Q - \lambda I| = \left| \begin{array}{c|c} (\lambda^* - \lambda)I_s & B \\ \hline 0 & C - \lambda I_{n-s} \end{array} \right| = (\lambda - \lambda^*)^s \cdot |C - \lambda I|$$

This means that $(\lambda - \lambda^*)^s$ is a factor in the characteristic equation of Q, and therefore of A, and this implies that $s \leq m$. □

4.3 Diagonalization

Let A be an $n \times n$ matrix, and let $T : \mathbb{R}^n \to \mathbb{R}^n$ be the linear transformation given by $T(\mathbf{v}) = A \cdot \mathbf{v}$. We say that A is *diagonalizable* if there are n linearly independent eigenvectors $\mathbf{v}_1, \mathbf{v}_2, \ldots, \mathbf{v}_n$ of A. In that case, we have by definition that $T(\mathbf{v}_i) = \lambda_i \mathbf{v}_i$ for $1 \leq i \leq n$, where λ_i is the eigenvalue of the eigenvector $\mathbf{v}_i$ of A.

If A is diagonalizable, we can form a new $n \times n$ matrix P with the eigenvectors $\mathbf{v}_1, \mathbf{v}_2, \ldots, \mathbf{v}_n$ as columns. The matrix P is invertible since the vectors are linearly independent, and we have

$$A \cdot P = A \cdot \left(\mathbf{v}_1 \mid \mathbf{v}_2 \mid \ldots \mid \mathbf{v}_n \right) = \left(A\mathbf{v}_1 \mid A\mathbf{v}_2 \mid \ldots \mid A\mathbf{v}_n \right)$$

$$= \left(\lambda_1 \mathbf{v}_1 \mid \lambda_2 \mathbf{v}_2 \mid \ldots \mid \lambda_n \mathbf{v}_n \right)$$

Let D be the diagonal matrix with the eigenvalues $\lambda_1, \lambda_2, \ldots, \lambda_n$ on the diagonal. It follows that $AP = PD$ since we have

$$P \cdot D = \left(\mathbf{v}_1 \mid \mathbf{v}_2 \mid \ldots \mid \mathbf{v}_n \right) \cdot \begin{pmatrix} \lambda_1 & 0 & \ldots & 0 \\ 0 & \lambda_2 & \ldots & 0 \\ \vdots & \vdots & \ddots & \vdots \\ 0 & 0 & \ldots & \lambda_n \end{pmatrix}$$

$$= \left(\lambda_1 \mathbf{v}_1 \mid \lambda_2 \mathbf{v}_2 \mid \ldots \mid \lambda_n \mathbf{v}_n \right)$$

This means that if A is diagonalizable, then $AP = PD$ for a diagonal matrix D and an invertible matrix P. This equation can also be written as $P^{-1}AP = D$, or $A = PDP^{-1}$.

Proposition 4.4. Let A be an $n \times n$ matrix. Then A is diagonalizable if and only if $P^{-1}AP = D$ for an invertible matrix P and a diagonal matrix D.

Proof. If A is diagonalizable, then the argument above shows that $P^{-1}AP = D$ with P an invertible and D a diagonal matrix. Conversely, if $P^{-1}AP = D$ for an invertible matrix P and a diagonal matrix D, then the columns of P are linearly independent eigenvectors of A, and the diagonal entries of D are the corresponding eigenvalues, since $AP = PD$. □

4.3 Diagonalization

To find a diagonalization of a square matrix A, we find all eigenvalues and eigenvectors of A. The idea is to form the matrix D using eigenvalues and the matrix P using eigenvectors, and that A is diagonalizable if there are enough eigenvalues and eigenvectors. When A is an $n \times n$ matrix, we need n eigenvalues of A (counted with multiplicity) and n linearly independent eigenvectors of A. Let us consider the following example:

$$A = \begin{pmatrix} 4 & 1 & 1 \\ 1 & 4 & 1 \\ 1 & 1 & 4 \end{pmatrix}$$

We computed eigenvalues and eigenvectors of A in Section 4.1: We found the eigenvalues $\lambda = 3$ of multiplicity $m = 2$ and $\lambda = 6$ with multiplicity $m = 1$. Since $n = 3$ in this case, and we have 3 eigenvalues (counted with multiplicity), we choose the diagonal matrix

$$D = \begin{pmatrix} 3 & 0 & 0 \\ 0 & 3 & 0 \\ 0 & 0 & 6 \end{pmatrix}$$

We also found a base $B_1 = \{\mathbf{v}_1, \mathbf{v}_2\}$ of the eigenspace E_3, with $\mathbf{v}_1 = (-1, 1, 0)$ and $\mathbf{v}_2 = (-1, 0, 1)$, and a base $B_2 = \{\mathbf{v}_3\}$ of the eigenspace E_6, with $\mathbf{v}_3 = (1, 1, 1)$. As we shall show below, it is a fact that if we combine the bases of the eigenspaces E_λ for all the different eigenvalues λ of A, we obtain a set of eigenvectors of A that are linearly independent:

$$B_1 \cup B_2 = \{\mathbf{v}_1, \mathbf{v}_2, \mathbf{v}_3\} = \left\{ \begin{pmatrix} -1 \\ 1 \\ 0 \end{pmatrix}, \begin{pmatrix} -1 \\ 0 \\ 1 \end{pmatrix}, \begin{pmatrix} 1 \\ 1 \\ 1 \end{pmatrix} \right\}$$

It follows that we have $n = 3$ linearly independent eigenvectors, and we may use them to form an invertible matrix P such that $P^{-1}AP = D$:

$$P = \begin{pmatrix} -1 & -1 & 1 \\ 1 & 0 & 1 \\ 0 & 1 & 1 \end{pmatrix}$$

Since there are n eigenvalues (counted with multiplicity) and n linearly independent eigenvectors, the $n \times n$ matrix A is diagonalizable. Note that the matrices P and D are not unique, and it is essential that the order of the eigenvectors in P correspond to the order of the eigenvalues in D.

Proposition 4.5. Let $\mathbf{v}_i$ be an eigenvector of A with eigenvalues λ_i for $1 \leq i \leq r$. If all eigenvalues $\lambda_1, \lambda_2, \ldots, \lambda_r$ are distinct, then the eigenvectors $\{\mathbf{v}_1, \mathbf{v}_2, \ldots, \mathbf{v}_r\}$ are linearly independent.

Proof. We prove this statement by induction on r. For $r = 1$, we must prove that one eigenvector is linearly independent, and this is clear since eigenvectors are nonzero: If $c_1 \mathbf{v}_1 = \mathbf{0}$, then $c_1 = 0$. For the induction step, we assume that any $r - 1$ eigenvectors with distinct eigenvalues are linearly independent, and we must prove that r eigenvectors with distinct eigenvalues are linearly independent. We consider the equation $c_1 \mathbf{v}_1 + c_2 \mathbf{v}_2 + \ldots + c_r \mathbf{v}_r = \mathbf{0}$. To show that $c_1 = c_2 = \ldots = c_r = 0$, we multiply it by $A - \lambda_r I$ from the left. We get

$$c_1(\lambda_1 - \lambda_r)\mathbf{v}_1 + c_2(\lambda_2 - \lambda_r)\mathbf{v}_2 + \ldots c_{r-1}(\lambda_{r-1} - \lambda_r)\mathbf{v}_{r-1} = \mathbf{0}$$

Since $\mathbf{v}_1, \ldots, \mathbf{v}_{r-1}$ are $r - 1$ eigenvectors with distinct eigenvalues, it follows by the induction assumption that $c_i(\lambda_i - \lambda_r) = 0$ for $1 \le i \le r - 1$, and this means that $c_1 = c_2 = \ldots = c_{r-1} = 0$, since the eigenvalues are distinct. Hence $c_r \mathbf{v}_r = \mathbf{0}$, and this means that $c_r = 0$, since $\mathbf{v}_r \ne \mathbf{0}$. □

We notice that if $\lambda_1, \lambda_2, \ldots, \lambda_r$ are the distinct eigenvalues of A, and we choose a base B_i of the eigenspace E_{λ_i} for $1 \le i \le r$, it follows from the proposition above that $B_1 \cup B_2 \cup \ldots \cup B_r$ is a set of linearly independent eigenvectors of A. In fact, the number of vectors in this set is the maximal number of linearly independent eigenvectors of A.

One important special case is the case when A has n distinct eigenvalues. Then the set above contains one eigenvector from each eigenspace, and a total of n linearly independent eigenvectors. It follows that any $n \times n$ matrix A with n distinct eigenvalues is diagonalizable. More generally, we have the following conditions for the diagonalizability of A:

Conditions for diagonalizability

An $n \times n$ matrix A with distinct eigenvalues $\lambda_1, \lambda_2, \ldots \lambda_r$ of multiplicities $m_1, m_2, \ldots, m_r$ is diagonalizable if and only if the following conditions hold:

a) A has n eigenvalues, counted with multiplicity $\Leftrightarrow m_1 + \ldots + m_r = n$

b) A has n linearly independent eigenvectors $\Leftrightarrow \dim E_{\lambda_1} + \ldots + \dim E_{\lambda_r} = n$

4.3 Diagonalization

Computing powers of square matrices. Let A be an $n \times n$ matrix. In general, it is hard to compute A^m directly for large exponents m. However, if A has a diagonalization $P^{-1}AP = D$, then we have

$$A = PDP^{-1} \quad \Rightarrow \quad A^m = (PDP^{-1})(PDP^{-1})(PDP^{-1})\cdots(PDP^{-1}) = PD^mP^{-1}$$

In fact, $P^{-1}P = I$, hence the last factor P^{-1} in one parenthesis cancels the first P in the next parenthesis. Moreover, we can compute D^m by the following formula, since D is a diagonal matrix:

$$D^m = \begin{pmatrix} \lambda_1 & 0 & \cdots & 0 \\ 0 & \lambda_2 & \cdots & 0 \\ \vdots & \vdots & \ddots & \vdots \\ 0 & 0 & \cdots & \lambda_n \end{pmatrix}^m = \begin{pmatrix} \lambda_1^m & 0 & \cdots & 0 \\ 0 & \lambda_2^m & \cdots & 0 \\ \vdots & \vdots & \ddots & \vdots \\ 0 & 0 & \cdots & \lambda_n^m \end{pmatrix}$$

We can therefore compute $A^m = PD^mP^{-1}$ for any exponent m using the matrices D and P found in the diagonalization, and the inverse matrix P^{-1} of P, which we can compute as $P^{-1} = 1/|P| \cdot \mathrm{Adj}(P)$.

As an example, let us compute the power A^m when A is the 2×2 matrix we considered earlier in this chapter, given by

$$A = \begin{pmatrix} 4 & -2 \\ -2 & 1 \end{pmatrix}$$

We found the eigenvalues $\lambda_1 = 5$ and $\lambda_2 = 0$ in Section 4.1. We can use this to compute D^m:

$$D = \begin{pmatrix} 5 & 0 \\ 0 & 0 \end{pmatrix} \quad \Rightarrow \quad D^m = \begin{pmatrix} 5^m & 0 \\ 0 & 0^m \end{pmatrix} = \begin{pmatrix} 5^m & 0 \\ 0 & 0 \end{pmatrix}$$

We also found bases of E_0 and E_5, consisting of the eigenvectors $\mathbf{v}_1 = (-2, 1)$ in E_5 and $\mathbf{v}_2 = (1, 2)$ in E_0. We can use these to determine P, and compute P^{-1}:

$$P = \begin{pmatrix} -2 & 1 \\ 1 & 2 \end{pmatrix} \quad \Rightarrow \quad P^{-1} = \frac{1}{-5}\begin{pmatrix} 2 & -1 \\ -1 & -2 \end{pmatrix} = \frac{1}{5}\begin{pmatrix} -2 & 1 \\ 1 & 2 \end{pmatrix}$$

Combining these results, we can compute $A^m = PD^mP^{-1}$, and we find the following expression for the power A^m:

$$A^m = PD^mP^{-1}$$

$$= \begin{pmatrix} -2 & 1 \\ 1 & 2 \end{pmatrix}\begin{pmatrix} 5^m & 0 \\ 0 & 0 \end{pmatrix} \cdot \frac{1}{5}\begin{pmatrix} -2 & 1 \\ 1 & 2 \end{pmatrix} = \frac{1}{5}\begin{pmatrix} -2 \cdot 5^m & 0 \\ 1 \cdot 5^m & 0 \end{pmatrix}\begin{pmatrix} -2 & 1 \\ 1 & 2 \end{pmatrix}$$

$$= \frac{1}{5}\begin{pmatrix} 4 \cdot 5^m & -2 \cdot 5^m \\ -2 \cdot 5^m & 1 \cdot 5^m \end{pmatrix} = \frac{5^m}{5}\begin{pmatrix} 4 & -2 \\ -2 & 1 \end{pmatrix} = 5^{m-1} \cdot A$$

4 • Eigenvectors and eigenvalues

For $m = 2$, this gives $A^2 = 5A$, and the expression for A^m follows from this formula. For example, we have $A^3 = A^2 \cdot A = 5A \cdot A = 5A^2 = 5(5A) = 5^2 A$. We notice that $A^2 = 5A$ can be written $p(A) = 0$, where the left-hand side is obtained by replacing λ with the matrix A in the characteristic polynomial $p(\lambda)$ of A:

$$p(\lambda) = (-1)^2(\lambda - 5)(\lambda - 0) = \lambda^2 - 5\lambda$$

In this case, $p(A) = 0$ gives $A^2 - 5A = 0$, or $A^2 = 5A$. The fact that $p(A) = 0$ is no coincidence; it follows from a general result called the Cayley-Hamilton Theorem:

Theorem 4.6 (Cayley-Hamilton). Let A be an $n \times n$ matrix with characteristic polynomial $p(\lambda) = |A - \lambda I|$. Then $p(A) = 0$.

Proof. Write $p(\lambda) = (-\lambda)^n + c_1(-\lambda)^{n-1} + \ldots + c_{n-1}(-\lambda) + c_n$ for the characteristic polynomial of A, and consider an eigenvector $\mathbf{v}$ of A with eigenvalue λ. Then we have

$$p(A) \cdot \mathbf{v} = ((-A)^n + c_1(-A)^n - 1 + \ldots + c_{n-1}(-A) + c_n I) \cdot \mathbf{v}$$
$$= ((-\lambda)^n + c_1(-\lambda)^{n-1} + \ldots + c_{n-1}(-\lambda) + c_n)\mathbf{v}$$
$$= 0 \cdot \mathbf{v} = \mathbf{0}$$

since $A\mathbf{v} = \lambda\mathbf{v}$ implies that $A^i\mathbf{v} = \lambda^i\mathbf{v}$. Hence $p(A)\mathbf{v} = \mathbf{0}$ for any eigenvector of A, and this implies that $p(A) = 0$ when A has n linearly independent eigenvectors. This proves the result in case when A is diagonalizable. In the general case, the result is still true, but the proof is more complicated and we shall not give it in this book. □

4.4 Nonnegative matrices and Markov chains

Let $n > 1$ be positive integer, and assume that any member of a population can be in one of n different states, which we call $1, 2, \ldots, n$. We write v_i for the share of the population in state i, and call $\mathbf{v} = (v_1, v_2, \ldots, v_n)$ the *state vector* of the system. Clearly, a state vector satisfies the conditions $0 \le v_i \le 1$ for $1 \le i \le n$, and that the sum $v_1 + v_2 + \ldots + v_n = 1$. We can picture the states as nodes in a diagram:

$$\begin{array}{ccccc} 1 & 2 & 3 & \cdots & n \end{array}$$

As a simple example, let us assume that any member of the adult population is classified as employed or unemployed. In this case, we have $n = 2$ states, and we may consider state 1 to be employed and state 2 to be unemployed. The state vector $\mathbf{v} = (v_1, v_2)$ will give information about the share of the population that is employed

We have $\mathbf{v}_m = A^m \mathbf{v}_0$, and its limit as $m \to \infty$ is given by

$$\lim_{m \to \infty} \frac{1}{5} \begin{pmatrix} 4 + 0.85^m & 4 - 4 \cdot 0.85^m \\ 1 - 0.85^m & 1 + 4 \cdot 0.85^m \end{pmatrix} \begin{pmatrix} 0.94 \\ 0.06 \end{pmatrix} = \frac{1}{5} \begin{pmatrix} 4 & 4 \\ 1 & 1 \end{pmatrix} \cdot \begin{pmatrix} 0.94 \\ 0.06 \end{pmatrix}$$

$$= \frac{1}{5} \begin{pmatrix} 4 \\ 1 \end{pmatrix}$$

since $0.85^m \to 0$ as $m \to \infty$. The limit $\mathbf{v} = (4/5, 1/5) = (0.80, 0.20)$ is called the long term *equilibrium state* of the Markov chain. Its interpretation is that the long term unemployment rate is 20 % with the given assumptions.

A matrix $A = (a_{ij})$ is called *positive* if $a_{ij} > 0$ for $1 \leq i, j \leq n$, and *nonnegative* if $a_{ij} \geq 0$ for $1 \leq i, j \leq n$. We write $A > 0$ if A is positive, and $A \geq 0$ if it is nonnegative. We also use this notation for vectors, and write $\mathbf{v} > 0$ for a positive vector, and $\mathbf{v} \geq 0$ for a nonnegative vector. In many applications, we use positive, or at least nonnegative matrices, and it is clear that the transition matrix of a Markov chain is nonnegative (and often, but not always, it is a positive matrix).

We define a nonnegative matrix A to be *irreducible* if $A^m > 0$ is positive for some positive integer $m > 0$, and *primitive* if for any position (i, j) with $1 \leq i, j \leq n$, we have $(A^m)_{ij} > 0$ for some integer m. We notice that A positive $\Rightarrow$ A primitive (with $m = 1$), and that A primitive $\Rightarrow$ A irreducible. When A is the transition matrix of a Markov chain, we have the following interpretations:

- positive: movement from any state to any other state is possible in one time period
- irreducible: movement from any state to any other state is possible in a finite number of time periods
- primitive: there is a fixed positive integer $m > 0$ such that movement from any state to any other state is possible in m time periods

We say that a Markov chain is *regular* if the transition matrix A is a primitive matrix. Let us look at some examples of transition matrices:

a) $A = \begin{pmatrix} 0.97 & 0.12 \\ 0.03 & 0.88 \end{pmatrix}$

b) $A = \begin{pmatrix} 0.85 & 0.07 & 0.10 \\ 0.15 & 0.90 & 0.01 \\ 0 & 0.03 & 0.89 \end{pmatrix}$

c) $A = \begin{pmatrix} 0 & 1 \\ 1 & 0 \end{pmatrix}$

Example a) is the Markov chain in the example above. Since A is positive, it is also primitive, and the Markov chain is regular. In example b) we have that $A \geq 0$ is nonnegative, and primitive since $A^2 > 0$ is positive, hence the Markov chain is regular. In fact, movement from any state to any other state is possible in one step in a) and in two steps in b). Example c) is *not* a regular Markov chain: Movement from one state to the opposite state is possible in an odd number of steps, and to the same state in an even number of steps. But there is no fixed $m > 0$ such that movement from any state to any other state is possible in m steps.

Proposition 4.7. Let A be the transition matrix of a Markov chain with n states. If the Markov chain is regular, then the following holds:

a) $\lambda = 1$ is an eigenvalue of A of multiplicity $m = 1$, and $|\lambda| < 1$ for any other eigenvalue λ of A

b) there is a unique eigenvector $\mathbf{v}$ with eigenvalue $\lambda = 1$ that is a state vector, and for any initial state vector $\mathbf{v}_0$, we have that $\mathbf{v}_m = A^m \mathbf{v}_0 \to \mathbf{v}$ as $m \to \infty$

If a Markov chain is regular, then we can find the equilibrium state $\mathbf{v}$ without computing all eigenvalues and eigenvectors: By Proposition 4.7, it is enough to find the unique eigenvector $\mathbf{v}$ with eigenvalue $\lambda = 1$ that is a state vector: We find all eigenvectors with eigenvalue $\lambda = 1$, and impose the extra condition that the sum of the components in the eigenvector should be 1. We also notice that $A^m \mathbf{v}_0 \to \mathbf{v}$ as $m \to \infty$ for any initial state $\mathbf{v}_0$, hence the limit is independent of $\mathbf{v}_0$.

In the example above, this would give a much simpler computation to find the equilibrium state: The eigenvectors with eigenvalue $\lambda = 1$ are given by $\mathbf{v} = (x, y)$ with $x = 4y$ and y free, since the linear system has echelon form

$$\left(\begin{array}{cc|c} -0.03 & 0.12 & 0 \\ 0.03 & -0.12 & 0 \end{array} \right) \to \left(\begin{array}{cc|c} 1 & -4 & 0 \\ 0 & 0 & 0 \end{array} \right)$$

We write $\mathbf{v} = (4y, y)$, and impose the condition $4y + y = 1$, which gives $5y = 1$, or $y = 1/5$. This means that the equilibrium state is $\mathbf{v} = (4/5, 1/5) = (0.80, 0.20)$. It also means that the unemployment rate of 20 % in the long term is independent of the initial unemployment rate 6 %.

We shall not give a proof of Proposition 4.7 in this book, but we shall provide some context to it: It follows from the theorems of Perron and Frobenius on positive and nonnegative matrices. The version of the Perron-Frobenius theory relevant for our case, with A primitive, is given by the following result:

Theorem 4.8 (Perron-Frobenius). Let A be a nonnegative $n \times n$ matrix. If A is primitive, then there is a positive eigenvalue $\lambda_A > 0$ of A and a positive eigenvector $\mathbf{v}_A > \mathbf{0}$ with eigenvalue λ_A such that the following holds.

a) λ_A has multiplicity $m = 1$

b) $|\lambda| < \lambda_A$ for all eigenvalues $\lambda \neq \lambda_A$ of A

c) Any nonnegative eigenvector $\mathbf{v} \geq \mathbf{0}$ of A is a positive multiple of $\mathbf{v}_A$

Moreover, $\min\{s_1, s_2, \ldots, s_n\} \leq \lambda_A \leq \max\{s_1, s_2, \ldots, s_n\}$ when $s_1, s_2, \ldots, s_n$ are the column sums in the matrix A.

Proposition 4.7 follows from this theorem when the Markov chain is regular. In fact, the last part gives $\lambda_A = 1$ when A is the transition matrix of a Markov chain, and the equilibrium state $\mathbf{v}$ is the unique positive multiple of $\mathbf{v}_A$ that is a state vector.

4.5 Spectral theory of symmetric matrices

Let $\mathbf{v}, \mathbf{w}$ be vectors in $\mathbb{R}^n$. We say that $\mathbf{v}$ and $\mathbf{w}$ are orthogonal if their inner product $\mathbf{v} \cdot \mathbf{w} = 0$. We recall from Chapter 2 that the inner product

$$\mathbf{v} \cdot \mathbf{w} = v_1 w_1 + v_2 w_2 + \ldots + v_n w_n$$

and that $\mathbf{v} \cdot \mathbf{w} = 0$ means that the vectors are perpendicular, which we write $\mathbf{v} \perp \mathbf{w}$. We shall expand this definition to a set $\mathfrak{B} = \{\mathbf{v}_1, \mathbf{v}_2, \ldots, \mathbf{v}_r\}$ of vectors: We say that $\mathfrak{B}$ is an *orthogonal* set of vectors if $\mathbf{v}_i \cdot \mathbf{v}_j = 0$ when $i \neq j$. An orthogonal set of vectors where each vector has unit length $\|\mathbf{v}_i\| = 1$ is called an *orthonormal* set of vectors. Since the dot product $\mathbf{v}_i \cdot \mathbf{v}_j$ is the same as the matrix product $\mathbf{v}_i^T \mathbf{v}_j$, $\mathfrak{B}$ is an orthonormal set if and only if

$$\mathbf{v}_i^T \mathbf{v}_j = \begin{cases} 1, & i = j \\ 0, & i \neq j \end{cases}$$

for $1 \leq i, j \leq r$. This condition can be written $A^T A = I$ when A is the matrix with $\mathbf{v}_1, \ldots, \mathbf{v}_r$ as columns.

Let us consider the three vectors $\mathbf{v}_1 = (1, 0, 1)$, $\mathbf{v}_2 = (0, 1, 0)$ and $\mathbf{v}_3 = (-1, 0, 1)$ in $\mathbb{R}^3$ as an example. The set $\mathfrak{B} = \{\mathbf{v}_1, \mathbf{v}_2, \mathbf{v}_3\}$ is an orthogonal set of vectors since we have

$$\mathbf{v}_1 \cdot \mathbf{v}_2 = 0, \quad \mathbf{v}_1 \cdot \mathbf{v}_3 = 0, \quad \mathbf{v}_2 \cdot \mathbf{v}_3 = 0$$

When A is the 3×3 matrix with these three vectors as columns, we have that

$$A^T A = \begin{pmatrix} 1 & 0 & 1 \\ 0 & 1 & 0 \\ -1 & 0 & 1 \end{pmatrix} \begin{pmatrix} 1 & 0 & -1 \\ 0 & 1 & 0 \\ 1 & 0 & 1 \end{pmatrix} = \begin{pmatrix} 2 & 0 & 0 \\ 0 & 1 & 0 \\ 0 & 0 & 2 \end{pmatrix}$$

That this a diagonal matrix confirms that $\mathfrak{B}$ is an orthogonal set of vectors. But the fact that $A^T A \neq I$ means that $\mathfrak{B}$ is not an orthonormal set. In fact, we can read off the lengths of the vectors from the matrix product $A^T A$ and see that

$$\|\mathbf{v}_1\| = \|\mathbf{v}_3\| = \sqrt{2}, \quad \|\mathbf{v}_2\| = 1$$

since the diagonal entries are given by $\mathbf{v}_i^T \mathbf{v}_i = \mathbf{v}_i \cdot \mathbf{v}_i = \|\mathbf{v}_i\|^2$. This means that we can obtain an orthonormal set of vectors

$$\frac{1}{\sqrt{2}} \begin{pmatrix} 1 \\ 0 \\ 1 \end{pmatrix}, \quad \begin{pmatrix} 0 \\ 1 \\ 0 \end{pmatrix}, \quad \frac{1}{\sqrt{2}} \begin{pmatrix} -1 \\ 0 \\ 1 \end{pmatrix}$$

by dividing each vector by its length.

Let A be an $n \times n$ matrix. We say that A is an *orthogonal matrix* if $A^T A = I$. According to the comments above, the matrix A is orthogonal if and only if its column vectors form an orthonormal set of vectors. We also see that if A is an orthogonal matrix, then

$$\det(I) = \det(A^T A) = \det(A^T) \det(A) = \det(A)^2$$

Since $\det(I) = 1$, an orthogonal matrix has determinant $\det(A) = 1$ or $\det(A) = -1$.

Lemma 4.9. Let A be an $n \times n$ matrix. Then A is orthogonal if and only if it is invertible with inverse $A^{-1} = A^T$.

Proof. If A is orthogonal, then $A^T A = I$ and $|A| = \pm 1$ by the comments above. In particular, A is invertible and we have

$$A^T A = I \quad \Rightarrow \quad (A^T A) A^{-1} = I A^{-1} \quad \Rightarrow \quad A^T = A^{-1}$$

Conversely, if $A^T = A^{-1}$, then $A^T A = A^{-1} A = I$, so A is an orthogonal matrix.

□

Let A be an $n \times n$ matrix, and let $T : \mathbb{R}^n \to \mathbb{R}^n$ be the corresponding linear transformation, given by $T(\mathbf{v}) = A \cdot \mathbf{v}$. We say that A has an *orthogonal diagonalization* if there is an orthonormal set $\mathfrak{B} = \{\mathbf{v}_1, \mathbf{v}_2, \ldots, \mathbf{v}_n\}$ of eigenvectors of A. By definition, this means that $T(\mathbf{v}_i) = \lambda_i \mathbf{v}_i$ for $1 \leq i \leq n$. Note that since $\mathfrak{B}$ is orthonormal, it is a linearly independent set of vectors. In fact, if P is the matrix with the vectors in $\mathfrak{B}$ as columns, then P is orthogonal with $P^{-1} = P^T$. Hence, an orthonormal diagonalization is a special case of the diagonalization defined in the previous section, and A has an orthogonal diagonalization if and only if there is an orthogonal matrix P and a diagonal matrix D such that $P^T A P = D$.

4.5 Spectral theory of symmetric matrices

To find an orthogonal diagonalization of an $n \times n$ matrix A, we must therefore find an orthonormal set $\mathfrak{B} = \{\mathbf{v}_1, \mathbf{v}_2, \ldots, \mathbf{v}_n\}$ of eigenvectors of A and let

$$P = \left(\mathbf{v}_1 \middle| \mathbf{v}_2 \middle| \ldots \middle| \mathbf{v}_n \right), \quad D = \begin{pmatrix} \lambda_1 & 0 & \ldots & 0 \\ 0 & \lambda_2 & \ldots & 0 \\ \vdots & \vdots & \ddots & \vdots \\ 0 & 0 & \ldots & \lambda_n \end{pmatrix}$$

where λ_i is the eigenvalue of the eigenvector $\mathbf{v}_i$ for $1 \leq i \leq n$. This is very similar to the way we find a general diagonalization, and the extra requirement is simply that the set $\mathfrak{B}$ of eigenvectors is orthonormal.

If a square matrix A has an orthogonal diagonalization, then it is a symmetric matrix. This is not difficult to see; in fact, an orthonormal diagonalization $P^T A P = D$ can be written $A = PDP^T$, since $P^{-1} = P^T$, and this implies that

$$A^T = (PDP^T)^T = (P^T)^T D^T P^T = PDP^T = A$$

The converse statement is also true: Any symmetric matrix A has an orthogonal diagonalization. The proof is more difficult and requires complex numbers; it will not be given here.

Theorem 4.10. *A square matrix A has an orthogonal diagonalization if and only if it is symmetric. In particular, any symmetric matrix is diagonalizable.*

Corollary 4.11. *Let A be a symmetric $n \times n$ matrix. Then it has n eigenvalues, counted with multiplicity, and $\dim E_\lambda = m$ for any eigenvalue λ of multiplicity m.*

We shall look more closely into how to find an orthogonal diagonalization when A is a symmetric matrix. Let us first look at the following example:

$$A = \begin{pmatrix} 4 & -2 \\ -2 & 1 \end{pmatrix}$$

This is a symmetric matrix, and we computed all eigenvalues and eigenvectors of A in Section 4.1: We found eigenvalues $\lambda_1 = 5$ and $\lambda_2 = 0$, and bases $\{\mathbf{v}_1\}$ for E_5 and $\{\mathbf{v}_2\}$ for E_0, with $\mathbf{v}_1 = (-2, 1)$, $\mathbf{v}_2 = (1, 2)$. It follows that A is diagonalizable, and we may choose

$$P = \begin{pmatrix} -2 & 1 \\ 1 & 2 \end{pmatrix}, \quad D = \begin{pmatrix} 5 & 0 \\ 0 & 0 \end{pmatrix}$$

We notice that $\{\mathbf{v}_1, \mathbf{v}_2\}$ are orthogonal in this case since $\mathbf{v}_1 \cdot \mathbf{v}_2 = -2 \cdot 1 + 1 \cdot 2 = 0$. However, this is not an orthonormal set of vectors, since $\|\mathbf{v}_1\| = \sqrt{(-2)^2 + 1^2} = \sqrt{5}$, and $\|\mathbf{v}_2\| = \sqrt{1^2 + 2^2} = \sqrt{5}$. Notice that we could read off the inner product of the vectors and their lengths from the matrix product $P^T P$:

$$P^T P = \begin{pmatrix} -2 & 1 \\ 1 & 2 \end{pmatrix} \begin{pmatrix} -2 & 1 \\ 1 & 2 \end{pmatrix} = \begin{pmatrix} 5 & 0 \\ 0 & 5 \end{pmatrix} = \begin{pmatrix} \mathbf{v}_1 \cdot \mathbf{v}_1 & \mathbf{v}_1 \cdot \mathbf{v}_2 \\ \mathbf{v}_1 \cdot \mathbf{v}_2 & \mathbf{v}_2 \cdot \mathbf{v}_2 \end{pmatrix}$$

We conclude that P is not an orthogonal matrix. However, A is symmetric and has an orthogonal diagonalization by Theorem 4.10: By choosing different bases for E_5 and E_0, we could make P orthogonal. When $\{\mathbf{v}_1, \mathbf{v}_2\}$ is an orthogonal set of vectors, it is easy to change it into an orthonormal set of eigenvectors: We divide each vector by its length, which gives $\mathbf{w}_i = (1/\|\mathbf{v}_i\|)\mathbf{v}_i$ for $1 \leq i \leq 2$:

$$\mathbf{w}_1 = \frac{1}{\sqrt{5}} \begin{pmatrix} -2 \\ 1 \end{pmatrix}, \quad \mathbf{w}_2 = \frac{1}{\sqrt{5}} \begin{pmatrix} 1 \\ 2 \end{pmatrix}$$

Then $\{\mathbf{w}_1, \mathbf{w}_2\}$ is an orthonormal set of eigenvectors for A, since $\mathbf{w}_1 \cdot \mathbf{w}_2 = 0$ and $\mathbf{w}_i\| = 1$ for $1 \leq i \leq 2$. The orthogonal diagonalization $P^T A P = D$ of A is given by

$$P = \frac{1}{\sqrt{5}} \begin{pmatrix} -2 & 1 \\ 1 & 2 \end{pmatrix}, \quad D = \begin{pmatrix} 5 & 0 \\ 0 & 0 \end{pmatrix}$$

where P is an orthogonal matrix.

We showed how to change an orthogonal set of eigenvectors into an orthonormal set in the example above. In many cases, using this technique is enough to find an orthogonal diagonalization of a symmetric matrix. In general, vectors from different eigenspaces are orthogonal when the matrix is symmetric:

Proposition 4.12. Let $\mathbf{v}_1, \mathbf{v}_2$ be eigenvectors of A with distinct eigenvalues $\lambda_1 \neq \lambda_2$. If A is a symmetric matrix, then $\mathbf{v}_1$ and $\mathbf{v}_2$ are orthogonal vectors.

Proof. For any vectors $\mathbf{v}, \mathbf{w}$, we have that the inner product $\mathbf{v} \cdot \mathbf{w}$ can be written as a matrix multiplication $\mathbf{v}^T \mathbf{w}$. Hence $(A\mathbf{v}_1) \cdot \mathbf{v}_2 = (A\mathbf{v}_1)^T \mathbf{v}_2 = \mathbf{v}_1^T A^T \mathbf{v}_2 = \mathbf{v}_1 \cdot (A^T \mathbf{v}_2)$. Since A is symmetric, it follows that the following two expressions are equal:

$$(A\mathbf{v}_1) \cdot \mathbf{v}_2 = (\lambda_1 \mathbf{v}_1) \cdot \mathbf{v}_2 = \lambda_1 \mathbf{v}_1 \cdot \mathbf{v}_2$$
$$\mathbf{v}_1 \cdot (A\mathbf{v}_2) = \mathbf{v}_1 \cdot (\lambda_2 \mathbf{v}_2) = \lambda_2 \mathbf{v}_1 \cdot \mathbf{v}_2$$

Hence $(\lambda_1 - \lambda_2)\mathbf{v}_1 \cdot \mathbf{v}_2 = 0$, and it follows that $\mathbf{v}_1 \cdot \mathbf{v}_2 = 0$ since $\lambda_1 \neq \lambda_2$. □

When there are eigenvalues of multiplicity $m > 1$, it is more complicated to find an orthogonal diagonalization. By Proposition 4.12, we know that eigenvectors from different eigenspaces are orthogonal. But we also have to make sure that the base vectors in each eigenspace E_λ are orthogonal. This is always possible, using an algorithm called the *Gram-Schmidt process*.

4.5 Spectral theory of symmetric matrices

We shall not explain this method in the general case, but rather show how it works for small values of the multiplicity m, such as $m = 2$. We consider the following example.

$$A = \begin{pmatrix} 4 & 1 & 1 \\ 1 & 4 & 1 \\ 1 & 1 & 4 \end{pmatrix}$$

We computed eigenvalues and eigenvectors of A in Section 4.1, and used them to find a diagonalization of A in Section 4.3: The eigenvalue $\lambda = 3$ has multiplicity $m = 2$, $\lambda = 6$ has multiplicity $m = 1$, the vectors $\{\mathbf{v}_1, \mathbf{v}_2\}$ form a base of E_3, and $\{\mathbf{v}_3\}$ form a base of E_3, with $\mathbf{v}_1 = (-1, 1, 0)$, $\mathbf{v}_2 = (-1, 0, 1)$ and $\mathbf{v}_3 = (1, 1, 1)$. Hence a diagonalization $P^{-1}AP = D$ of A is given by

$$P = \begin{pmatrix} -1 & -1 & 1 \\ 1 & 0 & 1 \\ 0 & 1 & 1 \end{pmatrix}, \quad D = \begin{pmatrix} 3 & 0 & 0 \\ 0 & 3 & 0 \\ 0 & 0 & 6 \end{pmatrix}$$

We see that $\mathbf{v}_1 \cdot \mathbf{v}_3 = \mathbf{v}_2 \cdot \mathbf{v}_3 = 0$, and this is what we expect; these are vectors from different eigenspaces E_3 and E_6 and therefore orthogonal. However, we have that

$$\mathbf{v}_1 \cdot \mathbf{v}_2 = (-1)(-1) + 1(0) + 0(1) = 1 \neq 0$$

Hence the diagonalization from Section 4.3 is not an orthogonal diagonalization. However, we may choose a new base for the eigenspace E_3, given by

$$\mathbf{w}_1 = \mathbf{v}_1, \quad \mathbf{w}_2 = \mathbf{v}_2 - \mathrm{Proj}_{\mathbf{v}_1}(\mathbf{v}_2)$$

where $\mathrm{Proj}_{\mathbf{v}_1}(\mathbf{v}_2)$ is the orthogonal projection of $\mathbf{v}_2$ onto the linear subspace spanned by $\mathbf{v}_1$. The idea is that $\mathbf{v}_2$ can be decomposed as a sum of a vector along $\mathbf{v}_1$ and a component that is orthogonal to $\mathbf{v}_1$. This is shown geometrically in the figure below, where $\mathbf{v}_1$ and $\mathbf{v}_2$ are shown in blue, and the new vector $\mathbf{w}_2$ is shown in red.

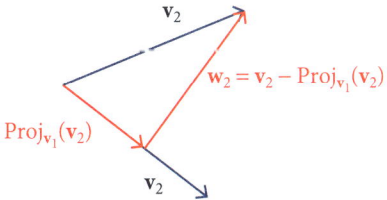

We use the formula from Section 2.5 to compute the projection, and find that

$$\mathrm{Proj}_{\mathbf{v}_1}(\mathbf{v}_2) = \frac{\mathbf{v}_1 \cdot \mathbf{v}_2}{\mathbf{v}_1 \cdot \mathbf{v}_1} \cdot \mathbf{v}_1 = \frac{1}{2}\mathbf{v}_1$$

and therefore that

$$\mathbf{w}_2 = \mathbf{v}_2 - \mathrm{Proj}_{\mathbf{v}_1}(\mathbf{v}_2) = \begin{pmatrix} -1 \\ 0 \\ 1 \end{pmatrix} - \frac{1}{2}\begin{pmatrix} -1 \\ 1 \\ 0 \end{pmatrix} = \frac{1}{2}\begin{pmatrix} -1 \\ -1 \\ 2 \end{pmatrix}$$

By construction, $\mathbf{w}_2$ is orthogonal to $\mathbf{w}_1$. It is an eigenvector in E_3, since it is a linear combination of $\mathbf{v}_1$ and $\mathbf{v}_2$. We have that $\|\mathbf{w}_1\| = \sqrt{(-1)^2 + 1^2 + 0^2} = \sqrt{2}$ and that $\|\mathbf{w}_2\| = \sqrt{(-1)^2 + (-1)^2 + 2^2}/2 = \sqrt{6}/2$. We divide each vector by its length, and obtain an orthonormal base of E_3:

$$\frac{1}{\sqrt{2}}\mathbf{w}_1 = \frac{1}{\sqrt{2}}\begin{pmatrix} -1 \\ 1 \\ 0 \end{pmatrix}, \quad \frac{2}{\sqrt{6}}\mathbf{w}_2 = \frac{1}{\sqrt{6}}\begin{pmatrix} -1 \\ -1 \\ 2 \end{pmatrix}$$

Since $\|\mathbf{v}_3\| = \sqrt{1^2 + 1^2 + 1^2} = \sqrt{3}$, we may take $\mathbf{v}_3/\sqrt{3}$ as an orthonormal base of E_6. It follows that an orthogonal diagonalization $P^T A P = D$ of A is given by

$$P = \frac{1}{\sqrt{6}}\begin{pmatrix} -\sqrt{3} & -1 & \sqrt{2} \\ \sqrt{3} & -1 & \sqrt{2} \\ 0 & 2 & \sqrt{2} \end{pmatrix}, \quad D = \begin{pmatrix} 3 & 0 & 0 \\ 0 & 3 & 0 \\ 0 & 0 & 6 \end{pmatrix}$$

where P is an orthogonal matrix.

4.6 Definiteness of quadratic forms

A function f in n variables is called a *quadratic form* if the functional expression $f(x_1, x_2, \ldots, x_n)$ can be written as a sum of terms of the form $c_{ij} x_i x_j$ with constant coefficients c_{ij}. In other words, f is a quadratic form if

$$f(x_1, x_2, \ldots, x_n) = c_{11}x_1^2 + c_{12}x_1x_2 + c_{13}x_1x_3 + \ldots + c_{nn}x_n^2$$

where c_{ij} are given numbers for $1 \leq i \leq j \leq n$. An example of a quadratic form in three variables is

$$f(x, y, z) = x^2 + y^2 + z^2 + 2xy - 2yz$$

Note that $xy = yx$, $xz = zx$ and $yz = zy$, hence there are only six different kinds of terms in any quadratic form in these three variables: The squares x^2, y^2 and z^2, and the cross terms xy, xz and yz. This is why we only included terms $c_{ij} x_i x_j$ for $i \leq j$ in the expression above.

Let us write $\mathbf{x} = (x_1, x_2, \ldots, x_n)$ and consider $\mathbf{x}$ as a column vector. For any $n \times n$ matrix A, we have that

$$\mathbf{x}^T A \mathbf{x} = \begin{pmatrix} x_1 & x_2 & \ldots & x_n \end{pmatrix} \begin{pmatrix} a_{11} & a_{12} & \ldots & a_{1n} \\ a_{21} & a_{22} & \ldots & a_{2n} \\ \vdots & \vdots & \ddots & \vdots \\ a_{n1} & a_{n2} & \ldots & a_{nn} \end{pmatrix} \begin{pmatrix} x_1 \\ x_2 \\ \vdots \\ x_n \end{pmatrix} = \sum_{i,j} a_{ij} x_i x_j$$

4.6 Definiteness of quadratic forms

To be more precise, the matrix product is a 1×1 matrix with an entry given by the sum on the right-hand side. It follows that $f(\mathbf{x}) = \mathbf{x}^T A \mathbf{x}$ is a quadratic form for any $n \times n$ matrix A. We call the expression $f(\mathbf{x}) = \mathbf{x}^T A \mathbf{x}$ the *matrix form* of f. As we shall see, there are many advantages to writing quadratic forms in this way. It is a more compact notation, but more importantly, we can apply what we know about vectors and matrices to analyze quadratic forms.

Let us look at an example: We compute the matrix product $\mathbf{x}^T A \mathbf{x}$ for the following 3×3 matrix A:

$$A = \begin{pmatrix} 1 & 1 & 0 \\ 1 & 1 & -1 \\ 0 & -1 & 1 \end{pmatrix}$$

$$\Downarrow$$

$$\mathbf{x}^T A \mathbf{x} = (x \ y \ z) \begin{pmatrix} 1 & 1 & 0 \\ 1 & 1 & -1 \\ 0 & -1 & 1 \end{pmatrix} \begin{pmatrix} x \\ y \\ z \end{pmatrix} = (x \ y \ z) \begin{pmatrix} x+y \\ x+y-z \\ -y+z \end{pmatrix}$$

$$= x(x+y) + y(x+y-z) + z(-y+z)$$
$$= x^2 + xy + yx + y^2 - yz - zy + z^2$$

Hence A corresponds to the quadratic form $f(x, y, z) = x^2 + y^2 + z^2 + 2xy - 2yz$. Notice that the entries on the diagonal of the matrix give rise to the coefficients of the squares x^2, y^2 and z^2, while pairs of entries in symmetric positions off the diagonal give rise to the coefficients of the cross terms xy, xz and yz.

Lemma 4.13. *Let f be a quadratic form in n variables. Then $f(\mathbf{x}) = \mathbf{x}^T A \mathbf{x}$ for an $n \times n$ matrix A, and there is a unique symmetric matrix A such that $f(\mathbf{x}) = \mathbf{x}^T A \mathbf{x}$.*

Proof. The quadratic form can be written $f(\mathbf{x}) = \sum c_{ij} x_i x_j$, where the sum is taken over pairs (i, j) of indices with $i \leq j$. We let A be an $n \times n$ matrix where $a_{ij} = c_{ij}$ if $i = j$, and where $a_{ij} + a_{ji} = c_{ij}$ if $i < j$. There are many ways to choose the matrix A with this property, but for A to be symmetric, we must choose $a_{ij} = a_{ji} = c_{ij}/2$ when $i < j$. □

As an example, we consider $f(x, y, z, w) = x^2 + y^2 + z^2 + w^2 - 2xw + 2yz$, a quadratic form in $n = 4$ variables. In matrix form, with $\mathbf{x} = (x, y, z, w)$, it can be written $f(\mathbf{x}) = \mathbf{x}^T A \mathbf{x}$ where A is the symmetric matrix

$$A = \begin{pmatrix} 1 & 0 & 0 & -1 \\ 0 & 1 & 1 & 0 \\ 0 & 1 & 1 & 0 \\ -1 & 0 & 0 & 1 \end{pmatrix}$$

For example, a_{11} must be equal to the coefficient of x^2 (since x is the first variable), and $a_{14} + a_{41} = -2$, since these entries will contribute to xw terms (where x is the first and w is the fourth variable), and this means that $a_{14} = a_{41} = -2/2 = -1$. We call A the *symmetric matrix* of the quadratic form. Notice that if we change the order of the variables $\mathbf{x} = (x, y, z, w)$, the matrix A would change. For example, if we choose the order $\mathbf{x} = (w, x, y, z)$, then the corresponding symmetric matrix would be

$$A = \begin{pmatrix} 1 & -1 & 0 & 0 \\ -1 & 1 & 0 & 0 \\ 0 & 0 & 1 & 1 \\ 0 & 0 & 1 & 1 \end{pmatrix}$$

It is a new symmetric matrix obtained by changing the order of both rows and columns.

Let us consider the quadratic form $f(\mathbf{x})$ as a function, and $\mathbf{x} = (x_1, x_2, \ldots, x_n)$ as a point in n-dimensional space. One of the most important properties of quadratic forms is their *definiteness*. We define a quadratic form f to be *positive semidefinite* if $f(\mathbf{x}) \geq 0$ for all $\mathbf{x} = (x_1, x_2, \ldots, x_n)$, to be *negative semidefinite* if $f(\mathbf{x}) \leq 0$ for all $\mathbf{x} = (x_1, x_2, \ldots, x_n)$, and to be *indefinite* in all other cases. In other words, the quadratic form is indefinite if and only if it takes both positive and negative values.

In some cases, it is easy to determine the definiteness by considering the form of the functional expression. For example, $f(x, y) = x^2 + 3y^2$ is positive semidefinite: We have that $f(x, y) \geq 0$ for all points (x, y), since it is a sum of squares. On the other hand, $f(x, y) = x^2 - y^2$ is indefinite, since $f(1, 0) = 1 > 0$ and $f(0, 1) = -1 < 0$. In a similar way, $f(x, y) = xy$ is indefinite, since $f(1, 1) = 1 > 0$ and $f(1, -1) = -1 < 0$.

We notice that for any quadratic form, we have $f(\mathbf{0}) = 0$, since $x_i x_j = 0$ when $x_i = 0$ and $x_j = 0$. Hence the point $\mathbf{x} = \mathbf{0}$ at the origin is a global minimum point for f when f is positive semidefinite, and a global maximum point for f when f is negative semidefinite. We call a quadratic form *positive definite* if $f(\mathbf{x}) > 0$ for all $\mathbf{x} \neq \mathbf{0}$ and *negative definite* if $f(\mathbf{x}) < 0$ for all $\mathbf{x} \neq \mathbf{0}$. Clearly, positive and negative definite quadratic forms are special cases of positive and negative semidefinite quadratic forms.

4.6 Definiteness of quadratic forms

Let us consider the special case of a quadratic form f without any cross terms. In general, it has the form $f(\mathbf{x}) = d_1 x_1^2 + d_2 x_2^2 + \ldots + d_n x_n^2$ for coefficients $d_1, d_2, \ldots, d_n$, and its symmetric matrix is the diagonal matrix with these coefficients on the diagonal. In this case, we have that

- f is positive semidefinite if and only if $d_1, d_2, \ldots, d_n \geq 0$
- f is negative semidefinite if and only if $d_1, d_2, \ldots, d_n \leq 0$
- f is indefinite in all other cases

This means that f is indefinite if and only if there are both positive and negative coefficients among $d_1, d_2, \ldots, d_n$. Moreover, we have that

- f is positive definite if and only if $d_1, \ldots, d_n > 0$
- f is negative definite if and only if $d_1, \ldots, d_n < 0$

For example, we have that $f(x, y, z) = x^2 + z^2$ is positive semidefinite, but not positive definite. In fact, $f(x, y, z) \geq 0$, since it is a sum of squares, but $f(0, y, 0) = 0$ for all values of y. Hence f is not positive definite. In this case, all points of the form $(0, y, 0)$ are global minimum points for f, while a positive definite quadratic form such as $f(x, y, z) = x^2 + 2y^2 + 3z^2$ would have $\mathbf{0} = (0, 0, 0)$ as the unique global minimum point.

Proposition 4.14. Let $f(\mathbf{x}) = \mathbf{x}^T A \mathbf{x}$ be a quadratic form in n variables, and let $\lambda_1, \ldots, \lambda_n$ denote the eigenvalues of its symmetric matrix A. Then we have

a) f is positive definite if and only if $\lambda_1, \ldots, \lambda_n > 0$
b) f is positive semidefinite if and only if $\lambda_1, \ldots, \lambda_n \geq 0$
c) f is negative definite if and only if $\lambda_1, \ldots, \lambda_n < 0$
d) f is negative semidefinite if and only if $\lambda_1, \ldots, \lambda_n \leq 0$
e) f is indefinite if and only if A has both positive and negative eigenvalues

Proof. Since A is a symmetric $n \times n$ matrix, we know from Theorem 4.10 that A has n eigenvalues $\lambda_1, \ldots, \lambda_n$ counted with multiplicity, and that there is an orthogonal diagonalization $P^T A P = D$ of A. This means that if we introduce new variables $\mathbf{u}$, given by $\mathbf{u} = P^T \mathbf{x}$, or $\mathbf{x} = P\mathbf{u}$, then the quadratic form can be written

$$f(\mathbf{x}) = \mathbf{x}^T A \mathbf{x} = \mathbf{u}^T D \mathbf{u} = \lambda_1 u_1^2 + \lambda_2 u_2^2 + \ldots + \lambda_n u_n^2$$

This means that we can transform $f(\mathbf{x})$ to a quadratic form without cross terms in the new variables $\mathbf{u}$, and the rest follows from the comments above. □

Let us consider the quadratic form $f(\mathbf{x}) = 4x^2 + 4y^2 + 4z^2 + 2xy + 2xz + 2yz$ as an example. Its symmetric matrix is

$$A = \begin{pmatrix} 4 & 1 & 1 \\ 1 & 4 & 1 \\ 1 & 1 & 4 \end{pmatrix}$$

and we found a orthogonal diagonalization $P^T A P = D$ of this matrix in Section 4.5, with

$$P = \frac{1}{\sqrt{6}} \begin{pmatrix} -\sqrt{3} & -1 & \sqrt{2} \\ \sqrt{3} & -1 & \sqrt{2} \\ 0 & 2 & \sqrt{2} \end{pmatrix}, \quad D = \begin{pmatrix} 3 & 0 & 0 \\ 0 & 3 & 0 \\ 0 & 0 & 6 \end{pmatrix}$$

This means that $f(\mathbf{x}) = 3u^2 + 3v^2 + 6w^2$ in the new coordinates $\mathbf{u} = (u, v, w)$, given by $\mathbf{u} = P^T \mathbf{x}$, or

$$\begin{pmatrix} u \\ v \\ w \end{pmatrix} = \frac{1}{\sqrt{6}} \begin{pmatrix} -\sqrt{3} & \sqrt{3} & 0 \\ -1 & -1 & 2 \\ \sqrt{2} & \sqrt{2} & \sqrt{2} \end{pmatrix} \begin{pmatrix} x \\ y \\ z \end{pmatrix} = \frac{1}{\sqrt{6}} \begin{pmatrix} -\sqrt{3}x + \sqrt{3}y \\ -x - y + 2z \\ \sqrt{2}x + \sqrt{2}y + \sqrt{2}z \end{pmatrix}$$

It follows that $f(\mathbf{x}) = 4x^2 + 4y^2 + 4z^2 + 2xy + 2xz + 2yz$ is a positive definite quadratic form, with a global minimum point $f(0, 0, 0) = 0$.

In principle, we can use eigenvalues to determine the definiteness of any quadratic form. However, this is not always practical, as it can be hard to compute eigenvalues; we must solve an n'th order polynomial equation. We shall explain an alternative method, using principal minors.

Let A be an $n \times n$ matrix. We recall that the r-minor $M_{I,J}$ of A is defined to be the determinant of the $r \times r$ submatrix of A obtained by keeping the r rows specified by I and the r columns specified by J, and deleting all the other rows and columns. For example, these are some 2-minors of the matrix A:

$$A = \begin{pmatrix} 2 & 1 & 1 \\ 1 & 2 & 1 \\ 1 & 1 & 2 \end{pmatrix} \Rightarrow M_{12,13} = \begin{vmatrix} 2 & 1 \\ 1 & 1 \end{vmatrix} = 1, \; M_{12,12} = \begin{vmatrix} 2 & 1 \\ 1 & 2 \end{vmatrix} = 3$$

In the first case, $I = \{1, 2\}$ and $J = \{1, 3\}$ means that we keep the first two rows (and delete the third row), and keep the first and third column (and delete the second column). In the second case, $I = J = \{1, 2\}$ means that we keep the first two rows and columns (and delete the third row and column). We sometimes write $I = 12$ instead of $I = \{1, 2\}$ to simplify the notation. In general, an r-minor of an $n \times n$ matrix A has the form M_{IJ}, where I, J are subsets of $\{1, 2, \ldots, n\}$ with r elements.

We define a *principal minor* of a symmetric $n \times n$ matrix to be a minor M_{IJ}, where $I = J$. We write $M_I = M_{II}$ for the principal minor defined by the subset I of rows and columns, and A_I for the corresponding submatrix with $|A_I| = M_I$. For example, we have the following principal 2-minors of the matrix A given above:

$$A = \begin{pmatrix} 2 & 1 & 1 \\ 1 & 2 & 1 \\ 1 & 1 & 2 \end{pmatrix}$$

$$\Downarrow$$

$$M_{12} = \begin{vmatrix} 2 & 1 \\ 1 & 2 \end{vmatrix} = 3, \quad M_{23} = \begin{vmatrix} 2 & 1 \\ 1 & 2 \end{vmatrix} = 3, \quad M_{13} = \begin{vmatrix} 2 & 1 \\ 1 & 2 \end{vmatrix} = 3$$

We shall write Δ_r for any of the principal r-minors of A. There are in general $\binom{n}{r}$ such minors, and the principal r-minors are special cases of all r-minors of A. In the example above, there are $\binom{3}{2} = 3$ principal 2-minors of A. They are all written above, and Δ_2 refers to any of these principal 2-minors.

We define the *leading principal r-minor* of A to be the principal r-minor M_I for $I = \{1, 2, \ldots, r\}$, and we write D_r for the leading principal r-minor. It is the minor we obtain by keeping the first r rows and columns of A. For example, for the matrix A given above, we have

$$A = \begin{pmatrix} 2 & 1 & 1 \\ 1 & 2 & 1 \\ 1 & 1 & 2 \end{pmatrix}$$

$$\Downarrow$$

$$D_1 = |2| = 2, \quad D_2 = \begin{vmatrix} 2 & 1 \\ 1 & 2 \end{vmatrix} = 3, \quad D_3 = |A| = \begin{vmatrix} 2 & 1 & 1 \\ 1 & 2 & 1 \\ 1 & 1 & 2 \end{vmatrix} = 4$$

Notice that there is a unique leading principal r-minor D_r of A for $1 \leq r \leq n$, and that the last leading principal minor is $D_n = |A|$.

The idea is that we can determine the definiteness of a quadratic form f using the principal minors of its symmetric matrix A, and it is far easier to compute principal minors than eigenvalues. From now on, we shall refer to the definiteness of A and the definiteness of f interchangeably.

It is instructional to first consider the special case where the quadratic form $f(\mathbf{x}) = d_1 x_1^2 + d_2 x_2^2 + \ldots + d_n x_n^2$ has no cross terms. In this case, the symmetric matrix A is diagonal and its diagonal entries $d_1, \ldots, d_n$ are the eigenvalues of A:

$$A = \begin{pmatrix} d_1 & 0 & 0 & +\ldots & 0 \\ 0 & d_2 & 0 & \ldots & 0 \\ 0 & 0 & d_3 & \ldots & 0 \\ \vdots & \vdots & \vdots & \ddots & \vdots \\ 0 & 0 & 0 & \ldots & d_n \end{pmatrix}$$

Hence the leading principal minors are $D_1 = d_1, D_2 = d_1 d_2, \ldots, D_n = d_1 d_2 \cdots d_n$. We know that f is positive definite if and only if all eigenvalues are positive, which holds if and only if
$$D_1 = d_1 > 0, D_2 = d_1 d_2 > 0, \ldots, D_n = d_1 d_2 \cdots d_n > 0$$
Hence f is positive definite if and only if all leading principal minors are positive. We also know that f is negative definite if and only if all eigenvalues are negative, which holds if and only if
$$D_1 = d_1 < 0, D_2 = d_1 d_2 > 0, \ldots$$
In other words, f is negative definite if the leading principal minors follow an alternating pattern, with $D_1 < 0$. This condition can be written $(-1)^i D_i > 0$ for $1 \leq i \leq n$. It turns out that these conclusions hold in all cases, not only when f has no cross terms:

Proposition 4.15. *Let A be a symmetric $n \times n$ matrix. Then we have*

a) *A is positive definite if and only if $D_i > 0$ for $1 \leq i \leq n$*

b) *A is negative definite if and only if $(-1)^i D_i > 0$ for $1 \leq i \leq n$*

Proof. It is enough to prove the first statement, since the second follows from the first applied to $-A$.

We first prove that if A is positive definite, then all leading principal minors are positive: If A is positive definite, then the leading principal submatrix A_i, obtained by keeping the first i rows and columns of A, is also positive definite. In fact, A_i is the symmetric matrix of the quadratic form f_i in $x_1, \ldots, x_i$ obtained by letting $x_{i+1} = \ldots = x_n = 0$ in f. It is clear that when f is positive definite, then all the quadratic forms f_i are also positive definite. Since $D_i = |A_i|$ is the product of the eigenvalues of A_i, which are all positive since A_i is positive definite, it follows that $D_i > 0$ for $1 \leq i \leq n$.

We shall prove the converse statement by induction on n. The case $n = 1$ is trivial. We therefore assume that $n \geq 2$ and that $D_i > 0$ for $1 \leq i \leq n$, and shall prove that A is positive definite: Assume that A is not positive definite. Then there must be at least two negative eigenvalues $\lambda_1, \lambda_2 < 0$ of A. Since A is symmetric, there is an orthogonal diagonalization of A, and we may choose orthogonal eigenvectors $\mathbf{v}_1, \mathbf{v}_2$ with eigenvalues λ_1, λ_2. We fix coefficients α_1, α_2 such that $\mathbf{v} = \alpha_1 \mathbf{v}_1 + \alpha_2 \mathbf{v}_2 \neq \mathbf{0}$ has the last component equal to zero. Then
$$\mathbf{v}^T A \mathbf{v} = \alpha_1^2 \lambda_1 \|\mathbf{v}_1\|^2 + \alpha_2^2 \lambda_2 \|\mathbf{v}_2\|^2 < 0$$
Since the last component of $\mathbf{v}$ is zero, this means that the leading $(n-1) \times (n-1)$ submatrix A_{n-1} of A is not positive definite. By the assumption in the induction step, this is impossible. Hence A must be positive definite. □

4.6 Definiteness of quadratic forms

Let us consider the quadratic form $f(x, y, z) = x^2 + 2y^2 + 3z^2 - 2xy + 2yz$ as an example. Its symmetric matrix is given by

$$A = \begin{pmatrix} 1 & -1 & 0 \\ -1 & 2 & 1 \\ 0 & 1 & 3 \end{pmatrix}$$

Hence the leading principal minors are $D_1 = 1$, $D_2 = 2 - 1 = 1$ and $D_3 = |A|$ is given by $D_3 = 1(6 - 1) - (-1)(-3 - 0) = 5 - 3 = 2$ by cofactor expansion along the first row. Since all leading principal minors are positive, f is positive definite.

Let us consider the quadratic form $f(x, y, z) = x^2 + 2y^2 + z^2 - 2xy + 2yz$ as another example. Its symmetric matrix is given by

$$A = \begin{pmatrix} 1 & -1 & 0 \\ -1 & 2 & 1 \\ 0 & 1 & 1 \end{pmatrix}$$

Hence the leading principal minors are $D_1 = 1$, $D_2 = 2 - 1 = 1$ and $D_3 = |A|$ is given by $D_3 = 1(2 - 1) - (-1)(-1 - 0) = 1 - 1 = 0$ by cofactor expansion along the first row. All leading principal minors $D_i \geq 0$, but not all of the leading principal minors are strictly positive, since $D_3 = 0$. Hence we cannot use Proposition 4.15 in this case and in general, it is not true that quadratic forms with $D_i \geq 0$ for $1 \leq i \leq n$ are positive semidefinite; they may also be indefinite.

We can determine the definiteness in more difficult cases, where Proposition 4.15 is not enough, by computing all the principal minors Δ_i of all orders. This includes computing all leading principal minors D_i, but also the remaining principal minors that are not leading. We use the following result:

Proposition 4.16. Let A be a symmetric $n \times n$ matrix, and let Δ_i denote any principal minor of A of order i. Then we have

a) A is positive semidefinite if and only if $\Delta_i \geq 0$ for all Δ_i with $1 \leq i \leq n$

b) A is negative semidefinite if and only if $(-1)^i \Delta_i \geq 0$ for all Δ_i with $1 \leq i \leq n$

c) A is indefinite in all other cases

Let us use this result in the more difficult case $f(x, y, z) = x^2 + 2y^2 + z^2 - 2xy + 2yz$ mentioned above. Its symmetric matrix A has the following principal minors: There are three principal minors M_1, M_2 and M_3 of order one, and they are the diagonal entries of A:

$$A = \begin{pmatrix} 1 & -1 & 0 \\ -1 & 2 & 1 \\ 0 & 1 & 1 \end{pmatrix} \quad \Rightarrow \quad \Delta_1 = \begin{cases} M_1 = 1 \\ M_2 = 2 \\ M_3 = 1 \end{cases}$$

113

There are three principal minors M_{12}, M_{23} and M_{13} of order two, and they are the 2-minors of A obtained by using symmetric positions $I = J$:

$$A = \begin{pmatrix} 1 & -1 & 0 \\ -1 & 2 & 1 \\ 0 & 1 & 1 \end{pmatrix} \Rightarrow \Delta_2 = \begin{cases} M_{12} = \begin{vmatrix} 1 & -1 \\ -1 & 2 \end{vmatrix} = 1 \\ M_{23} = \begin{vmatrix} 2 & 1 \\ 1 & 1 \end{vmatrix} = 1 \\ M_{13} = \begin{vmatrix} 1 & 0 \\ 0 & 1 \end{vmatrix} = 1 \end{cases}$$

There is only one principal minor $M_{123} = D_3$ of order three. It is the determinant $M_{123} = |A|$ of the matrix, and we computed $|A| = 0$ earlier in this section. Since $\Delta_i \geq 0$ for all principal minors of all orders, it follows from Proposition 4.16 that f is positive semidefinite.

We shall not give a proof of Proposition 4.16 in this book. In fact, most textbooks omit the proof. Instead, we shall take another approach that was suggested by Mandy as recently as 2017. He shows the following result, which does not seem to be well-known:

Theorem 4.17. Let A be a symmetric $n \times n$ matrix. Assume that A_I is a principal submatrix of A such that the following conditions hold:

a) A_I is positive definite

b) No higher order principal submatrix of A is positive definite

c) If J is a subset of indices containing I, then $M_J \geq 0$

Then A is positive semidefinite.

We shall not give the proof of Theorem 4.17; the interested reader can find a proof in Mandy's paper *Leading principal minors and semidefiniteness* (2018). However, we shall comment on some of its applications.

First, we notice that there is a version of the theorem for negative semidefiniteness, obtained by applying Theorem 4.17 to the matrix $-A$:

Corollary 4.18. Let A be a symmetric $n \times n$ matrix. Assume that A_I is a principal submatrix of A such that the following conditions hold:

a) A_I is negative definite

b) No higher order principal submatrix of A is negative definite

c) If J is a subset of j indices containing I, then $(-1)^j M_J \geq 0$

Then A is negative semidefinite.

Next, we notice that Proposition 4.16 follows from Theorem 4.17. The proof is a straightforward application of the theorem:

Proof. We prove the positive semidefinite version of Proposition 4.16; the negative semidefinite version has a similar proof. Assume that all principal minors $\Delta_i \geq 0$. If all diagonal entries in A are zero, we claim that $A = 0$, and this means that A is trivially positive semidefinite. In fact, for any principal 2-minor, we have

$$\Delta_2 = \begin{vmatrix} 0 & a_{ij} \\ a_{ij} & 0 \end{vmatrix} = -a_{ij}^2 \geq 0 \quad \Rightarrow \quad a_{ij} = 0$$

We may therefore assume that there is a diagonal entry $a_{ii} \neq 0$, and since this is a principal 1-minor $\Delta_1 = a_{ii}$, it follows that $a_{ii} > 0$. Hence there is a maximal principal submatrix A_I of A containing a_{ii} that is positive definite, and A is therefore positive semidefinite by Theorem 4.17. □

The most important application of Theorem 4.17 is the following result, which we call the *reduced rank criterion*. It is a special case of the theorem and gives a useful criterion to determine the definiteness of symmetric matrices in many cases with $|A| = 0$ (also called reduced rank since $|A| = 0$ implies that rk $A < n$). In these cases, we would otherwise have to use Proposition 4.16 and compute the sign of all principal minors to determine the definiteness.

Corollary 4.19 (Reduced rank criterion). Let A be a symmetric $n \times n$ matrix with rank rk $A = r < n$. Then we have:

a) If $D_i > 0$ for $1 \leq i \leq r$, then A is positive semidefinite

b) If $(-1)^i D_i > 0$ for $1 \leq i \leq r$, then A is negative semidefinite

Proof. Let $I = \{1, 2, \ldots, r\}$ and let A_I be the corresponding principal submatrix of A order r. If the assumption in a) holds, then A_I satisfies the three conditions of Theorem 4.17, and it follows from the theorem that A is positive semidefinite. The proof in the negative semidefinite case is similar. □

Let us consider the quadratic form $f(x, y, z, w) = 2xw + 2yz - x^2 - y^2 - z^2 - w^2$ as an example. Its symmetric matrix is

$$A = \begin{pmatrix} -1 & 0 & 0 & 1 \\ 0 & -1 & 1 & 0 \\ 0 & 1 & -1 & 0 \\ 1 & 0 & 0 & -1 \end{pmatrix}$$

A quick computation shows that $D_1 = -1$ and $D_2 = 1$. We also see that the rank rk $A = 2$, since the last two rows would become rows of zeros after a couple of elementary row operations. From the reduced rank criterion, it follows that A, and therefore f, is negative semidefinite. There are in this case four principal minors of order one, six of order two, four of order three, and one of order four. Even if we realized that rk $A = 2$, so that all minors of order three or four are zero, we avoid computing a lot of principal minors when we use the reduced rank criterion.

Another example is $f(x, y, z) = 2x^2 + 8y^2 + 18z^2 + 8xy + 12xz + 24yz$. It has symmetric matrix

$$A = \begin{pmatrix} 2 & 4 & 6 \\ 4 & 8 & 12 \\ 6 & 12 & 18 \end{pmatrix}$$

A quick computation show that $D_1 = 2$ and $D_2 = 16 - 16 = 0$. The rank is rk $A = 1$, since all rows are multiples of the first row. By the reduced rank criterion, it follows that A is positive semidefinite.

We end this section with the following remark: We cannot use the reduced rank criterion in all cases with $|A| = 0$. But sometimes it can help to change the order of the variables. For example, if $f(x, y, z, w) = x^2 + y^2 + z^2 + w^2 + 2xy + 2zw$, then the usual ordering gives the symmetric matrix A and the ordering (w, x, y, z) gives the symmetric matrix B, where A and B are given by

$$A = \begin{pmatrix} 1 & 1 & 0 & 0 \\ 1 & 1 & 0 & 0 \\ 0 & 0 & 1 & 1 \\ 0 & 0 & 1 & 1 \end{pmatrix}, \quad B = \begin{pmatrix} 1 & 0 & 0 & 1 \\ 0 & 1 & 1 & 0 \\ 0 & 1 & 1 & 0 \\ 1 & 0 & 0 & 1 \end{pmatrix}$$

We have rk A = rk $B = 2$. Since the matrix A gives $D_1 = 1$ and $D_2 = 0$, we cannot use the reduced criterion. However, the matrix B gives $D_1 = 1$ and $D_2 = 1$, hence B is positive semidefinite by the reduced rank criterion. This means that the quadratic form f is positive semidefinite. Of course, the matrix A is also positive semidefinite, as we could check by computing all principal minors of A.

Problems

Problem 4.1 Check that the vector **v** is an eigenvector of the matrix A, and find the corresponding eigenvalue:
$$A = \begin{pmatrix} 6 & 2 \\ 2 & 6 \end{pmatrix}, \quad \mathbf{v} = \begin{pmatrix} -1 \\ 1 \end{pmatrix}$$

Problem 4.2 Find all eigenvalues and eigenvectors of the matrix A:

a) $A = \begin{pmatrix} 6 & -7 \\ 3 & -4 \end{pmatrix}$
b) $A = \begin{pmatrix} 1 & 4 \\ -2 & -5 \end{pmatrix}$
c) $A = \begin{pmatrix} 3 & 4 \\ 6 & 1 \end{pmatrix}$

Problem 4.3 Find the eigenvalues and eigenvectors of the matrix A, and determine whether A is diagonalizable:

a) $A = \begin{pmatrix} 1 & -1 & 1 \\ 0 & 7 & 2 \\ 0 & 0 & -2 \end{pmatrix}$
b) $A = \begin{pmatrix} 2 & 1 & 5 \\ 0 & -1 & 0 \\ 3 & 0 & 4 \end{pmatrix}$

c) $A = \begin{pmatrix} 1 & 0 & -1 \\ 2 & 1 & 1 \\ 3 & 1 & 0 \end{pmatrix}$

Problem 4.4 Show that if A is an invertible matrix and λ is an eigenvalue of A, then $\lambda \neq 0$ and $1/\lambda$ is an eigenvalue of A^{-1}.

Problem 4.5 Compute A^m when A is the matrix

a) $A = \begin{pmatrix} 0.75 & 0.15 \\ 0.25 & 0.85 \end{pmatrix}$
b) $A = \begin{pmatrix} 0 & 1 \\ 1 & 0 \end{pmatrix}$
c) $A = \begin{pmatrix} 0 & -1 \\ 1 & 0 \end{pmatrix}$

Problem 4.6 Show that the characteristic equation of a 3×3 matrix A is given by
$$-\lambda^3 + c_1 \lambda^2 - c_2 \lambda + c_3 = 0$$
where $c_1 = \text{tr}(A)$, $c_2 = M_{12} + M_{23} + M_{13}$ is the sum of all principal 2-minors of A, and $c_3 = \det(A)$. Use this to find the eigenvalues of the matrix A:

a) $A = \begin{pmatrix} 1 & 4 & 2 \\ 2 & -1 & 1 \\ 3 & 3 & 3 \end{pmatrix}$
b) $A = \begin{pmatrix} 3 & 1 & 4 \\ 1 & 2 & 3 \\ 4 & 3 & 7 \end{pmatrix}$
c) $A = \begin{pmatrix} 2 & 1 & 1 \\ 1 & 2 & 1 \\ 1 & 1 & 2 \end{pmatrix}$

Problem 4.7 Determine the values of s such that the matrix A is diagonalizable:

a) $A = \begin{pmatrix} 1 & s & 0 \\ 0 & 1 & 0 \\ 0 & 0 & 2 \end{pmatrix}$
b) $A = \begin{pmatrix} 1 & s & 0 \\ 0 & s & 0 \\ 0 & 0 & 2 \end{pmatrix}$
c) $A = \begin{pmatrix} 1 & 0 & s \\ 0 & 1 & 0 \\ 0 & 0 & 2 \end{pmatrix}$

4 • Eigenvectors and eigenvalues

Problem 4.8 Find the equilibrium state for the Markov chain with transition matrix A, if it exists:

a) $A = \begin{pmatrix} 0.75 & 0.15 \\ 0.25 & 0.85 \end{pmatrix}$
b) $A = \begin{pmatrix} 0.40 & 0.20 & 0.10 \\ 0.40 & 0.60 & 0.10 \\ 0.20 & 0.20 & 0.80 \end{pmatrix}$

Problem 4.9 Determine whether the Markov chain with transition matrix A is regular and determine the equilibrium state of the system, if it exists:

a) $A = \begin{pmatrix} 0.15 & 0.30 & 0 \\ 0.85 & 0.45 & 0.70 \\ 0 & 0.25 & 0.30 \end{pmatrix}$
b) $A = \begin{pmatrix} 0.80 & 0.00 & 0.00 \\ 0.10 & 0.00 & 1.00 \\ 0.10 & 1.00 & 0.00 \end{pmatrix}$

Problem 4.10 Let A be the transition matrix of a regular Markov chain with 5 states. Show that if A is symmetric then $\mathbf{v} = (0.20, 0.20, 0.20, 0.20, 0.20)$ is the equilibrium state of the system.

Problem 4.11 Find an orthogonal diagonalization of A:

a) $A = \begin{pmatrix} 2 & 1 \\ 1 & 2 \end{pmatrix}$
b) $A = \begin{pmatrix} 2 & 1 & 1 \\ 1 & 2 & 1 \\ 1 & 1 & 2 \end{pmatrix}$
c) $A = \begin{pmatrix} 2 & 7 & 0 & 0 \\ 7 & 2 & 0 & 0 \\ 0 & 0 & 5 & 2 \\ 0 & 0 & 2 & 5 \end{pmatrix}$

Problem 4.12 Write down the symmetric matrix A of the quadratic form f, and determine its definiteness:

a) $f(x, y) = x^2 + 6xy + 4y^2$

b) $f(x, y, z) = x^2 + y^2 + z^2 + xy - xz + yz$

c) $f(x, y, z) = x^2 + 4xy + 2xz + 4y^2 + 4yz$

d) $f(x, y, z, w) = 2xy + 2xz + 2xw + 2yw$

e) $f(x, y, z, w) = x^2 + y^2 + z^2 + w^2 - xw - yz$

f) $f(x, y, z) = x^2 + y^2 + z^2 + xy - xz + 2yz$

g) $f(x, y, z, w) = x^2 - yz + w^2$

Problem 4.13 Determine the definiteness of the symmetric matrix A:

a) $A = \begin{pmatrix} 1 & -2 \\ -2 & 4 \end{pmatrix}$
b) $A = \begin{pmatrix} 3 & 1 & 0 \\ 1 & 3 & 0 \\ 0 & 0 & 1 \end{pmatrix}$

c) $A = \begin{pmatrix} -1 & 2 & 1 & 0 \\ 2 & -5 & 0 & 0 \\ 1 & 0 & -6 & 0 \\ 0 & 0 & 0 & -1 \end{pmatrix}$

Problem 4.14 Determine the definiteness of the quadratic form $f(\mathbf{x}) = \mathbf{x}^T A \mathbf{x}$ when A is the matrix

$$A = \begin{pmatrix} 1 & 2 & 0 & 2 \\ 2 & 4 & 2 & 0 \\ 0 & 0 & 5 & 6 \\ 0 & 0 & 6 & 10 \end{pmatrix}$$

Problem 4.15 Let $\mathbf{v}, \mathbf{w}$ be eigenvectors of a symmetric matrix A with eigenvalues λ_1, λ_2, and assume that $\|\mathbf{v}\| = 2$ and $\|\mathbf{w}\| = 3$. Determine $f(\mathbf{v} - \mathbf{w})$ when f is the quadratic form $f(\mathbf{x}) = \mathbf{x}^T A \mathbf{x}$.

Problem 4.16 Let $f(x, y) = x^2 + xy + y^2$ be a quadratic form.

a) Find the symmetric matrix A of f and determine its definiteness

b) Find an orthogonal diagonalization $P^T A P = D$ of A with $|P| = 1$

c) Express f in terms of the new coordinates $\mathbf{u} = P^T \mathbf{x}$, and show that the level curves $f(x, y) = c$ are ellipses when $c > 0$

d) Draw the ellipse $f(x, y) = 2$ in the xy-coordinate system

Problem 4.17 Let $f(x, y) = x^2 + 4xy + y^2$ be a quadratic form.

a) Find the symmetric matrix A of f and determine its definiteness

b) Find an orthogonal diagonalization $P^T A P = D$ of A with $|P| = 1$

c) Express f in terms of the new coordinates $\mathbf{u} = P^T \mathbf{x}$

d) Draw the level curve $f(x, y) = 5$ in the xy-coordinate system, and show that it is a hyperbola

CHAPTER 5

Unconstrained optimization

5.1 Functions in several variables

The function $f(x, y, z) = x^3 + y^3 + z^3 - 3xyz$ is an example of a function in several variables. It is a polynomial function of degree three in the three variables x, y, z, and its domain of definition is the $D_f = \mathbb{R}^3$. In other words, $f(x, y, z)$ is defined for all points (x, y, z) in $\mathbb{R}^3$. Another example is the rational function

$$f(x, y, z) = \frac{xy + xz + yz}{x + y + z}$$

in three variables x, y, z. It is defined for all points (x, y, z) such that $x + y + z \neq 0$, and we write $D_f = \{(x, y, z) : x + y + z \neq 0\} \subseteq \mathbb{R}^3$ for its domain of definition.

When u is a function of several variables, and h is a function in one variable, then the composite function $f(x_1, x_2, \ldots, x_n) = h(u)$ with $u = u(x_1, x_2, \ldots, x_n)$ gives a new function in several variables. For example, we can construct the functions

$$f(x, y, z) = \ln(4 - x^2 - y^2 - z^2),$$
$$f(x, y, z) = e^{xyz},$$
$$f(x, y, z) = \sqrt{x^2 + y^2 + z^2}$$

using the natural logarithm, the exponential function, or the square root as the outer function h, and a polynomial as the inner function u.

In general, the *domain of definition* D_f of a function f in n variables is the set of points $(x_1, x_2, \ldots, x_n)$ that we can use as inputs in f. It is either all of $\mathbb{R}^n$ or a subset of $\mathbb{R}^n$. The *function value* $f(x_1, x_2, \ldots, x_n)$ at a point $(x_1, x_2, \ldots, x_n)$ in D_f is usually given by a functional expression, which can be any well-defined expression in n variables. In some cases, there are several functional expressions, for different regions of the domain of definition, as in the following example:

$$f(x, y) = \begin{cases} \dfrac{1 + xy}{x^2 + y^2}, & (x, y) \neq (0, 0) \\ 1, & (x, y) = (0, 0) \end{cases}$$

In this case, we say that f is a *piecewise defined* function.

We define the *range* V_f of f to be the set of all function values $f(x_1, x_2, \ldots, x_n)$ of f, and it is a subset of $\mathbb{R}$. It can be difficult to determine V_f for a given function f. For example, when f is the function given by $f(x, y, z) = x^3 + y^3 + z^3 - 3xyz$, we would have to find the maximum and minimum value of f to find its range. We will study this problem later in this chapter, as finding maximum and minimum values of functions in several variables is the main topic of Chapter 5.

The *graph* of f is the set of points $(x_1, x_2, \ldots, x_n, y)$, where $(x_1, x_2, \ldots, x_n) \in D_f$ and $y = f(x_1, x_2, \ldots, x_n)$. This is a subset of $\mathbb{R}^{n+1}$, and the geometric picture of the graph lies in the $(n+1)$-dimensional coordinate system with coordinates $(x_1, x_2, \ldots, x_n, y)$. When $n = 2$, the graph of f is a surface in $\mathbb{R}^3$ given by the equation $y = f(x_1, x_2)$, which we sometimes write as $z = f(x, y)$, and we can "see" the geometric picture of the graph in simple examples. When $n \geq 3$, it is difficult to imagine what the graph of f looks like geometrically.

Matrix notation. We often form the vector $\mathbf{x} = (x_1, x_2, \ldots, x_n)$ from the variables of f, and write $f(\mathbf{x})$ instead of $f(x_1, x_2, \ldots, x_n)$. This notation is shorter, and it is especially useful when the function is given by matrices and vectors. As an example, we write $f(\mathbf{x}) = \mathbf{x}^T A \mathbf{x}$ for a quadratic form with symmetric matrix A, following the notation of Section 4.6. For instance, the function $f(x, y, z) = x^2 + 4xy + 8xz - y^2 + z^2$ can be written as $f(\mathbf{x}) = \mathbf{x}^T A \mathbf{x}$, where A is the symmetric matrix

$$A = \begin{pmatrix} 1 & 2 & 4 \\ 2 & -1 & 0 \\ 4 & 0 & 1 \end{pmatrix}$$

A *linear form* is a polynomial function where all terms have degree one, and they can also be written in matrix form, as $f(\mathbf{x}) = B\mathbf{x}$, where B is a $1 \times n$ matrix (also called a row vector). For example, $f(x, y, z, w) = x + y - z - w$ can be written as $f(\mathbf{x}) = B\mathbf{x}$, where B is the row vector $B = \begin{pmatrix} 1 & 1 & -1 & -1 \end{pmatrix}$.

Continuity. Let f be a function in n variables with the domain of definition D_f. We say that f is *continuous* at a specific point $\mathbf{x}^*$ in D_f if

$$f(\mathbf{x}^*) = \lim_{\mathbf{x} \to \mathbf{x}^*} f(\mathbf{x})$$

This means that the limit exists and equals the function value at the point $\mathbf{x}^*$. We say that f is *continuous* if it is continuous at all points in its domain of definition D_f.

5.1 Functions in several variables

We remark that it can be quite difficult to compute limits of functions in several variables. When $f(x)$ is a function in one variable, and we want to find the limit

$$\lim_{x \to a} f(x)$$

we only have to consider what happens with the function value $f(x)$ when x tends towards a from below or from above, which we write $x \to a^-$ and $x \to a^+$. When $f(\mathbf{x})$ is a function of $n \geq 2$ variables, there are many ways for $\mathbf{x}$ to approach a specific point $\mathbf{a}$: For every curve in n-dimensional space passing through $\mathbf{a}$, given by

$$\mathbf{x}(t) = (x_1(t), x_2(t), \ldots, x_n(t)) \text{ with } \mathbf{x}(0) = \mathbf{a}$$

we can consider the limit of $f(\mathbf{x}(t))$ as $t \to 0$. We define that $f(\mathbf{x}) \to L$ as $\mathbf{x} \to \mathbf{a}$ if the above limit exists and equals L for every choice of a curve through $\mathbf{a}$. For instance, this includes all straight lines through $\mathbf{a}$, of which there are infinitely many.

For example, the function $f(x, y) = x^y$ is defined when $x, y \geq 0$ and $(x, y) \neq (0, 0)$. For points $(x, 0)$ with $x > 0$, we have $f(x, 0) = x^0 = 1$. Hence $f(x, y) \to 1$ when $(x, y) \to (0, 0)$ along the positive x-axis. For points $(0, y)$ with $y > 0$, we have $f(0, y) = 0^y = 0$. Hence $f(x, y) \to 0$ when $(x, y) \to (0, 0)$ along the positive y-axis. Since there is no common limit for $f(x, y) = x^y$ when $(x, y) \to (0, 0)$ along different curves, we have that the limit

$$\lim_{(x,y) \to (0,0)} f(x, y) = \lim_{(x,y) \to (0,0)} x^y$$

does not exist. This means that the function defined by

$$f(x, y) = \begin{cases} x^y, & x, y \geq 0, (x, y) \neq (0, 0) \\ a, & (x, y) = (0, 0) \end{cases}$$

is *not* a continuous function on $D = \{(x, y) : x, y \geq 0\}$ for any number a.

This is essentially the simplest example of a function that is not continuous. In fact, functions that are not piecewise defined, with a functional expression involving the "usual" mathematical operations, are continuous. One may show a more precise version of this statement using the following facts (the list is not complete, and can be extended):

a) All polynomial functions and rational functions are continuous

b) Any sum, difference, product, or quotient of continuous functions is continuous

c) Any composition of continuous functions is continuous

d) The exponential function and the natural logarithm are continuous

e) For any positive exponent $a > 0$, the function $f(x) = x^a$, $x > 0$ is continuous

For instance, the function f given by $f(x, y, z) = \ln(4 - x^2 - y^2 - z^2)$ is continuous, since it is a composition of a polynomial function and the natural logarithm, which are both continuous functions.

5 • Unconstrained optimization

5.2 Partial derivatives

Let f be a function in n variables and let $\mathbf{x}^*$ be a point in its domain of definition. For $1 \leq i \leq n$, we define $f'_i(\mathbf{x}^*)$ to be the limit

$$f'_i(\mathbf{x}^*) = \lim_{h \to 0} \frac{f(x_1^*, x_2^*, \ldots, x_i^* + h, \ldots, x_n^*) - f(x_1^*, x_2^*, \ldots, x_i^*, \ldots, x_n^*)}{h}$$

if it exists. If the limit does not exist, we say that $f'_i(\mathbf{x}^*)$ does not exist. We call $f'_1(\mathbf{x}^*), f'_2(\mathbf{x}^*), \ldots, f'_n(\mathbf{x}^*)$ the *partial derivatives of f at $\mathbf{x}^*$*.

The interpretation of the partial derivative $f'_i(\mathbf{x}^*)$ is the slope of the tangent to the curve $y = f(x_1^*, x_2^*, \ldots, x_i, \ldots, x_n^*)$ at the point $x_i = x_i^*$. This is the curve we obtain by keeping $x_j = x_j^*$ constant for $j \neq i$, and consider y as a function of x_i. It means that the partial derivative $f'_i(\mathbf{x}^*)$ is the marginal change in the function value of f at the point $\mathbf{x}^*$ when we change x_i and keep the other variables constant.

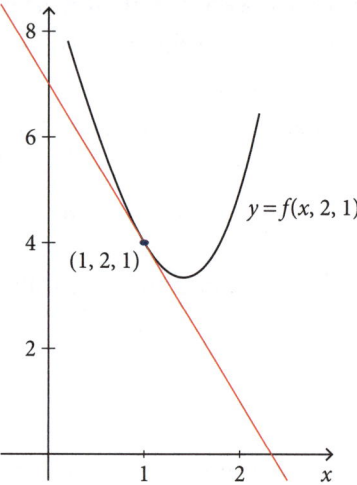

Figure 5.1 The cut of the graph of $f(x, y, z) = x^3 + y^3 + z^3 - 3xyz$ through $y = 2$ and $z = 1$

We use the function $f(x, y, z) = x^3 + y^3 + z^3 - 3xyz$ as an example, and look at its first partial derivative $f'_x(1, 2, 1)$ at the point $\mathbf{x}^* = (1, 2, 1)$. Note that we write f'_x instead of f'_1 when the variables are x, y, z. The cut we obtain by keeping $y = 2$ and $z = 1$ constant is given by

$$f(x, 2, 1) = x^3 + 2^3 + 1^3 - 6x = x^3 - 6x + 9$$

Since $(x^3 - 6x + 9)' = 3x^2 - 6$, it follows that $f'_x(1, 2, 1) = 3 \cdot 1^2 - 6 = -3$. This means that the slope of the tangent line of the graph of $f(x, 2, 1)$ at $x = 1$ is -3. The cut is shown in the figure above, with the tangent line of slope -3 shown in red. We interpret the partial derivative $f'_x(1, 2, 1) = -3$ as the marginal change in the function value of f at the point $(1, 2, 1)$, when we change x and keep $y = 2$ and $z = 1$ constant. In other words, we have that

$$f(1 + h, 2, 1) \approx f(1, 2, 1) + h \cdot f'_x(1, 2, 1) = 4 - 3h$$

when h is small.

For many functions, such as polynomials, the partial derivatives $f'_1(\mathbf{x}), \ldots, f'_n(\mathbf{x})$ exist at all points $\mathbf{x}$ in $\mathbb{R}^n$. In fact, the partial derivatives can be viewed as functions $f'_i(\mathbf{x})$, and we can find the functional expression of $f'_i(\mathbf{x})$ in the following way: We consider the variables x_j with $j \neq i$ as constants, and take the derivative of f with respect to x_i using the derivation rules for functions in one variable. For example, the polynomial function $f(x, y, z) = x^3 + y^3 + z^3 - 3xyz$ has partial derivatives

$$f'_x(x, y, z) = 3x^2 - 3yz \qquad f'_y(x, y, z) = 3y^2 - 3xz \qquad f'_z(x, y, z) = 3z^2 - 3xy$$

Note that we often write $f'_x = 3x^2 - 3yz$ instead of $f'_x(x, y, z) = 3x^2 - 3zy$, when it is clear from the context that f'_x is a function of the variables x, y, z. Sometimes, we use Leibniz's notation, and write

$$\frac{\partial f}{\partial x}, \quad \frac{\partial f}{\partial y}, \quad \frac{\partial f}{\partial z}$$

for the partial derivatives f'_x, f'_y, f'_z. Note the use of the Greek letter ∂ in the partial derivatives.

Open and closed sets. Let $\mathbf{x} = (x_1, x_2, \ldots, x_n)$ be a point in $\mathbb{R}^n$, and let $r > 0$ be a positive number. We define the *open ball* with center $\mathbf{x}$ and radius r to be the set

$$B_r(\mathbf{x}) = \{\mathbf{y} : d(\mathbf{x}, \mathbf{y}) < r\}$$

This is the set of points with distance less than r from $\mathbf{x}$. Recall from Chapter 2 the formula $d(\mathbf{x}, \mathbf{y}) = \sqrt{(y_1 - x_1)^2 + \ldots + (y_n - x_n)^2}$ for the distance between $\mathbf{x}$ and $\mathbf{y}$ in $\mathbb{R}^n$, and notice that the points with $d(\mathbf{x}, \mathbf{y}) = r$ are not part of the open ball $B_{\mathbf{x}}(r)$.

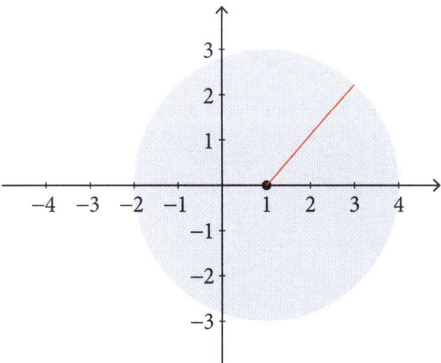

Figure 5.2 The open ball $B_r(\mathbf{x})$ in $\mathbb{R}^2$ with center $\mathbf{x} = (1, 0)$ and $r = 3$

5 • Unconstrained optimization

A subset $D \subseteq \mathbb{R}^n$ is called an *open subset* if the following condition holds: For any point $\mathbf{x} \in D$, there is a small radius $r > 0$ such that $B_r(\mathbf{x}) \subseteq D$. This means that if $\mathbf{x}$ is in D and $\mathbf{y}$ is sufficiently close to $\mathbf{x}$, then $\mathbf{y}$ is also in D. In concrete terms, if D is defined by open inequalities (given by $<$, $>$, or $\neq$), then D is an open set. For example, when f is the function

$$f(x, y, z) = \frac{xy + xz + yz}{x + y + z}$$

with the domain of definition $D_f = \{(x, y, z) : x + y + z \neq 0\}$, then D_f is an open subset of $\mathbb{R}^3$.

We define the *boundary* of a subset $D \subseteq \mathbb{R}^n$ to be the set of points $\mathbf{y} \in \mathbb{R}^n$ such that $B_r(\mathbf{y})$ contains both points from D and points outside of D for any radius $r > 0$, and write ∂D for the boundary of D. We say that D is a *closed subset* if D contains all its boundary points. In concrete terms, if D is defined by equations or closed inequalities (given by $=$, $\leq$ or $\geq$), then D is a closed set. For example, when f is the function

$$f(x, y, z) = \sqrt{x - y + z}$$

then the domain of definition $D_f = \{(x, y, z) : x - y + z \geq 0\}$ is closed; it contains its boundary $\partial D_f = \{(x, y, z) : x - y + z = 0\}$.

The points in a subset $D \subseteq \mathbb{R}^n$ that are not boundary points of D, are called *interior points*. It follows that a set D is open if and only if all points in D are interior points.

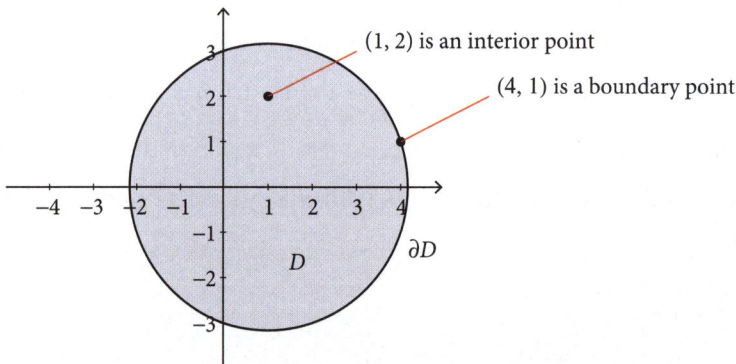

Figure 5.3 The set $D = \{(x, y) : (x - 1)^2 + y^2 \leq 10\}$ with marked interior points and boundary points

Differentiable functions. Let us return to the definition of the partial derivative $f'_i(\mathbf{x}^*)$ of f. For any point $\mathbf{x}^*$ in the domain of definition D_f, it is given by the limit

$$f'_i(\mathbf{x}^*) = \lim_{h \to 0} \frac{f(x_1^*, x_2^*, \ldots, x_i^* + h, \ldots, x_n^*) - f(x_1^*, x_2^*, \ldots, x_i^*, \ldots, x_n^*)}{h}$$

We notice that when $\mathbf{x}^*$ is an interior point of D_f, then $f(x_1^*, x_2^*, \ldots, x_i^* + h, \ldots, x_n^*)$ is defined for all small values of h; if $\mathbf{x}^*$ is a boundary point, this is not necessarily the case. Therefore, we only consider the partial derivatives at interior points of D_f.

Let f be a function in n variables defined on an open subset $D \subseteq \mathbb{R}^n$. We say that f is *continuously differentiable* on D, or simply C^1 on D, if all the partial derivatives $f'_1(\mathbf{x}), f'_2(\mathbf{x}), \ldots, f'_n(\mathbf{x})$ exist and are continuous functions on D. It is a fact that all polynomial functions are C^1 on all of $\mathbb{R}^n$. For example, the polynomial function $f(x, y, z) = x^3 + y^3 + z^3 - 3xyz$ has partial derivatives

$$f'_x(x, y, z) = 3x^2 - 3yz \qquad f'_y(x, y, z) = 3y^2 - 3xz \qquad f'_z(x, y, z) = 3z^2 - 3xy$$

These partial derivatives are continuous functions on all of $\mathbb{R}^3$, hence f is C^1 on $\mathbb{R}^3$. It is also a fact that any function that is C^1 is continuous.

When f is a continuously differentiable function on D, and $\mathbf{x}^*$ is a point in D, we define the *derivative* of f at $\mathbf{x}^*$ to be the $1 \times n$ matrix $\mathbf{f}'(\mathbf{x}^*)$ given by

$$\mathbf{f}'(\mathbf{x}^*) = (f'_1(\mathbf{x}^*) \quad f'_2(\mathbf{x}^*) \quad \ldots \quad f'_n(\mathbf{x}^*))$$

For any vector $\mathbf{h} = (h_1, h_2, \ldots, h_n)$ where $h_1, h_2, \ldots, h_n$ are small numbers, we have the first order approximation

$$f(x_1^* + h_1, x_2^* + h_2, \ldots, x_n^* + h_n) \approx$$
$$f(\mathbf{x}^*) + h_1 f'_1(\mathbf{x}^*) + h_2 f'_2(\mathbf{x}^*) + \ldots + h_n f'_n(\mathbf{x}^*)$$

This can be written $f(\mathbf{x}^* + \mathbf{h}) \approx f(\mathbf{x}^*) + \mathbf{f}'(\mathbf{x}^*) \cdot \mathbf{h}$ in matrix notation, where we consider the derivative $\mathbf{f}'(\mathbf{x}^*)$ as a row vector and $\mathbf{h}$ as a column vector. In fact, we have that $f(\mathbf{x}^* + \mathbf{h}) = f(\mathbf{x}^*) + \mathbf{f}'(\mathbf{x}^*) \cdot \mathbf{h} + \varepsilon_1(\mathbf{h})$, where the error term $\varepsilon_1(\mathbf{h})$ has the property that

$$\lim_{\mathbf{h} \to \mathbf{0}} \frac{\varepsilon_1(\mathbf{h})}{\|\mathbf{h}\|} = 0$$

Notice that $\mathbf{h}$ is close to $\mathbf{0}$ if $\|\mathbf{h}\| < r$ for a small positive radius $r > 0$, and this means that $h_1^2 + h_2^2 + \ldots + h_n^2 < r^2$, and in particular that $|h_i| < r$ is small for $1 \leq i \leq n$.

5.3 The Hessian matrix

Let f be a C^1 function on an open set $D \subseteq \mathbb{R}^n$, and let $\mathbf{x}^*$ be a point in D. For $1 \le i, j \le n$, we define $f''_{ij}(\mathbf{x}^*)$ to be the partial derivative of f'_i with respect to the variable x_j at the point $\mathbf{x}^*$. We call $f''_{ij}(\mathbf{x}^*)$ the *second order partial derivatives* of f, and say that f is a C^2 function on D if the second order partial derivatives $f''_{ij}(\mathbf{x})$ exist for all points $\mathbf{x} \in D$ and are continuous functions on D.

If the second order partial derivatives $f''_{ij}(\mathbf{x}^*)$ of f at $\mathbf{x}^*$ exist for $1 \le i, j \le n$, we define the *Hessian matrix* of f at $\mathbf{x}^*$ to be the $n \times n$ matrix

$$H(f)(\mathbf{x}^*) = \begin{pmatrix} f''_{11}(\mathbf{x}^*) & f''_{12}(\mathbf{x}^*) & \cdots & f''_{1n}(\mathbf{x}^*) \\ f''_{21}(\mathbf{x}^*) & f''_{22}(\mathbf{x}^*) & \cdots & f''_{2n}(\mathbf{x}^*) \\ \vdots & \vdots & \ddots & \vdots \\ f''_{n1}(\mathbf{x}^*) & f''_{n2}(\mathbf{x}^*) & \cdots & f''_{nn}(\mathbf{x}^*) \end{pmatrix}$$

Let us consider the function $f(x, y, z) = x^2 + 6xy + 3y^2 - 2yz + z^2$ as an example, with first order partial derivatives given by

$$f'_x(x, y, z) = 2x + 6y \qquad f'_y(x, y, z) = 6x + 6y - 2z \qquad f'_z(x, y, z) = -2y + 2z$$

Taking partial derivatives of each of the first order partial derivatives, we find the second order partial derivatives and the Hessian matrix of f:

$$H(f) = \begin{pmatrix} f''_{xx} & f''_{xy} & f''_{xz} \\ f''_{yx} & f''_{yy} & f''_{yz} \\ f''_{zx} & f''_{zy} & f''_{zz} \end{pmatrix} = \begin{pmatrix} 2 & 6 & 0 \\ 6 & 6 & -2 \\ 0 & -2 & 2 \end{pmatrix}$$

Notice that we write $H(f)$ for the Hessian matrix $H(f)(x, y, z)$ to simplify notation. In this case, $H(f)$ is a constant matrix. In fact, the function f is a quadratic form and the Hessian matrix $H(f) = 2A$, where A is the symmetric matrix of f. We shall prove that this holds for any quadratic form in Section 5.6.

Another example is the function $f(x, y, z) = x^3 + y^3 + z^3 - 3xyz$, with first order partial derivatives given by

$$f'_x(x, y, z) = 3x^2 - 3yz \qquad f'_y(x, y, z) = 3y^2 - 3xz \qquad f'_z(x, y, z) = 3z^2 - 3xy$$

Taking partial derivatives of each of the first order partial derivatives, we find the second order partial derivatives and the Hessian matrix of f:

$$H(f) = \begin{pmatrix} f''_{xx} & f''_{xy} & f''_{xz} \\ f''_{yx} & f''_{yy} & f''_{yz} \\ f''_{zx} & f''_{zy} & f''_{zz} \end{pmatrix} = \begin{pmatrix} 6x & -3z & -3y \\ -3z & 6y & -3x \\ -3y & -3x & 6z \end{pmatrix}$$

We notice that also in this case, the Hessian matrix is a symmetric matrix. This is not a coincidence, but follows from Young's Lemma:

Lemma 5.1 (Young). Let f be a C^2 function defined on an open set $D \subseteq \mathbb{R}^n$. Then the Hessian matrix $H(f)(\mathbf{x})$ is a symmetric $n \times n$ matrix for all points $\mathbf{x}$ in D.

When f is a C^2 function on an open set D, and $\mathbf{x}^*$ is a point in D, we can extend the first order approximation $f(\mathbf{x}^* + \mathbf{h}) = f(\mathbf{x}^*) + \mathbf{f}'(\mathbf{x}^*) \cdot \mathbf{h} + \varepsilon_1(\mathbf{h})$ from Section 5.2 to a *second order approximation* of f for points close to $\mathbf{x}^*$: For any vector $\mathbf{h}$, we have that

$$f(\mathbf{x}^* + \mathbf{h}) = f(\mathbf{x}^*) + \mathbf{f}'(\mathbf{x}^*) \cdot \mathbf{h} + \frac{1}{2} \mathbf{h}^T H(f)(\mathbf{x}^*) \mathbf{h} + \varepsilon_2(\mathbf{h})$$

The quadratic term is the quadratic form in $\mathbf{h}$ with symmetric matrix $1/2 \cdot H(f)(\mathbf{x}^*)$, and the factor $1/2$ comes from the fact that $H(f) = 2A$ for a quadratic form with symmetric matrix A. The error term $\varepsilon_2(\mathbf{h})$ in the quadratic approximation satisfies

$$\lim_{\mathbf{h} \to \mathbf{0}} \frac{\varepsilon_2(\mathbf{h})}{\|\mathbf{h}\|^2} = 0$$

This means that when $\mathbf{h} \to \mathbf{0}$, the error term $\varepsilon_2(\mathbf{h})$ will tend towards zero even faster than $\varepsilon_1(\mathbf{h})$.

5.4 Unconstrained optimization

We consider the *unconstrained optimization problem* for a function f in n variables. It can be written

$$\max f(\mathbf{x}) \text{ or } \min f(\mathbf{x})$$

We shall assume that f is a C^2 function defined on an open subset $D = D_f$ of $\mathbb{R}^n$. Hence the points in the domain of definition D are the admissible points for this problem; there are no additional constraints.

Let $\mathbf{x}^*$ be a point in D, and let $f(\mathbf{x}^*)$ be the corresponding function value. We say that $\mathbf{x}^*$ is a *maximum point* of f if $f(\mathbf{x}^*) \geq f(\mathbf{x})$ for all points $\mathbf{x} \in D$. If this is the case, we say that $f(\mathbf{x}^*)$ is the *maximum value* of f. Moreover, we say that $\mathbf{x}^*$ is a *minimum point* of f if $f(\mathbf{x}^*) \leq f(\mathbf{x})$ for all points $\mathbf{x} \in D$. If this is the case, we say that $f(\mathbf{x}^*)$ is the *minimum value* of f.

We define a *stationary point* of f to be a point $\mathbf{x}^*$ where the *first order conditions* hold:

$$f'_1(\mathbf{x}^*) = f'_2(\mathbf{x}^*) = \ldots = f'_n(\mathbf{x}^*) = 0$$

A *critical point* of f is a point that is either a stationary point, or a point in the domain of definition D where at least one of the partial derivatives does not exist.

Let us consider the function $f(x, y) = x^2 y^3 + y^2 - 2y$, a polynomial function that is C^2 on all of $\mathbb{R}^2$. The first order conditions are

$$f'_x = 2xy^3 = 0, \quad f'_y = 3x^2 y^2 + 2y - 2 = 0$$

To find the stationary points of f, we must solve these equations. The first gives $x = 0$ or $y = 0$. Substituting this in the second equation, we see that $x = 0$ gives $2y - 2 = 0$, or $y = 1$, and $y = 0$ gives $-2 = 0$, which has no solutions. Hence f has one stationary point $(x, y) = (0, 1)$. There are no more critical points, and this will be the case for any C^2 function, since the partial derivatives exist at all points in D.

In general, it is not difficult to see that if $\mathbf{x}^*$ is a maximum or minimum point of a function f, then $\mathbf{x}^*$ is either a critical point for f or a boundary point for its domain of definition $D = D_f$. In fact, if $\mathbf{x}^*$ is an interior point where all the partial derivatives exist, then $f'_i(\mathbf{x}^*) > 0$ means that the function value of f will increase (decrease) when x_i^* is replaced by $x_i^* + h$ and h is a small positive (negative) number, and $f'_i(\mathbf{x}^*) < 0$ means that the function value of f will decrease (increase) when x_i^* is replaced by $x_i^* + h$ and h is a small positive (negative) number. Hence $\mathbf{x}^*$ cannot be a maximum or minimum point unless $f'_i(\mathbf{x}^*) = 0$ for $1 \leq i \leq n$.

Proposition 5.2. Let f be a C^2 function on an open subset $D \subseteq \mathbb{R}^n$. Any maximum or minimum point of f is a stationary point.

Proof. Since D is open, it has no boundary points, and the only critical points of f are the stationary points, since f is C^2. Hence the result follows from the argument above. □

We call the stationary points of f the *candidate points* for maximum or minimum. Note that for $\mathbf{x}^*$ to be a maximum or minimum point, it must be a stationary point according to the proposition above, but this is not enough to ensure that it is a maximum or minimum point. We say that the first order condition is a necessary, but not a sufficient, condition for maximum or minimum.

Classification of stationary points. Let $\mathbf{x}^*$ be a stationary point for f. We say that $\mathbf{x}^*$ is a *local maximum point* for f if $f(\mathbf{x}^*) \geq f(\mathbf{x})$ for all points $\mathbf{x}$ close to $\mathbf{x}^*$. More precisely, we require that there is a small radius $r > 0$ such that $f(\mathbf{x}^*) \geq f(\mathbf{x})$ for all points $\mathbf{x} \in B_r(\mathbf{x}^*)$. In a similar way, we say that $\mathbf{x}^*$ is a *local minimum point* for f if $f(\mathbf{x}^*) \leq f(\mathbf{x})$ for all points $\mathbf{x}$ close to $\mathbf{x}^*$. A stationary point that is neither a local maximum nor a local minimum is called a *saddle point* for f.

We would like to classify stationary points of f as local maxima, local minima, or saddle points. The idea is that the local maxima for f are the candidates for maximum points, and the local minima are the candidates for minimum points. The saddle points for f are certainly neither maximum nor minimum points of f.

5.4 Unconstrained optimization

Proposition 5.3 (Second derivative test). Let f be a C^2 function on an open set D, and let $\mathbf{x}^* \in D$ be a stationary point for f. Then we have:

a) If $H(f)(\mathbf{x}^*)$ is positive definite, then $\mathbf{x}^*$ is a local minimum point for f
b) If $H(f)(\mathbf{x}^*)$ is negative definite, then $\mathbf{x}^*$ is a local maximum point for f
c) If $H(f)(\mathbf{x}^*)$ is indefinite, then $\mathbf{x}^*$ is a saddle point for f

Proof. Since $\mathbf{x}^*$ is a stationary point of f, we have that $\mathbf{f}'(\mathbf{x}^*) = \mathbf{0}$. Hence the second order approximation from Section 5.3 can be written in the form

$$f(\mathbf{x}^* + \mathbf{h}) - f(\mathbf{x}^*) = \frac{1}{2}\mathbf{h}^T H(f)(\mathbf{x}^*)\mathbf{h} + \varepsilon_2(\mathbf{h})$$

We notice that any point close to $\mathbf{x}^*$ can be written as $\mathbf{x}^* + \mathbf{h}$, where $\mathbf{h}$ is close to $\mathbf{0}$. Hence the sign of the left-hand side when $\|\mathbf{h}\|$ is small determines whether $\mathbf{x}^*$ is a local maximum, local minimum or saddle point. We have that

$$H(f)(\mathbf{x}^*) \text{ positive definite} \quad \Rightarrow \quad f(\mathbf{x}^* + \mathbf{h}) - f(\mathbf{x}^*) > 0$$
$$H(f)(\mathbf{x}^*) \text{ negative definite} \quad \Rightarrow \quad f(\mathbf{x}^* + \mathbf{h}) - f(\mathbf{x}^*) < 0$$

when $\|\mathbf{h}\|$ is small. This follows from the fact that the quadratic term is the dominant term. If $H(f)(\mathbf{x}^*)$ is indefinite, then the difference $f(\mathbf{x}^* + \mathbf{h}) - f(\mathbf{x}^*)$ takes both positive and negative values, and this means that $\mathbf{x}^*$ is a saddle point. $\square$

In most cases, we can classify a stationary point $\mathbf{x}^*$ for f as a local maximum, local minimum, or saddle point using the second derivative test, but there are some notable exceptions: If $H(f)(\mathbf{x}^*)$ is positive semidefinite but not positive definite, then $\mathbf{x}^*$ can be a local maximum, a local minimum or a saddle point. We say that the second derivative test is inconclusive. The same applies to the case when $H(f)(\mathbf{x}^*)$ is negative semidefinite but not negative definite. For example, the point $x = 0$ is a stationary point for the functions

$$f(x) = -x^4, \quad f(x) = x^4, \quad f(x) = x^3$$

Even though $H(f)(0) = 0$ in each case, which means that $H(f)(0)$ is both positive and negative semidefinite, $x = 0$ is respectively a local maximum, a local minimum, and a saddle point for these functions. The reason is that the proof of the second derivative test breaks down when $\mathbf{h}^T H(f)(\mathbf{x}^*)\mathbf{h} = 0$. In fact, at the points where this happens, we have that

$$f(\mathbf{x}^* + \mathbf{h}) - f(\mathbf{x}^*) = \varepsilon_2(\mathbf{h})$$

The quadratic term is no longer dominant, and we have no control over the sign of the error term.

5 • Unconstrained optimization

To show how to use the second derivative test to classify stationary points, we consider $f(x, y) = x^2 y^3 + y^2 - 2y$ as an example. Earlier, we found that the partial derivatives of f and the first order conditions were given by

$$f'_x = 2xy^3 = 0, \quad f'_y = 3x^2 y^2 + 2y - 2 = 0$$

and that $(x, y) = (0, 1)$ was the only stationary point of f. We compute the Hessian matrix at this point:

$$H(f) = \begin{pmatrix} 2y^3 & 6xy^2 \\ 6xy^2 & 6x^2 y + 2 \end{pmatrix} \Rightarrow H(f)(0, 1) = \begin{pmatrix} 2 & 0 \\ 0 & 2 \end{pmatrix}$$

Since $H(f)(0, 1)$ is positive definite, the stationary point $(x^*, y^*) = (0, 1)$ is a local minimum point for f. It follows that the unconstrained optimization problem

$$\max / \min f(x, y) = x^2 y^3 + y^2 - 2y$$

has no maximum, since f has no local maximum point, and the only candidate for a minimum value of f is $f(0, 1) = -1$, since f has a single local minimum point $(0, 1)$. In general, it is a nontrivial task to determine whether local maxima or minima are in fact global maxima or minima. In this case, we can look at the cut $x = 1$ through the graph of f. This gives

$$f(1, y) = 1^2 \cdot y^3 + y^2 - 2y = y^3 + y^2 - 2y$$

Since this is a polynomial with the leading term y^3, we have that $f(1, y) \to -\infty$ when $y \to -\infty$. Hence f has no minimum value in this case.

Let us consider the function $f(x, y, z) = x^3 + y^3 + z^3 - 3xyz$ as another example. We have earlier computed the first order partial derivatives

$$f'_x(x, y, z) = 3x^2 - 3yz$$

and the Hessian matrix

$$H(f) = \begin{pmatrix} f''_{xx} & f''_{xy} & f''_{xz} \\ f''_{yx} & f''_{yy} & f''_{yz} \\ f''_{zx} & f''_{zy} & f''_{zz} \end{pmatrix} = \begin{pmatrix} 6x & -3z & -3y \\ -3z & 6y & -3x \\ -3y & -3x & 6z \end{pmatrix}$$

When we solve the first order conditions, we find infinitely many stationary points in this case. In fact, to solve the equations

$$f'_x = 3x^2 - 3yz = 0, \quad f'_y = 3y^2 - 3xz = 0, \quad f'_z = 3z^2 - 3xy = 0$$

we first consider the case where one of the variables is equal to zero. This implies that the other variables are zero as well, and we find the solution $(x, y, z) = (0, 0, 0)$

in this case. Next, we consider the case where all the variables are nonzero. Then we have

$$3x^2 - 3yz \to 3x^3 - 3xyz,$$
$$3y^2 - 3xz \to 3y^3 - 3xyz,$$
$$3z^2 = 3xy \Rightarrow 3z^3 = 3xyz$$

This implies that $3x^3 = 3y^3 = 3z^3$, or $x = y = z$. Hence $(x, y, z) = (t, t, t)$ with $t \neq 0$ are stationary points, as well as the point $(0, 0, 0)$ with $t = 0$. Let us try to classify the stationary points $(x, y, z) = (t, t, t)$ using the second derivative test. The Hessian matrix is given by

$$H(f)(t, t, t) = \begin{pmatrix} 6t & -3t & -3t \\ -3t & 6t & -3t \\ -3t & -3t & 6t \end{pmatrix} = tA, \text{ where } A = \begin{pmatrix} 6 & -3 & -3 \\ -3 & 6 & -3 \\ -3 & -3 & 6 \end{pmatrix}$$

By the reduced rank criterion, A is positive semidefinite, since $D_1 = 6$, $D_2 = 27$, and $D_3 = |A| = 0$. Hence $H(f)(t, t, t)$ is positive semidefinite for $t \geq 0$ and negative semidefinite for $t \leq 0$. This means that the second derivative test is inconclusive for all stationary points of f. We need to use another method to determine their type, and we shall use the stationary point $(x, y, z) = (0, 0, 0)$ as an example. When we consider points $(h, 0, 0)$ close to $(0, 0, 0)$, where only the x-coordinate has changed, we have that

$$f(h, 0, 0) - f(0, 0, 0) = h^3$$

Since h^3 has the same sign as h, there are points with function values greater than $f(\mathbf{x}^*) = 0$ and other points with function values less than $f(\mathbf{x}^*) = 0$ in any open ball $B_r(\mathbf{x}^*)$ around $\mathbf{x}^* = (0, 0, 0)$. This means that $\mathbf{x}^* = (0, 0, 0)$ is a saddle point for f.

5.5 Convex and concave functions

Let f be a function in n variables with the domain of definition D. We say that $D \subseteq \mathbb{R}^n$ is a *convex set* if the following condition holds: For any points $P, Q \in D$, the line segment $[P, Q]$ from P to Q is contained in D. When we identify P and Q with vectors $\mathbf{x}$ and $\mathbf{y}$, this line segment can be expressed in concrete terms as

$$[P, Q] = \{\mathbf{x} + t(\mathbf{y} - \mathbf{x}) : 0 \leq t \leq 1\} = \{(1 - t)\mathbf{x} + t\mathbf{y} : 0 \leq t \leq 1\}$$

using the parametrization of the line through P and Q from Section 2.3. It follows that the set $D = \mathbb{R}^n$ is a convex set, and a subset of $\mathbb{R}^n$ is convex if it is without "holes". The set $D = \{(x, y) : (x - 1)^2 + y^2 \leq 9\} \subseteq \mathbb{R}^2$ is an example of a convex set. It is shown in the figure below, and consists of the points on the circle with center $(1, 0)$ and radius 3, and all points inside this circle.

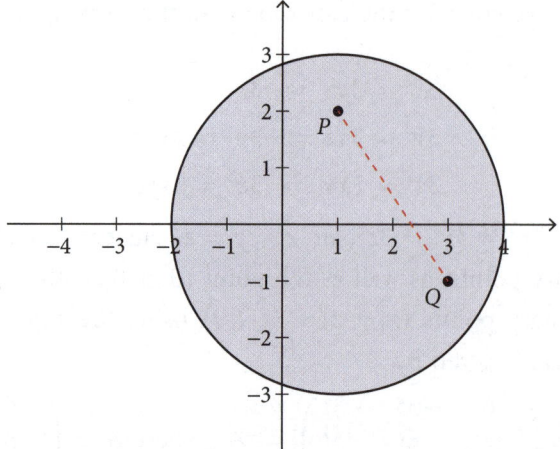

When f is a function defined on a convex set D, we say that the function f is *convex* if the line segment $[P, Q]$ lies on or over the graph of f whenever P, Q are two different points on the graph of f. To be more precise, f is convex if and only if

$$f((1-t)\mathbf{x} + t\mathbf{y}) \leq (1-t)f(\mathbf{x}) + tf(\mathbf{y})$$

for all $\mathbf{x}, \mathbf{y} \in D$ and all $t \in [0, 1]$. The left-hand side is the function value of a point on the line segment $[\mathbf{x}, \mathbf{y}]$, which is well-defined since D is a convex set, and the right-hand side is the corresponding point on the line segment $[f(\mathbf{x}), f(\mathbf{y})]$.

In a similar way, we say that f is *concave* if the line segment $[P, Q]$ lies on or under the graph of f whenever P, Q are two different points on the graph of f. To be more precise, f is concave if and only if

$$f((1-t)\mathbf{x} + t\mathbf{y}) \geq (1-t)f(\mathbf{x}) + tf(\mathbf{y})$$

for all $\mathbf{x}, \mathbf{y} \in D$. Also in this case, f must be defined on a convex set D for this definition to make sense. It follows from the definition that f is concave if and only if $-f$ is convex.

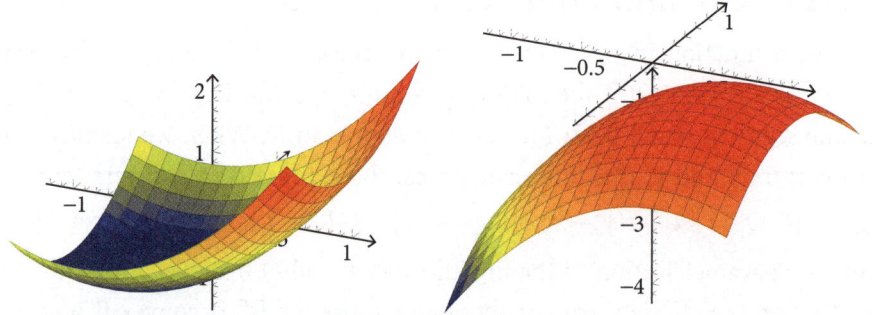

Figure 5.4 The graph of a convex function (left) and a concave function (right)

5.5 Convex and concave functions

In Figure 5.4, we show an example of a convex and a concave function in two variables. The property of being a convex or a concave function is a global property; it is a requirement on the sign of the curvature of the graph of f at any point $\mathbf{x}$. In fact, this can be measured by the definiteness of the Hessian matrix $H(f)(\mathbf{x})$ at each point $\mathbf{x} \in D$ in the domain of definition of f.

Proposition 5.4. Let f be a C^2 function defined on an open convex subset $D \subseteq \mathbb{R}^n$. Then we have:

a) f is convex if and only if $H(f)(\mathbf{x})$ is positive semidefinite for all $\mathbf{x} \in D$

b) f is concave if and only if $H(f)(\mathbf{x})$ is negative semidefinite for all $\mathbf{x} \in D$

We consider the function $f(x, y, z) = x^4 + 2x^2 + y^2 + 2z^2 + z^4 - 4xz$ as an example. This is a C^2 function on $\mathbb{R}^3$, with first order partial derivatives

$$f'_x = 4x^3 + 4x - 4z, \quad f'_y = 2y, \quad f'_z = 4z + 4z^3 - 4x$$

and its Hessian matrix $H(f) = H(f)(\mathbf{x})$ is given by

$$H(f) = \begin{pmatrix} 12x^2 + 4 & 0 & -4 \\ 0 & 2 & 0 \\ -4 & 0 & 12z^2 + 4 \end{pmatrix}$$

We must determine the definiteness of $H(f)(\mathbf{x})$ for all points $\mathbf{x} \in \mathbb{R}^3$ to decide if f is convex or concave. We have that $D_1 = 12x^2 + 4$, so $D_1 > 0$ for all points $\mathbf{x}$, and $D_2 = 2D_1$, hence $D_2 > 0$ for all points $\mathbf{x}$ as well. We compute D_3 by cofactor expansion:

$$D_3 = 2((12x^2 + 4)(12z^2 + 4) - 16) = 2(144x^2z^2 + 12x^2 + 12z^2)$$
$$= 288x^2z^2 + 24x^2 + 24z^2$$

Hence $D_3 \geq 0$ for all points $\mathbf{x} \in \mathbb{R}^3$. At the points (x, y, z) with $x = z = 0$, $H(f)(\mathbf{x})$ is positive semidefinite by the reduced rank criterion, since $D_3 = 0$ and $D_1, D_2 > 0$. At all other points, $H(f)(\mathbf{x})$ is positive definite, since $D_1, D_2, D_3 > 0$. Hence $H(f)(\mathbf{x})$ is positive semidefinite for all points $\mathbf{x} \in \mathbb{R}^3$, and therefore f is a convex function.

When we consider the unconstrained optimization problem $\max/\min f(\mathbf{x})$ for a convex or concave function f, we have the following strong result:

Theorem 5.5 (Convex optimization). Let f be a C^2 function on an open convex subset $D \subseteq \mathbb{R}^n$, and let $\mathbf{x}^*$ be a stationary point of f. Then we have:

a) If f is convex, then $\mathbf{x}^*$ is a minimum point for f

b) If f is concave, then $\mathbf{x}^*$ is a maximum point for f

5.6 Quadratic functions

We have seen that any quadratic form f in n variables can be written in matrix form as $f(\mathbf{x}) = \mathbf{x}^T A \mathbf{x}$, where A is the symmetric matrix of the quadratic form, and that any linear form can be written as $f(\mathbf{x}) = B\mathbf{x}$, where B is a row vector. Therefore, any polynomial function in n variables of degree two can be written

$$f(\mathbf{x}) = \mathbf{x}^T A \mathbf{x} + B\mathbf{x} + C$$

where A is an $n \times n$ symmetric matrix, B is a $1 \times n$ matrix, and C is a number. For example, the function $f(x, y, z) = 3x^2 - 6xy + 4y^2 + 4yz + 5z^2 - 2y - 4z + 3$ can be written as

$$f(\mathbf{x}) = (x \ y \ z) \begin{pmatrix} 3 & -3 & 0 \\ -3 & 4 & 2 \\ 0 & 2 & 5 \end{pmatrix} \begin{pmatrix} x \\ y \\ z \end{pmatrix} + (0 \ -2 \ -4) \begin{pmatrix} x \\ y \\ z \end{pmatrix} + 3$$

In this section, we shall study the unconstrained optimization problem for quadratic polynomials, or polynomials of degree two, using matrices. The following formulas for the derivative and the Hessian matrix are very useful. We write $\mathbf{f}'(\mathbf{x})^T$ for the derivative of f expressed as a column vector, since the derivative $\mathbf{f}'(\mathbf{x})$ is defined to be a row vector.

Lemma 5.6. Let Q be a quadratic form $Q(\mathbf{x}) = \mathbf{x}^T A \mathbf{x}$ with symmetric matrix A, and let L be a linear form $L(\mathbf{x}) = B\mathbf{x}$. Then we have

a) $\mathbf{Q}'(\mathbf{x})^T = 2A\mathbf{x}$ and $H(Q)(\mathbf{x}) = 2A$

b) $\mathbf{L}'(\mathbf{x})^T = B^T$ and $H(L)(\mathbf{x}) = 0$

Proof. The terms in $Q(\mathbf{x})$ have the form $a_{ii}x_i^2$ or $(a_{ij} + a_{ji})x_i x_j$ for $i \neq j$, and since A is symmetric, we can write $(a_{ij} + a_{ji})x_i x_j = 2a_{ij}x_i x_j$. The derivative of $a_{ii}x_i^2$ with respect to x_i is $2a_{ii}x_i$, and the derivative of $2a_{ij}x_i x_j$ with respect to x_i is $2a_{ij}x_j$. Therefore we have that

$$\mathbf{Q}'(\mathbf{x})^T = \begin{pmatrix} Q'_1 \\ Q'_2 \\ \vdots \\ Q'_n \end{pmatrix} = \begin{pmatrix} 2a_{11}x_1 + 2a_{12}x_2 + \ldots + 2a_{1n}x_n \\ 2a_{21}x_1 + 2a_{22}x_2 + \ldots + 2a_{2n}x_n \\ \vdots \\ 2a_{n1}x_1 + 2a_{n2}x_2 + \ldots + 2a_{nn}x_n \end{pmatrix} = 2A\mathbf{x}$$

It follows from this that $H(Q)(\mathbf{x}) = 2A$. The linear form L can be written in the form $L(\mathbf{x}) = B\mathbf{x} = b_1 x_1 + b_2 x_2 + \ldots + b_n x_n$. It follows from this that $L'_i = b_i$, hence $\mathbf{L}'(\mathbf{x}) = B$, or $\mathbf{L}'(\mathbf{x})^T = B^T$, and $H(L)(\mathbf{x}) = 0$. □

5.6 Quadratic functions

Let us use Lemma 5.6 to find the maximum and minimum values of the quadratic polynomial $f(x,y,z) = 3x^2 - 6xy + 4y^2 + 4yz + 5z^2 + 2y + 4z + 3$, if they exist. We have written f in the form $f(\mathbf{x}) = \mathbf{x}^T A \mathbf{x} + B \mathbf{x} + C$ earlier in this section, with

$$A = \begin{pmatrix} 3 & -3 & 0 \\ -3 & 4 & 2 \\ 0 & 2 & 5 \end{pmatrix}, \quad B = \begin{pmatrix} 0 & -2 & -4 \end{pmatrix}, \quad C = 3$$

We have that $\mathbf{f}'(\mathbf{x})^T = 2A\mathbf{x} + B^T$ and $H(f)(\mathbf{x}) = 2A$. Hence the stationary points are given by the linear system $2A\mathbf{x} + B^T = 0$, or $2A\mathbf{x} = -B^T$. We solve this system by Gaussian elimination:

$$\begin{pmatrix} 6 & -6 & 0 & | & 0 \\ -6 & 8 & 4 & | & 2 \\ 0 & 4 & 10 & | & 4 \end{pmatrix} \to \begin{pmatrix} 6 & -6 & 0 & | & 0 \\ 0 & 2 & 4 & | & 2 \\ 0 & 4 & 10 & | & 4 \end{pmatrix} \to \begin{pmatrix} 6 & -6 & 0 & | & 0 \\ 0 & 2 & 4 & | & 2 \\ 0 & 0 & 2 & | & 0 \end{pmatrix}$$

Back substitution gives one stationary point $(x,y,z) = (1,1,0)$. To classify this point, we determine the definiteness of $2A$. We have $D_1 = 6$ and $D_2 = 48 - 36 = 12$, and $D_3 = |2A| = 6 \cdot 2 \cdot 2 = 24$ using the Gaussian process. Hence $2A$ is positive definite, and $\mathbf{x}^* = (1,1,0)$ is a local minimum point for f. We notice that $H(f)(\mathbf{x}) = 2A$ is constant, and therefore positive definite for all $\mathbf{x}$, hence f is also a convex function. This means that $\mathbf{x}^* = (1,1,0)$ is a minimum point, and the minimum value of f is $f_{\min} = f(1,1,0) = 2$. Clearly, it has no maximum value.

Proposition 5.7. Let $f(\mathbf{x}) = \mathbf{x}^T A \mathbf{x} + B\mathbf{x} + C$ be a quadratic polynomial, where A is a symmetric matrix. Then the stationary points of f are given by the linear system $2A\mathbf{x} = -B^T$. Moreover, we have:

a) If A is positive definite, then f is convex and has a unique minimum point

b) If A is negative definite, then f is concave and has a unique maximum point

c) If A is positive (negative) semidefinite, then f is convex (concave) and stationary points are minima (maxima)

d) If A is indefinite, then stationary points of f are saddle points

Proof. Since $\mathbf{f}'(\mathbf{x}) = 2A\mathbf{x} + B^T$, the first order conditions give the linear system $2A\mathbf{x} + B^T = \mathbf{0}$, or $2A\mathbf{x} = -B^T$. The Hessian matrix $H(f) = 2A$, which is constant and has the same definiteness as A. The rest follows from the theory in the earlier sections of the chapter, since A positive (negative) definite implies that $D_n = |A| \neq 0$, and this means that $2A\mathbf{x} = -B^T$ has the unique solution $\mathbf{x} = -(2A)^{-1} \cdot B^T$. □

5.7 Envelope theorem

Many optimization problems have parameters, in addition to the variables that we optimize for. This applies in particular to economic problems, which often depend on prices and other parameters outside our control. We think of the parameters as given, and search for optimal solutions for each given value of the parameters. It is therefore essential to determine how the optimal value changes when the parameters of the problem vary.

Let us start by considering a very simple example of an optimization problem with a parameter: We consider the maximum problem

$$\max_x f(x;a) = 1 + ax - x^2$$

We write $f(x;a)$ when we want to make it clear that x is the variable we are optimizing for, and that we consider a to be a parameter. This means that we want to find the optimal value of x for each given value of the parameter a. We shall write $x = x^*(a)$ for optimal value of x, if it exists, and $f^*(a)$ for the corresponding optimal value $f^*(a) = f(x^*(a); a)$. We call f^* the *optimal value* function, since it gives the optimal value (in this case, the maximal value) for each value of the parameter a.

For a specific value of a, such as $a = 2$, it is not difficult to solve the problem. The function $f(x) = 1 + 2x - x^2$ has derivative $f'(x) = 2 - 2x$, and stationary point $x = 1$. Since $f''(x) = -2 < 0$, the function is concave. Hence $x^* = 1$ is a maximum point for f, and the maximum value of f is $f(1) = 2$. We write $x^*(2) = 1$ and $f^*(2) = 2$, since this is the maximum point and the maximum value of the optimization problem when $a = 2$.

This particular example is very simple (almost trivial), and we can easily compute the optimal value function $f^*(a)$ explicitly. For any value of a, we have that

$$f'_x(x;a) = (1 + ax - x^2)'_x = a - 2x = 0 \quad \Rightarrow \quad x = \frac{a}{2}$$

and the stationary point $x = a/2$ is a maximum point since $f''_{xx}(x;a) = -2 < 0$ means that $f(x;a)$ is concave. We conclude that $x = x^*(a) = a/2$ maximizes $f(x;a)$ for any value of a, and the optimal value function is given by

$$f^*(a) = f(x^*(a); a) = f(a/2; a) = 1 + a(a/2) - (a/2)^2 = 1 + a^2/4$$

In particular $f^*(2) = 2$, in agreement with what we found for $a = 2$. We illustrate these results in the figure below. The figure shows the graph $y = f(x;a)$ for some values of a, with the maximum points marked on each graph. The optimal value function is shown in blue. The graph of the optimal value function is called an *envelope of all the curves* $y = f(x;a)$.

5.7 Envelope theorem

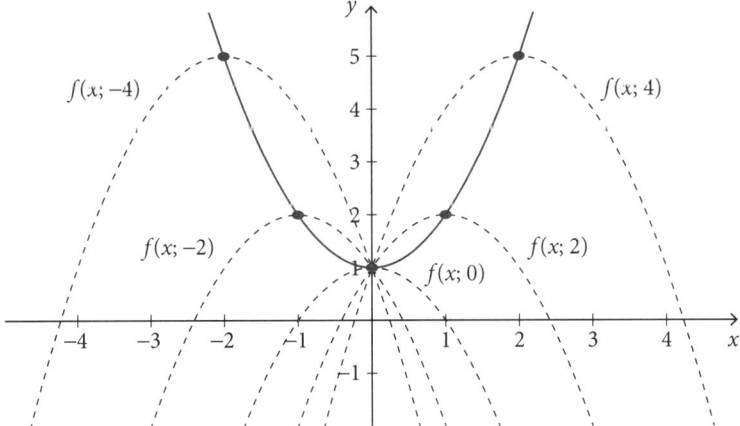

Figure 5.5 The graph of $f(x;a)$ for $a = -4, -2, 0, 2, 4$, and their envelope

Notice that the graph of the optimal value function describes how the maximal value changes when we vary the parameter a, and that its derivative

$$\frac{df^*(a)}{da} = \left(1 + \frac{a^2}{4}\right)'_a = \frac{a}{2}$$

is the marginal change in the optimal value function $f^*(a)$. We can plot the graph of the optimal value function $f^*(a)$ with the parameter a on the first axis; the marginal change in $f^*(a)$ is the slope of the tangent line to this graph.

In more complicated examples, it is can be difficult to compute the optimal value function explicitly, as we have done in this example. We shall show how we can use the envelope theorem to compute the marginal change in the optimal value function. The idea is to use this as a proxy for $f^*(a)$: When h is small, we can use the approximation

$$f^*(a+h) \approx f^*(a) + h \cdot \frac{df^*(a)}{da}$$

to estimate the change in the optimal value, at least when the optimal value function is differentiable.

In general, let $f(\mathbf{x}; a)$ be a function defined for $\mathbf{x} \in D$ and $a \in U$, where $D \subseteq \mathbb{R}^n$ and $U \subseteq \mathbb{R}$ are open subsets, and consider the unconstrained optimization problem

$$\max_{\mathbf{x} \in D} f(\mathbf{x}; a) \quad \text{or} \quad \min_{\mathbf{x} \in D} f(\mathbf{x}; a)$$

in n variables $\mathbf{x}$ with a parameter a. We may consider $f(\mathbf{x}; a)$ as a function on the open set $D \times U \subseteq \mathbb{R}^{n+1}$. We write $\mathbf{x}^*(a)$ for the maximum or minimum point, if it exists, and $f^*(a) = f(\mathbf{x}^*(a); a)$ for the corresponding optimal value.

5 • Unconstrained optimization

Theorem 5.8 (Envelope theorem). Let $f(\mathbf{x}; a)$ be a C^1 function on an open set $D \times U \subseteq \mathbb{R}^{n+1}$, and consider the unconstrained optimization problem

$$\max_{\mathbf{x} \in D} f(\mathbf{x}; a) \quad \text{or} \quad \min_{\mathbf{x} \in D} f(\mathbf{x}; a)$$

for any parameter value a in U. If there is an optimal point $\mathbf{x} = \mathbf{x}^*(a)$ for all $a \in U$ such that $a \mapsto \mathbf{x}^*(a)$ is a C^1 function on U, then

$$\frac{df^*(a)}{da} = \frac{\partial f}{\partial a}(\mathbf{x}^*(a); a)$$

for any $a \in U$.

Proof. It is clear that $f^*(a) = f(\mathbf{x}^*(a); a)$ is a C^1 function on U, and that its total derivative is given by the chain rule. This gives

$$\frac{df^*(a)}{da} = f_1'(\mathbf{x}^*(a)) \cdot \frac{dx_1^*(a)}{da} + \ldots + f_n'(\mathbf{x}^*(a)) \cdot \frac{dx_n^*(a)}{da} + \frac{\partial f}{\partial a}(\mathbf{x}^*(a))$$

$$= \frac{\partial f}{\partial a}(\mathbf{x}^*(a))$$

since $f_1' = \ldots = f_n' = 0$ at $\mathbf{x}^*(a)$; it follows from Proposition 5.2 that the maximum or minimum point $\mathbf{x}^*(a)$ in the unconstrained optimization problem is a stationary point. $\square$

Let us consider the unconstrained optimization problem $\min f(x, y, z, w; a)$ with parameter a when f is the function given by

$$f(x, y, z, w; a) = x^2 + y^2 + z^2 + w^2 - a\,xw - 2x + 2z - 4w$$

as an example. Let us consider the case $a = 0$ as our starting point. In this case, we have first order conditions

$$f_x' = 2x - 2 = 0, \quad f_y' = 2y = 0, \quad f_z' = 2z + 2 = 0, \quad f_w' = 2w - 4 = 0$$

and therefore a unique stationary point $(x, y, z, w) = (1, 0, -1, 2)$. We compute the Hessian matrix and find that

$$H(f) = \begin{pmatrix} 2 & 0 & 0 & 0 \\ 0 & 2 & 0 & 0 \\ 0 & 0 & 2 & 0 \\ 0 & 0 & 0 & 2 \end{pmatrix}$$

and this matrix is clearly positive definite. Hence f is convex when $a = 0$. We write $\mathbf{x}^*(0) = (1, 0, -1, 2)$ for the unique minimum point of f when $a = 0$, and we write $f^*(0) = f(1, 0, -1, 2) = -6$ for the corresponding minimum value of f.

5.7 Envelope theorem

Let us try to use the envelope theorem to estimate the minimum value of f when a is close to 0: If the assumptions of the envelope theorem are satisfied, then we have

$$f'_a = -xw \quad \Rightarrow \quad \frac{df^*(a)}{da} = -x^*(a) \cdot w^*(a)$$

In particular, this means that the marginal change in the minimum value at $a = 0$ is given by $-x^*(0) \cdot w^*(0) = -1 \cdot 2 = -2$, and for values of a close to 0 we have the estimate

$$f^*(a) \approx f^*(0) + a \cdot \frac{df^*(a)}{da}(0) = -6 - 2a$$

Hence a small positive value of a would mean a smaller minimum value, and small negative values of a would give a greater minimum value.

Let us check that the assumptions of the envelope theorem are satisfied, at least when a is close to 0, as we expect: The first condition is that $f(x, y, z, w; a)$ is a C^1 function, and this is clearly the case on all of $\mathbb{R}^4 \times \mathbb{R}$ since f is a polynomial in (x, y, z, w, a). The second condition is that there is a minimum point $\mathbf{x}^*(a)$ for each value of a: We compute the Hessian matrix for a general a, and find that

$$H(f) = \begin{pmatrix} 2 & 0 & 0 & -a \\ 0 & 2 & 0 & 0 \\ 0 & 0 & 2 & 0 \\ -a & 0 & 0 & 2 \end{pmatrix}$$

We have $D_1 = 2$, $D_2 = 4$, $D_3 = 8$ and $D_4 = 16 - 4a^2$, and f is convex if $16 - 4a^2 > 0$. This gives $a^2 < 4$, or $-2 < a < 2$. This implies that f is convex for all $a \in U$, when U is the open interval $U = (-2, 2)$. The stationary points of f are given by the linear system $H(f) \cdot \mathbf{x} = \mathbf{0}$ by Lemma 5.6, and $|H(f)| = D_4 > 0$ for all $a \in U$, hence there is a unique stationary point $\mathbf{x}^*(a)$ for all $a \in U$. In fact, the first order conditions

$$f'_x = 2x - aw - 2 = 0,$$
$$f'_y = 2y = 0,$$
$$f'_z = 2z + 2 = 0,$$
$$f'_w = -ax + 2w - 4 = 0$$

give $y = 0$ and $z = -1$ from the middle equations. From the first and last equation, we get

$$\begin{pmatrix} 2 & -a \\ -a & 2 \end{pmatrix} \begin{pmatrix} x \\ w \end{pmatrix} = \begin{pmatrix} 2 \\ 4 \end{pmatrix}$$
$$\Downarrow$$
$$\begin{pmatrix} x \\ w \end{pmatrix} = \begin{pmatrix} 2 & -a \\ -a & 2 \end{pmatrix}^{-1} \begin{pmatrix} 2 \\ 4 \end{pmatrix} = \frac{1}{4 - a^2} \begin{pmatrix} 2 & a \\ a & 2 \end{pmatrix} \begin{pmatrix} 2 \\ 4 \end{pmatrix}$$

which gives $x = (4 + 4a)/(4 - a^2)$ and $w = (2a + 8)/(4 - a^2)$. This means that there is a unique minimum point

$$\mathbf{x}^*(a) = \left(\frac{4 + 4a}{4 - a^2},\ 0,\ -1,\ \frac{2a + 8}{4 - a^2} \right)$$

for all $a \in U = (-2, 2)$, and $\mathbf{x}^*(a)$ is clearly a C^1 function, since it is given by rational expressions in a. This means that the assumptions of the envelope theorem are satisfied for $a \in U = (-2, 2)$. We could replace the estimate $f^*(a) \approx -6 - 2a$ with an exact value for $f^*(a)$ when $a \in U$. To compute this exact value, we would have to substitute the minimum point $\mathbf{x}^*(a)$ that we found above into the expression for f, and compute

$$f^*(a) = f\left(\frac{4 + 4a}{4 - a^2},\ 0,\ -1,\ \frac{2a + 8}{4 - a^2} \right) \text{ for } a \in U = (-2, 2)$$

The simple estimate $f^*(a) \approx -6 - 2a$ for values of a close to 0 obtained from the envelope theorem clearly has computational advantages. In addition, the envelope theorem gives a clear and conceptual answer to the following question: How does the minimum value $f^*(0) = -6$ change when the parameter a changes from $a = 0$ to a small value of a?

Problems

Problem 5.1 Find the stationary points and classify their type:

a) $f(x, y) = x^4 + x^2 - 6xy + 3y^2$
b) $f(x, y) = x^2 - 6xy + 2y^2 + 10x + 2y$
c) $f(x, y) = xy^2 + x^3y - xy$
d) $f(x, y) = 3x^4 + 3x^2y - y^3$
e) $f(x, y) = e^{xy}$
f) $f(x, y) = \ln(x^2 + y^2 + 1)$
g) $f(x, y, z) = x^2 + 6xy + y^2 - 3yz + 4z^2 - 10x - 5y - 21z$

Problem 5.2 Find the stationary points and classify their type:

a) $f(x, y) = e^{xy}$ b) $f(x, y) = \ln(x^2 + y^2 + 1)$

Problem 5.3 Determine whether the function is convex or concave:

a) $f(x, y) = x^4 + x^2 - 6xy + 3y^2$
b) $f(x, y) = x^2 - 6xy + 2y^2 + 10x + 2y$
c) $f(x, y) = xy^2 + x^3y - xy$
d) $f(x, y) = 3x^4 + 3x^2y - y^3$
e) $f(x, y) = e^{xy}$
f) $f(x, y) = \ln(x^2 + y^2 + 1)$
g) $f(x, y, z) = x^2 + 6xy + y^2 - 3yz + 4z^2 - 10x - 5y - 21z$

Problem 5.4 Consider the subset $D = \{(x, y) : x \geq 0, y \geq 0, xy \leq 1\}$ of $\mathbb{R}^2$.

a) Sketch the set D
b) Describe the boundary points of D.
c) Determine if D is open or closed.
d) Determine if D is a convex set.

Problem 5.5 Let f be the function given by
$$f(x, y) = -6x^2 + (2a + 4)xy - y^2 + 4ay$$
where x, y are variables and a is a parameter. Determine the values of a such that f is a concave function.

Problem 5.6 Let $D = \{(x, y, z) : x > 0,; y > 0, z > 0\}$ and $E = \{(x, y, z) : xyz > 0\}$. Determine whether D or E is a convex set. Is the function $f(x, y, z) = \ln(xyz)$ convex or concave when we consider f as a function defined on D or E?

Problem 5.7 Consider the function $f(x, y) = x^4 + 16y^4 + 32xy^3 + 8x^3y + 24x^2y^2$ defined on $D = \mathbb{R}^2$. Determine if this function is convex or concave.

Problem 5.8 Consider the function $f(x, y) = e^{x+y} + e^{x-y}$ defined on $\mathbb{R}^2$. Determine whether f is convex or concave.

Problem 5.9 Solve the unconstrained optimization problems $\max / \min f(\mathbf{x})$ when f is the function given by $f(x, y, z) = x^4 + y^4 + z^4 + x^2 + y^2 + z^2$.

Problem 5.10 Find the range of the composite function f given by:

a) $f(x, y, z) = \ln(u + 1)$ with $u = 2x^2 + 2xy + 3y^2 - 2xz + z^2$
b) $f(x, y, z) = e^{1-u}$ with $u = x^2 + 2xy + 3y^2 + 2yz + z^2$
c) $f(x, y, z) = u \ln(u)$ with $u = 5x^2 - 8xy - 4xz + 5y^2 - 4yz + 8z^2 + 1$

Problem 5.11 We consider the function $f(x, y, z) = x^3 + 3xy + 3xz + y^3 + 3yz + z^3$. Find all its stationary points, and classify their type.

Problem 5.12 Show that the function $f(x, y, z) = x^4 + y^4 + z^4 + x^2 - xy + y^2 + yz + z^2$ is convex.

Problem 5.13 Let $f(x, y, z; h) = 12 - x^4 - hx^2 - 3y^2 + 6xz - 6z^2 + h^2$ be a function with parameter h.

a) Compute the Hessian matrix of f, and show that f is concave if and only if $h \geq H$ for a constant H. What is the value of H?
b) Find the global maximum point $(x^*(h), y^*(h), z^*(h))$ of f when $h \geq H$.
c) Will the global maximum value $f^*(h)$ increase or decrease when the value of the parameter h increases? We assume that the initial value of h satisfies $h > H$.

Problem 5.14 Let $f(x, y; a) = xy^2 + 5x^3y - a^2xy$ be a function with parameter a, and assume that $a > 0$.

a) Compute the partial derivatives and the Hessian matrix of f.
b) Compute all stationary points of f. Show that there is exactly one stationary point $(x^*(a), y^*(a))$ that is a local maximum, and find it.
c) Will the local maximum value $f^*(a) = f(x^*(a), y^*(a))$ increase or decrease when the value of the parameter a increases?

CHAPTER 6

Constrained optimization

6.1 Constrained optimization problems

We consider the *constrained optimization problem* for a function f in n variables, characterized by the fact that additional constraints are imposed, limiting the points $\mathbf{x} = (x_1, x_2, \ldots, x_n)$ we allow in the problem. This is an example of a constrained optimization problem:

$$\min f(x, y, z) = \sqrt{x^2 + y^2 + z^2} \quad \text{when} \quad x + 2y + 3z = 6$$

The function f that we want to optimize in a constrained optimization problem is called the *objective function*, and the set $D \subseteq \mathbb{R}^n$ of points satisfying all constraints in the problem is called the *set of admissible points*. In the example above, the set $D = \{(x, y, z) : x + 2y + 3z = 6\}$ of admissible points is a plane in $\mathbb{R}^3$, and since $f(x, y, z) = \sqrt{x^2 + y^2 + z^2}$ is the distance between the origin $(0, 0, 0)$ and the point (x, y, z), the geometric interpretation of the constrained optimization problem is to determine the shortest distance from a point in the plane D to the origin.

When the set D of admissible points is an open subset of $\mathbb{R}^n$, we may use the methods of Chapter 5 to solve the problem. Let us consider the example

$$\min f(x, y, z) = x^2 + y^2 + z^2 - 4x + 2y - 6z \quad \text{when} \quad x + 2y + 3z > 6$$

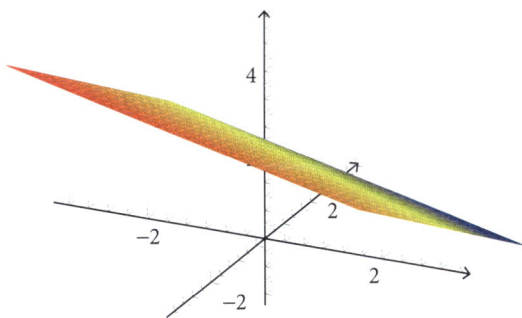

Figure 6.1 The plane $D \subseteq \mathbb{R}^3$ given by the equation $x + 2y + 3z = 6$

145

Since the set $D = \{(x, y, z) : x + 2y + 3z > 6\}$ of admissible points is open, it has no boundary points, and therefore any minimum point must be a stationary point of f that is an interior point of D. The first order conditions for f are

$$f'_x = 2x - 4 = 0, \quad f'_y = 2y + 2 = 0, \quad f'_z = 2z - 6 = 0$$

hence $(x, y, z) = (2, -1, 3)$ is the unique stationary point of f. This is a point in D, and therefore an interior point of D, since $x + 2y + 3z = 9 > 6$ at $(2, -1, 3)$. We have that f is a convex function on the convex set D, since

$$H(f) = \begin{pmatrix} 2 & 0 & 0 \\ 0 & 2 & 0 \\ 0 & 0 & 2 \end{pmatrix}$$

is positive definite. This means that $\mathbf{x}^* = (2, -1, 3)$ is a minimum point, and that

$$\min_{\mathbf{x} \in D} f(\mathbf{x}) = f(2, -1, 3) = -14$$

We conclude that with small modifications (for instance, we must check that the stationary point that we found satisfies the constraint), the methods of Chapter 5 can still be used when the set of admissible points is an open subset.

When the set D of admissible points is a closed subset of $\mathbb{R}^n$, the candidate points for maximum or minimum in the constrained optimization problem

$$\max_{\mathbf{x} \in D} f(\mathbf{x}) \text{ or } \min_{\mathbf{x} \in D} f(\mathbf{x})$$

are either stationary points of f that are interior points of D, or boundary points of D. In this chapter, we shall explain methods for solving these kinds of optimization problems.

6.2 The Extreme Value Theorem

We say that a subset $D \subseteq \mathbb{R}^n$ is *bounded* if there are fixed numbers $a_1, a_2, \ldots, a_n$ and $b_1, b_2, \ldots, b_n$ such that

$$a_1 \leq x_1 \leq b_1, \ a_2 \leq x_2 \leq b_2, \ \ldots, \ a_n \leq x_n \leq b_n$$

for all points $\mathbf{x} = (x_1, x_2, \ldots, x_n) \in D$. When D is a subset of $\mathbb{R}^2$, this condition means that there is a rectangle $[a_1, b_1] \times [a_2, b_2]$ that contains all the points of D, and when D is a subset of $\mathbb{R}^3$, it means that there is a three-dimensional rectangular box $[a_1, b_1] \times [a_2, b_2] \times [a_3, b_3]$ that contains all the points of D.

In the figure below, we show two subsets of $\mathbb{R}^2$. The subset shown to the left is given by $D = \{(x, y) : 4x^2 + 9y^2 < 36\}$. Its boundary has the equation $4x^2 + 9y^2 = 36$, which can be written $x^2/9 + y^2/4 = 1$, hence it is an ellipse with center $(0, 0)$ and half-axes $a = 3$ and $b = 2$. The set D contains all points inside the ellipse, and it follows that D is bounded, since it is contained in the rectangle $[-3, 3] \times [-2, 2]$. The subset shown to the right is given by $D = \{(x, y) : xy = 1\}$, and its boundary points (which are all the points in D) are given by the equation $xy = 1$, or $y = 1/x$. Hence D is the graph of $y - 1/x$. This subset is not bounded, since the x- and y-values of points in D are not bounded. For example, for arbitrary large numbers a, the point $(a, 1/a)$ is in D.

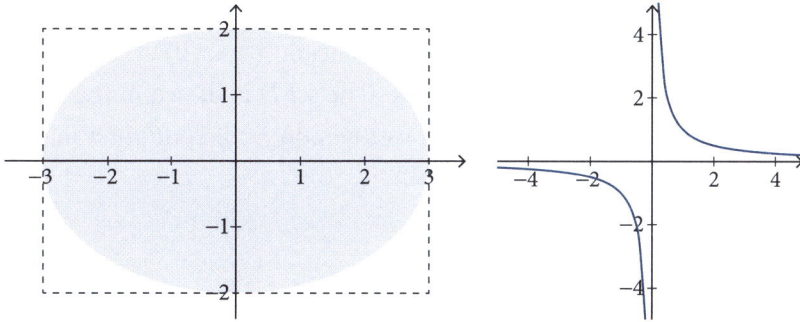

Figure 6.2 The sets given by $4x^2 + 9y^2 < 36$ (bounded) and $xy = 1$ (not bounded)

We say that a subset $D \subseteq \mathbb{R}^n$ is *compact* if it is closed and bounded. The following result explains why compactness matters in optimization problems:

Theorem 6.1 (Extreme Value Theorem). Let f be a continuous function on a compact subset $D \subseteq \mathbb{R}^n$. Then f attains a maximum and a minimum value on D.

Proof. When f is a continuous function and K is a compact set, one may show that $f(K)$ is a compact set. This means that $f(D)$ is a closed and bounded subset of $\mathbb{R}$, and therefore a closed interval $[a, b]$, or a union of such closed intervals, with $a = f(\mathbf{x}_0)$ and $b = f(\mathbf{x}_1)$ for $\mathbf{x}_0, \mathbf{x}_1 \in D$. This proves the result. □

The conditions that D is closed and bounded are both necessary to ensure that a maximum or minimum exists. To see this, consider the following examples: In the problem

$$\max f(x, y) = y \quad \text{when} \quad 4x^2 + 9y^2 < 36$$

the set $D = \{(x, y) : 4x^2 + 9y^2 < 36\}$ is bounded but not closed. No maximum exists in this case: At $(x, y) = (0, 2)$, we have $f(0, 2) = 2$, but this point is not admissible, since it is at the boundary of D. But there are admissible points infinitely close to $(0, 2)$. In fact, $f(x, y) = y$ attains all values in $(-2, 2)$ on D, but there is no maximum (or minimum) value. The set D is shown in the figure above (left-hand side). On the other hand, in the problem

$$\max f(x, y) = x \quad \text{when} \quad xy = 1$$

the set $D = \{(x, y) : xy = 1\}$ is closed but not bounded. No maximum exists in this case: For any number $a \neq 0$, the point $(a, 1/a)$ is admissible, and we have that

$$\lim_{a \to \infty} f(a, 1/a) = \lim_{a \to \infty} a = \infty$$

In fact, the function $f(x, y) = x$ attains all values in $(-\infty, 0) \cup (0, \infty)$ on D, and there is no maximum (or minimum) value. The set D is shown in the figure above (right-hand side). Of course, a continuous function f could attain a maximum or minimum on D even if D is not compact.

6.3 Introduction to the method of Lagrange multipliers

We consider a constrained optimization problem where the set of admissible points is closed. To find candidate points for maximum or minimum among the boundary points, we use the *method of Lagrange multipliers*. In this section, we present the ideas behind this method, and explain how to use it in simple examples.

Let us consider the problem $\min f(x, y) = x^2 + y^2$ when $xy = 1$. The graph of $y = 1/x$, shown in blue in Figure 6.3, is the set of admissible points. We show the level curves $f(x, y) = c$ in the same figure for some values of $c > 0$. The level curves have equation $x^2 + y^2 = c$, and are circles with center $(0, 0)$ and radius $\sqrt{c}$.

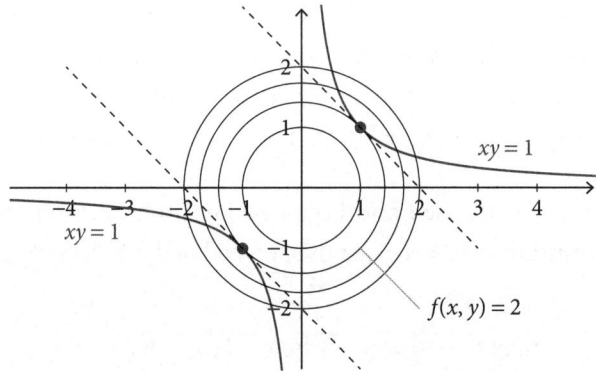

Figure 6.3 Level curves $f(x, y) = x^2 + y^2 = c$ for $c = 1, 2, 3, 4$ and the admissible curve $xy = 1$

The idea behind the method of Lagrange multipliers is that the candidate points for maximum or minimum are the points where a level curve $f(x, y) = c$ meets the admissible curve $xy = 1$ at a tangent. There are two such points in this example, shown in Figure 6.3 with their tangent lines. To see why these points are candidates for maximum or minimum, notice that if a level curves intersects the admissible curve transversally (that is, not at a tangent), then we can find admissible points with higher and lower function values by moving along the admissible curve.

For example, the point $(2, 1/2)$ is an admissible point with $f(2, 1/2) = 17/4$, and we see from the figure below that the level curve $f(x, y) = 17/4$ and the admissible curve do not meet at a tangent at this point. When we move along the curve $xy = 1$, we have $f(a, 1/a) > 17/4$ when $a > 2$, and $f(a, 1/a) < 17/4$ when $a < 2$. The admissible point $(2, 1/2)$ is therefore not a candidate for minimum in this example.

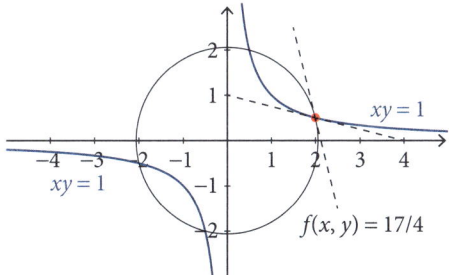

Figure 6.4 The admissible curve and the level curve intersects transversally at $(2, 1/2)$

Let us make some computations to see how we can find admissible points such that the admissible curve $g(x, y) = a$ intersects the level curve $f(x, y) = c$ at a tangent in the more general optimization problem

$$\max / \min f(x, y) \quad \text{when} \quad g(x, y) = a$$

Implicit derivation of the equation $g(x, y) = a$ gives $g'_x + g'_y \cdot y' = 0$, hence the slope of the tangent line of the admissible curve is given by $y' = -g'_x/g'_y$. Similarly, implicit derivation of the equation $f(x, y) = c$ gives $f'_x + f'_y \cdot y' = 0$, hence the slope of the level curve is given by $y' = -f'_x/f'_y$. It follows that the two curves meet at a tangent in an admissible point (x^*, y^*) if and only if the following condition is satisfied:

$$-\frac{g'_x(x^*, y^*)}{g'_y(x^*, y^*)} = -\frac{f'_x(x^*, y^*)}{f'_y(x^*, y^*)}$$

We define the *Lagrangian* to be the function $\mathscr{L}(x, y; \lambda) = f(x, y) - \lambda(g(x, y) - a)$ in the two variables x, y, and a new variable λ that we introduce. We notice that the stationary points of $\mathscr{L}$ are given by

$$\mathscr{L}'_x = f'_x - \lambda g'_x = 0, \quad \mathscr{L}'_y = f'_y - \lambda g'_y = 0, \quad \mathscr{L}'_\lambda = -(g(x, y) - a) = 0$$

We claim that the admissible points where the admissible curve $g(x, y) = a$ and a level curve $f(x, y) = c$ meet at a tangent are exactly the stationary points of $\mathscr{L}$: In fact, the condition $g(x, y) - a = 0$ means the the point (x, y) is admissible, and the other conditions mean that

$$-\frac{f'_x(x^*, y^*)}{f'_y(x^*, y^*)} = -\frac{\lambda g'_x(x^*, y^*)}{\lambda g'_y(x^*, y^*)} = -\frac{g'_x(x^*, y^*)}{g'_y(x^*, y^*)}$$

or that the level curve and the admissible curve meet at a tangent. The new variable λ is called a *Lagrange multiplier*, and the method of Lagrange multipliers can be described in the following way: We compute the stationary points of the Lagrangian to find candidates for maximum or minimum.

In the example $\min f(x, y) = x^2 + y^2$ when $xy = 1$, the Lagrangian is given by $\mathscr{L}(x, y; \lambda) = x^2 + y^2 - \lambda(xy - 1)$, and its stationary points are given by

$$\mathscr{L}'_x = 2x - \lambda y = 0, \quad \mathscr{L}'_y = 2y - \lambda x = 0, \quad \mathscr{L}'_\lambda = -1(xy - 1) = 0$$

The first two conditions give $x = \lambda y/2$ and

$$2y - \lambda \cdot \frac{\lambda y}{2} = 0 \quad \Rightarrow \quad \frac{y}{2}(4 - \lambda^2) = 0$$

This gives $y = 0$ or $\lambda = \pm 2$. If $y = 0$, then $xy = 1$ gives a contradiction. If $\lambda = 2$, then $x = y$, and $xy = 1$ gives $x^2 = 1$, or $x = \pm 1$. If $\lambda = -2$, then $x = -y$, and $xy = 1$ gives $-x^2 = 1$, a contradiction. We conclude that $\mathscr{L}$ has exactly two stationary points $(x, y; \lambda) = (1, 1; 2), (-1, -1; 2)$. When we compare this with Figure 6.3, we see that $(x, y) = (1, 1)$ and $(x, y) = (-1, -1)$ are the admissible points where the level curve and the admissible curve meet at a tangent.

6.4 Lagrange problems

A *Lagrange problem* is a constrained optimization problem where all constraints are equality constraints. In the general case, we may consider a Lagrange problem where the objective function f has n variables $\mathbf{x} = (x_1, x_2, \ldots, x_n)$, and where there are m equality constraints of the form $g_i(\mathbf{x}) = a_i$, where g_i is a function in n variables and a_i is a constant for $1 \leq i \leq m$:

$$\max/\min f(\mathbf{x}) \quad \text{when} \quad \begin{cases} g_1(\mathbf{x}) = a_1 \\ g_2(\mathbf{x}) = a_2 \\ \quad \vdots \\ g_m(\mathbf{x}) = a_m \end{cases} \tag{6.1}$$

We assume that $f, g_1, \ldots, g_m$ are C^1 functions on an open set that contains all admissible points. This is an example of a Lagrange problem in four variables $\mathbf{x} = (x, y, z, w)$ with two equality constraints:

$$\max f(\mathbf{x}) = xw - yz \quad \text{when} \quad \begin{cases} x^2 + 4y^2 = 4 \\ 4z^2 + 9w^2 = 36 \end{cases}$$

In this example, the subset $D = \{(x, y, z, w) : x^2 + 4y^2 = 4, 4z^2 + 9w^2 = 36\} \subseteq \mathbb{R}^4$ of admissible points is compact: It is closed since it is given by two equations, and it is bounded since $x^2 + 4y^2 = 4$ and $4z^2 + 9w^2 = 36$ implies that $-2 \leq x \leq 2$, $-1 \leq y \leq 1$, $-3 \leq z \leq 3$ and $-2 \leq w \leq 2$. According to the Extreme Value Theorem, it follows that there is a maximum in this Lagrange problem.

The general method of Lagrange multipliers. To find candidates for maximum and minimum points in a Lagrange problem, we consider the *Lagrangian function*. For a general Lagrange problem in the form (6.1), the Lagrangian is given by

$$\mathscr{L}(\mathbf{x}; \boldsymbol{\lambda}) = f(\mathbf{x}) - \lambda_1(g_1(\mathbf{x}) - a_1) - \lambda_2(g_2(\mathbf{x}) - a_2) - \ldots - \lambda_m(g_m(\mathbf{x}) - a_m)$$

where $\mathbf{x} = (x_1, x_2, \ldots, x_n)$ are the variables of the problem, and $\boldsymbol{\lambda} = (\lambda_1, \lambda_2, \ldots, \lambda_m)$ are new variables that we introduce, called the *Lagrange multipliers*. In the example above, the Lagrangian is the function

$$\mathscr{L}(\mathbf{x}; \boldsymbol{\lambda}) = xw - yz - \lambda_1(x^2 + 4y^2 - 4) - \lambda_2(4z^2 + 9w^2 - 36)$$

in the variables $\mathbf{x} = (x, y, z, w)$ and the Lagrange multipliers $\boldsymbol{\lambda} = (\lambda_1, \lambda_2)$.

The idea is that the stationary points of the Lagrangian are the candidates for maxima and minima in the Lagrange problem. We therefore have to solve the $n + m$ equations in $n + m$ variables consisting of the *first order conditions*

$$\mathscr{L}'_{x_1} = \mathscr{L}'_{x_2} = \ldots = \mathscr{L}'_{x_n} = 0$$

and the *constraints*

$$\mathscr{L}'_{\lambda_1} = \mathscr{L}'_{\lambda_2} = \ldots = \mathscr{L}'_{\lambda_m} = 0$$

We call the first order conditions and the constraints the *Lagrange conditions*. Note that the solutions of the Lagrange conditions will have the form $(\mathbf{x}; \boldsymbol{\lambda})$, where $\mathbf{x}$ is the candidate point and $\boldsymbol{\lambda}$ is its Lagrange multipliers.

Let us write down all the Lagrange conditions in the example above, and solve the resulting system of equations to find candidate points. We write the first order conditions in the first column and the constraints in the second:

$$\begin{aligned} \mathscr{L}'_x &= w - \lambda_1 \cdot 2x = 0 & x^2 + 4y^2 &= 4 \\ \mathscr{L}'_y &= -z - \lambda_1 \cdot 8y = 0 & 4z^2 + 9w^2 &= 36 \\ \mathscr{L}'_z &= -y - \lambda_2 \cdot 8z = 0 \\ \mathscr{L}'_w &= x - \lambda_2 \cdot 18w = 0 \end{aligned}$$

Since there are $n = 4$ variables and $m = 2$ constraints in the Lagrange problem, we obtain a system of 6 equations in 6 variables.

From the first of the first order conditions (FOC's), we get $w = 2\lambda_1 x$, and when we substitute this into the last FOC, we get

$$x - 18\lambda_2(2\lambda_1 x) = x - 36\lambda_1\lambda_2 x = 0 \quad \Rightarrow \quad x(1 - 36\lambda_1\lambda_2) = 0$$

This means that $x = 0$ or $\lambda_1\lambda_2 = 1/36$. Similarly, from the second FOC, we get $z = -8\lambda_1 y$, and when we substitute this into the third FOC, we get

$$-y - 8\lambda_2(-8\lambda_1 y) = -y + 64\lambda_1\lambda_2 y = 0 \quad \Rightarrow \quad -y(1 - 64\lambda_1\lambda_2) = 0$$

This means that $y = 0$ or $\lambda_1\lambda_2 = 1/64$. Since each group of two FOC's gives two subcases, there are four cases in all to consider:

Case 1: When $x = 0$ and $y = 0$, it follows from the FOC's that $w = 0$ and $z = 0$ as well. This is impossible, since $\mathbf{x} = (0, 0, 0, 0)$ does not satisfy the constraints.

Case 2: When $x = 0$ and $\lambda_1\lambda_2 = 1/64$, we have that $w = 0$ from the first FOC, and this means that $4y^2 = 4$ and $4z^2 = 36$ from the constraints, so $y = \pm 1$ and $z = \pm 3$. When y, z have the same sign, we find that $\lambda_1 = -3/8$ and $\lambda_2 = -1/24$ from the two middle FOC's. Similarly, if y and z have opposite signs, then $\lambda_1 = 3/8$ and $\lambda_2 = 1/24$. This gives the following candidate points:

$$(\mathbf{x}; \boldsymbol{\lambda}) = (0, 1, 3, 0; -3/8, -1/24), \ (0, 1, -3, 0; 3/8, 1/24),$$
$$(0, -1, 3, 0; 3/8, 1/24), \ (0, -1, -3, 0; -3/8, -1/24)$$

Note that the objective function f has values $f(0, 1, -3, 0) = f(0, -1, 3, 0) = 3$ and $f(0, 1, 3, 0) = f(0, -1, -3, 0) = -3$ at these points.

Case 3: When $y = 0$ and $\lambda_1\lambda_2 = 1/36$, we have $z = 0$ from the second FOC, and this means that $x^2 = 4$ and $9w^2 = 36$ from the constraints, so $x = \pm 2$ and $w = \pm 2$. When x, w have the same sign, we find that $\lambda_1 = 1/2$ and $\lambda_2 = 1/18$ from the first and last FOC's. Similarly, if x and w has opposite signs, then $\lambda_1 = -1/2$ and $\lambda_2 = -1/18$. This gives the following candidate points:

$$(\mathbf{x}; \boldsymbol{\lambda}) = (2, 0, 0, 2; 1/2, 1/18), \ (2, 0, 0, -2; -1/2, -1/18),$$
$$(-2, 0, 0, 2; -1/2, -1/18), \ (-2, 0, 0, -2; 1/2, 1/18)$$

Note that the objective function f has values $f(2, 0, 0, 2) = f(-2, 0, 0, -2) = 4$ and $f(2, 0, 0, -2) = f(-2, 0, 0, 2) = -4$ at these points.

Case 4: When $\lambda_1\lambda_2 = 1/36$ and $\lambda_1\lambda_2 = 1/64$, there are clearly no solutions.

6.4 Lagrange problems

In total, we find eight candidate points $(\mathbf{x}; \boldsymbol{\lambda})$ that satisfy the Lagrange conditions. Among these, the best candidates for maximum points are $(2, 0, 0, 2; 1/2, 1/18)$ and $(-2, 0, 0, -2; 1/2, 1/18)$ with the function value $f = 4$.

Normally, we would conclude from this that $f_{\max} = 4$ is the maximum value in the Lagrange problem, with maximum points $\mathbf{x} = (2, 0, 0, 2), (-2, 0, 0, -2)$. The argument is that the problem has a maximum using the Extreme Value Theorem, and these points are the best candidate points. However, there is a technical condition that has to be checked before we can conclude.

Nondegenerate constraint qualification. We say that an admissible point $\mathbf{x}$ in a Lagrange problem of the form (6.1) satisfy the *nondegenerate constraint qualification* if the Jacobian matrix

$$J = \begin{pmatrix} \dfrac{\partial g_1}{\partial x_1} & \dfrac{\partial g_1}{\partial x_2} & \cdots & \dfrac{\partial g_1}{\partial x_n} \\ \dfrac{\partial g_2}{\partial x_1} & \dfrac{\partial g_2}{\partial x_2} & \cdots & \dfrac{\partial g_2}{\partial x_n} \\ \vdots & \vdots & \ddots & \vdots \\ \dfrac{\partial g_m}{\partial x_1} & \dfrac{\partial g_m}{\partial x_2} & \cdots & \dfrac{\partial g_m}{\partial x_n} \end{pmatrix}$$

has maximal rank at $\mathbf{x}$. In most Lagrange problems, we have that $m < n$. In this case, the nondegenerate constraint qualification (NDCQ) is satisfied at an admissible point $\mathbf{x}$ if rk $J(\mathbf{x}) = m$.

Let us consider the example above, with constraints given by $x^2 + 4y^2 = 4$ and $4z^2 + 9w^2 = 36$. The Jacobian matrix is in this case

$$J = \begin{pmatrix} 2x & 8y & 0 & 0 \\ 0 & 0 & 8z & 18w \end{pmatrix}$$

Since J is a 2×4-matrix, it has maximal rank if rk $J = 2$. This means that the NDCQ fails if $rkJ < 2$, and it is not hard to see that for this to happen, we must have $x = y = 0$ or $z = w = 0$. Hence this cannot happen at an admissible point: If $x = y = 0$, then the constraint $x^2 + 4y^2 = 4$ is not satisfied, and if $z = w = 0$, then the constraint $4z^2 + 9w^2 = 36$ is not satisfied. We conclude that there are no admissible points where NDCQ fails in the Lagrange problem

$$\max f(\mathbf{x}) = xw - yz \quad \text{when} \quad \begin{cases} x^2 + 4y^2 = 4 \\ 4z^2 + 9w^2 = 36 \end{cases}$$

153

This means that the maximum value is $f(2, 0, 0, 2) = f(-2, 0, 0, -2) = 4$: There is a maximum according to the Extreme Value Theorem. Moreover, the maximum is attained at a point $(\mathbf{x}; \boldsymbol{\lambda})$ that satisfies the Lagrange conditions or at an admissible point where NDCQ fails. The last statement follows from the following key result:

Theorem 6.2. *If $f(\mathbf{x}^*)$ is a maximum or minimum in a Lagrange problem, and the nondegenerate constraint qualification holds at $\mathbf{x}^*$, then there are Lagrange multipliers $\boldsymbol{\lambda}^*$ such that $(\mathbf{x}^*; \boldsymbol{\lambda}^*)$ satisfies the Lagrange conditions.*

It follows from Theorem 6.2 that the candidates for maximum or minimum in a Lagrange problem include both points $(\mathbf{x}; \boldsymbol{\lambda})$ that satisfy the Lagrange conditions, and admissible points $\mathbf{x}$ that do not satisfy the NDCQ. Let us give an example that shows that we must consider both types of candidate points:

$$\max f(x, y) = y \quad \text{when} \quad x^2 + y^3 = 0$$

It is clear that $(x, y) = (0, 0)$ is the maximum point, with maximum value $f(0, 0) = 0$. In fact, any admissible point (x, y) must have $y \leq 0$, since $y > 0$ gives $x^2 + y^3 > 0$, and the point $(0, 0)$ is admissible, since it satisfies $x^2 + y^3 = 0$. Let us first write down the Lagrange conditions using the Lagrangian $\mathscr{L} = y - \lambda(x^2 + y^3)$:

$$\mathscr{L}'_x = -\lambda \cdot 2x = 0 \qquad x^2 + y^3 = 0$$
$$\mathscr{L}'_y = 1 - \lambda \cdot 3y^2 = 0$$

From the first FOC, we must have $x = 0$ or $\lambda = 0$, and $x = 0$ gives $y = 0$ by the constraint. When we substitute $\lambda = 0$ or $(x, y) = (0, 0)$ in the second FOC, we get a contradiction. Hence there are no points $(x, y; \lambda)$ that satisfy the Lagrange conditions. The Jacobian matrix is

$$J = \begin{pmatrix} 2x & 3y^2 \end{pmatrix}$$

The NDCQ is that $\operatorname{rk} J = 1$, and the only point where this condition fails is the point $(0, 0)$, where $\operatorname{rk} J(0, 0) = 0$. Since $(0, 0)$ is admissible, we have one admissible point where NDCQ fails. As we have seen, this is the maximum point.

> **Method of Lagrange multipliers**
>
> Candidate points for maximum or minimum in a Lagrange problem are either
>
> a) Points $(\mathbf{x}; \boldsymbol{\lambda})$ that satisfy the Lagrange conditions
> b) Admissible points $\mathbf{x}$ that do not satisfy the NDCQ

Second order conditions. As for unconstrained optimization problems, we have strong results for Lagrange problems when the underlying functions are convex or concave in the following sense:

Theorem 6.3. Let $(\mathbf{x}^*; \boldsymbol{\lambda}^*)$ be a point that satisfies the Lagrange conditions in a Lagrange problem, and consider the function $h(\mathbf{x}) = \mathscr{L}(\mathbf{x}; \boldsymbol{\lambda}^*)$. Then we have:

a) If h is convex, then $\mathbf{x}^*$ is a minimum point
b) If h is concave, then $\mathbf{x}^*$ is a maximum point

Proof. The point $(\mathbf{x}^*; \boldsymbol{\lambda}^*)$ satisfies the first order conditions, and it follows that $\mathbf{x}^*$ is a stationary point for h. This means that when h is convex, $\mathbf{x}^*$ is a minimum point for h. In particular, we have that $h(\mathbf{x}^*) \leq h(\mathbf{x})$ for any admissible point $\mathbf{x}$. We note that $\lambda_i^*(g_i(\mathbf{x}^*) - a_i) = \lambda_i^*(g_i(\mathbf{x}) - a_i)$ for $1 \leq i \leq m$, since $\mathbf{x}^*, \mathbf{x}$ satisfy the constraints. This means that

$$f(\mathbf{x}^*) = h(\mathbf{x}^*) + \lambda_1^* g_1(\mathbf{x}^*) + \ldots + \lambda_m^* g_m(\mathbf{x}^*) = h(\mathbf{x}^*) + \lambda_1^* a_1 + \ldots + \lambda_m^* a_m$$
$$f(\mathbf{x}) = h(\mathbf{x}) + \lambda_1^* g_1(\mathbf{x}) + \ldots + \lambda_m^* g_m(\mathbf{x}) = h(\mathbf{x}) + \lambda_1^* a_1 + \ldots + \lambda_m^* a_m$$

For any admissible point $\mathbf{x}$, we have $h(\mathbf{x}^*) \leq h(\mathbf{x})$, and therefore that

$$f(\mathbf{x}^*) = h(\mathbf{x}^*) + \lambda_1^* a_1 + \ldots + \lambda_m^* a_m \leq h(\mathbf{x}) + \lambda_1^* a_1 + \ldots + \lambda_m^* a_m = f(\mathbf{x})$$

It follows that $\mathbf{x}^*$ is a minimum point in the Lagrange problem. The proof in the case when h is concave is similar. □

Notice that when we find a point $(\mathbf{x}^*; \boldsymbol{\lambda}^*)$ that satisfies the Lagrange conditions, and which is such that $h(\mathbf{x}) = \mathscr{L}(\mathbf{x}; \boldsymbol{\lambda}^*)$ is convex or concave, then $\mathbf{x}^*$ is a minimum or maximum in the Lagrange problem. In particular, it is not necessary to find the other candidate points, to check the NDCQ condition, or to check that the set D of admissible points is bounded in such cases.

6 • Constrained optimization

We end this section with another example. This time we consider a minimum problem where the set D of admissible points is given by a linear equation, and therefore is not bounded:

$$\min f(x, y, z) = x^2 + y^2 + z^2 - xy + xz - yz \text{ subject to } x + y + z = 11$$

The Lagrangian of this problem is $\mathscr{L} = x^2 + y^2 + z^2 - xy + xz - yz - \lambda(x + y + z - 11)$, and the Lagrange conditions are

$$\begin{aligned}\mathscr{L}'_x &= 2x - y + z - \lambda = 0 \\ \mathscr{L}'_y &= -x + 2y - z - \lambda = 0 \\ \mathscr{L}'_z &= x - y + 2z - \lambda = 0\end{aligned} \qquad x + y + z = 11$$

We see that the Lagrange conditions form a linear system, and when we use (x, y, z, λ) as variables, the augmented matrix is given by

$$\begin{pmatrix} 2 & -1 & 1 & -1 & 0 \\ -1 & 2 & -1 & -1 & 0 \\ 1 & -1 & 2 & -1 & 0 \\ 1 & 1 & 1 & 0 & 11 \end{pmatrix}$$

We solve the linear system using Gaussian elimination. We add the second row to the first row to simplify the computations:

$$\begin{pmatrix} 1 & 1 & 0 & -2 & 0 \\ -1 & 2 & -1 & -1 & 0 \\ 1 & -1 & 2 & -1 & 0 \\ 1 & 1 & 1 & 0 & 11 \end{pmatrix} \rightarrow \begin{pmatrix} 1 & 1 & 0 & -2 & 0 \\ 0 & 3 & -1 & -3 & 0 \\ 0 & -2 & 2 & 1 & 0 \\ 0 & 0 & 1 & 2 & 11 \end{pmatrix}$$

$$\rightarrow \begin{pmatrix} 1 & 1 & 0 & -2 & 0 \\ 0 & 1 & 1 & -2 & 0 \\ 0 & 0 & 1 & 2 & 11 \\ 0 & -2 & 2 & 1 & 0 \end{pmatrix}$$

In the last step, we added the third row to the second row, and switched the third and fourth row. Next, we proceed until we get an echelon form:

$$\begin{pmatrix} 1 & 1 & 0 & -2 & 0 \\ 0 & 1 & 1 & -2 & 0 \\ 0 & 0 & 1 & 2 & 11 \\ 0 & 0 & 4 & -3 & 0 \end{pmatrix} \rightarrow \begin{pmatrix} \underline{1} & 1 & 0 & -2 & 0 \\ 0 & \underline{1} & 1 & -2 & 0 \\ 0 & 0 & \underline{1} & 2 & 11 \\ 0 & 0 & 0 & \underline{-11} & -44 \end{pmatrix}$$

$$\rightarrow \begin{pmatrix} \underline{1} & 1 & 0 & -2 & 0 \\ 0 & \underline{1} & 1 & -2 & 0 \\ 0 & 0 & \underline{1} & 2 & 11 \\ 0 & 0 & 0 & \underline{1} & 4 \end{pmatrix}$$

Using back substitution in the linear system obtained from the echelon form, we find that $\lambda = 4$, that $z = 11 - 2 \cdot 4 = 3$, that $y = -3 + 2 \cdot 4 = 5$, and that

$x = -5 + 2 \cdot 4 = 3$. From this computation, it follows that $(x, y, z; \lambda) = (3, 5, 3; 4)$ is the unique solution of the Lagrange condition. We test this candidate point using Theorem 6.3, and see that

$$h(x, y, z) = \mathscr{L}(x, y, z; 4) = f(x, y, z) - 4(x + y + z - 11)$$

has the same Hessian matrix as f. Moreover, we have that $H(f) = 2A$, where A is the symmetric matrix of the quadratic form f, and this gives

$$H(f) = 2A = \begin{pmatrix} 2 & -1 & 1 \\ -1 & 2 & -1 \\ 1 & -1 & 2 \end{pmatrix}$$

This matrix has leading principal minors $D_1 = 2$, $D_2 = 4 - 1 = 3$, and $D_3 = |A|$. We compute the determinant by cofactor expansion along the first row:

$$D_3 = \begin{vmatrix} 2 & -1 & 1 \\ -1 & 2 & -1 \\ 1 & -1 & 2 \end{vmatrix} = 2(4 - 1) - (-1)(-2 + 1) + 1(1 - 2) = 4$$

It follows that $H(f)$ is positive definite, and this means that f and therefore h is convex. Using Theorem 6.3, we conclude that $f_{min} = f(3, 5, 3) = 22$ is the minimum value in the Lagrange problem.

6.5 Kuhn-Tucker problems

A *Kuhn-Tucker problem* is a constrained optimization problem where all constraints are closed inequality constraints. This is an example of a Kuhn-Tucker problem:

$$\min f(x, y, z) = 2x^2 + y^2 + 3z^2 \quad \text{subject to} \quad \begin{cases} x - y + 2z \geq 3 \\ x + y \geq 3 \end{cases}$$

We say that a Kuhn-Tucker problem is in *standard form* if it is written as a maximum problem with all constraints on the form $g(\mathbf{x}) \leq a$:

$$\max f(\mathbf{x}) \quad \text{when} \quad \begin{cases} g_1(\mathbf{x}) \leq a_1 \\ g_2(\mathbf{x}) \leq a_2 \\ \quad \vdots \\ g_m(\mathbf{x}) \leq a_m \end{cases} \quad (6.2)$$

It is not difficult to rewrite any Kuhn-Tucker problem into one in standard form. Constraints of the form $g(\mathbf{x}) \geq a$ can be rewritten as $-g(\mathbf{x}) \leq -a$, and minimum problems can be transformed into maximum problems by changing the sign of the objective function, since a minimizer of f is a maximizer of $-f$. For example, we can write the problem in the example above in standard form as

$$\max -f(x, y, z) = -2x^2 - y^2 - 3z^2 \text{ subject to } \begin{cases} -x + y - 2z & \leq -3 \\ -x - y & \leq -3 \end{cases}$$

For any Kuhn-Tucker problem in standard form (6.2), we assume that $f, g_1, \ldots, g_m$ are C^1 functions on an open set that contains all admissible points.

Let $\mathbf{x}^*$ be an admissible point in a Kuhn-Tucker problem, and consider one of the constraints $g(\mathbf{x}) \leq a$. We have that $g(\mathbf{x}^*) = a$ or $g(\mathbf{x}^*) < a$ since $\mathbf{x}^*$ is admissible, and say that the constraint $g(\mathbf{x}) \leq a$ is *binding* at $\mathbf{x}^*$ in the first case, and that it is *nonbinding* at $\mathbf{x}^*$ in the second case.

As an example, let us consider the set D of admissible points in the following Kuhn-Tucker problem:

$$\max f(x, y) = 9x^2 + 4y^2 \quad \text{when} \quad \begin{cases} 2x + 3y & \geq 12 \\ x^2 + y^2 & \leq 16 \end{cases}$$

The set D is shown in Figure 6.5: The intersection points marked in the figure are the points where both constraints are binding. We can find these points by solving the equations $2x + 3y = 12$ and $x^2 + y^2 = 16$: We get $y = (12 - 2x)/3$, and

$$x^2 + \frac{(12 - 2x)^2}{3^2} = \frac{9x^2 + (12 - 2x)^2}{9} = 16 \Rightarrow 9x^2 + 144 - 48x + 4x^2 = 9 \cdot 16$$

Hence $13x^2 - 48x = 0$, which gives $x = 0$ or $x = 48/13$. We conclude that the two points are $(0, 4)$ and $(48/13, 20/13)$. The line segment and circle segment shown in blue consists of admissible points where one constraint is binding and the other is nonbinding. The points between the line segment and the circle segment are the interior points of D, where both constraints are nonbinding.

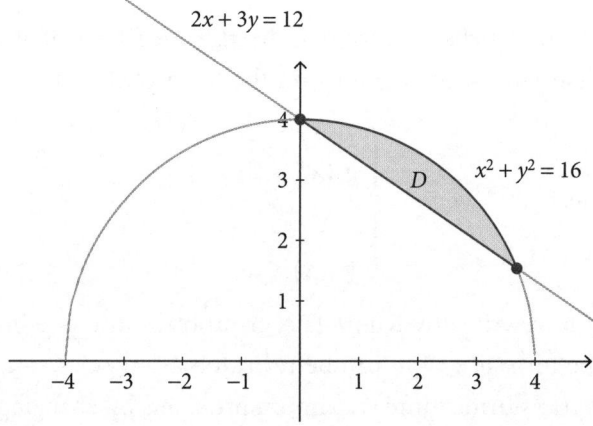

Figure 6.5 The set $D = \{(x, y) : 2x + 3y \geq 12, x^2 + y^2 \leq 16\}$ of admissible points

In a general Kuhn-Tucker problem, we may group the admissible points in D as we have done in the example above:

a) **Admissible points where all constraints are nonbinding:** These are interior points of D, and we can use the methods of Chapter 5 to find candidates for maximum points among them: We look for stationary points of f that are in the interior of D.

b) **Admissible points where all constraints are binding:** These are boundary points of D, and we can use the methods in Section 6.4 to find candidates for maximum points among them: We look for stationary points of the Lagrangian.

c) **Admissible points with binding and nonbinding constraints:** These are also boundary points of D, and we must use mixed methods to find the candidates for maximum points among them.

We shall explain a version of the method of Lagrange multipliers that is adapted to Kuhn-Tucker problems in standard form. It is especially useful when there are many constraints and therefore many mixed cases (where some constraints are binding and others are nonbinding).

The method of Lagrange multipliers for Kuhn-Tucker problems. We consider a Kuhn-Tucker problem in the standard form (6.2), and form the Lagrangian function

$$\mathscr{L}(\mathbf{x}; \boldsymbol{\lambda}) = f(\mathbf{x}) - \lambda_1(g_1(\mathbf{x}) - a_1) - \lambda_2(g_2(\mathbf{x}) - a_2) - \ldots - \lambda_m(g_m(\mathbf{x}) - a_m)$$

where $\mathbf{x} = (x_1, x_2, \ldots, x_n)$ are the variables of the problem, and $\boldsymbol{\lambda} = (\lambda_1, \lambda_2, \ldots, \lambda_m)$ are new variables that we introduce, called the Lagrange multipliers. We define the first order conditions of the Kuhn-Tucker problem to be the n equations

$$\mathscr{L}'_{x_1} = \mathscr{L}'_{x_2} = \ldots = \mathscr{L}'_{x_n} = 0$$

and we define the *complimentary slackness conditions* to be the conditions

$$\lambda_i \geq 0 \text{ and } \lambda_i(g_i(\mathbf{x}) - a_i) = 0 \text{ for } 1 \leq i \leq m$$

The *Kuhn-Tucker conditions* consist of the first order conditions, the constraints and the complementary slackness conditions. The idea is that when we solve this system of equations and inequalities, we find candidate points for maximum in the Kuhn-Tucker problem. The solutions of the Kuhn-Tucker conditions will have the form $(\mathbf{x}; \boldsymbol{\lambda})$, where $\mathbf{x}$ is the candidate point and $\boldsymbol{\lambda}$ is its Lagrange multipliers.

6 • Constrained optimization

The complimentary slackness conditions require that all Lagrange multipliers $\lambda_i \geq 0$, and that $\lambda_i = 0$ if the constraint $g_i(\mathbf{x}) \leq a_i$ is nonbinding. We will discuss the interpretation of the Lagrange multipliers in detail in the next section, but the idea is that if $\lambda_i > 0$, then an increase in the constant a_i would increase the value $f(\mathbf{x})$ of the objective function at points $\mathbf{x}$ where $g_i(\mathbf{x}) \leq a_i$ is binding. This means that for a Kuhn-Tucker problem in standard form, we should have $\lambda_i \geq 0$ for every candidate point for maximum where $g_i(\mathbf{x}) \leq a_i$ is binding. Notice that for interior points of D, where all constraints are nonbinding, the complimentary slackness conditions are $\lambda_1 = \lambda_2 = \ldots = \lambda_m = 0$; this means that we require $\mathbf{x}$ to be a stationary point of f.

We remark that for Kuhn-Tucker problems that are *not in standard form*, we need to consider if we should require $\lambda_i \geq 0$ or $\lambda_i \leq 0$ in each case. The answer would depend on whether the problem was a maximum or minimum problem, and whether the constraint had the form $g_i(\mathbf{x}) \leq a_i$ or $g_i(\mathbf{x}) \geq a_i$.

As an example, we find candidates for maximum in the Kuhn-Tucker problem we mentioned earlier in this section. We use standard form we found earlier to write down the Kuhn-Tucker conditions:

$$\max -f(x,y,z) = -2x^2 - y^2 - 3z^2 \quad \text{subject to} \quad \begin{cases} -x + y - 2z \leq -3 \\ -x - y \leq -3 \end{cases}$$

The Lagrangian is $\mathcal{L} = -2x^2 - y^2 - 3z^2 - \lambda_1(-x + y - 2z + 3) - \lambda_2(-x - y + 3)$, and the first order conditions and the constraints are given by

$$\mathcal{L}'_x = -4x + \lambda_1 + \lambda_2 = 0 \qquad x - y + 2z \geq 3$$
$$\mathcal{L}'_y = -2y - \lambda_1 + \lambda_2 = 0 \qquad x + y \geq 3$$
$$\mathcal{L}'_z = -6z + 2\lambda_1 = 0$$

Moreover, the complementary slackness conditions can be written

$$\lambda_1 \geq 0 \qquad \lambda_1(x - y + 2z - 3) = 0$$
$$\lambda_2 \geq 0 \qquad \lambda_2(x + y - 3) = 0$$

Notice that in the constraint and in the complementary slackness condition, it does not matter if we use the form $g(\mathbf{x}) \geq a$ or $-g(\mathbf{x}) \leq -a$. To find all solutions of the Kuhn-Tucker conditions, we start with the first order conditions, which are easy to solve for x, y, z:

$$x = \frac{\lambda_1 + \lambda_2}{4}, \quad y = \frac{-\lambda_1 + \lambda_2}{2}, \quad z = \frac{2\lambda_1}{6} = \frac{\lambda_1}{3}$$

We use these expressions when we consider the different combinations of binding and nonbinding constraints.

6.5 Kuhn-Tucker problems

The case $x - y + 2z = 3$ and $x + y = 3$. The constraints give the following equations:

$$\frac{\lambda_1 + \lambda_2}{4} - \frac{-\lambda_1 + \lambda_2}{2} + 2\frac{\lambda_1}{3} = 3 \Rightarrow 3(\lambda_1 + \lambda_2) - 6(-\lambda_1 + \lambda_2) + 8(\lambda_1) = 36$$

$$\frac{\lambda_1 + \lambda_2}{4} + \frac{-\lambda_1 + \lambda_2}{2} = 3 \Rightarrow (\lambda_1 + \lambda_2) + 2(-\lambda_1 + \lambda_2) - 12$$

We therefore find that $17\lambda_1 - 3\lambda_2 = 36$ and $-\lambda_1 + 3\lambda_2 = 12$. Adding the two equations, we get $16\lambda_1 = 48$, or $\lambda_1 = 3$. Hence $\lambda_2 = 5$, and this gives $(x, y, z) = (2, 1, 1)$ in the FOC's. Since we have used the FOC's and the constraints to find this point, it remains to check the complementary slackness conditions (CSC's). Since both constraints are binding, the CSC's are $\lambda_1, \lambda_2 \geq 0$, and these conditions hold since $\lambda_1 = 3$ and $\lambda_2 = 5$. It follows that $(\mathbf{x}; \boldsymbol{\lambda}) = (1, 1, 2; 3, 5)$ is the unique candidate point in this case.

The case $x - y + 2z = 3$ and $x + y > 3$. Since the last constraint is nonbinding, we have $\lambda_2 = 0$ by the CSC's. The first constraint reduces to the equation $17\lambda_1 = 36$ when $\lambda_2 = 0$, or $\lambda_1 = 36/17 \geq 0$, and the FOC's with $\lambda_2 = 0$ give $(x, y, z) = (9/17, -18/17, 12/17)$. Since $x + y = -9/17 < 3$, this point does not satisfy the first constraint, and there are no candidate points in this case.

The case $x - y + 2z > 3$ and $x + y = 3$. The first constraint is nonbinding, hence $\lambda_1 = 0$ by the CSC's. The last constraint reduces to the equation $3\lambda_2 = 12$ when $\lambda_1 = 0$, or $\lambda_2 = 4 \geq 0$, and the FOC's with $\lambda_1 = 0$ give that $(x, y, z) = (1, 2, 0)$. Since $x - y + 2z = -1 < 3$, this point does not satisfy the second constraint, and there are no candidate points in this case.

The case $x - y + 2z > 3$ and $x + y > 3$. Both constraints are nonbinding, hence $\lambda_1 = \lambda_2 = 0$ by the CSC's, and this means that $(x, y, z) = (0, 0, 0)$ by the FOC's. Since $x - y + 2z = 0 < 3$, this point does not satisfy the first constraint, and there are no candidate points in this case.

In conclusion, we find a single candidate point for maximum $(\mathbf{x}; \boldsymbol{\lambda}) = (2, 1, 1; 3, 5)$ that satisfies the Kuhn-Tucker conditions, and it has the value $-f(2, 1, 1) = -12$ of the objective function. In other words, there is a single candidate point for minimum in the original problem (which was a minimum problem in nonstandard form), with function value $f(2, 1, 1) = 12$.

If the Kuhn-Tucker problem has a solution, then we would expect the candidate point that we have found to be the optimal one. However, note that the set D of admissible points is not compact in this case, and we cannot use the Extreme Value Theorem. In fact, if we let $x = a$ and $y = z = 0$, then the point $(x, y, z) = (a, 0, 0)$ is admissible if and only if $a \geq 3$, and hence the x-values in D are not bounded from above.

Non-degenerate constraint qualification. Let $\mathbf{x}$ be an admissible point in a Kuhn-Tucker problem, and let $J(\mathbf{x})$ be the matrix obtained from the Jacobian matrix

$$J = \begin{pmatrix} \frac{\partial g_1}{\partial x_1} & \frac{\partial g_1}{\partial x_2} & \cdots & \frac{\partial g_1}{\partial x_n} \\ \frac{\partial g_2}{\partial x_1} & \frac{\partial g_2}{\partial x_2} & \cdots & \frac{\partial g_2}{\partial x_n} \\ \vdots & \vdots & \ddots & \vdots \\ \frac{\partial g_m}{\partial x_1} & \frac{\partial g_m}{\partial x_2} & \cdots & \frac{\partial g_m}{\partial x_n} \end{pmatrix}$$

by deleting the rows corresponding to constraints that are nonbinding at $\mathbf{x}$, and keeping the rows corresponding to constraints that are binding at $\mathbf{x}$. We say that $\mathbf{x}$ satisfies the *nondegenerate constraint qualification* if the matrix $J(\mathbf{x})$ has maximal rank.

Let us consider the example above, with constraints given by $x - y + 2z \geq 3$ and $x + y \geq 3$. The Jacobian matrix is in this case

$$J = \begin{pmatrix} 1 & -1 & 2 \\ 1 & 1 & 0 \end{pmatrix}$$

Let us check, case by case, if there are admissible points that do not satisfy the NDCQ:

The case $x - y + 2z = 3$ and $x + y = 3$. Both constraints are binding, hence we consider the full Jacobian matrix:

$$J(\mathbf{x}) = \begin{pmatrix} 1 & -1 & 2 \\ 1 & 1 & 0 \end{pmatrix}$$

It is a constant matrix of rank 2 since $M_{12,12} = 2 \neq 0$, hence all admissible points satisfy the NDCQ in this case.

The case $x - y + 2z = 3$ and $x + y > 3$. The first constraint is binding, hence we consider the matrix obtained by deleting the last row in the Jacobian matrix:

$$J(\mathbf{x}) = \begin{pmatrix} 1 & -1 & 2 \end{pmatrix}$$

All admissible points satisfy the NDCQ in this case, since $\operatorname{rk} J(\mathbf{x}) = 1$.

6.5 Kuhn-Tucker problems

The case $x - y + 2z > 3$ and $x + y = 3$. The second constraint is binding, hence we consider the matrix obtained by deleting the first row in the Jacobian matrix:

$$J(\mathbf{x}) = \begin{pmatrix} 1 & 1 & 0 \end{pmatrix}$$

All admissible points satisfy the NDCQ in this case, since rk $J(\mathbf{x}) = 1$.

The case $x - y + 2z > 3$ and $x + y > 3$. There is no condition to check, since $J(\mathbf{x})$ is the empty matrix obtained by deleting both rows, and all admissible points satisfy the NDCQ in this case.

In conclusion, we see that all admissible points satisfy the NCDQ in this example.

Theorem 6.4. If $f(\mathbf{x}^*)$ is a maximum in a Kuhn-Tucker problem in standard form, and the nondegenerate constraint qualification holds at $\mathbf{x}^*$, then there are Lagrange multipliers $\boldsymbol{\lambda}^*$ such that $(\mathbf{x}^*; \boldsymbol{\lambda}^*)$ satisfy the Kuhn-Tucker conditions.

It follows from Theorem 6.4 that the candidates for maximum in a Kuhn-Tucker problem in standard form include both points $(\mathbf{x}; \boldsymbol{\lambda})$ that satisfy the Kuhn-Tucker conditions, and admissible points $\mathbf{x}$ that do not satisfy the NDCQ.

> **Method of Lagrange multipliers for Kuhn-Tucker problems**
> Candidate points for maximum in a Kuhn-Tucker problem in standard form are either
> a) Points $(\mathbf{x}; \boldsymbol{\lambda})$ that satisfy the Kuhn-Tucker conditions
> b) Admissible points $\mathbf{x}$ that do not satisfy the NDCQ

Second order conditions. There is a second order condition for Kuhn-Tucker problems, that is very similar to the second order condition for Lagrange problems given in Theorem 6.3:

Theorem 6.5. Let $(\mathbf{x}^*; \boldsymbol{\lambda}^*)$ be a point that satisfies the Kuhn-Tucker conditions in a Kuhn-Tucker problem in standard form, and consider the function $h(\mathbf{x}) = \mathscr{L}(\mathbf{x}; \boldsymbol{\lambda}^*)$. If h is a concave function, then $\mathbf{x}^*$ is a maximum point in the Kuhn-Tucker problem.

Proof. The point $(\mathbf{x}^*; \boldsymbol{\lambda}^*)$ satisfies the first order conditions, and it follows that $\mathbf{x}^*$ is a stationary point for h. This means that when h is concave, $\mathbf{x}^*$ is a maximum point for h. In particular, we have that $h(\mathbf{x}^*) \geq h(\mathbf{x})$ for any admissible point $\mathbf{x}$. We note that $\lambda_i^*(g_i(\mathbf{x}^*) - a_i) = 0$ for $1 \leq i \leq m$, since $\mathbf{x}^*$ satisfies the complementary slackness conditions, and we have that $\lambda_i^*(g_i(\mathbf{x}) - a_i) \leq 0$ for $1 \leq i \leq m$ when $\mathbf{x}$ is an admissible point, since $\lambda_i^* \geq 0$ and $g_i(\mathbf{x}) \leq a_i$. This means that

$$f(\mathbf{x}^*) = h(\mathbf{x}^*) + \lambda_1^* g_1(\mathbf{x}^*) + \ldots + \lambda_m^* g_m(\mathbf{x}^*) = h(\mathbf{x}^*) + \lambda_1^* a_1 + \ldots + \lambda_m^* a_m$$
$$f(\mathbf{x}) = h(\mathbf{x}) + \lambda_1^* g_1(\mathbf{x}) + \ldots + \lambda_m^* g_m(\mathbf{x}) \leq h(\mathbf{x}) + \lambda_1^* a_1 + \ldots + \lambda_m^* a_m$$

For any admissible point $\mathbf{x}$, we have $h(\mathbf{x}^*) \geq h(\mathbf{x})$, and therefore

$$f(\mathbf{x}^*) = h(\mathbf{x}^*) + \lambda_1^* a_1 + \ldots + \lambda_m^* a_m \geq h(\mathbf{x}) + \lambda_1^* a_1 + \ldots + \lambda_m^* a_m \geq f(\mathbf{x})$$

It follows that $\mathbf{x}^*$ is a maximum point in the Kuhn-Tucker problem. $\square$

Note that when we find a point $(\mathbf{x}^*; \boldsymbol{\lambda}^*)$ that satisfies the Kuhn-Tucker conditions, which is such that $h(\mathbf{x}) = \mathscr{L}(\mathbf{x}; \boldsymbol{\lambda}^*)$ is concave, then $\mathbf{x}^*$ is a maximum point in the Kuhn-Tucker problem. In particular, it is not necessary to find the other candidate points, to check the NDCQ condition, or to check that the set D of admissible points is bounded in such cases.

Let us show how to use Theorem 6.5 in an example: We look at the candidate point $(\mathbf{x}; \boldsymbol{\lambda}) = (1, 1, 2; 3, 5)$ that we found earlier in this section when we solved the Kuhn-Tucker conditions for the following problem in standard form:

$$\max -f(x, y, z) = -2x^2 - y^2 - 3z^2 \quad \text{subject to} \quad \begin{cases} -x + y - 2z \leq -3 \\ -x - y \leq -3 \end{cases}$$

The Lagrangian is $\mathscr{L} = -2x^2 - y^2 - 3z^2 - \lambda_1(-x + y - 2z + 3) - \lambda_2(-x - y + 3)$, and to use Theorem 6.5, we find the function $h(\mathbf{x}) = \mathscr{L}(x, y, z; 3, 5)$:

$$h(\mathbf{x}) = -2x^2 - y^2 - 3z^2 - 3(-x + y - 2z + 3) - 5(-x - y + 3)$$
$$= -2x^2 - y^2 - 3z^2 + 8x + 2y + 6z - 24$$

The Hessian of the function h is clearly negative definite, since it is the constant matrix

$$H(h) = \begin{pmatrix} -4 & 0 & 0 \\ 0 & -2 & 0 \\ 0 & 0 & -6 \end{pmatrix}$$

Therefore h is a concave function, and by Theorem 6.5, we have that $\mathbf{x} = (2, 1, 1)$ is the maximum point in the Kuhn-Tucker problem in standard form. The maximum value $-f(2, 1, 1) = -12$. This means that $f(2, 1, 1) = 12$ is the minimum value in the original Kuhn-Tucker problem from the start of this section. Notice that there is a minimum value even though the set of admissible points is not compact.

6.6 Envelope theorem

In this section, we shall consider constrained optimization problems that depend on parameters. A Lagrange problem that depends on a parameter a can be written as

$$\max/\min f(\mathbf{x}; a) \quad \text{when} \quad \begin{cases} g_1(\mathbf{x}; a) = 0 \\ g_2(\mathbf{x}; a) = 0 \\ \vdots \\ g_m(\mathbf{x}; a) = 0 \end{cases} \quad (6.3)$$

Notice the form of the constraints: We can always write the constraints in this way. For instance, we could write $x^2 - y^2 + 3z^2 = 10$ as $x^2 - y^2 + 3z^2 - 10 = 0$. To state the envelope theorem, it is preferable to have all coefficients that may be considered parameters on the left-hand side in the constraint. If we write the constraints in the usual way $g(\mathbf{x}) = a_i$, we would have to take into account that both the function $g(\mathbf{x})$ and the constant a_i could depend on the parameter a in general.

As an example, let us turn the Lagrange problem we considered in Section 6.4 into a Lagrange problem with a parameter a:

$$\max f(\mathbf{x}) = xw - yz \quad \text{when} \quad \begin{cases} x^2 + 4y^2 = 4 \\ 4z^2 + aw^2 = 36 \end{cases}$$

In a concrete case such as this, it is not important rewrite the constraints into the form $x^2 + 4y^2 - 4 = 0$ and $4z^2 + aw^2 - 36 = 0$. The Lagrangian function would in either case be given by

$$\mathscr{L}(\mathbf{x}; \boldsymbol{\lambda}; a) = xw - yz - \lambda_1(x^2 + 4y^2 - 4) - \lambda_2(4z^2 + aw^2 - 36)$$

Recall that we solved this problem for $a = 9$ in Section 6.4, and found the maximum value $f_{\max} = 4$ at $\mathbf{x} = (2, 0, 0, 2), (-2, 0, 0, -2)$ with Lagrange multipliers $\boldsymbol{\lambda} = (3, 5)$.

In a Lagrange problem with parameter a of the form (6.3), the Lagrangian is given by

$$\mathscr{L}(\mathbf{x}; \boldsymbol{\lambda}; a) = f(\mathbf{x}; a) - \lambda_1 \cdot g_1(\mathbf{x}, a) - \lambda_2 \cdot g_2(\mathbf{x}; a) - \ldots - \lambda_m \cdot g_m(\mathbf{x}; a)$$

For each value of the parameter a such that a maximum or a minimum exists, we write $\mathbf{x}^*(a)$ for the maximum or minimum point, $\boldsymbol{\lambda}^*(a)$ for its Lagrange multipliers, and $f^*(a) = f(\mathbf{x}^*(a); a)$ for the maximum or minimum value. We want to determine how the optimal value $f^*(a)$ changes when the parameter a of the problem varies. For instance, we could ask how the maximum value in the example above would change if we changed the value of the parameter from $a = 9$ to $a = 10$.

6 • Constrained optimization

We recall that for unconstrained optimization problems $\max / \min f(\mathbf{x}; a)$, the envelope theorem answered this question. For Lagrange problems that depend on a parameter, we have a similar result:

Theorem 6.6 (Envelope theorem). Let $f(\mathbf{x}; a)$ and $g_i(\mathbf{x}; a)$ for $1 \leq i \leq m$ be C^1 functions on an open set $D \times U \subseteq \mathbb{R}^{n+1}$, and consider the Lagrange problem (6.3) with Lagrangian

$$\mathscr{L}(\mathbf{x}; \boldsymbol{\lambda}; a) = f(\mathbf{x}; a) - \lambda_1 \cdot g_1(\mathbf{x}, a) - \lambda_2 \cdot g_2(\mathbf{x}; a) - \ldots - \lambda_m \cdot g_m(\mathbf{x}; a)$$

If there is an optimal point $\mathbf{x}^*(a)$ with Lagrange multipliers $\boldsymbol{\lambda}^*(a)$ for all $a \in U$ such that $a \mapsto \mathbf{x}^*(a)$ and $a \mapsto \boldsymbol{\lambda}^*(a)$ are C^1 functions on U, then

$$\frac{df^*(a)}{da} = \frac{\partial \mathscr{L}}{\partial a}(\mathbf{x}^*(a), \boldsymbol{\lambda}^*(a); a)$$

for any $a \in U$.

Proof. Since $\mathbf{x}^*(a)$ is admissible, we have that $g_i(\mathbf{x}^*(a); a) = 0$ for $1 \leq i \leq m$. Hence $f^*(a) = f(\mathbf{x}^*(a); a) = \mathscr{L}(\mathbf{x}^*(a); \boldsymbol{\lambda}^*(a); a)$. It follows from the assumptions that $f^*(a)$ is a C^1 function on U, and its total derivative is given by the chain rule:

$$\frac{df^*(a)}{da} = \mathscr{L}'_{x_1}(\mathbf{x}^*(a); \boldsymbol{\lambda}^*(a); a) \cdot \frac{dx_1^*(a)}{da} + \ldots + \mathscr{L}'_{x_n}(\mathbf{x}^*(a); \boldsymbol{\lambda}^*(a); a) \cdot \frac{dx_n^*(a)}{da}$$

$$+ \mathscr{L}'_{\lambda_1}(\mathbf{x}^*(a); \boldsymbol{\lambda}^*(a); a) \cdot \frac{d\lambda_1^*(a)}{da} + \ldots + \mathscr{L}'_{\lambda_n}(\mathbf{x}^*(a); \boldsymbol{\lambda}^*(a); a) \cdot \frac{d\lambda_n^*(a)}{da}$$

$$+ \frac{\partial \mathscr{L}}{\partial a}(\mathbf{x}^*(a); \boldsymbol{\lambda}^*(a); a)$$

$$= \frac{\partial \mathscr{L}}{\partial a}(\mathbf{x}^*(a); \boldsymbol{\lambda}^*(a); a)$$

The last equality follows from the fact that $\mathscr{L}'_{x_1} = \ldots = \mathscr{L}'_{x_n} = \mathscr{L}'_{\lambda_1} = \ldots = \mathscr{L}'_{\lambda_n} = 0$ at $(\mathbf{x}^*(a); \boldsymbol{\lambda}^*(a))$ since the Lagrange conditions are satisfied at this point. □

Let us use the envelope theorem to estimate the maximum value in the problem mentioned above when we change the parameter from $a = 9$ to $a = 10$. In this case, we have that

$$\mathscr{L}(\mathbf{x}; \boldsymbol{\lambda}; a) = xw - yz - \lambda_1(x^2 + 4y^2 - 4) - \lambda_2(4z^2 + aw^2 - 36)$$
$$\Downarrow$$
$$\mathscr{L}'_a = -\lambda_2 w^2$$

At $a = 9$, we have $-\lambda_2^*(9) w^*(9)^2 = -1/18 \cdot 4 = -2/9 \approx -0.22$. If the conditions of the envelope theorem are satisfied for values of a close to $a = 9$, including $a = 10$, then it follows that

$$f^*(10) \approx f^*(9) + (10 - 9) \cdot \mathscr{L}'_a(\pm 2, 0, 0, \pm 2; 1/2, 1/18) = 4 - 2/9 \approx 3.78$$

One may find the exact solution $f^*(10) = 6\sqrt{2/5} \approx 3.79$, so the estimate is quite good in this case.

Finally, let us make some comments regarding the conditions in the envelope theorem as they apply to this case: It is clear that f, g_1, g_2 are C^1 functions, since they are polynomials. The constraints $x^2 + 4y^2 = 4$ and $4z^2 + aw^2 = 36$ define a compact set for all $a > 0$, since the two equations define two ellipses, and the maximum is therefore attained at a candidate point $(\mathbf{x}^*(a); \boldsymbol{\lambda}^*(a))$ satisfying the Lagrange conditions for $a > 0$. It turns out that we may choose the candidate point $(\mathbf{x}^*(a), \boldsymbol{\lambda}^*(a))$ such that it depends smoothly on a, and this is the most difficult condition to check. In fact, solving the Lagrange conditions for any $a > 0$ shows that we can choose

$$(\mathbf{x}^*(a), \boldsymbol{\lambda}^*(a)) = \left(2, 0, 0, \frac{6}{\sqrt{a}}; \frac{3}{2\sqrt{a}}, \frac{1}{6\sqrt{a}}\right)$$

which is C^1 for $a > 0$. Hence the conditions of the envelope theorem are satisfied in this case when $U = (0, \infty)$.

Interpretation of the Lagrange multipliers. When we solve a Lagrange problem using the method of Lagrange multipliers, we usually obtain a solution of the form $(\mathbf{x}^*; \boldsymbol{\lambda}^*)$, where $\mathbf{x}^*$ is the maximum or minimum point. The Lagrange multipliers $\boldsymbol{\lambda}^*$ have an interesting interpretation, which we shall discuss using the envelope theorem. Let us consider the Lagrange problem

$$\max/\min f(\mathbf{x}) \quad \text{when} \quad \begin{cases} g_1(\mathbf{x}) = a_1 \\ g_2(\mathbf{x}) = a_2 \\ \vdots \\ g_m(\mathbf{x}) = a_m \end{cases}$$

where we consider the constants $a_1, a_2, \ldots, a_m$ as parameters. In many economic applications, the constraint $g_i(\mathbf{x}) = a_i$ is a budget constraint, and a_i is the number of units available of a scarce resource. The Lagrangian for this problem is

$$\mathscr{L}(\mathbf{x}; \boldsymbol{\lambda}; a_i) = f(\mathbf{x}) - \lambda_1(g_1(\mathbf{x}) - a_1) - \lambda_2(g_2(\mathbf{x}) - a_2) - \ldots - \lambda_m(g_m(\mathbf{x}) - a_m)$$

and it follows that $\mathscr{L}'_{a_i} = \lambda_i$ for $1 \leq i \leq m$.

This means that if the conditions of the relevant envelope theorem are satisfied, then we have that
$$\frac{df^*(a_i)}{da_i} = \lambda_i^*(a_i)$$
for $1 \leq i \leq m$. In other words, the Lagrange multiplier λ_i is marginal change in optimal value when we vary the parameter a_i. If $g_i(\mathbf{x}) = a_i$ is budget constraint for a scarce resource, the Lagrange multiplier λ_i is often called a *shadow price* for a unit of the scarce resource in question.

Envelope theorem in the Kuhn-Tucker case. We remark that there is a similar interpretation of Lagrange multipliers in Kuhn-Tucker problems. In fact, we have an Envelope Theorem in the Kuhn-Tucker case that is very similar to the result in the Lagrange case. A Kuhn-Tucker problem that depends on a parameter a can be written in standard form as

$$\max f(\mathbf{x}; a) \quad \text{when} \quad \begin{cases} g_1(\mathbf{x}; a) \leq 0 \\ g_2(\mathbf{x}; a) \leq 0 \\ \vdots \\ g_m(\mathbf{x}; a) \leq 0 \end{cases} \quad (6.4)$$

For each value of the parameter a such that a maximum exists, we write $\mathbf{x}^*(a)$ for the maximum point, $\boldsymbol{\lambda}^*(a)$ for its Lagrange multipliers, and $f^*(a) = f(\mathbf{x}^*(a); a)$ for the maximum value. We have the following result:

Theorem 6.7 (Envelope theorem). Let $f(\mathbf{x}; a)$ and $g_i(\mathbf{x}; a)$ for $1 \leq i \leq m$ be C^1 functions on an open set $D \times U \subseteq \mathbb{R}^{n+1}$, and consider the Kuhn-Tucker problem in standard form (6.4) with Lagrangian

$$\mathcal{L}(\mathbf{x}; \boldsymbol{\lambda}; a) = f(\mathbf{x}; a) - \lambda_1 \cdot g_1(\mathbf{x}, a) - \lambda_2 \cdot g_2(\mathbf{x}; a) - \ldots - \lambda_m \cdot g_m(\mathbf{x}; a)$$

If there is a maximum point $\mathbf{x}^*(a)$ with Lagrange multipliers $\boldsymbol{\lambda}^*(a)$ for all $a \in U$ such that $a \mapsto \mathbf{x}^*(a)$ and $a \mapsto \boldsymbol{\lambda}^*(a)$ are C^1 functions on U, then

$$\frac{df^*(a)}{da} = \frac{\partial \mathcal{L}}{\partial a}(\mathbf{x}^*(a), \boldsymbol{\lambda}^*(a); a)$$

for any $a \in U$.

6.7 Minimum variance portfolios

Let $n \geq 1$ be a positive integer, and let $S_1, S_2, \ldots, S_n$ be n securities. For instance, we may think of $S_1, S_2, \ldots, S_n$ as the shares of all the companies we can invest in. We define R_i to be the return of the security S_i, which we think of as a stochastic variable. We write $\mu_i = E(R_i)$ for the expected return and $\sigma_i^2 = \text{Var}(R_i)$ for the variance of R_i, and write $\sigma_{i,j} = \text{Cov}(R_i, R_j)$ for the covariance of R_i and R_j for $1 \leq i, j \leq n$.

When we hold a collection of securities chosen from $S_1, S_2, \ldots, S_n$, we refer to this as a *portfolio*. Let w_i be the share of our total investment held in security S_i for $1 \leq i \leq n$. Then the vector $\mathbf{w} = (w_1, w_2, \ldots, w_n)$ of *portfolio weights* clearly satisfies $w_1 + w_2 + \ldots + w_n = 1$. We remark that we do not require that $w_i \geq 0$. This means that we allow negative portfolio weights $w_i < 0$ (selling the security S_i short). It also means that we allow $w_i > 1$.

The return of the portfolio is $R = w_1 R_1 + w_2 R_2 + \ldots + w_n R_n$, and its expected return is given by
$$E(R) = w_1 \mu_1 + w_2 \mu_2 + \ldots w_n \mu_n$$
since $E(aX + bY) = aE(X) + bE(Y)$ for any stochastic variables X, Y and any constants a, b. Let us write $\boldsymbol{\mu} = (\mu_1, \mu_2, \ldots, \mu_n)$ for the vector of expected returns, and think of this as a column vector. Then the expected portfolio return is $E(R) = \boldsymbol{\mu}^T \cdot \mathbf{w}$, and it is a linear form in the portfolio weights $\mathbf{w}$. The variance of the portfolio return is given by
$$\text{Var}(R) = w_1^2 \sigma_1^2 + 2 w_1 w_2 \sigma_{12} + \ldots + w_n^2 \sigma_n^2$$
since $\text{Var}(aX + bY) = a^2 \text{Var}(X) + 2ab \text{Cov}(X, Y) + b^2 \text{Var}(Y)$ for any stochastic variables X, Y and any constants a, b. Let us write Σ for the covariance matrix

$$\begin{pmatrix} \text{Var}(R_1) & \text{Cov}(R_1, R_2) & \ldots & \text{Cov}(R_1, R_n) \\ \text{Cov}(R_2, R_1) & \text{Var}(R_2) & \ldots & \text{Cov}(R_2, R_n) \\ \vdots & \vdots & \ddots & \vdots \\ \text{Cov}(R_n, R_1) & \text{Cov}(R_n, R_2) & \ldots & \text{Var}(R_n) \end{pmatrix} = \begin{pmatrix} \sigma_1^2 & \sigma_{12} & \ldots & \sigma_{1n} \\ \sigma_{12} & \sigma_2^2 & \ldots & \sigma_{2n} \\ \vdots & \vdots & \ddots & \vdots \\ \sigma_{1n} & \sigma_{2n} & \ldots & \sigma_n^2 \end{pmatrix}$$

Then the variance of the portfolio is $\text{Var}(R) = \mathbf{w}^T \Sigma \mathbf{w}$, and it is a quadratic form in the portfolio weights $\mathbf{w}$ with symmetric matrix Σ. Notice that since $\text{Var}(R) \geq 0$ for any portfolio weights $\mathbf{w}$, the symmetric matrix Σ is positive semidefinite.

6 • Constrained optimization

> **Portfolio returns**
> When $R = w_1 R_1 + w_2 R_2 + \ldots + w_n R_n$ is the return of a portfolio of securities $S_1, S_2, \ldots, S_n$ with portfolio weights $\mathbf{w} = (w_1, w_2, \ldots, w_n)$, we have that
>
> a) $E(R) = \boldsymbol{\mu}^T \mathbf{w}$
> b) $\mathrm{Var}(R) = \mathbf{w}^T \Sigma \mathbf{w}$
>
> where $\boldsymbol{\mu}$ is the vector of expected returns and Σ is the covariance matrix of the returns of the securities $S_1, S_2, \ldots, S_n$.

Let us consider the return R of the portfolio given by the portfolio weights $\mathbf{w}$. We write $\mu_{\mathbf{w}} = E(R)$ for its expected return and $\sigma_{\mathbf{w}}^2 = \mathrm{Var}(R)$ for the variance of its return. Moreover, we write $\sigma_{\mathbf{w}} = \sqrt{\mathrm{Var}(R)}$ for the *standard deviation* of its return, which is often more convenient to use in applications than the variance. We shall study the geometric picture that we get if we plot the points $(\sigma_{\mathbf{w}}, \mu_{\mathbf{w}})$ for all possible portfolio weights $\mathbf{w}$ in a two-dimensional coordinate system. This figure is called the *feasible region*.

In the rest of this section, we assume that $\boldsymbol{\mu}$ and Σ are known, and that they satisfy the following additional conditions:

(A) $\boldsymbol{\mu}$ and $\mathbf{1} = (1, 1, \ldots, 1)$ are linearly independent vectors

(B) Σ is a positive definite symmetric matrix

Under these assumptions, we solve several optimization problems: First, we find the portfolio with minimal variance, and then the portfolio with minimal variance among the portfolios with given expected return μ. Of course, all portfolio weights must satisfy $w_1 + w_2 + \ldots + w_n = 1$, which can be written as $\mathbf{1}^T \cdot \mathbf{w} = 1$ in matrix form. The portfolio that minimizes the variance will of course also minimize the standard deviation, and the idea is that among the portfolios with given expected return, the portfolios with smaller standard deviation are preferable. The standard deviation is often used as a proxy for risk in finance.

Before we consider the optimization problems, let us discuss the assumptions mentioned above and their interpretations. We start with (A): If $\boldsymbol{\mu}$ and $\mathbf{1}$ are linearly dependent vectors, it means that are scalars $(x, y) \neq (0, 0)$ such that

$$x\boldsymbol{\mu} + y\mathbf{1} = \mathbf{0} \quad \Rightarrow \quad \boldsymbol{\mu} = -\frac{y}{x}\mathbf{1} \text{ with } x \neq 0$$

Therefore, the first assumption means that not all securities have the same expected return. The assumption (B) is equivalent to the fact that $\mathbf{w}^T \Sigma \mathbf{w} \neq 0$ for all portfolio weights $\mathbf{w}$, since Σ is positive semidefinite and $\mathbf{w} \neq \mathbf{0}$. In other words, the second assumption means that there is no portfolio with $\text{Var}(R) = 0$. In fact, if $\text{Var}(R) = 0$, then $w_1 R_1 + w_2 R_2 + \ldots + w_n R_n = c$ for a constant c. If $c = 0$, this implies that one of the securities has a return that is a linear combination of the returns of the other securities, which means that one of the securities could be omitted. If $c \neq 0$, the portfolio **w** is an *arbitrage opportunity*; that is, a portfolio with a positive or negative return that is not uncertain.

Minimum variance portfolio. Let us first try to minimize the portfolio variance $\text{Var}(R)$. We therefore consider the optimization problem

$$\min \text{Var}(R) = \mathbf{w}^T \Sigma \mathbf{w} \quad \text{subject to} \quad \mathbf{1}^T \mathbf{w} = 1$$

This is a Lagrange problem with Lagrangian $\mathscr{L} = \mathbf{w}^T \Sigma \mathbf{w} - \lambda(\mathbf{1}^T \mathbf{w} - 1)$, and the first order conditions are given by $2\Sigma \mathbf{w} - \lambda \mathbf{1} = \mathbf{0}$ in accordance with the results of Section 5.6. We claim that there is a unique solution of the Lagrange conditions: Since Σ is positive definite, its eigenvalues $\lambda_1, \ldots, \lambda_n > 0$ are positive. This implies that Σ is invertible, and that Σ^{-1} is a symmetric, positive definite matrix, since its eigenvalues $1/\lambda_1, \ldots, 1/\lambda_n > 0$ are positive. The FOC's therefore give

$$2\Sigma \mathbf{w} - \lambda \mathbf{1} = \mathbf{0} \quad \Rightarrow \quad \Sigma \mathbf{w} = \frac{\lambda}{2} \mathbf{1} \quad \Rightarrow \quad \mathbf{w} = \Sigma^{-1}\left(\frac{\lambda}{2}\mathbf{1}\right) = \frac{\lambda}{2}\Sigma^{-1}\mathbf{1}$$

When we substitute this into the constraint $\mathbf{1}^T \mathbf{w} = 1$, we find that

$$\mathbf{1}^T \mathbf{w} = \mathbf{1}^T \left(\frac{\lambda}{2}\Sigma^{-1}\mathbf{1}\right) = \frac{\lambda}{2} \mathbf{1}^T \Sigma^{-1} \mathbf{1} = 1 \quad \Rightarrow \quad \lambda = \frac{2}{\mathbf{1}^T \Sigma^{-1} \mathbf{1}}$$

Note that Σ^{-1} is positive definite by the comments above, hence $\mathbf{1}^T \Sigma^{-1} \mathbf{1} > 0$. We substitute the value of λ into the expression for **w**, and find the unique solution of the Lagrange conditions

$$(\mathbf{w}^*; \lambda^*) = \left(\frac{1}{\mathbf{1}^T \Sigma^{-1} \mathbf{1}} \Sigma^{-1} \mathbf{1}; \frac{2}{\mathbf{1}^T \Sigma^{-1} \mathbf{1}}\right)$$

To show that this is a minimum in the Lagrange problem, we use the second order condition: We consider the function $h(\mathbf{w}) = \mathscr{L}(\mathbf{w}; \lambda^*) = \mathbf{w}^T \Sigma \mathbf{w} - \lambda^*(\mathbf{1}^T \mathbf{w} - 1)$. Since the first term is a positive definite quadratic form and the last term is linear in **w**, it follows that h is convex. It follows from Theorem 6.3 that $(\mathbf{w}^*; \lambda^*)$ is a minimum in the Lagrange problem. The minimum variance portfolio with portfolio weights $\mathbf{w}^*$ has variance

$$\text{Var}(R) = \left(\frac{1}{\mathbf{1}^T \Sigma^{-1} \mathbf{1}}\right)^2 (\Sigma^{-1}\mathbf{1})^T \Sigma (\Sigma^{-1}\mathbf{1})$$

$$= \left(\frac{1}{\mathbf{1}^T \Sigma^{-1} \mathbf{1}}\right)^2 \mathbf{1}^T \Sigma^{-1} \mathbf{1} = \frac{1}{\mathbf{1}^T \Sigma^{-1} \mathbf{1}}$$

6 • Constrained optimization

since $(\Sigma^{-1}\mathbf{1})^T = \mathbf{1}^T(\Sigma^{-1})^T = \mathbf{1}^T\Sigma^{-1}$. The expected return of the minimum variance portfolio is

$$E(R) = \boldsymbol{\mu}^T\mathbf{w} = \boldsymbol{\mu}^T\left(\frac{1}{\mathbf{1}^T\Sigma^{-1}\mathbf{1}}\Sigma^{-1}\mathbf{1}\right) = \frac{1}{\mathbf{1}^T\Sigma^{-1}\mathbf{1}}\mathbf{1}^T\Sigma^{-1}\boldsymbol{\mu}$$

since $\boldsymbol{\mu}^T\Sigma^{-1}\mathbf{1} = (\boldsymbol{\mu}^T\Sigma^{-1}\mathbf{1})^T = \mathbf{1}^T\Sigma^{-1}\boldsymbol{\mu}^T$. In fact, this expression gives a 1×1 matrix and it is therefore symmetric by definition.

Minimum variance portfolio with given expected return. There are of course portfolios with higher expected return than the minimum variance portfolio. We shall try to minimize the portfolio variance $\text{Var}(R)$ among portfolios of a given level of expected return $E(R) = a$. This leads to the following Lagrange problem with parameter a:

$$\min \text{Var}(R) = \mathbf{w}^T\Sigma\mathbf{w} \quad \text{subject to} \quad \begin{cases} \mathbf{1}^T\mathbf{w} = 1 \\ \boldsymbol{\mu}^T\mathbf{w} = a \end{cases}$$

The Lagrangian is $\mathscr{L} = \mathbf{w}^T\Sigma\mathbf{w} - \lambda_1(\mathbf{1}^T\mathbf{w} - 1) - \lambda_2(\boldsymbol{\mu}^T\mathbf{w} - a)$, and the first order conditions are given by $2\Sigma\mathbf{w} - \lambda_1\mathbf{1} - \lambda_2\boldsymbol{\mu} = \mathbf{0}$ by the results of Section 5.6. We claim that there is a unique solution of the Lagrange conditions: The FOC's give

$$\Sigma\mathbf{w} = \frac{\lambda_1}{2}\mathbf{1} + \frac{\lambda_2}{2}\boldsymbol{\mu}$$
$$\Downarrow$$
$$\mathbf{w} = \Sigma^{-1}\left(\frac{\lambda_1}{2}\mathbf{1} + \frac{\lambda_2}{2}\boldsymbol{\mu}\right) = \frac{\lambda_1}{2}\Sigma^{-1}\mathbf{1} + \frac{\lambda_2}{2}\Sigma^{-1}\boldsymbol{\mu}$$

When we substitute this expression for $\mathbf{w}$ into the two constraints, we get

$$\mathbf{1}^T\left(\frac{\lambda_1}{2}\Sigma^{-1}\mathbf{1} + \frac{\lambda_2}{2}\Sigma^{-1}\boldsymbol{\mu}\right) = 1 \quad \Rightarrow \quad (\mathbf{1}^T\Sigma^{-1}\mathbf{1})\lambda_1 + (\mathbf{1}^T\Sigma^{-1}\boldsymbol{\mu})\lambda_2 = 2$$

$$\boldsymbol{\mu}^T\left(\frac{\lambda_1}{2}\Sigma^{-1}\mathbf{1} + \frac{\lambda_2}{2}\Sigma^{-1}\boldsymbol{\mu}\right) = a \quad \Rightarrow \quad (\boldsymbol{\mu}^T\Sigma^{-1}\mathbf{1})\lambda_1 + (\boldsymbol{\mu}^T\Sigma^{-1}\boldsymbol{\mu})\lambda_2 = 2a$$

We see that the two constraints give a 2×2 linear system in the variables (λ_1, λ_2) with coefficient matrix

$$\begin{pmatrix} \mathbf{1}^T\Sigma^{-1}\mathbf{1} & \mathbf{1}^T\Sigma^{-1}\boldsymbol{\mu} \\ \boldsymbol{\mu}^T\Sigma^{-1}\mathbf{1} & \boldsymbol{\mu}^T\Sigma^{-1}\boldsymbol{\mu} \end{pmatrix} = (\mathbf{1}|\boldsymbol{\mu})^T \cdot \Sigma^{-1} \cdot (\mathbf{1}|\boldsymbol{\mu})$$

Since $\boldsymbol{\mu}$ and $\mathbf{1}$ are linearly independent vectors by assumption (A), we have that $\text{rk}(\mathbf{1}|\boldsymbol{\mu}) = 2$. Moreover, since Σ^{-1} is invertible, we have that

$$\text{rk}\left[(\mathbf{1}|\boldsymbol{\mu})^T \cdot \Sigma^{-1} \cdot (\mathbf{1}|\boldsymbol{\mu})\right] = \text{rk}(\mathbf{1}|\boldsymbol{\mu}) = 2$$

Hence there is a unique solution for (λ_1, λ_2) in the 2×2 linear system, and therefore a unique solution $(\mathbf{w}^*; \lambda_1^*, \lambda_2^*)$ of the Lagrange conditions for any value of a. Since $\mathbf{w}^T \Sigma \mathbf{w}$ is positive definite, it follows from Theorem 6.5 that $\mathbf{w}^*$ is a minimum in the Lagrange problem. The formulas for the optimal portfolio weights $\mathbf{w}^*$ and its variance are possible to write down also in this case, but they are quite complicated.

Numerical examples. We consider concrete numerical data for the three securities Microsoft, Nordstrom and Starbucks, which we call S_1, S_2, S_3. The monthly data for continuously compounded returns in the five-year period from January 1995 to January 2000 give

$$\boldsymbol{\mu} = \begin{pmatrix} 0.0427 \\ 0.0015 \\ 0.0285 \end{pmatrix}, \quad \Sigma = \begin{pmatrix} 0.0100 & 0.0018 & 0.0011 \\ 0.0018 & 0.0109 & 0.0026 \\ 0.0011 & 0.0026 & 0.0199 \end{pmatrix}$$

It is not difficult to see that the assumptions we have used in this section are satisfied for these data. Using the results of this section and some computational tools, we can easily compute the expected return and variance of the minimum variance portfolio, and the minimal variance of a portfolio of given expected return. For instance, one may use the python script given at the end of this section.

The minimal variance portfolio has portfolio weights $\mathbf{w}_M = (0.441, 0.366, 0.193)$, and has expected return $\mu_M = 0.0249$ with standard deviation $\sigma_M = 0.0727$. We have also computed the minimal variance portfolio with given expected return μ for some selected values of μ, and the standard deviation σ of their return. We plot (σ, μ) for these portfolios in the figure below. The feasible region consists of this curve and points to the right of the curve. The minimal variance portfolio corresponds to the point farthest to the left on the curve.

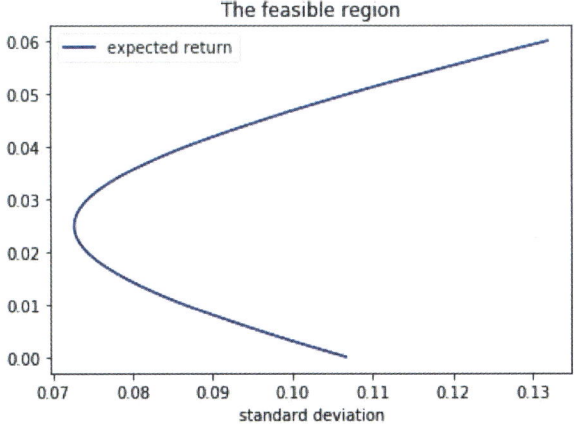

6 • Constrained optimization

We remark, with the gift of hindsight, that it is the company with the *maximum variance* that has performed best since January 2000: As I finish writing this book on March 16 2021, Starbucks has grown by an 18.3 % compounded annual growth rate (CAGR) since the end of January 2000, while Microsoft and Nordstrom have grown by respectively 9.48 % and 9.61 % CAGR since that date.

```python
# Python code: Optimal portfolio theory

import numpy as
np import pandas as pd

# Data for three stock portfolio (Microsoft, Nordstrom, Starbucks)
Mu = np.array([[0.0427],[0.0015],[0.0285]])
Sigma = np.array([[0.0100,0.0018,0.0011],[0.0018,0.0109,0.0026],
    [0.0011,0.0026,0.0199]])

# Compute minimum variance portfolio and its expected return and
# standard deviation
u = np.ones((Mu.shape[0],1)
SigmaInv = np.linalg.inv(Sigma)
w_M = SigmaInv.dot(u)/u.transpose().dot(SigmaInv.dot(u))
mu_M = Mu.transpose().dot(w_M)[0,0]
sigma_M = w_M.transpose().dot(Sigma.dot(w_M))[0,0]**0.5

# Compute standard deviation of minimum variance portfolio with
# expected return mu_0
def stddev(mu_0,Mu,Sigma):
    u = np.ones((Mu.shape[0],1))
    U = np.concatenate((u,Mu),axis=1)
    SigmaInv = np.linalg.inv(Sigma)
    B = U.transpose().dot(SigmaInv).dot(U)
    BInv = np.linalg.inv(B)
    lvec = np.array([[1],[mu_0]])
    w = SigmaInv.dot(U).dot(BInv.dot(lvec))
    sigma = w.transpose().dot(Sigma.dot(w))[0,0]**0.5
    return(sigma)

# Curve showing the standard deviation of the minimum variance
# portfolio with expected returns mu_0
points=[]
for mu in np.linspace(0,0.06,50):
    sigma = stddev(mu,Mu,Sigma)
    points.append((sigma,mu))
p = pd.DataFrame(points, columns=['standard deviation',
    'expected return'])
p.plot(kind='line',x='standard deviation',y='expected return',
    color='blue',title='The feasible region')
```

Problems

Problem 6.1 Sketch each set and determine if it is open, closed, bounded or convex:

a) $\{(x, y) : x^2 + y^2 < 1\}$
b) $\{(x, y) : x^2 + y^2 \geq 2\}$
c) $\{(x, y) : xy \leq 1\}$
d) $\{(x, y, z) : x \geq 0, y \geq 0, z \geq 0\}$
e) $\{(x, y) : x \geq 0, y \geq 0, xy \geq 1\}$
f) $\{(x, y) : \ln(x) + \ln(y) \leq 5\}$

Problem 6.2 Determine whether the subset $D = \{(x, y, z, w) : xw - yz \leq -2\} \subseteq \mathbb{R}^4$ is compact.

Problem 6.3 Solve the following optimization problems:

a) $\max f(x, y) = xy$ subject to $2x + 3y = 12$
b) $\max f(x, y) = x^2 y$ subject to $2x^2 + 5y^2 = 15$
c) $\max f(x, y) = xy$ subject to $x^2 + y^2 \leq 1$
d) $\min f(x, y, z) = x^2 + y^2 + z^2$ subject to $2x^2 + 6y^2 + 3z^2 \geq 36$

Problem 6.4 Solve the Lagrange problem
$$\max f(x, y, z) = xyz \quad \text{subject to} \quad \begin{cases} x^2 + y^2 = 1 \\ x + z = 1 \end{cases}$$

Problem 6.5 Solve the Kuhn-Tucker problem
$$\max f(x, y, z) = xyz \quad \text{subject to} \quad \begin{cases} x + y + z \leq 1 \\ x \geq 0 \\ y \geq 0 \\ z \geq 0 \end{cases}$$

Problem 6.6 We consider the Kuhn-Tucker problem $\max f(x, y, z) = x^2 yz$ subject to $x^2 + 2y^2 - 2z^2 \leq 32$.

a) Solve the Kuhn-Tucker conditions.

b) Does the maximum problem have a solution?

Problem 6.7 We consider the following optimization problem:
$$\max \ln(x^2 y) - x - y \quad \text{subject to} \quad \begin{cases} x + y \geq 4 \\ x \geq 1 \\ y \geq 1 \end{cases}$$

Sketch the set of admissible points, and solve the optimization problem.

6 • Constrained optimization

Problem 6.8 Consider the Lagrange problem
$$\max f(x, y, z) = 100 - x^2 - y^2 - z^2 \quad \text{subject to} \quad x + 2y + z = a$$
with parameter a. Find the solution $(\mathbf{x}^*(a); \lambda^*(a))$ of the Lagrange conditions, show that it is a maximum point, and that
$$\lambda^*(a) = \frac{df^*(a)}{da}$$
where $f^*(a) = f(\mathbf{x}^*(a))$ is the optimal value function.

Problem 6.9 Solve the Lagrange problem
$$\max f(x, y, z) = x + 4y + z \quad \text{subject to} \quad \begin{cases} x^2 + y^2 + z^2 = 216 \\ x + 2y + 3z = 0 \end{cases}$$
Use the Lagrange multiplier to estimate the new maximum value when the constraints are changed to $x^2 + y^2 + z^2 = 220$ and $x + 2y + 3z = -1$.

Problem 6.10 We consider the following Kuhn-Tucker problem:
$$\max f(x, y) = x^2 y^2 \quad \text{subject to} \quad x^2 + y^2 + x^2 y^2 \le 3$$
a) Write down all Kuhn-Tucker conditions for this problem.

b) Find all points $(x, y; \lambda)$ with $x, y \ne 0$ that satisfy the Kuhn-Tucker conditions.

c) Show that the Kuhn-Tucker problem has a maximum, and find the maximum value.

Problem 6.11 We consider the Lagrange problem given by
$$\min f(x, y, z, w) =$$
$$- 4x^2 - 10y^2 - 5z^2 - 5w^2 + 4xz + 4xw - 4yz + 4yw + 6zw$$
$$\text{subject to} \quad x^2 + y^2 + z^2 + w^2 = 6$$

a) Determine whether f is convex or concave.

b) Find all solutions $(x, y, z, w; \lambda)$ of the Lagrange conditions with $\lambda = -12$.

c) Show that any solution in (b) solves the minimum problem.

d) Solve $\max f(x, y, z, w)$ subject to $x^2 + y^2 + z^2 + w^2 = 6$.

CHAPTER 7

Differential equations

7.1 Introduction to differential equations

An *ordinary differential equation* is an equation containing the derivative or higher derivatives of a function in one variable. These are examples of ordinary differential equations:

$$y'(t) + 2y(t) = 6, \qquad y''(t) + y(t) = 1, \qquad y'(t) + y(t) \cdot y''(t) = t^2$$

We shall write $y = y(t)$ for the unknown function and use the name t for the input variable, since it usually represents time.

To simplify notation, we often write y, y', and y'' for $y(t)$, $y'(t)$, and $y''(t)$. For example, we would write the differential equations above simply as

$$y' + 2y = 6, \qquad y'' + y = 1, \qquad y' + yy'' = t^2$$

This is easier to read, when it is understood that $y = y(t)$, $y' = y'(t)$, and $y'' = y''(t)$. The notation $\dot{y}$ for y' and $\ddot{y}$ for y'' is also used in some books.

The *order* of a differential equation is the highest order derivative that appears in the equation. A *first order* differential equation contains the derivative y', but no other derivatives. Hence, any first order differential equation can be written in the form

$$F(t, y, y') = 0$$

for some function F. A *second order* differential equation contains y'', but no higher order derivatives. For example, $y' + 2y = 1$ is a first order differential equation, while $y'' + y = 1$ and $y' + yy'' = t^2$ are second order differential equations.

A *solution* of a differential equation is a function $y(t)$ that satisfies the equation. For example, the function $y(t) = e^{-2t} + 3$ is a solution of the differential equation $y' + 2y = 6$, since $y = e^{-2t} + 3$ gives $y' = -2e^{-2t}$, and therefore that

$$y' + 2y = \left(-2e^{-2t}\right) + 2\left(e^{-2t} + 3\right) = -2e^{-2t} + 2e^{-2t} + 6 = 6$$

To find all solutions of differential equations, we need systematic methods. In this chapter, we shall study systematic methods for solving some classes of first and second order differential equations (including the differential equation $y' + 2y = 6$).

7 • Differential equations

Let us start by considering all differential equations that can be written on the form $y' = f(t)$ for some function $f(t)$. These differential equations are quite easy to solve using integration.

An example is the differential equation $y' = 2t$. The solutions of $y' = 2t$ are all functions $y(t)$ with derivative $y'(t) = 2t$. That is, the solutions are all antiderivatives of $2t$, given by the indefinite integral

$$\int 2t \, dt = t^2 + C$$

The integration constant C is called an *undetermined coefficient*, since there is no information in the differential equation that can be used to determine the value of C. Hence, there is one solution $y(t) = t^2 + C$ for each value of C, and these solutions form an infinite family. We call $y(t) = t^2 + C$ the *general solution* of $y' = 2t$, since this family contains all solutions of the differential equation. For any given value of C, we obtain a *particular solution* of $y' = 2t$, such as

$$y(t) = t^2, \quad y(t) = t^2 - 1, \quad y(t) = t^2 + 3/4$$

corresponding to the (randomly chosen) values $C = 0$, $C = -1$ and $C = 3/4$. We show the graphs of these particular solutions below. One may easily imagine the shape of the graph of other particular solutions, corresponding to other values of C.

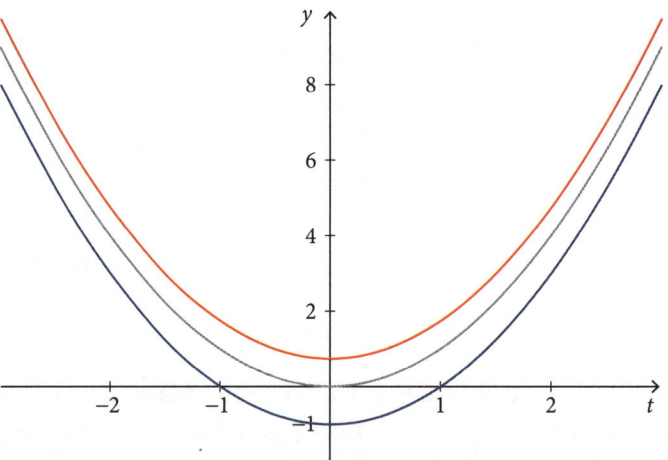

It is not difficult to see that any differential equation of the form $y' = f(t)$ can be solved in the same way, using integration. The solution method is simply given by

$$y' = f(t) \quad \Rightarrow \quad y = \int f(t) \, dt = F(t) + C$$

where $F(t)$ is an antiderivative of $f(t)$, such that $F'(t) = f(t)$. It is not surprising that we need to compute indefinite integrals to find the general solution, and we review methods for computing indefinite integrals in Appendix B. We also note that the general solution contains one undetermined coefficient.

> **Differential equations solvable by simple integration**
>
> Let f be a continuous function. The first order differential equation $y' = f(t)$ has the general solution
>
> $$y(t) = \int f(t)\,dt = F(t) + C$$
>
> where $F(t)$ is an antiderivative of $f(t)$. The general solution depends on one undetermined coefficient C.

Of course, not all first order differential equations are of the form $y' = f(t)$. However, it is typical for first order differential equations that the general solution depends on *one* undetermined coefficient, and we often need to compute indefinite integrals to find the general solution.

It is a hopeless task to solve differential equations in general, even first order differential equations. In this chapter, we shall explain some techniques and methods that can be used to solve certain first and second order differential equations. Others are simply too difficult to solve in this way, and we must use approximation techniques (and often computers) to solve them.

7.2 Modeling change using differential equations

To model how a variable y changes, we use a differential equation in the function $y(t)$. We write t for the independent variable and think of this variable as the *time*. In this situation, we interpret the derivative

$$y' = \lim_{\Delta t \to 0} \frac{\Delta y}{\Delta t} = \lim_{h \to 0} \frac{y(t+h) - y(t)}{h}$$

as the *rate of change* in the variable y. A first order differential equation can often be written in the form $y' = F(t, y)$, and this equation specifies the rate of change in $y = y(t)$ using the expression $F(t, y)$. This is exactly what we mean by a model for change. Let us show some examples.

7 • Differential equations

Example 7.1. Let $y(t)$ denote the UK population (in millions) t years after 1980. The UK population was 56.3 millon in 1980 and 58.9 millon in 2000. This gives us the data points $y(0) = 56.3$ and $y(20) = 58.9$. In order to model the population $y = y(t)$ as a function of t, we need to make an assumption about the growth of the population. Recall that the *rate of change* of the population $y = y(t)$ is its derivative

$$y' = \lim_{\Delta t \to 0} \frac{\Delta y}{\Delta t} = \lim_{h \to 0} \frac{y(t+h) - y(t)}{h}$$

where $\Delta y / \Delta t$ is the average rate of change in the period $[t, t+h]$. For example, in the period 1980–2000, the population increased by the average rate of change

$$\frac{y(20) - y(0)}{20} = \frac{58.9 - 56.3}{20} = 0.13$$

or 0.13 million/year. An assumption about the rate of change leads to a differential equation. One choice of model is the *simple exponential growth model*. In this model, we assume that

$$y' = r \cdot y$$

for a constant r. In other words, the rate of change $y' = y'(t)$ is proportional to the population $y = y(t)$. It turns out that the general solution of this differential equation is $y(t) = C \cdot e^{rt}$, where C is an undetermined coefficient. You may verify that this is a solution of $y' = ry$, and we will show how to obtain the general solution of this equation in Section 7.4 - 7.5. When we fit the general solution $y(t) = C e^{rt}$ to the given data points, we see that $y(0) = 56.3$ gives

$$56.3 = C \cdot e^{r \cdot 0} = C \quad \Rightarrow \quad C = 56.3$$

and that $y(20) = 58.9$ gives

$$58.9 = 56.3 e^{r \cdot 20} \quad \Rightarrow \quad e^{20r} = 58.9/56.3 \quad \Rightarrow \quad r = \frac{\ln(58.9/56.3)}{20} \approx 0.00226$$

This means that $y(t) = 56.3 \, e^{0.00226 \, t}$. The graph of the solution is shown below.

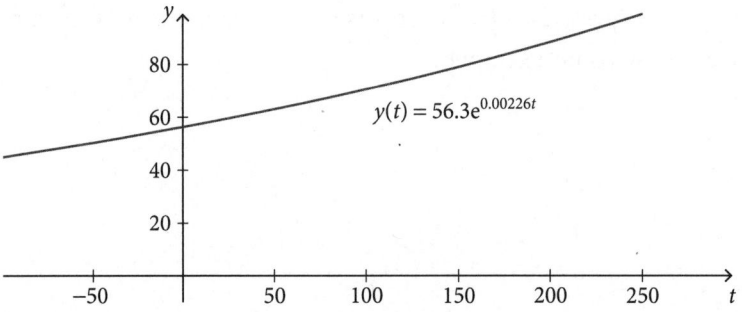

According to this model, the UK population will reach 80 million around the year 2135, since

$$56.3\, e^{0.00226\, t} = 80 \;\rightarrow\; e^{0.00226\, t} = 80/56.3 \;\rightarrow\; t = \frac{\ln(80/56.3)}{0.00226} \approx 155$$

and $t = 155$ corresponds to the year 2135. In the long term, the population will increase without bounds, since

$$\lim_{t \to \infty} y(t) = \lim_{t \to \infty} 56.3 \cdot e^{0.00226\, t} = \infty$$

A differential equation in $y(t)$, where t is time, gives a model for the changes in the variable $y = y(t)$. The derivative y' is interpreted as the rate of change in y. We need additional information about the initial state to determine the solution $y = y(t)$ completely.

Example 7.2. The simple exponential growth model is seldom a realistic model. In most practical situations, the growth of $y = y(t)$ would be restricted by the size of y. For example, when y is a population, limited resources would keep the growth rate y' in the population from growing equally fast as y. Instead of the differential equation $y' = ry$, we could consider

$$y' = r \cdot y \left(1 - \frac{y}{K}\right)$$

This is called a *logistic growth model*. The positive constant K is called the *carrying capacity*. We see that when y is much smaller than K, the factor $1 - y/K$ is close to 1, and $y(t)$ will have close to simple exponential growth. However, when y grows large and approaches K, the factor $1 - y/K$ is close to zero, and $y(t)$ will have close to zero growth. The graph of the solution of the logistic growth model is shown below (blue curve). The carrying capacity K (dotted) and the corresponding solution of the simple exponential growth model (red curve) is shown for comparison. The solution of the logistic growth model is sometimes called an S-curve.

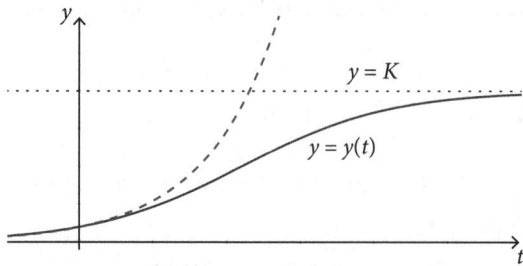

It turns out that the general solution of the logistic differential equation is

$$y(t) = K \cdot \frac{C e^{rt}}{1 + C e^{rt}}$$

where C is an undetermined coefficient. It is possible to verify that this function is a solution of $y' = ry(1 - y/K)$, and we will show how to obtain the general solution of this equation in Section 7.4. Note that if $r > 0$, then $y(t) \to K$ when $t \to \infty$.

7.3 First order differential equations

A first order differential equation in the unknown function $y = y(t)$ is an equation that involves expressions in t, y and y'. Many first order differential equations can be written in the form

$$y' = F(t, y)$$

for some function F, and we shall only consider first order differential equations of this type. Examples of first order differential equations are

$$y' = -y^2 e^t, \quad y' = ty - 1, \quad y' = \frac{y^2 - 3t^2 y}{t^3 - 2yt}$$

In Section 7.4 - 7.7, we shall explain methods for solving *certain*, but not all, first order differential equations that can be written as $y' = F(t, y)$.

For a general first order differential equation $y' = F(t, y)$, we expect that a general solution $y = y(t)$ exists and that it depends on one undetermined coefficient C. For example, the differential equation $y' = 2t$ has the general solution $y(t) = t^2 + C$. If the value of $y = y(t)$ at an initial time $t = t_0$ is given, this is called an *initial value* for the differential equation. In this case, we expect that there is a unique solution of $y' = F(t, y)$ such that $y(t_0) = y_0$. For example, the differential equation $y' = 2t$ with initial value $y(0) = 1$ has a unique solution $y(t) = t^2 + 1$, since the condition $y(0) = 1$ in the general solution $y(t) = t^2 + C$

gives $1 = 0^2 + C$, which we can solve for C to determine that $C = 1$. The unique particular solution passing through the point $(t_0, y_0) = (0, 1)$, corresponding to the initial condition $y(0) = 1$, is shown below (blue curve).

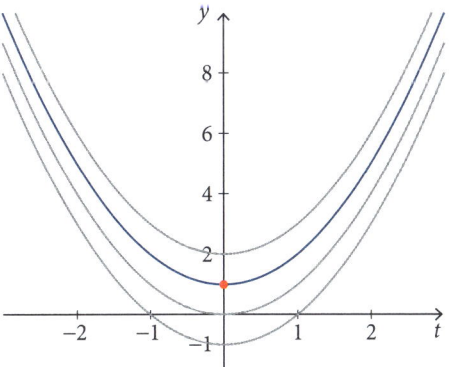

A first order differential equation $y' = F(t, y)$ with an initial condition $y(t_0) = y_0$ is called an *initial value problem*. Recall that $F = F(t, y)$ is called a C^1 function if it is continuous and has continuous partial derivatives; we will only consider initial value problems where this assumption holds. We state the following precise result on the solutions of initial value problems $y' = F(t, y)$, $y(t_0) = y_0$ where F is C^1:

Theorem 7.3. Let $y' = F(t, y)$, $y(t_0) = y_0$ be a first order initial value problem. If F is a C^1 function in a neighborhood around the point (t_0, y_0), then the initial value problem has a unique solution $y = y(t)$.

7.4 Separable differential equations

A first order differential equation is called *separable* if it can be written in the form
$$y' = f(t) \cdot g(y)$$
for functions $f(t)$ and $g(y)$. An example of a separable differential equation is $y' + 2y = 6$, which can be written in the form $y' = 6 - 2y = 2 \cdot (3 - y)$. Another example is $y' + y = 2ty$, which can be written in the form $y' = 2ty - y = (2t - 1) \cdot y$. An example of a first order differential equation that is *not* separable is $y' = y + t$.

We note that the first order differential equations $y' = f(t)$ solvable by simple integration that we studied in Section 7.1 are special cases of separable differential equations, since they can be written in the form $y' = f(t) \cdot 1$. However, far from all separable differential equations are of this type, and we need additional methods to be able to solve separable differential equations where y appears explicitly.

7 • Differential equations

In general, any separable differential equation can be solved by a technique called *separation of variables*. When the equation is written in the form $y' = f(t) \cdot g(y)$, the solution method is given by the following steps:

$$y' = f(t) \cdot g(y)$$

$$\frac{1}{g(y)} \cdot y' = f(t)$$

$$\int \frac{1}{g(y)} \cdot y' \, dt = \int f(t) \, dt$$

$$\int \frac{1}{g(y)} \, dy = \int f(t) \, dt$$

We have divided both sides with $g(y)$ and integrated both sides with respect to t. To rewrite the integral on the left-hand side, we use the chain rule for the composite function $1/g(y)$ with $y = y(t)$, which can be written in the form $dy = y' \, dt$. We obtain two indefinite integrals that we can solve, at least in principle.

Separable differential equations

Let f, g be continuous functions. The first order separable differential equation $y' = f(t) \cdot g(y)$ has the general solution given by

$$\int \frac{1}{g(y)} \, dy = \int f(t) \, dt$$

In particular, the general solution can be written as $G(y) + C_1 = F(t) + C_2$ in implicit form, and rewritten as $G(y) = F(t) + C$ with $C = C_2 - C_1$. It depends on one undetermined coefficient C.

When we use this method, we obtain the general solution as $G(y) = F(t) + C$. It is called an *implicit form* of the solution. We prefer to solve this equation for y, to obtain a solution $y = y(t)$ in *explicit form*, if possible.

To illustrate this method, consider the differential equation $y' = 2y$ as an example. Using the factorization $2y = 2 \cdot y$, with $f(t) = 2$ and $g(y) = y$, we obtain

$$y' = 2 \cdot y$$

$$\frac{1}{y} \cdot y' = 2$$

$$\int \frac{1}{y} \cdot y' \, dt = \int 2 \, dt$$

$$\int \frac{1}{y} \, dy = \int 2 \, dt$$

Then we have to compute these integrals. The integrals are in this case not difficult to compute, and we get

$$\int \frac{1}{y}\,dy = \ln|y| + C_1 \quad \text{and} \quad \int 2\,dt = 2t + C_2$$

and therefore $\ln|y| + C_1 = 2t + C_2$ is the general solution in implicit form. We solve for y to get it in the explicit form $y = y(t)$. We get

$$\ln|y| + C_1 = 2t + C_2$$
$$\ln|y| = 2t + C_2 - C_1$$
$$|y| = e^{2t + C_2 - C_1} = e^{2t} \cdot e^{C_2 - C_1}$$
$$y = \pm e^{C_2 - C_1} \cdot e^{2t} = K e^{2t}$$

with $K = \pm e^{C_2 - C_1}$, which is an undetermined coefficient. The general solution of the differential equation in explicit form is therefore $y(t) = K e^{2t}$.

7.5 Linear first order differential equation

A first order differential equation $y' = F(t, y)$ is *linear* if $F(t, y)$ is linear in y. More precisely, the differential equation is linear if and only if it can be written in the form

$$y' + a(t) \cdot y = b(t) \quad \Leftrightarrow \quad y' = b(t) - a(t) \cdot y$$

for functions $a(t)$ and $b(t)$. Examples of linear first order differential equations are $y' + 2y = 6$ and $y' = t^2 - ty$. The form $y' + a(t) \cdot y = b(t)$ is called the *standard form* of linear first order differential equations, and it is the one we use when we solve these equations. The form $y' = b(t) - a(t) \cdot y$ is included to show that these equations can be written as $y' = F(t, y)$ for a function $F(t, y)$ that is linear in y.

Let us postpone the general case for the moment, and start by considering the special case where $a(t)$ and $b(t)$ are constants. In this case, we write the equation as

$$y' + ay = b$$

where $a = a(t)$ and $b = b(t)$ are constants. If $a = 0$, then $y' = b$ is easy to solve by simple integration, and we get the general solution $y = bt + C$. When $a \neq 0$, we notice that the equation is separable, since it can be written

$$y' + ay = b \quad \Leftrightarrow \quad y' = b - ay = 1 \cdot (b - ay)$$

with factorization given by $f(t) = 1$ and $g(y) = b - ay$. By separation of variables, this gives

$$\int \frac{1}{b - ay}\,dy = \int 1\,dt$$

7 • Differential equations

The first integral is

$$\int \frac{1}{b-ay}\, dy = \int \frac{1}{u} \cdot \frac{du}{(-a)} = \frac{1}{-a} \cdot \ln|u| + C_1 = -\frac{1}{a}\ln|b-ay| + C_1$$

using the substitution $u = b - ay$ with $du = -a \cdot dy$ since $u' = -a$. This gives

$$-\frac{1}{a}\ln|b-ay| + C_1 = t + C_2$$

$$\ln|b-ay| = -a(t + C_2 - C_1) = -at - a(C_2 - C_1)$$

$$b - ay = \pm e^{-at - a(C_2 - C_1)} = Ke^{-at}$$

$$ay = b - Ke^{-at}$$

$$y = \frac{b}{a} - \frac{K}{a}e^{-at} = \frac{b}{a} + Ce^{-at}$$

with $K = \pm e^{-a(C_2 - C_1)}$ and $C = -K/a$. Therefore, $y = b/a + Ce^{-at}$ is the general solution of $y' + ay = b$ when a, b are constants with $a \neq 0$.

This a very useful special case. For instance, the differential equation $y' = ry$ of the simple exponential growth model can be solved using the formula above, since $y' = ry$ can be written $y' - ry = 0$ with $a = -r$ and $b = 0$. This gives the solution $y = b/a + Ce^{-at} = Ce^{rt}$. It also illustrates the fact that some first order differential equations are both separable and linear.

In general, linear first order differential equations can be solved using *integrating factors*: We choose an integrating factor $u = u(t)$ and multiply the differential equation by this factor. This gives

$$y' + a(t) \cdot y = b(t)$$
$$uy' + ua(t) \cdot y = ub(t)$$

We want to choose $u = u(t)$ such that the left-hand side of the above equation is $(uy)' = uy' + u'y$. For this to be the case, we see that we must choose $u = u(t)$ such that $u' = a(t)u$. This is a separable differential equation in $u = u(t)$ that we can solve by the separation of variables

$$u' = a(t) \cdot u$$
$$\frac{1}{u} \cdot u' = a(t)$$
$$\int \frac{1}{u}\, du = \int a(t)\, dt$$
$$\ln|u| = \int a(t)\, dt$$

and we therefore choose the integrating factor $u = u(t)$ to be given by

$$u(t) = e^{\int a(t)\, dt}$$

7.5 Linear first order differential equation

We know that this choice for $u = u(t)$ makes $u y' + u a(t) \cdot y$ equal to $(uy)'$. We use this to solve the equation:

$$y' + a(t) \cdot y = b(t)$$
$$uy' + ua(t) \cdot y = ub(t)$$
$$(uy)' = u(t) \cdot b(t)$$
$$uy = \int u(t) \cdot b(t) \, dt$$
$$y = \frac{1}{u} \int u(t) \cdot b(t) \, dt = \frac{1}{u(t)} \int u(t) \cdot b(t) \, dt$$

Note that $u = u(t)$, and we switch between using u and $u(t)$ above. Note also that the formula for the integrating factor gives an undetermined coefficient. For instance, in the differential equation $y' + y = e^t$, the formula gives

$$\int a(t) \, dt = \int 1 \, dt = t + C \quad \Rightarrow \quad u = e^{\int a(t) \, dt} = e^{t+c}$$

We choose the integrating factor as simple as possible. In this case, we choose $u = e^t$.

Linear first order differential equations

Let f, g be continuous functions. The linear first order differential equation $y' + a(t) y = b(t)$ has the general solution given by

$$y = \frac{1}{u(t)} \cdot \int u(t) \cdot b(t) \, dt$$

where $u(t) = e^{\int a(t) \, dt}$ is an integrating factor.

To illustrate the method, consider the differential equation $y' - 2y = 4t$ as an example. In this case, the differential equation is first order linear in standard form, with $a(t) = -2$ (a constant) and $b(t) = 4t$. We first compute an integrating factor:

$$\int a(t) \, dt = \int -2 \, dt = -2t + C \quad \Leftrightarrow \quad u = e^{-2t+C} = e^{-2t}$$

We have chosen the integrating factor $u = e^{-2t}$ with $C = 0$, as any value of C would work. This gives

$$y' - 2y = 4t$$
$$e^{-2t}y' - 2e^{-2t} \cdot y = 4te^{-2t}$$
$$(e^{-2t}y)' = 4te^{-2t}$$
$$e^{-2t}y = \int 4te^{-2t}\,dt$$
$$y = e^{2t}\int 4te^{-2t}\,dt$$

Notice that the step where we simplify the left-hand side to $(e^{-2t}y)'$ follows from the construction of $u(t)$; we have chosen u such that this would be the case. Finally, we have to solve the integral on the right-hand side using integration by parts

$$\int 4te^{-2t}\,dt = 4t \cdot \left(-\frac{1}{2}e^{-2t}\right) - \int 4 \cdot \left(-\frac{1}{2}e^{-2t}\right) dt$$
$$= -2te^{-2t} + \int 2e^{-2t}\,dft$$
$$= -2te^{-2t} - e^{-2t} + C$$

with $u' = e^{-2t}$ and $v = 4t$, which gives $u = -e^{-2t}/2$ and $v' = 4$. The general solution of the differential equation is therefore

$$y = e^{2t} \cdot \left(-2te^{-2t} - e^{-2t} + C\right) = -2t - 1 + Ce^{2t} = Ce^{2t} - 2t - 1$$

with an undetermined coefficient C.

7.6 Superposition principle

In this section, we explain the *superposition principle* and how to use it to solve linear first order differential equations. The principle gives a decomposition of the general solution $y = y(t)$ into two components

$$y(t) = y_h(t) + y_p(t)$$

and a description of the two components that gives an alternative method for solving linear first order differential equations. In many cases, this method is easier to use than integrating factors.

We shall introduce *operators* to explain the superposition principle. We think of an operator as a "function of functions", which takes a function as input and produces a new function as output. In concrete terms, the operators that we use

7.6 Superposition principle

in linear first order differential equations are the *first order differential operators* of the form $D = p(t) \, d/dt + q(t)$. It operates on an input function $y = y(t)$ by

$$D(y) = \left(p(t) \frac{d}{dt} + q(t) \right) y = p(t) \, y' + q(t) \, y$$

and is called a differential operator since it involves differentiating the input function $y = y(t)$.

Any linear first order differential equation $y' + a(t) \, y = b(t)$ can be written in the form $D(y) = b(t)$, where $y = y(t)$ is the unknown function, and $D = d/dt + a(t)$ is a differential operator, and we interpret a solution of the differential equation to be an input function $y = y(t)$ such that the output function $D(y)$ is $b(t)$. For example, we write the differential equation $y' + y = e^t$ as $D(y) = e^t$ with $D = d/dt + 1$. Using the (random) input functions $y(t) = t, t^2, e^t$, we get

$$D(t) = 1 + t, \quad D(t^2) = 2t + t^2, \quad D(e^t) = e^t + e^t = 2e^t$$

and neither of these input functions are solutions of the linear differential equation since the requirement is that $D(y) = e^t$.

In general, we say that an operator D is *linear* if $D(y_1 + y_2) = D(y_1) + D(y_2)$ and $D(cy) = cD(y)$ for all functions $y_1 = y_1(t), y_2 = y_2(t)$ and all constants c. It is not difficult to see that any first order differential operator $p(t) \, d/dt + q(t)$ is linear. To check the two requirements, we compute

$$D(y_1 + y_2) = p(t) \cdot (y_1 + y_2)' + q(t) \cdot (y_1 + y_2)$$
$$= p(t) \cdot y_1' + p(t) \cdot y_2' + q(t) y_1 + q(t) y_2 = D(y_1) + D(y_2)$$
$$D(cy) = p(t) \cdot (cy)' + q(t) \cdot (cy) = cp(t) y' + cq(t) y = cD(y)$$

The real reason why $y' + a(t) \, y = b(t)$ is called a *linear* differential equation is, of course, that it can be written as $D(y) = b(t)$ for a linear operator D.

First order differential operators

Any first order differential operator $D = p(t) \, d/dt + q(t)$ is linear.

A linear first order differential equation $y' + a(t) \, y = b(t)$ is called *homogeneous* if $b(t) = 0$, and *inhomogeneous* otherwise. We define $y_h(t)$ to be the general solution of the homogeneous equation

$$y' + a(t) \, y = 0$$

obtained by replacing $b(t)$ with zero. If $a(t) = a$ is constant, it is easy to find y_h. We can use the formula in the case $y' + ay = b$ from Section 7.5, which gives

$$y_h(t) = b/a + Ce^{-at} = Ce^{-at}$$

7 • Differential equations

We say that the equation has *constant coefficients* when $a(t) = a$ is a constant. If $a(t)$ is non-constant, we must use an integrating factor to find $y_h(t)$.

We call $y_p = y_p(t)$ a *particular solution* of $y' + a(t)y = b(t)$ if it is a solution. We can often find y_p by considering special cases. For example, in the differential equation $t^2 y' + \ln(t) y = \ln(t)$, we guess that a constant $y_p = A$ could be a solution. To verify this and find A, we substitute $y(t) = A$ and $y'(t) = 0$ into the differential equation, which gives $\ln(t) \cdot A = \ln(t)$, or $A = 1$. Therefore, $y_p(t) = 1$ is a particular solution in this case.

The differential equation $y' + a(t)y = b(t)$ can be written as $D(y) = b(t)$. If we have found a particular solution y_p of $D(y) = b(t)$, and the general solution y_h of the homogeneous equation $D(y) = 0$, then $y = y_h + y_p$ is clearly a solution of $D(y) = b(t)$ since

$$D(y) = D(y_h + y_p) = D(y_h) + D(y_p) = 0 + b(t) = b(t)$$

by definition. It also follows that any solution of the equation must be of the form $y = y_h + y_p$, since for any solution y we have

$$D(y - y_p) = D(y) - D(y_p) = b(t) - b(t) = 0$$

and therefore that $y - y_p$ is a homogeneous solution, or $y - y_p = y_h$, which gives $y = y_h + y_p$. This proves the superposition principle:

> **Superposition principle**
> The general solution of the linear differential equation $y' + a(t)y = b(t)$ can be written as $y = y_h + y_p$, where the y_h is the general solution of the *homogeneous* equation $y' + a(t)y = 0$, and y_p is any particular solution of $y' + a(t)y = b(t)$.

To illustrate the usefulness of the superposition principle, let us use it to solve the differential equation $y' + y = e^t$. By the superposition principle, the general solution is $y = y_h + y_p$. The homogeneous solution is easy to find, since $a(t) = 1$ is a constant:

$$y' + y = 0 \quad \Rightarrow \quad y = \frac{b}{a} + Ce^{-at} = Ce^{-t}$$

Therefore $y_h = Ce^{-t}$. To find y_p, we just need one particular solution of $y' + y = e^t$. We try $y = e^t$, which gives $D(y) = e^t + e^t = 2e^t$ with $D = d/dt + 1$. The first attempt $y = e^t$ is not a solution, but since $D(e^t/2) = D(e^t)/2 = 2e^t/2 = e^t$, it follows that $y_p = e^t/2$ is a particular solution. The general solution is therefore

$$y = y_h + y_p = Ce^{-t} + \frac{1}{2}e^t$$

by the superposition principle.

7.7 Exact differential equations

A first order differential equation $y' = F(t, y)$ is *exact* if it can be written in the form

$$\frac{\partial h}{\partial t} + \frac{\partial h}{\partial y} \cdot y' = 0$$

for a differentiable function $h = h(t, y)$. In this case, we call $h'_t + h'_y \cdot y' = 0$ an *exact form* of the differential equation. It is simple to write any first order differential equation $y' = F(t, y)$ as $p(t, y) + q(t, y) \cdot y' = 0$. However, the requirement that $p = h'_t$ and $q = h'_y$ for a common function $h = h(t, y)$ is restrictive and must be checked to see whether the differential equation is in exact form.

For example, the differential equation $y' = 2y$, which is both separable and linear, can be written in the form $p(t, y) + q(t, y) \cdot y' = 0$ in many different ways. Let us first write it as

$$-2y + 1 \cdot y' = 0$$

with $p(t, y) = -2y$ and $q(t, y) = 1$. There is no function $h(t, y)$ that satisfies the requirement that $h'_t = -2y$ and $h'_y = 1$. To see this, note that any function $h(t, y)$ satisfying $h'_y = 1$ must have the form $h(t, y) = y + \phi(t)$ for some function $\phi(t)$ that is constant in y. Using this, we see that $h'_t = 0 + \phi'(t) = \phi'(t)$. Since $\phi(t)$ and $\phi'(t)$ are expressions in t (that do not include y), it is impossible to have $\phi'(t) = 2y$.

Let us instead take advantage of the fact that the differential equation $y' = 2y$ is separable, and rewrite it as

$$\frac{1}{y} \cdot y' = 2 \iff -2 + \frac{1}{y} \cdot y' = 0$$

with $p(t, y) = -2$ and $q(t, y) = 1/y$. If we choose $h(t, y) = -2t + \ln |y|$, we see that $h'_t = -2 = p$ and $h'_y = 1/y = q$. Hence the differential equation $y' = 2y$ is exact, and we obtained an exact form by multiplying the equation $-2y + y' = 0$ with $1/y$.

We could also take advantage of the fact that the differential equation $y' = 2y$ is linear. Writing it as $y' - 2y = 0$, we see that its integrating factor is $u = e^{-2t}$. After multiplication with u, we can rewrite the differential equation as

$$y' - 2y = 0 \iff -2y e^{-2t} + e^{-2t} \cdot y' = 0$$

with $p(t, y) = -2y e^{-2t}$ and $q(t, y) = e^{-2t}$. It we choose $h(t, y) = y e^{-2t}$, we see that $h'_t = -2y e^{-2t} = p$ and $h'_y = e^{-2t} = q$. Hence the differential equation is exact, and we obtained an exact form by multiplying it by the integrating factor e^{-2t}.

Proposition 7.4. *If a first order differential equation is separable or linear, then it is exact.*

7 • Differential equations

In general, we use the following method for solving exact differential equations: First, we find a function $h = h(t, y)$ such that the differential equation can be written in the form

$$\frac{\partial h}{\partial t} + \frac{\partial h}{\partial y} \cdot y' = 0$$

This is the hard part. Then we recall that the solution of the differential equation is supposed to be a function $y = y(t)$. When we take this into consideration, and compute the derivative of $h = h(t, y) = h(t, y(t))$ with respect to t, we get

$$\frac{dh}{dt} = \frac{\partial h}{\partial t} + \frac{\partial h}{\partial y} \cdot \frac{dy}{dt} = \frac{\partial h}{\partial t} + \frac{\partial h}{\partial y} \cdot y'$$

This is sometimes called the *total derivative* of h. We can think of the two terms as the direct change in h as a result of a change in t, and the indirect change as a result of a change in y. The total derivative is equal to the left-hand side of the exact differential equation, which therefore simplifies to

$$\frac{\partial h}{\partial t} + \frac{\partial h}{\partial y} \cdot y' = 0 \quad \Leftrightarrow \quad \frac{dh}{dt} = 0$$

This means that $h(t, y)$ is a constant. Therefore, the general solution of the exact differential equation is given by $h(t, y) = C$.

> **Exact differential equations**
> Let $h = h(t, y)$ be a differentiable function. The exact differential equation
> $$\frac{\partial h}{\partial t} + \frac{\partial h}{\partial y} \cdot y' = 0$$
> has a general solution that can be written as $h(t, y) = C$ in implicit form.

Let us illustrate the method with an example, the first order differential equation $(2t + y) + (t - 4y)y' = 0$. This equation is neither separable nor linear. We can see this by transforming it to the form $y' = F(t, y)$, which gives

$$(2t + y) + (t - 4y)y' = 0 \quad \Leftrightarrow \quad y' = -\frac{2t + y}{t - 4y}$$

We shall attempt to solve this differential equation as an exact equation, and we therefore try to write the differential equation

$$(2t + y) + (t - 4y)y' = 0$$

in the form $h'_t + h'_y \cdot y' = 0$ for a function $h = h(t, y)$. The function h must have the properties that

$$h'_t = 2t + y \quad \text{and} \quad h'_y = t - 4y$$

7.7 Exact differential equations

Any function h that satisfies the first condition must have the form $h = t^2 + yt + \phi(y)$ for a function $\phi(y)$ that is constant in t. We see this by using the inverse operation of partial derivation with respect to t. We can think of this inverse operation as an integral

$$\int (2t + y)\, dt = t^2 + yt + C = t^2 + yt + \phi(y)$$

where we consider y to be constant. We interpret the integration constant C as any expression $\phi(y)$ that is constant in the integration variable t, since this gives $(\phi(y))'_t = 0$. After finding the functions $h(t, y) = t^2 + yt + \phi(y)$ that satisfy the first condition, we check if any of these functions also satisfy the second condition by computing

$$h'_y = \left(t^2 + yt + \phi(y)\right)'_y = 0 + t + \phi'(y) = t + \phi'(y)$$

This should equal $q(t, y) = t - 4y$, and this condition means that $\phi'(y) = -4y$, or that $\phi(y) = -2y^2 + K$. It follows that the function $h(t, y) = t^2 + yt - 2y^2$ satisfies both conditions. Therefore, the equation is exact with the implicit solution

$$t^2 + yt - 2y^2 = C$$

Note that it is enough to find one function $h(t, y)$ that satisfies the two conditions; we have used $h(t, y) = t^2 + ty - 2y^2 + K$ with $K = 0$. To find an explicit solution, we solve the implicit equation $t^2 + yt - 2y^2 = C$ for y, and get

$$-2y^2 + ty + (t^2 - C) = 0 \;\Rightarrow\; y = \frac{-t \pm \sqrt{t^2 - 4(-2)(t^2 - C)}}{2(-2)} = \frac{t \pm \sqrt{9t^2 - 8C}}{4}$$

using the formula for quadratic equations. This is the general solution of the exact differential equation in explicit form.

Proposition 7.5. Let $p(t, y)$, $q(t, y)$ be C^1 functions, and consider the first order differential equation $p(t, y) + q(t, y) \cdot y' = 0$. There is a function $h = h(t, y)$ such that $h'_t = p$ and $h'_y = q$ if and only if the condition

$$\frac{\partial p}{\partial y} = \frac{\partial q}{\partial t}$$

holds. In this case, the differential equation is exact and $p(t, y) + q(t, y) \cdot y' = 0$ is an exact form.

Notice that if we use the exactness criterion and find that it is satisfied, we just know that the function $h = h(t, y)$ exists; we still have to find h in order to solve the exact differential equation. If the exactness criterion is not satisfied, it just means that $p(t, y) + q(t, y) \cdot y' = 0$ is not in exact form; it could still be possible to transform it to an exact form by multiplying it by a factor (such as an integrating factor).

It is not difficult to explain why an exact differential equation satisfies the criterion: If $p = h'_t$ and $q = h'_y$ for a common function $h = h(t, y)$, then we have that

$$p'_y = h''_{ty}, \qquad q'_t = h''_{yt}$$

and we know that the Hessian matrix of h is symmetric, so that $h''_{ty} = h''_{yt}$. To prove the opposite implication, that any differential equation that satisfies the criterion must be exact, is much more difficult.

7.8 Equilibrium states and stability

A first order differential equation $y' = F(t, y)$ is called *autonomous* if the right-hand side $F(t, y)$ is independent of the variable t. In other words, autonomous first order differential equations can be written $y' = F(y)$. An example of an autonomous first order differential equation is the linear equation $y' + ay = b$, where a, b are constants. This equation can be written as $y' = b - ay$, where the right-hand side $F(y) = b - ay$ is independent of t.

Equilibrium states. Let $y' = F(y)$ be an autonomous differential equation, and let y_e be a number. If $F(y_e) = 0$, then we say that $y = y_e$ is an *equilibrium state* for $y' = F(y)$. If this is the case, then the constant function $y(t) = y_e$ is a solution of the differential equation $y' = F(y)$. This follows from the fact that $y' = 0$ for the constant function $y(t) = y_e$, and that $F(y) = 0$ at an equilibrium state $y = y_e$.

The particular solution of the differential equation $y' = F(y)$ with the initial condition $y(0) = y_e$ for an equilibrium state y_e must be the constant solution $y(t) = y_e$. In other words, if we start at the equilibrium state, we will stay there as time passes. This is the reason for the name equilibrium state.

Note that it is often much easier to compute equilibrium states than to solve the differential equation. For example, the differential equation $y' + ay = b$ can be written $y' = b - ay$, and we can find equilibrium states by solving the equation

$$F(y) = b - ay = 0 \quad \Rightarrow \quad y_e = \frac{b}{a}$$

Compare this with the general solution $y(t) = Ce^{-at} + b/a$ of $y' + ay = b$ found in Section 7.5. We notice that if $a > 0$, then the limit

$$\bar{y} = \lim_{t \to \infty} y(t) = \lim_{t \to \infty} \left(Ce^{-at} + \frac{b}{a} \right) = \frac{b}{a}$$

is the equilibrium state of this equation. If $a < 0$, then the limit above does not exist.

Another example is the logistic differential equation $y' = ry(1 - y/K)$, which is autonomous with $F(y) = ry(1 - y/K)$. The equilibrium states are given by

$$F(y) = ry\left(1 - \frac{y}{K}\right) = 0 \quad \Rightarrow \quad y = 0 \quad \text{or} \quad y = K$$

Therefore, this differential equation has two equilibrium states $y_e = 0$ and $y_e = K$. We may compare this with the general solution

$$y(t) = K \cdot \frac{Ce^{rt}}{1 + Ce^{rt}}$$

of $y' = ry(1 - y/K)$. Notice that the limit

$$\bar{y} = \lim_{t \to \infty} y(t) = \lim_{t \to \infty} \left(K \cdot \frac{Ce^{rt}}{1 + Ce^{rt}} \right) = \begin{cases} K, & r > 0 \\ 0, & r < 0 \end{cases}$$

is one of the two equilibrium states of this equation.

Proposition 7.6. Let $y' = F(y)$ be an autonomous first order differential equation with $y = y(t)$ as a particular solution. If the limit

$$\bar{y} = \lim_{t \to \infty} y(t)$$

exists, then $y = \bar{y}$ is a an equilibrium state for $y' = F(y)$.

Stability. Let $y' = F(y)$ be an autonomous first order differential equation with an equilibrium state $y = y_e$. We consider the initial value problem $y' = F(y), y(0) = y_0$ when y_0 is close to the equilibrium state y_e but $y_0 \neq y_e$. If the solution $y(t)$ of the initial value problem moves away from y_e as t increases, then the equilibrium $y = y_e$ is called *unstable*. If it moves towards y_e, or at least doesn't move further away from it, then the equilibrium $y = y_e$ is called *stable*.

We consider the linear differential equation $y' + ay = b$ as an example. We have seen that it can be written $y' = b - ay$ with $F(y) = b - ay$, and if $a \neq 0$, then it has one equilibrium state $y_e = b/a$. Let us determine the stability of $y_e = b/a$.

We first consider the special case $a = 1$ and $b = 2$ and look at the diagrams below. The diagram on the left shows the plot of $y' = F(y)$ in the (y, y')-plane.

7 • Differential equations

This is called a *phase diagram*. The intersection with the horizontal axis is the equilibrium state $y_e = b/a = 2$. The diagram on the right is the solution curve $y(t) = b/a + Ce^{-at}$ drawn in the (t, y)-plane for various initial values $y_0 \neq y_e = 2$. The equilibrium state is shown as the horizontal blue line $y = y_e = 2$.

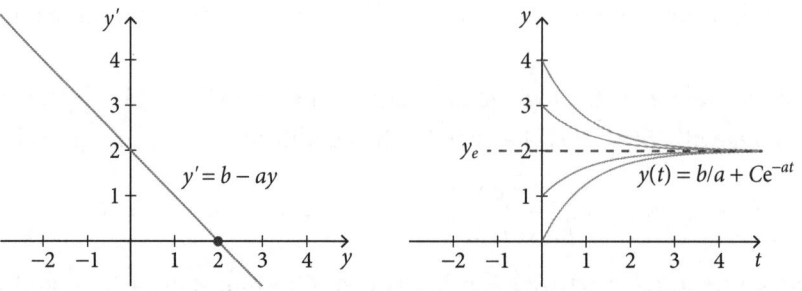

We see that the equilibrium state $y = y_e = 2$ is stable, since the solution curves in the right-hand side diagram move towards $y = 2$ as t increases when the initial state y_0 is close to $y_e = 2$ but $y_0 \neq y_e$. We can also see this in the phase diagram on the left-hand side: At points to the right of the equilibrium state $y = 2$, the graph of $y' = F(y)$ lies under the horizontal axis, meaning that $y' < 0$ and that $y = y(t)$ will decrease. At points to the left of $y = 2$, the graph of $y' = F(y)$ lies over the horizontal axis, meaning that $y' > 0$ and that $y = y(t)$ will increase. In either case, y will move towards the equilibrium state $y = 2$ when t increases.

Using the same methods, we analyze the equilibrium state $y = b/a$ of $y' = b - ay$ when a, b are general constants with $a \neq 0$. We see that $y_e = b/a$ is stable when $a > 0$ and unstable when $a < 0$. In fact, it turns out that the slope of the tangent line of $y' = F(y)$ at the equilibrium state $y = y_e$ determines the stability:

Theorem 7.7. Let $y' = F(y)$ be an autonomous first order differential equation with an equilibrium state $y = y_e$. Then we have the following:

a) If $F'(y_e) < 0$, then $y = y_e$ is a stable equilibrium state.

b) If $F'(y_e) > 0$, then $y = y_e$ is an unstable equilibrium state.

Stability of an equilibrium state $y = y_e$ is a local property, since it requires that $y(t)$ moves toward y_e when y_0 is close to y_e. We say that an equilibrium state $y = y_e$ is *globally asymptotically stable* if the particular solution $y = y(t)$ of the initial value problem $y' = F(y), y(0) = y_0$ moves towards y_e as t increases for all values of y_0.

For example, consider the linear differential equation $y' = b - ay$. We already know that $y_e = b/a$ is stable when $a > 0$. But since the general solution is given by $y(t) = b/a + Ce^{-at}$ with $C = y_0 - b/a$, it follows that

$$\lim_{t \to \infty} y(t) = \lim_{t \to \infty} \left(\frac{b}{a} + \left(y_0 - \frac{b}{a} \right) e^{-at} \right) = \frac{b}{a}$$

for all values of y_0 when $a > 0$. This means that the equilibrium $y_e = b/a$ is globally asymptotically stable when $a > 0$.

7.9 Second order differential equations

A second order differential equation contains the second derivative y'', and can often be written in the form $y'' = F(t, y, y')$ for some function F. We shall only consider second order differential equations of this type. A simple example is

$$y'' = 12t$$

We can solve this second order differential equation by simple integration in two steps. We get

$$y' = \int 12t \, dt = 6t^2 + C \quad \Rightarrow \quad y = \int (6t^2 + C) \, dt = 2t^3 + Ct + D$$

We notice that the general solution depends on two undetermined coefficients C and D. This is typical for second order differential equations, and it implies that we need two initial conditions to determine a unique solution. We can think of these as initial conditions for $y(t)$ and $y'(t)$.

For example, the initial value problem $y'' = 12$, $y(0) = 1$, $y'(0) = 2$ has the general solution $y(t) = 2t^3 + Ct + D$, and $y'(t) = 6t^2 + C$. The initial condition for $y'(t)$ is $y'(0) = 2$, and it gives $2 = 6 \cdot 0^2 + C$, or $C = 2$. The initial condition for $y(t)$ is $y(0) = 1$, and it gives $1 = 2 \cdot 0^3 + 2 \cdot 0 + D$, or $D = 1$. Therefore, the solution of the initial value problem is $y(t) = 2t^3 + 2t + 1$. We need both initial conditions to find a unique particular solution.

Theorem 7.8. Let $y'' = F(t, y, y')$, $y(t_0) = b$, $y'(t_0) = c$ be a second order initial value problem. If F is a C^1 function in a neighborhood around the point (t_0, b, c), then the initial value problem has a unique solution $y = y(t)$.

7.10 Linear second order differential equations

A second order differential equation $y'' = F(t, y, y')$ is *linear* if it can be written in the form
$$y'' + a(t)y' + b(t)y = h(t)$$
for functions $a(t)$, $b(t)$, $h(t)$. We may consider the left-hand side as $D(y)$, where D is the second order differential operator
$$D = \frac{d^2}{dt^2} + a(t)\frac{d}{dt} + b(t)$$
written using Leibniz's notation $dy/dt = y'$ and $d^2y/dt^2 = y''$. It operates on an input function $y = y(t)$ as
$$D(y) = \left(\frac{d^2}{dt^2} + a(t)\frac{d}{dt} + b(t)\right)y = y'' + a(t)y' + b(t)y$$

One may show that any second order differential operator D is a linear, just as first order differential operators were shown to be linear in Section 7.6, and therefore the superposition principle applies to linear second order differential equations.

> **Superposition principle for linear second order differential equations**
> The general solution of the differential equation $y'' + a(t)y' + b(t)y = h(t)$ can be written as $y = y_h + y_p$, where y_h is the general solution of the *homogeneous* equation $y'' + a(t)y' + b(t)y = 0$, and y_p is a particular solution of the equation $y'' + a(t)y' + b(t)y = h(t)$.

Let us consider the linear second order differential equation $y'' + 3y' + 2y = 10$ as an example. By the superposition principle, its general solution is $y = y_h + y_p$. Therefore, it is enough to find the general homogeneous solution y_h and a particular solution y_p to solve this differential equation. It turns out that $y_h = C_1 \cdot e^{-t} + C_2 \cdot e^{-2t}$ and that $y_p = 5$ in this case, and we shall explain in detail how to find y_h and y_p below. It follows that
$$y = y_h + y_p = C_1 \cdot e^{-t} + C_2 \cdot e^{-2t} + 5$$
is the general solution of $y'' + 3y' + 2y = 10$.

7.10 Linear second order differential equations

The homogeneous case. A homogeneous linear second order differential equation $y'' + a(t)\,y' + b(t)\,y = 0$ has *constant coefficients* if $a(t) = a$ and $b(t) = b$ are constants. In this case, we write the differential equation as

$$y'' + ay' + by = 0$$

We shall explain the solution method for this type of differential equation. It is based on the idea that $y = e^{rt}$ is a solution of $y'' + ay' + by = 0$ for certain values of r, and that we can determine those values of r by substituting $y = e^{rt}$ in the differential equation, using $y' = re^{rt}$ and $y'' = r^2 e^{rt}$. The left-hand side becomes

$$y'' + ay' + by = r^2 e^{rt} + a(re^{rt}) + b(e^{rt}) = e^{rt}(r^2 + ar + b)$$

Therefore, $y = e^{rt}$ is a solution of the differential equation $y'' + ay' + by = 0$ if and only if $r^2 + ar + b = 0$. This is the *characteristic equation*, and it has solutions

$$r = \frac{-a \pm \sqrt{a^2 - 4b}}{2}$$

The number of solutions depends on the sign of the *discriminant* $\Delta = a^2 - 4b$.

> **Characteristic equation**
>
> Let $y'' + ay' + by = 0$ be a linear second order differential equation that is homogeneous with constant coefficients. The function $y(t) = e^{rt}$ is a solution if and only if r is a root in the characteristic equation $r^2 + ar + b = 0$.

When $\Delta > 0$, we have two distinct (real) roots $r \neq s$, and therefore $y_1 = e^{rt}$ and $y_2 = e^{st}$ are distinct solutions. Since the differential operator D is linear, it follows that any linear combination

$$y(t) = C_1 \cdot y_1 + C_2 \cdot y_2 = C_1 \cdot e^{rt} + C_2 \cdot e^{st}$$

is a solution. This is the general solution, and it has two undetermined coefficients.

When $\Delta = 0$, we have a double root $r = -a/2$, and therefore $y_1 = e^{rt}$ is a solution. One may show that also $y_2 = t \cdot e^{rt}$ is a solution in the case of a double root. Since the differential operator D is linear, it follows that any linear combination

$$y(t) = C_1 \cdot y_1 + C_2 \cdot y_2 = C_1 \cdot e^{rt} + C_2 \cdot te^{rt} = (C_1 + C_2 t)e^{rt}$$

is a solution. This is the general solution in the case with a double root, and it also has two undetermined coefficients.

7 • Differential equations

When $\Delta < 0$, there are no real roots of the characteristic equation. But notice that formally, we can write the solutions

$$r = \frac{-a \pm \sqrt{a^2 - 4b}}{2} = \frac{-a}{2} \pm \frac{\sqrt{4b - a^2}\sqrt{-1}}{2} = \alpha + \beta \cdot \sqrt{-1}$$

with $\alpha = -a/2$ and $\beta = \sqrt{4b - a^2}/2$ since $4b - a^2 > 0$.

The general solution of $y'' + ay' + by = 0$ is in this case given by

$$y(t) = e^{\alpha t} \cdot (C_1 \cos(\beta t) + C_2 \sin(\beta t))$$

and it also has two undetermined coefficients. To show why the solutions are of the form given above, one has to work with *complex numbers*.

General solution in the homogeneous case

Let $y'' + ay' + by = 0$ be a linear second order differential equation that is homogeneous with constant coefficients. The general solution is given by

$$\Delta > 0: \quad y(t) = C_1 e^{rt} + C_2 e^{st}$$
$$\Delta = 0: \quad y(t) = (C_1 + C_2 t)e^{rt}$$
$$\Delta < 0: \quad y(t) = e^{\alpha t}(C_1 \cos(\beta t) + C_2 \sin(\beta t)$$

where $\alpha = -a/2$ and $\beta = \sqrt{4b - a^2}/2$.

As an example, let us consider the homogeneous equation $y'' + 3y' + 2y = 0$ with constant coefficients. Its characteristic equation is

$$r^2 + 3r + 2 = 0 \quad \Rightarrow \quad r = \frac{-3 \pm \sqrt{9 - 8}}{2} = \frac{-3 \pm 1}{2}$$

and there are two distinct characteristic roots $r = -1$ and $r = -2$. This corresponds to the case $\Delta > 0$, and the general solution of $y'' + 3y' + 2y = 0$ is therefore

$$y(t) = C_1 \cdot e^{-t} + C_2 \cdot e^{-2t}$$

The linear second order differential equation $y'' + 3y' + 2y = 10$ that we considered earlier in this section therefore has the general homogeneous solution

$$y_h = C_1 \cdot e^{-t} + C_2 \cdot e^{-2t}$$

Another example is $y'' + 4y' + 4y = 0$. It's characteristic equation is $r^2 + 4r + 4 = 0$, with double root $r = -2$. In this case, the general solution of the differential equation is $y(t) = (C_1 + C_2 t)e^{-2t}$.

Note that for a linear first order differential equation that is homogeneous with constant coefficients, we can use the characteristic equation in a similar way. For example, the first order differential equation $y' - 3y = 0$ has the characteristic equation $r - 3 = 0$, and therefore the general solution is $y = Ce^{3t}$. The characteristic equation always has one root for first order differential equations.

We remark that if the homogeneous linear second order differential equation $y'' + a(t)y' + b(t)y = 0$ does not have constant coefficients, then the characteristic equation cannot be used to find the general solution.

Particular solutions. It is usually much simpler to find a particular solution of a differential equation than to find the general solution by solving the equation. A useful technique is to make an assumption about the *form* of the solution, or to "guess" a solution $y = y(t)$, and then substitute this form into the differential equation to check whether any function of the chosen form is a solution. This is called the method of *undetermined coefficients*.

For example, to find a particular solution of $y'' + 3y' + 2y = 10$, we may "guess" that it has a constant solution $y = A$. To check whether or not this kind of solution could work in the equation, we assume that $y = A$, compute $y' = y'' = 0$, and substitute the values of y, y' and y'' into the differential equation $y'' + 3y' + 2y = 10$. This gives $2A = 10$, or $A = 5$. This means that $y = 5$ is a constant solution. We therefore say that $y_p = 5$ is a particular solution of $y'' + 3y' + 2y = 10$.

Note that it is a good idea to "guess" a solution $y = y(t)$ that depends on one or more parameters, called undetermined coefficients. This means that we guess a form of the solution (for example, a constant solution in the example above), rather than a specific solution. Note also that it may be that there are no solutions of the differential equation in the form that we have guessed. If this happens, we must change our assumptions.

We consider the linear second order differential equation $y'' + 7y' + 12y = t$ as an example. If we try to guess a constant solution $y = A$, we get $12A = t$ when we substitute it into the differential equation, and this has no solutions. Remember that A is assumed to be a constant. We notice that the problem is the non-constant function t on the right-hand side, and try to guess a linear form $y = At$ for a constant A instead. To substitute this into the differential equation, we compute $y' = A$ and $y'' = 0$. This gives

$$0 + 7(A) + 12(At) = t \quad \Rightarrow \quad (12A)t + (7A) = t$$

We compare coefficients of the linear functions on the left and right side of the equation, and get $12A = 1$ and $7A = 0$. There is no solution for A, and this means that the differential equation does not have any particular solutions of the form $y_p = At$ either. We must change our assumption, and this time we notice that the problem is that the equation $(12A)t + (7A) = t$ has a constant term as well as the degree one term. We shall therefore assume that the solution $y = At + B$ is a linear expression. We compute $y' = A$ and $y'' = 0$, and substitute it into the differential equation:

$$0 + 7(A) + 12(At + B) = t \quad \Rightarrow \quad (12A)t + (7A + 12B) = t$$

Comparing coefficients, this gives $12A = 1$ and $7A + 12B = 0$. The first equation gives $A = 1/12$, and the second gives $12B = -7A = -7/12$, or $B = -7/144$. We find a solution for A and B, and this means that there is a particular solution of the chosen form,

$$y_p = At + B = \frac{7}{12} \cdot t - \frac{7}{144}$$

We know that $y'' + 7y' + 12y = t$ has the general solution $y = y_h + y_p$ by the superposition principle. Since $y'' + 7y' + 12 = 0$ has the characteristic equation $r^2 + 7r + 12 = 0$, with roots $r = -3$ and $r = -4$, the homogeneous solution is

$$y_h = C_1 e^{-3t} + C_2 e^{-4t}$$

Therefore, the general solution of $y'' + 7y' + 12y = t$ is given by

$$y = y_h + y_p = C_1 e^{-3t} + C_2 e^{-4t} + \frac{7}{12} \cdot t - \frac{7}{144}$$

From this example, we notice that it is a good idea to choose $y = y(t)$ of the same form as the right-hand side of the linear second order differential equation: Since the right-hand side is a linear expression t, we guess that $y = y(t)$ is a linear expression $y = At + B$.

> **Method of undetermined coefficients**
> To find a particular solution of a linear second order differential equation $y'' + ay' + by = h(t)$, we guess a solution $y = y(t)$ and substitute it into the differential equation. We choose $y = y(t)$ such that
>
> a) $y = y(t)$ depends on one or more undetermined coefficients
> b) $y = y(t)$ has the same form as $h(t)$, $h'(t)$ and $h''(t)$
>
> If the initial guess $y = y(t)$ does not work, we try to replace $y(t)$ with $t \cdot y(t)$, and repeat the process until we find a particular solution.

Let us reconsider the differential equation $y'' + 7y' + 12y = t$. We first look at the right-hand side $h(t) = t$ and its derivatives $h'(t) = 1$ and $h''(t) = 0$, and then choose $y = At + B$. This is an expression with undetermined coefficients that has the same form as h, h' and h'', in the sense that all these functions are special cases of a linear function $At + B$. This means that we find a form $y = At + B$ that will give particular solutions when we substitute it into the differential equation; we avoid trying the forms $y = A$ and $y = At$ that do not work.

We note that when we solve a linear first order differential equation using the superposition principle, we can use similar principles for finding y_p. Let us consider $y' - 3y = te^t$ as an example. By the superposition principle, we have that $y = y_h + y_p$, and we find that $y_h = Ce^{3t}$ using the characteristic equation $r - 3 = 0$, which has the characteristic root $r = 3$. To find y_p, we make a "guess" of the same form as te^t and $(te^t)' = 1 \cdot e^t + te^t = (t+1)e^t$. We therefore try $y = (At + B)e^t$, which gives $y' = Ae^t + (At + B)e^t = (At + A + B)e^t$. When we substitute this into the differential equation, we get

$$y' - 3y = (At + A + B)e^t - 3(At + B)e^t = (-2At + A - 2B)e^t = te^t$$

This means that $-2A = 1$ and $A - 2B = 0$, and we find that $A = -1/2$ and $B = -1/4$ is a solution. Hence $y_p = (-t/2 - 1/4)e^t$ is a particular solution, and the general solution of $y' - 3y = te^t$ is given by

$$y = y_h + y_p = Ce^{3t} - \frac{1}{2}(t+2)e^t$$

It is instructive to try to solve this first order differential equation with alternative methods, such as integrating factors, and compare the two alternatives.

Problems

Problem 7.1 Show that $y = t - t^2$ is a solution of $y' + y = 1 - t - t^2$.

Problem 7.2 Determine all values of the constant r such that $y = e^{rt}$ is a solution of the differential equation $3y' + 6y = 0$.

Problem 7.3 Find the general solution of the differential equations:

a) $y' = 4t^3 + 1$ b) $ty' = 2\ln(t)$

c) $y' + t^3 = t^2$ d) $e^t y' = t$

Problem 7.4 Find the general solution of the differential equations $y'' = 12t + 6$, and show that it depends on two undetermined coefficients.

Problem 7.5 Show that $y = Ce^{rt}$ is a solution of the differential equation $y' = ry$.

Problem 7.6 Let $p = p(t)$ be the price of a product with demand function $d = d(t)$ and supply function $s = s(t)$. We consider the differential equation
$$p' = k(d - s)$$
for a positive constant $k > 0$. Explain the assumption on the rate of change in the price $p = p(t)$ that this differential equation expresses. What happens to the price when there is a demand surplus? What happens when there is a supply surplus?

Problem 7.7 We consider the logistic differential equation $y' = ry(1 - y/K)$. Find a particular solution such that $y(0) = 56.3$ and $y(20) = 58.9$, assuming that the carrying capacity $K = 80$. You may use that
$$y(t) = K \cdot \frac{Ce^{rt}}{1 + Ce^{rt}}$$
is the general solution of logistic differential equation. Use a tool such as Wolfram Alpha to draw the graph of the solution curve and describe what you see.

Problem 7.8 Solve the initial value problem $y' = 3t^2 + 6$, $y(1) = 1$.

Problem 7.9 Solve the initial value problem $y' = 3\sqrt{t}$, $y(0) = 1$.

Problem 7.10 Write $t^2 y' - ty = t + y$ in the form $y' = F(t, y)$, if possible. Is the differential equation solvable by simple integration?

Problem 7.11 Solve the initial value problem $ty' = 2\ln(t)$, $y(1) = 3$.

Problem 7.12 Find the general solution of the differential equation $y' = ry$ when r is a given constant. This is the differential equation in the simple exponential growth model considered in Section 7.2.

Problem 7.13 Determine whether the differential equations are separable or not, and find the general solution of the separable equations:

a) $yy' = t$
b) $y' + y = e^t$
c) $e^y y' = t + 1$
d) $ty' + y^2 = 1$
e) $y' - \ln(t) = 1$

Problem 7.14 Find the general solution of $y' = ry(1 - y/K)$ when r, K are given constants with $K > 0$. This is the differential equation in the logistic growth model considered in Section 7.2.

Problem 7.15 Show that the differential equation $y' = ry$ for a given constant r is both separable and linear, and solve it using an integrating factor.

Problem 7.16 Determine whether the differential equations are linear or not, and find the general solution of the linear equations:

a) $y' + y = e^t$
b) $yy' = t$
c) $y' = 2t + y$
d) $t^2 y' + \ln(t) y = \ln(t)$
e) $y' - 2ty = 2t$

Problem 7.17 Use the superposition principle to find the general solution of the linear first order differential equations:

a) $y' + 3y = 4e^t$
b) $y' - y = t$
c) $y' = 2t + y$
d) $6y' - 18y = 12t$

Problem 7.18 Use the superposition principle to find the general solution of the linear first order differential equation $t^2 y' + \ln(t) y = \ln(t)$.

Problem 7.19 Solve the initial value problem $ty' + 2y = t$, $y(1) = 1$.

Problem 7.20 Solve the differential equation $1 + 2ty^2 + 2t^2 y \cdot y' = 0$, and find all solutions that satisfy the initial condition $y(1) = -1$.

Problem 7.21 Solve the following differential equations:

a) $2t - y + (2y - t)y' = 0$
b) $ye^t + e^t \cdot y' = 0$
c) $ty^2 + y + (t^2 y + t)y' = 0$

7 • Differential equations

Problem 7.22 Show that any separable differential equation is exact.

Problem 7.23 Show that any first order linear differential equation is exact.

Problem 7.24 Determine all equilibrium states of $y' = 1 - y^2$, and determine their stability. Check if the stable equilibrium points are globally asymptotically stable.

Problem 7.25 Consider the differential equation $p' = k(d - s)$, where $p = p(t)$ is the price of a good with linear supply and demand functions
$$d = a - bp$$
$$s = c + dp$$
We assume that $a, b, c, d, k > 0$ are positive constants. Find all equilibrium states for the price p, and determine their stability.

Problem 7.26 Solve the differential equation $y'' = 0$.

Problem 7.27 Solve the differential equation $y'' = e^t - e^{-t}$, and find all solutions that satisfy the initial conditions $y(0) = -1$ and $y'(0) = 1$.

Problem 7.28 Solve the differential equation $y'' = 1 - y'$. It may be helpful to rewrite the equation as a differential equation in the variable $z = y'$.

Problem 7.29 Solve the initial value problem $y'' + y' - 2y = 4t$, $y(0) = 1$, $y'(0) = 0$.

Problem 7.30 Solve the following linear second order differential equations:

a) $y'' - 4y = t + 1$ b) $y'' + 3y' = e^{-t}$ c) $y'' + 5y' - 6y = t^2$

Problem 7.31 Solve the differential equation $y'' + 3y' - 4y = 2e^t$.

Problem 7.32 Show that if $y'' + ay' + by = 0$ has a characteristic equation with the double root r, then $y = te^{rt}$ is a solution of the differential equation.

Problem 7.33 Solve the linear first order differential equation $y' - 4y = te^t$ using the superposition principle and using integrating factors. Compare the methods.

Problem 7.34 Prove that the following second order differential operator is linear:
$$D = \frac{d^2}{dt^2} + a(t)\frac{d}{dt} + b(t)$$

CHAPTER 8

Difference equations

8.1 Introduction to difference equations

By a *sequence*, we mean a sequence $y_0, y_1, y_2, \ldots$ of numbers indexed by the nonnegative integers $t = 0, 1, 2, \ldots$, and we often write (y_t) for this sequence. We can describe a sequence by giving a formula for the general element in the sequence. For example, $y_t = 2^t$ denotes the sequence given by $y_0 = 1, y_1 = 2, y_2 = 4, y_3 = 8, \ldots$ where $y_t = 2^t$ for all integers $t \geq 0$.

We think of a sequence as a special type of a function, where the domain of definition is the set of nonnegative numbers $\{0, 1, 2, \ldots\}$. For example, the balance y_t of a bank account after t terms, where interest is capitalized at the end of each term with interest rate r per term, is described by the sequence $y_t = y_0 \cdot (1+r)^t$. Although it would make sense mathematically to substitute a non-integer value for t in this expression, the sequence y_t has values only when $t = 0, 1, 2, \ldots$ is a nonnegative number. In contrast, a continuous function $y(t)$ has a value for any real number t. We often use a continuous function to represent a quantity in continuous time, and a sequence to represent it in discrete time.

When (y_t) is a sequence, we use the *first difference* $y_{t+1} - y_t$ as the measure of change in y. We write $\Delta = \Delta(y_t)$ for the first difference of the sequence (y_t), and notice that (Δ_t) is a new sequence, given by $\Delta_t = y_{t+1} - y_t$. It is useful to contrast the case of a sequence (y_t) with that of a continuous function $y(t)$: For a continuous function, the derivative $y'(t)$ is the measure of change in y, and it is (usually) a new continuous function.

For example, the sequence $1, 2, 4, 8, 16, \ldots$ given by $y_t = 2^t$ has first difference $2-1, 4-2, 8-4, 16-8, \ldots = 1, 2, 4, 8, \ldots$. It seems that the first difference (Δ_t) is equal to the original sequence (y_t) in this case. In fact, this is the case since the first difference $\Delta_t = y_{t+1} - y_t$ is given by

$$\Delta_t = 2^{t+1} - 2^t = 2(2^t) - 2^t = (2-1)2^t = 2^t = y_t$$

8 • Difference equations

For another example, let $y_t = y_0(1+r)^t$ be the balance of a bank account after t terms. Then the first difference is given by

$$\Delta_t = y_0(1+r)^{t+1} - y_0(1+r)^t$$
$$= y_0(1+r)^t(1+r-1) = r \cdot y_0(1+r)^t = ry_t$$

In summary, we have that the first difference is given by $\Delta_t = y_t$ and $\Delta_t = ry_t$ in these two examples.

A *first order difference equation* is an equation that contains the first difference Δ_t of a sequence (y_t), and where the sequence (y_t) is the unknown. This is an example of a first order difference equation, written in several different ways:

$$\Delta_t = y_t \quad \Leftrightarrow \quad y_{t+1} - y_t = y_t \quad \Leftrightarrow \quad y_{t+1} = 2y_t$$

This equation means that $y_{t+1} = 2y_t$ for all integers $t \geq 0$, or that the next term in the sequence is twice the previous term, such that $y_1 = 2y_0$, $y_2 = 2y_1 = 2(2y_0) = 4y_0$, and so on. It is not difficult to see that the general solution of the difference equation is $y_t = C \cdot 2^t$, where the undetermined coefficient $C = y_0$. In general, the solution of a first order difference equation will depend on one undetermined coefficient.

If we consider the difference equation $y_{t+1} = 2y_t$ together with the initial condition $y_0 = 1$, we see that there is a unique solution $y_t = 2^t$, with $C = y_0 = 1$. We call $y_t = C \cdot 2^t$ the general solution of the difference equation, and $y_t = 2^t$ the particular solution satisfying the difference equation and the initial condition $y_0 = 1$.

First order difference equations can be written in the form $y_{t+1} = F(t, y_t)$ in most cases. We see that there are many similarities to first order differential equations. Difference equations provide a way to model change for variables in discrete time, in a similar way to differential equations that can model change in continuous time. Even though it is usually easiest to solve the difference equation when it is written on the form $y_{t+1} = F(t, y_t)$, it can also be rewritten as

$$y_{t+1} = F(t, y_t) \quad \Leftrightarrow \quad y_{t+1} - y_t = F(t, y_t) - y_t \quad \Leftrightarrow \quad \Delta_t = F(t, y_t) - y_t$$

where the left-hand side is the first difference $\Delta_t = y_{t+1} - y_t$. When it is written in this way, we see the underlying assumption on the measure of change that is built into the difference equation. For example, the difference equation $y_{t+1} = 1.04y_t + 10$ means that the first difference $\Delta_t = y_{t+1} - y_t = 0.04y_t + 10$.

8.2 Linear first order difference equations

A *linear first order difference equation* is a difference equation that can be written in the form $y_{t+1} + a_t y_t = b_t$, where a_t and b_t are sequences given by expressions in t. This is an example of a linear first order difference equation:

$$y_{t+1} - 1.04 y_t = 5 + t$$

Here, $a_t = 1.04$ is a constant sequence with $a_0 = a_1 = a_2 = \ldots = 1.04$, and $b_t = 5 + t$ is the sequence with $b_0 = 5$, $b_1 = 6$, $b_2 = 7$, …. We say that the difference equation has constant coefficients if $a_t = a$ is a constant sequence, and we shall explain how to solve the difference equation in this case.

> **Superposition principle**
> The general solution of the linear difference equation $y_{t+1} + a_t y_t = b_t$ can be written as $y_t = y_t^h + y_t^p$, where y_t^h is the general solution of the homogeneous difference equation $y_{t+1} + a_t y_t = 0$, and where y_t^p is a particular solution of $y_{t+1} + a_t y_t = b_t$.

If $a_t = a$ is a constant sequence, then the homogeneous equation $y_{t+1} + a y_t = 0$ can be written $y_{t+1} = -a \cdot y_t$. This means that $y_1 = -a y_0$, $y_2 = -a y_1 = (-a)^2 y_0$, and so on. It follows that the homogeneous solution is $y_t^h = C \cdot (-a)^t$ when $a_t = a$ is a constant.

We use the method of undetermined coefficients to find a particular solution: We choose an expression for y_t that depends on one or more undetermined coefficients, and try to adjust the undetermined coefficients so that this expression fits in the difference equation $y_{t+1} + a y_t = b_t$.

Let us consider the example $y_{t+1} - 1.04 y_t = 5 + t$. First, we have $y_t = y_t^h + y_t^p$ by the superposition principle, and $y_t^h = C \cdot 1.04^t$ since $a = -1.04$. To find a particular solution, we consider the expressions $b_t = 5 + t$ and $b_{t+1} = 5 + (t+1) = 6 + t$, which are linear expressions in t. Therefore, we look for a solution of the form $y_t = A + Bt$, which gives $y_{t+1} = A + B(t+1) = (A + B) + Bt$. We use this in the difference equation:

$$y_{t+1} - 1.04 y_t = 5 + t$$
$$(A + B) + Bt - 1.04(A + Bt) = 5 + t$$

The left-hand side gives $(B - 0.04A) + (-0.04B)t$, hence $B - 0.04A = 5$ and $-0.04B = 1$ by comparing coefficients. This gives $B = -1/0.04 = -25$, and $B - 0.04A = 5$ gives $-0.04A = 5 + 25 = 30$, or $A = -30/0.04 = -750$. It follows that $y_t^p = -750 - 25t$, and the general solution of the linear first order difference equation is

$$y_t = y_t^h + y_t^p = C \cdot 1.04^t - 750 - 25t$$

Notice that $t = 0$ gives $y_0 = C - 750$, hence $C = y_0 + 750$ in this case. In general, if the linear difference equation is not homogeneous, then C is not necessarily equal to y_0.

8.3 Equilibrium states and stability

A first order difference equation is called *autonomous* if it can be written in the form $y_{t+1} = F(y_t)$. An example of an autonomous first order difference equation is the linear equation $y_{t+1} = (1+r)y_t - b$, where r, b are constants. This equation can be written as $y_{t+1} - y_t = ry_t - b$, where the left-hand side is the first difference. In general, we shall write any first order autonomous difference equation $y_{t+1} = F(y_t)$ in the form $y_{t+1} - y_t = F(y_t) - y_t$ in this section.

Equilibrium states. An *equilibrium state* of the difference equation $y_{t+1} = F(y_t)$ is a number y_e such that $F(y_e) - y_e = 0$. If we rewrite the difference equation in the form $y_{t+1} - y_t = F(y_t) - y_t$, we see that if $y_t = y_e$ is an equilibrium state, then $y_{t+1} - y_t = 0$ or $y_{t+1} = y_e$. This means that if y_0 is an equilibrium state of the difference equation, then $y_t = y_e$ is a constant solution. In other words, if we start at an equilibrium state, we will stay there as time passes. This is the reason for the name equilibrium state.

Notice that it is often much easier to compute equilibrium states than to solve the difference equation. For example, the difference equation $y_{t+1} = (1+r)y_t + b$ can be written $y_{t+1} - y_t = ry_t - b$, and we can find equilibrium states by solving the equation

$$F(y_e) - y_e = ry_e - b = 0 \quad \Rightarrow \quad y_e = \frac{b}{r}$$

Compare this with the general solution $y_t = C(1+r)^t + b/r$ that we obtain with the methods of Section 8.2, when we use the superposition principle. We notice that if $r < 0$, then the limit

$$\bar{y} = \lim_{t \to \infty} y_t = \lim_{t \to \infty} \left(C(1+r)^t + \frac{r}{b} \right) = \frac{r}{b}$$

is the equilibrium state of this equation. If $r > 0$, then the limit above does not exist.

Stability. Let $y_{t+1} = F(y_t)$ be an autonomous first order difference equation with an equilibrium state $y = y_e$. We consider the initial value problem $y_{t+1} - y_t = F(y_t) - y_t$ with a given value of y_0 which is close to the equilibrium state y_e but with $y_0 \neq y_e$. If the solution y_t of the initial value problem moves away from y_e as t increases, then the equilibrium state $y_t = y_e$ is called *unstable*. If it moves towards y_e, or at least does not move further away from it, then the equilibrium state $y = y_e$ is called *stable*.

Stability of an equilibrium state y_e is a local property; it requires that y_t moves toward y_e when y_0 is close to y_e. We say that the equilibrium state $y = y_e$ is *globally asymptotically stable* if the particular solution $y = (y_t)$ of the initial value problem $y_{t+1} = F(y_t) - y_t$ for any given value of y_0 moves towards y_e as t increases.

For example, consider the linear differential equation $y_{t+1} = (1+r)y_t - b$. We already know that $y_e = b/r$ is stable when $r < 0$. But since the general solution is given by $y_t = b/r + C(1+r)^t$, and substituting $t = 0$ gives $C = y_0 - b/r$, it follows that

$$\lim_{t \to \infty} y_t = \lim_{t \to \infty} \left(\frac{b}{r} + \left(y_0 - \frac{b}{r} \right)(1+r)^t \right) = \frac{b}{r}$$

for all values of y_0 when $r < 0$. This means that the equilibrium state $y_e = b/r$ is globally asymptotically stable when $r < 0$.

8.4 Linear second order difference equations

For any sequence (y_t), the first difference $\Delta = \Delta(y_t)$ is a new sequence. Therefore, we may consider the second difference $\Delta^2 = \Delta(\Delta(y_t))$, and we have that

$$\Delta_t^2 = \Delta_{t+1} - \Delta_t = (y_{t+2} - y_{t+1}) - (y_{t+1} - y_t) = y_{t+2} - 2y_{t+1} + y_t$$

since the first difference is given by $\Delta_t = y_{t+1} - y_t$. The second difference is the difference of the difference, and plays the same role for sequences as the second derivative for continuous functions.

A difference equation that contains the second difference Δ_t^2 of a sequence (y_t), and where the sequence (y_t) is the unknown, is called a *second order difference equation*. This is an example of a second order difference equation, written in several different ways:

$$\Delta_t^2 = 1 \quad \Leftrightarrow \quad y_{t+2} - 2y_{t+1} + y_t = 1 \quad \Leftrightarrow \quad y_{t+2} = 2y_{t+1} - y_t + 1$$

It is usual to write second order difference equations in the form $y_{t+2} = F(t, y_t, y_{t+1})$.

The general solution of a second order difference equation will depend on two undetermined coefficients. To see this, let us consider the Fibonacci difference equation $y_{t+2} = y_{t+1} + y_t$, which means that each number of the sequence is the sum of the previous two. This gives $y_2 = y_1 + y_0$, $y_3 = y_2 + y_1 = (y_1 + y_0) + y_1 = 2y_1 + y_0$, and so on. Hence the expression y_t for the general element of the sequence will depend on two undetermined coefficients y_0 and y_1. We shall find this expression a bit later in this section.

A *linear second order difference equation* is a difference equation that can be written in the form $y_{t+2} + a_t y_{t+1} + b_t y_t = f_t$, where a_t, b_t and f_t are sequences given by expressions in t. We say that it has constant coefficients if $a_t = a$ and $b_t = b$ are constant sequences. This is an example of a linear second order difference equation:

$$y_{t+2} - 2y_{t+1} + y_t = 1$$

Here, $a = -2$, $b = 1$ and $f_t = 1$ are constant sequences. Another example is the Fibonacci difference equation

$$y_{t+2} = y_{t+1} + y_t \quad \Leftrightarrow \quad y_{t+2} - y_{t+1} - y_t = 0$$

Next, we shall explain how to use the superposition principle to solve linear second order difference equations with constant coefficients.

> **Superposition principle**
> The linear second order difference equation $y_{t+2} + a_t y_{t+1} + b_t y_t = f_t$ has a general solution of the form $y_t = y_t^h + y_t^p$, where y_t^h is the general solution of the homogeneous difference equation $y_{t+2} + a_t y_{t+1} + b_t y_t = 0$, and y_t^p is a particular solution of $y_{t+2} + a_t y_{t+1} + b_t y_t = f_t$.

Let us first see how to find the general solution of the homogeneous equation $y_{t+2} + a_t y_{t+1} + b_t y_t = 0$ when $a_t = a$ and $b_t = b$ are constants. In this case, the difference equation can be written

$$y_{t+2} + a\, y_{t+1} + b\, y_t = 0$$

We put $y_t = \lambda^t$ and compute $y_{t+2} = \lambda^{t+2} = \lambda^2 \cdot \lambda^t$ and $y_{t+1} = \lambda^{t+1} = \lambda \cdot \lambda^t$. In the difference equation, this gives

$$\lambda^2 \lambda^t + a\lambda \lambda^t + b\lambda^t = \lambda^t(\lambda^2 + a\lambda + b) = 0$$

It follows that $y_t = \lambda^t$ is a solution of the homogeneous difference equation if and only if λ is a root in the *characteristic equation* $\lambda^2 + a\lambda + b = 0$. The characteristic roots are given by

$$\lambda = \frac{-a \pm \sqrt{a^2 - 4b}}{2}$$

When the discriminant $\Delta = a^2 - 4b > 0$, there are two characteristic roots $\lambda_1 \neq \lambda_2$, and the homogeneous solutions is $y_t^h = C_1 \lambda_1^t + C_2 \lambda_2^t$ since λ_1^t and λ_2^t are solutions by the argument above. When the discriminant $\Delta = a^2 - 4b = 0$, there is a double root $\lambda_1 = \lambda_2 = -a/2$, which we simply write as $\lambda = -a/2$. The homogeneous solution is $y_t^h = C_1 \lambda^t + C_2 t \lambda^t = (C_1 + C_2 t)\lambda^t$ in this case. The reason is that λ^t and $t\lambda^t$ are solutions when λ is a double root.

When the discriminant $\Delta = a^2 - 4b < 0$, the characteristic equation has no roots among the real numbers, but one may show that there is a homogeneous solution also in this case, given by

$$y_t^h = \left(\sqrt{b}\right)^t (C_1 \cos(\theta t) + C_2 \sin(\theta t)), \quad \text{where} \quad \theta = \arccos\left(\frac{a}{2\sqrt{b}}\right)$$

To find this formula, one has to use complex numbers, and the explanation is outside the scope of this book.

General solution in the homogeneous case

Let $y_{t+2} + a_t y_{t+1} + b_t y_t = 0$ be the homogeneous linear second order difference equation with constant coefficients, and let $\Delta = a^2 - 4b$ be the discriminant in the characteristic equation $\lambda^2 + a\lambda + b = 0$. The general solution is given by

$$\Delta > 0: \quad y_t^h = C_1 \lambda_1^t + C_2 \lambda_2^t$$
$$\Delta = 0: \quad y_t^h = C_1 \lambda^t + C_2 t \lambda^t$$

where λ_1, λ_2 are the characteristic roots, and $\lambda = \lambda_1 = \lambda_2$ if $\lambda_1 = \lambda_2$.

As an example, we consider the Fibonacci difference equation $y_{t+2} = y_{t+1} + y_t$ with initial conditions $y_0 = y_1 = 1$. Recall that the difference equation means that each element in the sequence is the sum of the previous two elements, hence the solution is the sequence

$$1, 1, 2, 3, 5, 8, 13, 21, 34, \ldots$$

of positive integers, called the *Fibonacci sequence*. We write the difference equation in the form $y_{t+2} - y_{t+1} - y_t = 0$, the standard form of a second order difference equation, and notice that $y_t = y_t^h$ since this equation is homogeneous. To find a formula for the general element y_t in this sequence, we use the characteristic equation $\lambda^2 - \lambda - 1 = 0$. This gives

$$\lambda = \frac{1 \pm \sqrt{1 - 4(-1)}}{2} = \frac{1 \pm \sqrt{5}}{2}$$

Hence there are two distinct characteristic roots

$$\lambda_1 = \frac{1 + \sqrt{5}}{2}, \quad \lambda_2 = \frac{1 - \sqrt{5}}{2}$$

and the general solution is $y_t = C_1 \lambda_1^t + C_2 \lambda_2^t$. To determine the constants C_1, C_2 and the particular solution with $y_0 = y_1 = 1$, we put $t = 0$ and $t = 1$. This gives

$$1 = C_1 + C_2, \quad 1 = \lambda_1 C_1 + \lambda_2 C_2$$

Hence $C_2 = 1 - C_1$ and $1 = \lambda_1 C_1 + \lambda_2(1 - C_1)$. When we solve the last equation for C_1, we get

$$1 - \lambda_2 = C_1(\lambda_1 - \lambda_2)$$
$$\Downarrow$$
$$C_1 = \frac{1 - \lambda_2}{\lambda_1 - \lambda_2} = \frac{\lambda_1}{\lambda_1 - \lambda_2} = \frac{1 + \sqrt{5}}{2\sqrt{5}} = \frac{5 + \sqrt{5}}{10}$$

since $\lambda_1 + \lambda_2 = 1$. This gives the particular solution

$$y_t = \frac{5 + \sqrt{5}}{10} \cdot \left(\frac{1 + \sqrt{5}}{2}\right)^t + \frac{5 - \sqrt{5}}{10} \cdot \left(\frac{1 - \sqrt{5}}{2}\right)^t$$

since $C_2 = 1 - C_1 = (5 - \sqrt{5})/10$.

To solve a second order linear difference equation that is not homogeneous, of the form $y_{t+2} + a y_{t+1} + b y_t = f_t$, we use the method of undetermined coefficients to find the particular solution y_t^p. We show this method by example, as it is very similar to the method we used in the previous section to find the particular solutions for first order linear difference equations.

We consider the example $y_{t+2} - 5y_{t+1} + 6y_t = 4t$. The characteristic equation is $\lambda^2 - 5\lambda + 6 = 0$, which gives the roots $\lambda_1 = 2$ and $\lambda_2 = 3$, and the homogeneous solution is therefore

$$y_t^h = C_1 \cdot 2^t + C_2 \cdot 3^t$$

To find a particular solution, we consider the right-hand side $f_t = 4t$, which gives $f_{t+1} = 4(t+1) = 4t + 4$ and $f_{t+2} = 4(t+2) = 4t + 8$. These are all linear expressions. We therefore choose $y_t = At + B$, which gives $y_{t+1} = A(t+1) + B = At + (A + B)$, and $y_{t+2} = A(t+2) + B = At + (2A + B)$. In the differential equation, this gives

$$y_{t+2} - 5y_{t+1} + 6y_t = 4t$$
$$At + 2A + B - 5(At + A + B) + 6(At + B) = 4t$$
$$(A - 5A + 6A)t + (2A + B - 5A - 5B + 6B) = 4t$$
$$(2A)t + (-3A + 2B) = 4t$$

Comparing coefficients, we see that this holds if $2A = 4$ and $2B - 3A = 0$, and this gives $A = 2$ and $2B = 6$, or $B = 3$. Hence $y_t^p = 2t + 3$, and we see that

$$y_t = y_t^h + y_t^p = C_1 \cdot 2^t + C_2 \cdot 3^t + 2t + 3$$

is the general solution of the difference equation.

Problems

Problem 8.1 Solve the difference equation $y_{t+1} - 3y_t + 4$ with $y_0 - 1$.

Problem 8.2 Solve the difference equation $y_{t+1} = 1.1y_t + 100$.

Problem 8.3 Consider the difference equation $y_{t+1} - 1.4y_t = t$. Determine whether $y_t = At + B$ is a solution for constants A and B, and use this to solve the difference equation.

Problem 8.4 You borrow an amount K. The interest rate per period is r. The repayment is 500 in the first period, and increases with 50 for each subsequent period. Show that the outstanding balance b_t after period t satisfies the difference equation
$$b_{t+1} = (1+r)b_t - (500 + 50t), \quad b_0 = K$$
and solve this difference equation.

Problem 8.5 Solve the difference equation $y_{t+2} - 3y_{t+1} + 2y_t = 0$.

Problem 8.6 Solve the difference equation $3y_{t+2} - 12y_t = 4$.

Problem 8.7 We consider the difference equation $y_{t+2} + ay_{t+1} + by_t = 0$ in the case when $a^2 - 4b = 0$. Determine the double root λ of the characteristic equation, and show that $y_t = \lambda^t$ and $y_t = t\lambda^t$ are solutions of the difference equation.

Problem 8.8 Find the general solution of the following difference equations:

a) $y_{t+2} - 6y_{t+1} + 8y_t = 0$ b) $y_{t+2} - 8y_{t+1} + 16y_t = 0$
c) $y_{t+2} + 2y_{t+1} + 3y_t = 0$

Problem 8.9 Solve the difference equation $y_{t+2} + 2y_{t+1} + y_t = 9 \cdot 2^t$.

CHAPTER 9

Systems of differential and difference equations

9.1 Introduction to systems of differential equations

Let $y_i = y_i(t)$ be a function in one variable t for $1 \leq i \leq n$, and let $y'_i = y'_i(t)$ be its derivative. A first order differential equation of the form

$$y'_i = F_i(t, y_1, y_2, \ldots, y_n)$$

is called a *coupled* differential equation. For example, $y'_1 = y_1 + y_2$ is a coupled differential equation, since the derivative or growth rate of y_1 will depend on both y_1 and y_2, and the solution $y_1 = y_1(t)$ will therefore depend on $y_2 = y_2(t)$. In contrast, differential equations such as $y'_1 = 2y_1$ and $y'_2 = -y_2$ are *decoupled*.

A *coupled system* of first order differential equations in $y_1, y_2, \ldots, y_n$, or simply a *system of differential equations*, is a system of differential equations in the form

$$y'_1 = F_1(t, y_1, \ldots, y_n)$$
$$y'_2 = F_2(t, y_1, \ldots, y_n)$$
$$\vdots$$
$$y'_n = F_n(t, y_1, \ldots, y_n)$$

where $F_1, F_2, \ldots, F_n$ are functions in $(t, y_1, y_2, \ldots, y_n)$. It is called *autonomous* if $F_1, F_2, \ldots, F_n$ are independent of the time t, and only depend on the functions $(y_1, y_2, \ldots, y_n)$. This is an example of an autonomous system of differential equations:

$$y'_1 = y_1 + y_2$$
$$y'_2 = y_1$$

First order differential equations of the form $y'_i = F(t, y_i)$ are called *decoupled* in the context of systems of differential equations, and can often be solved using the methods introduced in Chapter 7. Decoupled differential equations $y'_i = F(t, y_i)$ are characterized by the fact that the solution $y_i = y_i(t)$ will not depend on the other variables $y_j = y_j(t)$ for $j \neq i$. For example, if $y'_2 = 2y_2$ is one of the equations

217

in a system of the differential equations in the variables y_1 and y_2, then it is decoupled, and we can solve it as a linear or separable equation. We find the general solution $y_2 = Ce^{2t}$, which is independent of y_1.

Given a system of differential equations, we may think of $(y_1, y_2, \ldots, y_n)$ as an n-vector. We call it the *state vector* of the system, and write it

$$\mathbf{y}(t) = \begin{pmatrix} y_1(t) \\ y_2(t) \\ \vdots \\ y_n(t) \end{pmatrix} \quad \text{or} \quad \mathbf{y} = \begin{pmatrix} y_1 \\ y_2 \\ \vdots \\ y_n \end{pmatrix}$$

That is, a state vector is a collection of n functions $y_1(t), y_2(t), \ldots, y_n(t)$. A *solution* of a system of differential equations is a state vector $\mathbf{y} = \mathbf{y}(t)$ that satisfies all differential equations in the system. An *initial condition* for a coupled system is an initial state vector at an initial time $t = t_0$, given by $\mathbf{y}(t_0) = \mathbf{b}$ for a vector $\mathbf{b}$; in other words, it is given by the conditions

$$y_1(t_0) = b_1, y_2(t_0) = b_2, \ldots, y_n(t_0) = b_n$$

where $b_1, b_2, \ldots, b_n$ are given numbers.

> **Solutions of initial value problems for coupled systems**
> Let $y'_1 = F_1(t, y_1, \ldots, y_n), \ldots, y'_n = F_n(t, y_1, \ldots, y_n)$, $y_1(t_0) = b_1, \ldots, y_n(t_0) = b_n$ be an initial value problem. If $F_1, \ldots, F_n$ are C^1 functions in a neighborhood around the point $(t_0, b_1, \ldots, b_n)$, then the initial value problem has a unique solution $\mathbf{y} = \mathbf{y}(t)$.

Planar systems. Coupled systems of differential equations are called *planar* in the special case $n = 2$, where there are two variables $y_1 = y_1(t)$ and $y_2 = y_2(t)$. This is the simplest case of nontrivial coupled systems, and many of the examples we consider in this chapter are planar autonomous coupled systems of differential equations. They can be written in the form

$$y'_1 = F(y_1, y_2)$$
$$y'_2 = G(y_1, y_2)$$

where F, G are functions in two variables. A simple example of a planar autonomous system is the *predator-prey system*, given by

$$y'_1 = y_1(-a + by_2)$$
$$y'_2 = y_2(c - dy_1)$$

where a, b, c, d are positive constants. We think of $y_1(t)$ and $y_2(t)$ as the population of two species (predator and prey) at time t, where the presence of predators has a negative impact on the growth of the prey population, and the presence of prey has a positive effect on the growth of the predator population.

Second order differential equations as coupled systems. We may rewrite any second order differential equation as a coupled system of differential equations, consisting of two first order differential equations. In fact, let us write the second order differential equation in the form $y'' = F(t, y, y')$, and let $y_1 = y$ and $y_2 = y'$. Then $y_1' = y_2$ and $y_2' = y'' = F(t, y, y') = F(t, y_1, y_2)$, and we obtain the following coupled system:
$$y_1' = y_2$$
$$y_2' = F(t, y_1, y_2)$$

Let us consider the second order differential equation $y'' - 4y' + 3y = 6$ as a simple example. It can be written as $y'' = 6 - 3y + 4y'$. Using $y_1 = y$ and $y_2 = y'$, we can therefore rewrite it as the planar coupled system
$$y_1' = y_2$$
$$y_2' = 6 - 3y_1 + 4y_2$$

In a similar way, any n'th order differential equation can be rewritten as a coupled system of n first order differential equations in n variables.

9.2 Linear systems of differential equations

An autonomous coupled system of first order differential equations is called *linear* if it can be written in the form
$$y_1' = a_{11}y_1 + a_{12}y_2 + \ldots + a_{1n}y_n + b_1$$
$$y_2' = a_{21}y_1 + a_{22}y_2 + \ldots + a_{2n}y_n + b_2$$
$$\vdots$$
$$y_n' = a_{n1}y_1 + a_{n2}y_2 + \ldots + a_{nn}y_n + b_n$$

It is called *homogeneous* if $b_1 = b_2 = \ldots = b_n = 0$. In other words, the coupled system is linear if and only if $F_1, \ldots, F_n$ are linear functions. Writing $\mathbf{y} = \mathbf{y}(t)$ for the state vector, and $\mathbf{y}' = \mathbf{y}'(t)$ for the vector of derivatives, we can write the system in matrix form as $\mathbf{y}' = A \cdot \mathbf{y} + \mathbf{b}$, or

$$\mathbf{y}'(t) = \begin{pmatrix} y_1'(t) \\ y_2'(t) \\ \vdots \\ y_n'(t) \end{pmatrix} = \begin{pmatrix} a_{11} & a_{12} & \cdots & a_{1n} \\ a_{21} & a_{22} & \cdots & a_{2n} \\ \vdots & \vdots & \ddots & \vdots \\ a_{n1} & a_{n2} & \vdots & a_{nn} \end{pmatrix} \cdot \begin{pmatrix} y_1(t) \\ y_2(t) \\ \vdots \\ y_n(t) \end{pmatrix} + \begin{pmatrix} b_1 \\ b_2 \\ \vdots \\ b_n \end{pmatrix}$$

$$= A \cdot \mathbf{y}(t) + \mathbf{b}$$

where A is an $n \times n$ matrix and $\mathbf{b}$ is an n-vector. It turns out that we can solve this system by decoupling it, and the decoupling uses the eigenvalues and eigenvectors of the matrix A.

The homogeneous case. We consider the case of a linear homogeneous system $\mathbf{y}' = A \cdot \mathbf{y}$, where A is an $n \times n$ diagonalizable matrix. In other words, we assume that $\mathbf{b} = \mathbf{0}$ and that A has n linearly independent eigenvectors $\mathbf{v}_1, \ldots, \mathbf{v}_n$ with eigenvalues $\lambda_1, \ldots, \lambda_n$ such that $A\mathbf{v}_i = \lambda_i \mathbf{v}_i$ for $1 \leq i \leq n$. This implies that $P^{-1}AP = D$ when

$$P = \begin{pmatrix} \mathbf{v}_1 | \mathbf{v}_2 | \cdots | \mathbf{v}_n \end{pmatrix}, \qquad D = \begin{pmatrix} \lambda_1 & 0 & \cdots & 0 \\ 0 & \lambda_2 & \cdots & 0 \\ \vdots & \vdots & \ddots & \vdots \\ 0 & 0 & \cdots & \lambda_n \end{pmatrix}$$

Let us introduce new variables $\mathbf{z} = (z_1, z_2, \ldots, z_n)$, given by $\mathbf{z} = P^{-1}\mathbf{y}$, or $\mathbf{y} = P\mathbf{z}$. We compute the left- and right-hand sides of the equation $\mathbf{y}' = A\mathbf{y}$ in terms of $\mathbf{z}$, and get

$$\mathbf{y}' = (P\mathbf{z})' = P\mathbf{z}', \quad A\mathbf{y} = (PDP^{-1})\mathbf{y} = PD(P^{-1}\mathbf{y}) = PD\mathbf{z}$$

The linear homogeneous system $\mathbf{y}' = A\mathbf{y}$ can therefore be written $P\mathbf{z}' = PD\mathbf{z}$. Since P is invertible, multiplication on the left by P^{-1} gives $\mathbf{z}' = D\mathbf{z}$, which is a decoupled system of differential equations:

$$\begin{pmatrix} z_1' \\ z_2' \\ \vdots \\ z_n' \end{pmatrix} = \begin{pmatrix} \lambda_1 & 0 & \cdots & 0 \\ 0 & \lambda_2 & \cdots & 0 \\ \vdots & \vdots & \ddots & \vdots \\ 0 & 0 & \cdots & \lambda_n \end{pmatrix} \cdot \begin{pmatrix} z_1 \\ z_2 \\ \vdots \\ z_n \end{pmatrix} \quad \Rightarrow \quad \begin{cases} z_1' = \lambda_1 z_1 \\ z_2' = \lambda_2 z_2 \\ \cdots \\ z_n' = \lambda_n z_n \end{cases}$$

The n equations are linear and separable first order differential equations, and we find the solution

$$z_1 = C_1 e^{\lambda_1 t}, \quad z_2 = C_2 e^{\lambda_2 t}, \quad \ldots \quad , z_n = C_n e^{\lambda_n t}$$

9.2 Linear systems of differential equations

using the methods in Section 7.4 or 7.5. In matrix form, we can write the general solution as

$$\mathbf{z} = \begin{pmatrix} C_1 e^{\lambda_1 t} \\ C_2 e^{\lambda_2 t} \\ \vdots \\ C_n e^{\lambda_n t} \end{pmatrix} \quad \Rightarrow \quad \mathbf{y} = P\mathbf{z} = \begin{pmatrix} \mathbf{v}_1 \big| \mathbf{v}_2 \big| \dots \big| \mathbf{v}_n \end{pmatrix} \cdot \begin{pmatrix} C_1 e^{\lambda_1 t} \\ C_2 e^{\lambda_2 t} \\ \vdots \\ C_n e^{\lambda_n t} \end{pmatrix}$$

Multiplication of the matrices above gives the general solution of the homogeneous linear system $\mathbf{y}' = A\mathbf{y}$ when A is diagonalizable:

$$\mathbf{y}(t) = C_1 \mathbf{v}_1 \, e^{\lambda_1 t} + C_2 \mathbf{v}_2 \, e^{\lambda_2 t} + \dots + C_n \mathbf{v}_n \, e^{\lambda_n t}$$

We remark that when A is not diagonalizable, it is also possible to solve this system with similar methods. We may need to use complex eigenvalues and generalized complex eigenvectors in this case, and this is outside the scope of this book.

Homogeneous linear systems of differential equations

The homogeneous linear system $\mathbf{y}' = A \cdot \mathbf{y}$ of first order differential equations has the general solution

$$\mathbf{y}(t) = C_1 \mathbf{v}_1 \, e^{\lambda_1 t} + C_2 \mathbf{v}_2 \, e^{\lambda_2 t} + \dots + C_n \mathbf{v}_n \, e^{\lambda_n t}$$

when A is diagonalizable with n linearly independent eigenvectors $\mathbf{v}_1, \dots, \mathbf{v}_n$ and eigenvalues $\lambda_1, \dots, \lambda_n$ such that $A\mathbf{v}_i = \lambda_i \mathbf{v}_i$ for $1 \leq i \leq n$.

As an example, let us consider the homogeneous linear system of differential equations in the variables (y_1, y_2), given by

$$y_1' = 3y_1 + 4y_2$$
$$y_2' = 4y_1 - 3y_2$$

In this case, A is symmetric and therefore diagonalizable, and we can use the method described above. We first compute the eigenvalues of A: The characteristic equation is given by

$$\det(A - \lambda I) = \lambda^2 - 25 = 0$$

Therefore, the eigenvalues are $\lambda_1 = 5$ and $\lambda_2 = -5$. Next, we find the corresponding eigenvectors. For $\lambda = 5$, the linear system becomes $-2y_1 + 4y_2 = 0$, $4y_1 - 8y_2 = 0$. Both equations give $y_1 = 2y_2$ with y_2 free. For $\lambda = -5$, the linear system becomes $8y_1 + 4y_2 = 0$, $4y_1 + 2y_2 = 0$. Both equations give $y_2 = -2y_1$ with y_1 free. We may therefore choose a base of eigenvectors in E_5 and E_{-5} given by

$$\mathbf{v}_1 = \begin{pmatrix} 2 \\ 1 \end{pmatrix}, \quad \mathbf{v}_2 = \begin{pmatrix} 1 \\ -2 \end{pmatrix}$$

9 • Systems of differential and difference equations

This gives $P^{-1}AP = D$ when

$$P = \begin{pmatrix} 2 & 1 \\ 1 & -2 \end{pmatrix}, \quad D = \begin{pmatrix} 5 & 0 \\ 0 & -5 \end{pmatrix}$$

We make the change of variables given by $\mathbf{z} = P^{-1}\mathbf{y}$, or $\mathbf{y} = P\mathbf{z}$. Explicitly, this gives the equations

$$\begin{pmatrix} y_1 \\ y_2 \end{pmatrix} = \begin{pmatrix} 2 & 1 \\ 1 & -2 \end{pmatrix} \begin{pmatrix} z_1 \\ z_2 \end{pmatrix}, \quad \text{or} \quad \begin{pmatrix} z_1 \\ z_2 \end{pmatrix} = \frac{1}{5} \begin{pmatrix} 2 & 1 \\ 1 & -2 \end{pmatrix} \begin{pmatrix} y_1 \\ y_2 \end{pmatrix}$$

In other words, $y_1 = 2z_1 + z_2$, $y_2 = z_1 - 2z_2$, or $z_1 = (2y_1 + y_2)/5$, $z_2 = (y_1 - 2y_2)/5$. The solutions for z_1 and z_2 are given by

$$\mathbf{z} = \begin{pmatrix} z_1 \\ z_2 \end{pmatrix} = \begin{pmatrix} C_1 e^{5t} \\ C_2 e^{-5t} \end{pmatrix}$$

since the decoupled system in z_1, z_2 is given by $z_1' = 5z_1$ and $z_2' = -5z_2$. This means that

$$\mathbf{y} = \begin{pmatrix} 2 & 1 \\ 1 & -2 \end{pmatrix} \cdot \begin{pmatrix} C_1 e^{5t} \\ C_2 e^{-5t} \end{pmatrix} = C_1 \begin{pmatrix} 2 \\ 1 \end{pmatrix} e^{5t} + C_2 \begin{pmatrix} 1 \\ -2 \end{pmatrix} e^{-5t} = \begin{pmatrix} 2C_1 e^{5t} + C_2 e^{-5t} \\ C_1 e^{5t} - 2C_2 e^{-5t} \end{pmatrix}$$

The general solution of the system is therefore given by $y_1(t) = 2C_1 e^{5t} + C_2 e^{-5t}$ and $y_2(t) = C_1 e^{5t} - 2C_2 e^{-5t}$.

Second order differential equations and characteristic equations. We consider a homogeneous linear second order differential equation $y'' + ay' + by = 0$, where a, b are constants. This differential equation can be written as $y'' = -by - ay'$, and when we set $y_1 = y$ and $y_2 = y'$, we obtain the planar system $y_1' = y' = y_2$ and $y_2' = y'' = -by - ay' = -by_1 - ay_2$, which can be written in the form

$$y_1' = y_2$$
$$y_2' = -by_1 - ay_2$$

In matrix form, this system of differential equations can be written $\mathbf{y}' = A\mathbf{y}$:

$$\mathbf{y}' = \begin{pmatrix} y_1' \\ y_2' \end{pmatrix} = \begin{pmatrix} 0 & 1 \\ -b & -a \end{pmatrix} \cdot \begin{pmatrix} y_1 \\ y_2 \end{pmatrix} = A \cdot \mathbf{y} \quad \Rightarrow \quad A = \begin{pmatrix} 0 & 1 \\ -b & -a \end{pmatrix}$$

The characteristic equation of the matrix A is $\lambda^2 - \text{tr}(A)\lambda + \det(A) = 0$, which gives $\lambda^2 + a\lambda + b = 0$. We notice that this coincides with the characteristic equation of $y'' + ay' + by = 0$ used in Section 7.10, given by

$$r^2 + ar + b = 0$$

when we substitute $r = \lambda$. This is the reason why $r^2 + ar + b = 0$ is called the characteristic equation of the homogeneous second order linear differential equation.

The inhomogeneous case. We consider the case of a linear system $\mathbf{y}' = A \cdot \mathbf{y} + \mathbf{b}$ of differential equations, where A is an $n \times n$ matrix and $\mathbf{b}$ is an n-vector. We say that a state vector $\mathbf{y}$ is an *equilibrium state* if $A \cdot \mathbf{y} + \mathbf{b} = \mathbf{0}$, and write $\mathbf{y}_e$ for any equilibrium state of the system. To find equilibrium states, we must solve the linear system $A\mathbf{y} = -\mathbf{b}$. Hence there is one equilibrium state when $\det(A) \neq 0$, and there may be none or infinitely many equilibrium states otherwise.

If $\mathbf{y}_e$ is an equilibrium state for the linear system $\mathbf{y}' = A \cdot \mathbf{y} + \mathbf{b}$, we make the change of variables $\mathbf{z} = \mathbf{y} - \mathbf{y}_e$. We compute that

$$\mathbf{z}' = (\mathbf{y} - \mathbf{y}_e)' = \mathbf{y}', \quad A\mathbf{z} = A(\mathbf{y} - \mathbf{y}_e) = A\mathbf{y} - A\mathbf{y}_e = A\mathbf{y} + \mathbf{b}$$

Therefore the linear system $\mathbf{y}' = A \cdot \mathbf{y} + \mathbf{b}$ takes the form $\mathbf{z}' = A\mathbf{z}$ in the variables $\mathbf{z}$. This is a homogeneous linear system, and we can solve it using eigenvalues and eigenvectors when A is diagonalizable.

9.3 Equilibrium states of systems of differential equations

We consider an autonomous coupled system of first order differential equations in $(y_1, y_2, \ldots, y_n)$ of the form

$$\begin{aligned} y_1' &= F_1(y_1, \ldots, y_n) \\ y_2' &= F_2(y_1, \ldots, y_n) \\ &\vdots \\ y_n' &= F_n(y_1, \ldots, y_n) \end{aligned}$$

An *equilibrium state* of the system of differential equations is a state vector $\mathbf{y}_e$ such that

$$F_1(\mathbf{y}_e) = F_2(\mathbf{y}_e) = \cdots = F_n(\mathbf{y}_e) = 0$$

If the system starts in an equilibrium state, it will remain there as time passes since $y_1' = y_2' = \cdots = y_n' = 0$. However, if the initial condition is $\mathbf{y}(0) = \mathbf{b}$, and $\mathbf{b}$ is close to the equilibrium state $\mathbf{y}_e$, then the state of the system can either approach the equilibrium state or move away from it as time passes. We say that $\mathbf{y}_e$ is a *stable equilibrium state* in the former case, and an *unstable equilibrium state* in the latter case. The equilibrium state $\mathbf{y}_e$ is called *globally asymptotically stable* if the state of the system approaches $\mathbf{y}_e$, no matter what the initial condition is.

For example, we have solved the following linear system of differential equations in the previous section:

$$\begin{aligned} y_1' &= 3y_1 + 4y_2 \\ y_2' &= 4y_1 - 3y_2 \end{aligned}$$

We found the general solution $y_1(t) = 2C_1 e^{5t} + C_2 e^{-5t}$ and $y_2(t) = C_1 e^{5t} - 2C_2 e^{-5t}$. This system has only one equilibrium state $\mathbf{y}_e = (0, 0)$, since $\det(A) = -25 \neq 0$, which means that $A\mathbf{y} = \mathbf{0}$ has a unique solution $\mathbf{y} = \mathbf{0}$. Given an initial condition $y_1(0) = b_1$ and $y_2(0) = b_2$, we can determine values for C_1 and C_2. We notice that if $C_1 \neq 0$, then

$$y_1(t) = 2C_1 e^{5t} + C_2 e^{-5t} \to \pm\infty, \qquad y_2(t) = C_1 e^{5t} - 2C_2 e^{-5t} \to \pm\infty$$

as $t \to \infty$. There are points close to the steady state $(0, 0)$ with $C_1 \neq 0$. For example, if $h > 0$ is small and the initial condition is $y_1(0) = 2h$ and $y_2(0) = h$, then $C_1 = h > 0$ and $C_2 = 0$. In fact, we have

$$y_1(0) = 2C_1 + C_2, \qquad y_2(0) = C_1 - 2C_2$$

and this means that $C_1 = h$, $C_2 = 0$ gives $y_1(0) = 2h$ and $y_2(0) = h$. We conclude that $\mathbf{y}_e = (0, 0)$ is an unstable equilibrium state for this linear system, since $\mathbf{y}(0) = (2h, h)$ with $h > 0$ small means that

$$\mathbf{y}(t) = \begin{pmatrix} 2h e^{5t} \\ h e^{5t} \end{pmatrix}$$

moves away from $\mathbf{y}_e = (0, 0)$ as t is increasing.

Proposition 9.1. Let $\mathbf{y}_e$ be an equilibrium state of a linear system $\mathbf{y}' = A\mathbf{y} + \mathbf{b}$ of differential equations. If A has n negative eigenvalues $\lambda_1, \lambda_2, \ldots, \lambda_n < 0$ then $\mathbf{y}_e$ is globally asymptotically stable.

Let $y'' = F(y, y')$ be a second order autonomous differential equation, and consider the corresponding system of differential equations

$$y_1' = y_2$$
$$y_2' = F(y_1, y_2)$$

given by $y_1 = y$ and $y_2 = y'$. We say that $y = y_e$ is an equilibrium state of $y'' = F(y, y')$ if $(y_1, y_2) = (y_e, 0)$ is an equilibrium state of the system of differential equations. This means that y_e is an equilibrium state if and only if $F(y_e, 0) = 0$. Moreover, we define the stability of $y = y_e$ to be the stability of $(y_1, y_2) = (y_e, 0)$ as an equilibrium state of this system of differential equations.

Proposition 9.2. Let $\mathbf{y}_e$ be an equilibrium state of a linear second order autonomous differential equation $y'' + ay' + by = c$. If its characteristic equation $r^2 + ar + b = 0$ has two negative characteristic roots $r_1, r_2 < 0$, then $\mathbf{y}_e$ is globally asymptotically stable.

9.4 Linear systems of difference equations

Let $y_i = (y_{it})$ be a sequence for $1 \le i \le n$. When we use this notation, we mean that $y_{i0}, y_{i1}, y_{i2}, \ldots$ is a sequence for $1 \le i \le n$. A first order difference equation of the form

$$y_{i,t+1} = F_i(t, y_{1t}, y_{2t}, \ldots, y_{nt})$$

is called a *coupled difference equation*. That the difference equation is coupled means that element $y_{i,t+1}$ in the sequence y_i at time $t+1$ depends on the values $y_{1t}, y_{2t}, \ldots, y_{nt}$ in the sequences $y_1, y_2, \ldots, y_n$ at time t. For example, the difference equation $y_{1,t+1} = 0.85 y_{1t} + 0.18 y_{2t}$ is coupled, and the solution for y_1 will depend on the sequence y_2.

A coupled system of first order difference equations is a system of difference equations that can be written in the form

$$y_{1,t+1} = F_1(t, y_{1t}, y_{2t}, \ldots, y_{nt})$$
$$y_{2,t+1} = F_2(t, y_{1t}, y_{2t}, \ldots, y_{nt})$$
$$\vdots$$
$$y_{n,t+1} = F_n(t, y_{1t}, y_{2t}, \ldots, y_{nt})$$

where $F_1, F_2, \ldots, F_n$ are functions in $(t, y_{1t}, \ldots, y_{nt})$. It is called *autonomous* if $F_1, F_2, \ldots, F_n$ are independent of t.

For example, $y_{1,t+1} = 0.85 y_{1t} + 0.18 y_{2t}$, $y_{2,t+1} = 0.15 y_{1t} + 0.82 y_{2t}$ is a coupled system of difference equations. In fact, this is an example of a Markov chain, since we can write it in matrix form as

$$\mathbf{y}_{t+1} = \begin{pmatrix} y_{1,t+1} \\ y_{2,t+1} \end{pmatrix} = \begin{pmatrix} 0.85 & 0.18 \\ 0.15 & 0.82 \end{pmatrix} \cdot \begin{pmatrix} y_{1t} \\ y_{2t} \end{pmatrix} = A \cdot \mathbf{y}_t$$

when we use vector notation $\mathbf{y}_t = (y_{1t}, y_{2t}, \ldots, y_{nt})$, and write A for the 2×2 matrix given above. We recognize A as the transition matrix of the Markov chain, and $\mathbf{y}_t$ as the state vector at time t.

A coupled autonomous system of first order difference equations is called *linear* if it can be written in the form

$$y_{1,t+1} = a_{11} y_{1t} + a_{12} y_{2t} + \ldots + a_{1n} y_{nt}) + b_1$$
$$y_{2,t+1} = a_{21} y_{1t} + a_{22} y_{2t} + \ldots + a_{2n} y_{nt}) + b_2$$
$$\vdots$$
$$y_{n,t+1} = a_{n1} y_{1t} + a_{n2} y_{2t} + \ldots + a_{nn} y_{nt}) + b_n$$

It is called *homogeneous* if, in addition, $b_1 = b_2 = \ldots = b_n = 0$. When we write $\mathbf{y}_t = (y_{1t}, y_{2t}, \ldots, y_{nt})$ for the state vector of the system, we can write any linear system of difference equations in matrix form as $\mathbf{y}_{t+1} = A\mathbf{y}_t + \mathbf{b}$, where A is an $n \times n$ matrix and $\mathbf{b}$ is an n-vector. Notice that any Markov chain is a linear homogeneous system of difference equations; it is the special case characterized by the fact that the matrix A is a nonnegative matrix where each column sum is equal to 1.

The homogeneous case. We consider the case of a linear homogeneous system $\mathbf{y}_{t+1} = A \cdot \mathbf{y}_t$, where A is an $n \times n$ diagonalizable matrix. That is, we assume that $\mathbf{b} = \mathbf{0}$ and that A has n linearly independent eigenvectors $\mathbf{v}_1, \ldots, \mathbf{v}_n$ with eigenvalues $\lambda_1, \ldots, \lambda_n$ such that $A\mathbf{v}_i = \lambda_i \mathbf{v}_i$ for $1 \leq i \leq n$. This implies that $P^{-1}AP = D$ when

$$P = \left(\mathbf{v}_1 \middle| \mathbf{v}_2 \middle| \ldots \middle| \mathbf{v}_n\right), \qquad D = \begin{pmatrix} \lambda_1 & 0 & \ldots & 0 \\ 0 & \lambda_2 & \ldots & 0 \\ \vdots & \vdots & \ddots & \vdots \\ 0 & 0 & \ldots & \lambda_n \end{pmatrix}$$

Let us introduce new sequences $\mathbf{z} = (z_1, z_2, \ldots, z_n)$, given by $\mathbf{z}_t = P^{-1}\mathbf{y}_t$, or $\mathbf{y}_t = P\mathbf{z}_t$. We compute the left- and right-hand sides of the equation $\mathbf{y}_{t+1} = A\mathbf{y}$ in terms of $\mathbf{z}$, and get

$$\mathbf{y}_{t+1} = P\mathbf{z}_{t+1}, \quad A\mathbf{y}_t = (PDP^{-1})\mathbf{y}_t = PD(P^{-1}\mathbf{y}_t) = PD\mathbf{z}_t$$

The linear homogeneous system $\mathbf{y}_{t+1} = A\mathbf{y}_t$ can therefore be written $P\mathbf{z}_{t+1} = PD\mathbf{z}_t$, or $\mathbf{z}_{t+1} = D\mathbf{z}_t$.

This is a decoupled system of difference equations:

$$\begin{pmatrix} z_{1,t+1} \\ z_{2,t+1} \\ \vdots \\ z_{n,t+1} \end{pmatrix} = \begin{pmatrix} \lambda_1 & 0 & \ldots & 0 \\ 0 & \lambda_2 & \ldots & 0 \\ \vdots & \vdots & \ddots & \vdots \\ 0 & 0 & \ldots & \lambda_n \end{pmatrix} \cdot \begin{pmatrix} z_{1t} \\ z_{2t} \\ \vdots \\ z_{nt} \end{pmatrix} \Rightarrow \begin{cases} z_{1,t+1} = \lambda_1 z_{1t} \\ z_{2,t+1} = \lambda_2 z_{2t} \\ \ldots \\ z_{n,t+1} = \lambda_n z_{nt} \end{cases}$$

The n equations are linear first order difference equations, and we find the solution

$$z_1 = C_1 \lambda_1^t, \quad z_2 = \lambda_2^t, \quad \ldots, \quad z_n = C_n \lambda_n^t$$

In matrix form, we can write the general solution as

$$\mathbf{z}_t = \begin{pmatrix} C_1 \lambda_1^t \\ C_2 \lambda_2^t \\ \vdots \\ C_n \lambda_n^t \end{pmatrix} \Rightarrow \mathbf{y}_t = P\mathbf{z}_t = \left(\mathbf{v}_1 \middle| \mathbf{v}_2 \middle| \ldots \middle| \mathbf{v}_n\right) \cdot \begin{pmatrix} C_1 \lambda_1^t \\ C_2 \lambda_2^t \\ \vdots \\ C_n \lambda_n^t \end{pmatrix}$$

Multiplication of the matrices above gives the general solution of the homogeneous linear system $\mathbf{y}_{t+1} = A\mathbf{y}_t$ of difference equations when A is diagonalizable:

$$\mathbf{y}_t = C_1 \mathbf{v}_1 \lambda_1^t + C_2 \mathbf{v}_2 \lambda_2^t + \ldots + C_n \mathbf{v}_n \lambda_n^t$$

We remark that when A is not diagonalizable, it is also possible to solve this system with similar methods. We may need to use complex eigenvalues and generalized complex eigenvectors in this case, and this is outside the scope of this book.

> **Homogeneous linear systems of difference equations**
>
> The homogeneous linear system $\mathbf{y}_{t+1} = A \cdot \mathbf{y}_t$ of first order differential equations has the general solution
>
> $$\mathbf{y}_t = C_1 \mathbf{v}_1 \lambda_1^t + C_2 \mathbf{v}_2 \lambda_2^t + \ldots + C_n \mathbf{v}_n \lambda_n^t$$
>
> when A is diagonalizable with n linearly independent eigenvectors $\mathbf{v}_1, \ldots, \mathbf{v}_n$ and eigenvalues $\lambda_1, \ldots, \lambda_n$ such that $A\mathbf{v}_i = \lambda_i \mathbf{v}_i$ for $1 \leq i \leq n$.

The inhomogeneous case. We consider the case of a linear system $\mathbf{y}_{t+1} = A \cdot \mathbf{y}_t + \mathbf{b}$ of difference equations, where A is an $n \times n$ matrix and $\mathbf{b}$ is an n-vector. We say that a state vector $\mathbf{y}$ is an *equilibrium state* if $A \cdot \mathbf{y} + \mathbf{b} = \mathbf{y}$ and write $\mathbf{y}_e$ for any equilibrium state of the system. The reason for this definition, is that we have $\mathbf{y}_{t+1} = \mathbf{y}_t$ if and only if $A\mathbf{y}_t + \mathbf{b} = \mathbf{y}_t$. To find equilibrium states, we must solve the linear system $A\mathbf{y} - \mathbf{y} = -\mathbf{b}$, which can be written in the form $(A - I)\mathbf{y} = -\mathbf{b}$. Hence there is one equilibrium state when $\det(A - I) \neq 0$, and there may be none or infinitely many equilibrium states otherwise.

If $\mathbf{y}_e$ is an equilibrium state for the linear system $\mathbf{y}_{t+1} = A \cdot \mathbf{y}_t + \mathbf{b}$, we make the change of variables $\mathbf{z}_t = \mathbf{y}_t - \mathbf{y}_e$. We compute that

$$\begin{aligned} A\mathbf{z}_t &= A(\mathbf{y}_t - \mathbf{y}_e) = A\mathbf{y}_t - A\mathbf{y}_e = A\mathbf{y}_t - (\mathbf{y}_e - \mathbf{b}) \\ &= A\mathbf{y}_t + \mathbf{b} - \mathbf{y}_e = \mathbf{y}_{t+1} - \mathbf{y}_e = \mathbf{z}_{t+1} \end{aligned}$$

since $A\mathbf{y}_e + \mathbf{b} = \mathbf{y}_e$. Therefore the linear system $\mathbf{y}_{t+1} = A \cdot \mathbf{y}_t + \mathbf{b}$ takes the form $\mathbf{z}_{t+1} = A\mathbf{z}_t$ in the variables $\mathbf{z}_t$. This is a homogeneous linear system, and we can solve it using eigenvalues and eigenvectors when A is diagonalizable.

9.5 Equilibrium states of systems of difference equations

We consider an autonomous coupled system of first order difference equations in $(y_1, y_2, \ldots, y_n)$ of the form

$$y_{1, t+1} = F_1(y_{1t}, y_{2t}, \ldots, y_{nt})$$
$$y_{2, t+1} = F_2(y_{1t}, y_{2t}, \ldots, y_{nt})$$
$$\vdots$$
$$y_{n, t+1} = F_n(y_{1t}, y_{2t}, \ldots, y_{nt})$$

An *equilibrium state* of the system of differential equations is a state vector $\mathbf{y}_e$ such that

$$(F_1(\mathbf{y}_e), F_2(\mathbf{y}_e), \ldots, F_n(\mathbf{y}_e)) = \mathbf{y}_e$$

If the system starts in an equilibrium state, it will remain there as time passes, since $y_{i,t+1} - y_{i,t} = 0$ for $1 \le i \le n$. However, if the initial condition is $\mathbf{y}_0 = \mathbf{b}$, and $\mathbf{b}$ is close to the equilibrium state $\mathbf{y}_e$, then the state of the system can either tend towards the equilibrium state or move away from it as time passes. We say that $\mathbf{y}_e$ is a *stable equilibrium state* in the former case, and an *unstable equilibrium state* in the latter case. The equilibrium state $\mathbf{y}_e$ is called *globally asymptotically stable* if the state of the system approaches $\mathbf{y}_e$, no matter what the initial condition is.

For example, when $\mathbf{y}_{t+1} = A\mathbf{y}_t$ is a regular Markov chain, it has an equilibrium state $\mathbf{y}$ such that $\mathbf{y}_t \to \mathbf{y}$ as $t \to \infty$ for any initial state $\mathbf{y}_0$ that is a state vector. We recall from Section 4.4 that a state vector in this context means a nonnegative vector $\mathbf{y}_0 \ge 0$ such that the sum of its components is 1, and that $\mathbf{y}$ is the unique eigenvector for A of eigenvalue $\lambda = 1$ that is a state vector in this sense. Hence the equilibrium state $\mathbf{y}$ of a regular Markov chain is globally asymptotically stable.

Proposition 9.3. Let $\mathbf{y}_e$ be an equilibrium state of a linear system $\mathbf{y}_{t+1} = A\mathbf{y}_t + \mathbf{b}$ of difference equations. If A has n eigenvalues $\lambda_1, \lambda_2, \ldots, \lambda_n$ with $|\lambda_i| < 1$, then $\mathbf{y}_e$ is globally asymptotically stable.

Problems

Problem 9.1 Solve the system of differential equations given by $y_1' = y_1 + y_2$ and $y_2' = 2y_2$, and find the particular solutions with $y_1(0) = 1$ and $y_2(0) = 2$.

Problem 9.2 Rewrite the second order differential equation $y'' - 7y' + 12y = 0$ as a system of differential equations, and use this to solve the second order differential equation.

Problem 9.3 Rewrite the second order differential equation $y'' + ay' + by = 0$ as a system of differential equations, and solve it as a system of differential equations when $a^2 > 4b$.

Problem 9.4 Consider the system of differential equations given by $\mathbf{y}' = A\mathbf{y}$, where

$$A = \begin{pmatrix} 6 & -3 \\ -2 & 1 \end{pmatrix}$$

Check that A is diagonalizable, and solve the system using the eigenvalues and eigenvectors of A.

Problem 9.5 Consider the system of differential equations given by $\mathbf{y}' = A\mathbf{y}$, for the following matrix A, and find its general solution:

$$A = \begin{pmatrix} 1 & 2 & 2 \\ 2 & 4 & 2 \\ 1 & 2 & 0 \end{pmatrix}$$

Problem 9.6 Consider the linear system of differential equations $\mathbf{y}' = A\mathbf{y} + \mathbf{b}$. Show that if A is a negative definite symmetric matrix, then there is a unique equilibrium state $\mathbf{y}_e$ that is globally asymptotically stable.

Problem 9.7 Consider the second order differential equation $y'' + 7y' + 12y = 3$. Find the equilibrium states of this system, and determine their stability. Are the steady states globally asymptotically stable?

Problem 9.8 Find the particular solution of the system of difference equations that satisfies the given initial condition:

$$\mathbf{y}_{t+1} = \begin{pmatrix} 4 & 0 & 6 \\ -1 & 3 & 0 \\ 1 & 1 & 2 \end{pmatrix} \cdot \mathbf{y}_t, \quad \mathbf{y}_0 = \begin{pmatrix} 1 \\ 1 \\ 1 \end{pmatrix}$$

CHAPTER A

Complex numbers and trigonometric functions

A.1 Complex numbers

The numbers that we know from school mathematics, and that we have used in most of this book, are called *real numbers*. We write $\mathbb{R}$ for the set of all real numbers. A real number has a decimal representation, and is represented by a point on the real number line. In the figure below, we show the real number line together with some examples of real numbers. The decimal representations $1/3 = 0.3333\ldots$, $\sqrt{2} = 1.4142\ldots$ and $e = 2.7182\ldots$ determine their position on the number line.

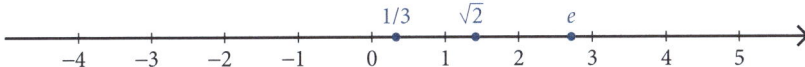

Not every polynomial equation with real coefficients has solutions among the real numbers. Let us consider the quadratic equation $x^2 - 4x + 5 = 0$ as an example. If we try to solve it by completing the square, we get

$$x^2 - 4x = -5 \quad \Rightarrow \quad x^2 - 4x + 4 = -5 + 4 \quad \Rightarrow \quad (x-2)^2 = -1$$

This equation has no real solutions, since the square of a real number cannot be negative. Alternatively, we could use the quadratic formula, which gives

$$x = \frac{-(-4) \pm \sqrt{(-4)^2 - 4 \cdot 1 \cdot 5}}{2 \cdot 1} = \frac{4 \pm \sqrt{-4}}{2}$$

The square root $\sqrt{-4}$ of a negative number does not exist among the real numbers. We conclude that the equation $x^2 - 4x + 5 = 0$ has no real solutions.

Let us introduce the number $i = \sqrt{-1}$. This is not a real number, since we have that $i^2 = -1$, and the square of a real number cannot be negative. The new number i is called an *imaginary number*, and it makes it possible to take square roots of negative numbers. For example, we have that $\sqrt{-4} = \sqrt{4} \cdot \sqrt{-1} = 2i$. This means that any quadratic equation has solutions. For example, if we write $x^2 - 4x + 5 = 0$

as $(x-2)^2 = -1$, then we get $x - 2 = \pm\sqrt{-1} = \pm i$, or that $x = 2 \pm i$. Alternatively, using the quadratic formula, we get

$$x = \frac{4 \pm \sqrt{-4}}{2} = \frac{4 \pm \sqrt{4}\sqrt{-1}}{2} = 2 \pm i$$

The idea behind complex numbers is that when we allow expressions involving $i = \sqrt{-1}$ in addition to real numbers, any quadratic equation has solutions.

We define a *complex number* to be a number of the form $z = a + bi$, where a and b are real numbers and $i = \sqrt{-1}$. We call a the *real part* and b the *imaginary part* of the complex number $z = a + bi$, and represent complex numbers as points $(x, y) = (a, b)$ in the complex plane shown in the figure below. Note that the complex plane contains the real number line as the x-axis.

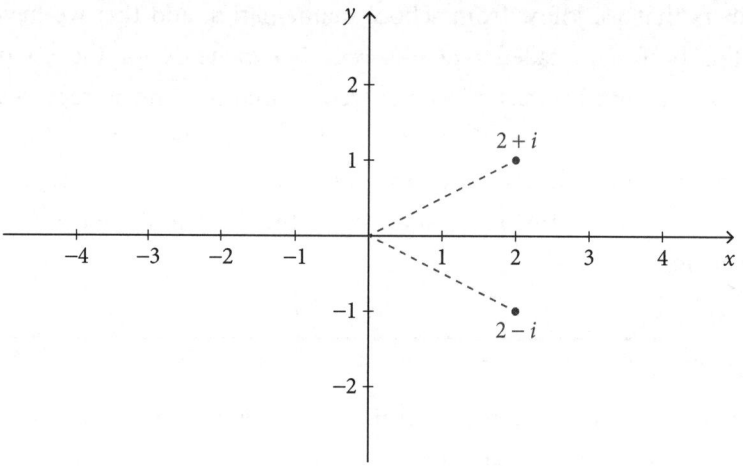

We can also think of a complex number $z = a + bi$ as a vector (a, b). Using the usual addition and subtraction of vectors, we can define addition and subtraction of complex numbers. We can also use scalar multiplication to define multiplication of a real number (a scalar) by a complex number.

Let $z_1 = a_1 + ib_1$ and $z_2 = a_2 + ib_2$ be any complex numbers. Then the formulas for adding and subtracting complex numbers are $z_1 + z_2 = (a_1 + a_2) + i(b_1 + b_2)$ and $z_1 - z_2 = (a_1 - a_2) + i(b_1 - b_2)$. For any real number r, the multiplication of r by z_1 is given by the formula $r \cdot (a_1 + ib_1) = (ra_1) + i(rb_1)$. For example, we have that

$$(2 + i) + (2 - i) = 4, \quad (2 + i) - (2 - i) = 2i, \quad 3 \cdot (2 + i) = 6 + 3i$$

Note that we sometimes write ib instead of bi when this makes it easier to read the complex numbers. The multiplication of the complex numbers z_1 and z_2 cannot be defined using the well-known vector operations. Instead, we must use algebraic laws and the fact that $i^2 = -1$, and get

$$z_1 \cdot z_2 = (a_1 + ib_1) \cdot (a_2 + ib_2) = a_1a_2 + ib_1a_2 + ia_1b_2 + i^2b_1b_2$$
$$= (a_1a_2 - b_1b_2) + i(a_1b_2 + a_2b_1)$$

For example, we have that

$$(2+i) \cdot (2-i) = 4 + 2i - 2i - i^2 = 4 - (-1) = 5$$

We see that the result of adding, subtracting and multiplying two complex numbers is again a complex number.

We define the *modulus* of the complex number $z = a + ib$ to be $|z| = \sqrt{a^2 + b^2}$. This represents the distance from the point $(x, y) = (a, b)$ to the origin of the complex plane. When z is a real number $z = a$ (that is, a complex number with $b = 0$), then the modulus $|z| = \sqrt{a^2} = |a|$, the absolute value of a.

When $z = a + ib$ is any complex number, we write $\bar{z} = a - ib$ and call $\bar{z}$ the *complex conjugate* of z. Geometrically, the complex conjugate $\bar{z}$ is the reflection of z across the x-axis (or the real number line). Note that

$$z \cdot \bar{z} = (a + ib)(a - ib) = a^2 + b^2 = |z|^2$$

It is clear that $\bar{z} = z$ if and only if z is a real number, and that $\bar{\bar{z}} = z$ for any complex number.

Lemma A.1. For any complex numbers z_1 and z_2, we have that

a) $\overline{z_1 + z_2} = \bar{z_1} + \bar{z_2}$
b) $\overline{z_1 - z_2} = \bar{z_1} - \bar{z_2}$
c) $\overline{z_1 z_2} = \bar{z_1} \cdot \bar{z_2}$

Proof. We will show the last statement; the proofs of the first two are similar. Since $z_1 z_2 = (a_1a_2 - b_1b_2) + i(a_1b_2 + a_2b_1)$, it follows that

$$\overline{z_1 z_2} = (a_1a_2 - b_1b_2) - i(a_1b_2 + a_2b_1)$$

On the other hand, $\bar{z_1} = a_1 - ib_1$ and $\bar{z_2} = a_2 - ib_2$, so we have that

$$\bar{z_1} \cdot \bar{z_2} = (a_1a_2 - b_1b_2) - i(a_1b_2 + a_2b_1)$$

Since the expressions are identical, we have that $\overline{z_1 z_2} = \bar{z_1} \cdot \bar{z_2}$. □

Lemma A.2. For any complex numbers z_1 and z_2, we have that $|z_1 z_2| = |z_1| \cdot |z_2|$. In particular, it follows that $|z^n| = |z|^n$.

Proof. Since $z_1 z_2 = (a_1 a_2 - b_1 b_2) + i(a_1 b_2 + a_2 b_1)$, it follows that its modulus is given by

$$\begin{aligned} |z_1 z_2| &= (a_1 a_2 - b_1 b_2)^2 + (a_1 b_2 + a_2 b_1)^2 \\ &= a_1^2 a_2^2 - 2a_1 a_2 b_1 b_2 + b_1^2 b_2^2 + a_1^2 b_2^2 + 2a_1 b_2 a_2 b_1 + a_2^2 b_1^2 \\ &= a_1^2 a_2^2 + b_1^2 b_2^2 + a_1^2 b_2^2 + a_2^2 b_1^2 \\ &= (a_1^2 + b_1^2)(a_2^2 + b_2^2) = |z_1| \cdot |z_2| \end{aligned}$$

This means that $|z_1^2| = |z_1| \cdot |z_1| = |z_1|^2$, and the formula for $|z^n|$ follows by induction. □

To define the division z_1/z_2 of complex numbers when $z_2 \neq 0$, we expand the fraction with $\bar{z}_2$. Since $z_2 \cdot \bar{z}_2 = |z_2|^2 = a_2^2 + b_2^2$, which is a nonzero real number, the result is a complex number:

$$\begin{aligned} \frac{z_1}{z_2} &= \frac{a_1 + ib_1}{a_2 + ib_2} = \frac{(a_1 + ib_1)(a_2 - ib_2)}{(a_2 + ib_2)(a_2 - ib_2)} = \frac{(a_1 a_2 + b_1 b_2) + i(a_2 b_1 - a_1 b_2)}{a_2^2 + b_2^2} \\ &= \left(\frac{a_1 a_2 + b_1 b_2}{a_2^2 + b_2^2} \right) + i \left(\frac{a_2 b_1 - a_1 b_2}{a_2^2 + b_2^2} \right) \end{aligned}$$

The two expressions in parentheses are real numbers, and give the real and imaginary part of z_1/z_2. This means that z_1/z_2 is a complex number when $z_2 \neq 0$. For example, we have

$$\frac{2+i}{2-i} = \frac{(2+i)(2+i)}{(2-i)(2+i)} = \frac{4 + 4i - 1}{4 + 1} = \frac{3 + 4i}{5} = \frac{3}{5} + i\frac{4}{5}$$

since $(2+i)(2-i) = |2+i|^2 = 5$.

A.2 Conjugation and complex roots

In the example $x^2 - 4x + 5 = 0$, we saw that the two solutions or roots $2 + i$ and $2 - i$ were complex conjugates. That is, $\overline{2 + i} = 2 - i$. This is not a coincidence:

Proposition A.3. Let $a_n x^n + a_{n-1} x^{n-1} + \ldots + a_1 x + a_0 = 0$ be a polynomial equation of degree n with real coefficients $a_0, a_1, \ldots, a_n$. If $z = a + ib$ is a complex solution of the polynomial equation, then its complex conjugate $\bar{z} = a - ib$ is also a solution.

Proof. If z is a solution, then $a_n z^n + a_{n-1} z^{n-1} + \ldots + a_1 z + a_0 = 0$. Taking complex conjugates on each side of the equation, we get

$$\overline{a_n z^n + a_{n-1} z^{n-1} + \ldots + a_1 z + a_0} = \overline{a_n}\,\overline{z}^n + \overline{a_{n-1}}\,\overline{z}^{n-1} + \ldots + \overline{a_1}\,\overline{z} + \overline{a_0} = 0$$

We have that $\overline{a_i} = a_i$ for $i = 0, 1, \ldots, n$ since a_i is a real number, and this means that $\bar{z}$ satisfies the equation $a_n x^n + a_{n-1} x^{n-1} + \ldots + a_1 x + a_0 = 0$. □

Let us consider the equation $x^3 - 5x^2 + 17x - 13 = 0$ as an example. We see that $x = 1$ is a solution, since $1^3 - 5 \cdot 1^2 + 17 \cdot 1 - 13 = 0$. Polynomial division gives

$$(x^3 - 5x^2 + 17x - 13) : (x - 1) = x^2 - 4x + 13$$

This means that $x^3 - 5x^2 + 17x - 13 = (x - 1)(x^2 - 4x + 13)$. To find the remaining solutions of $x^3 - 5x^2 + 17x - 13 = 0$, we solve $x^2 - 4x + 13 = 0$. This gives

$$x = \frac{-(-4) \pm \sqrt{(-4)^2 - 4(13)}}{2} = \frac{4 \pm \sqrt{-36}}{2} = \frac{4 \pm 6i}{2} = 2 \pm 3i$$

This means that $x^3 - 5x^2 + 17x - 13 = 0$ has the three complex solutions $z = 1$, $z = 2 + 3i$, and $z = 2 - 3i$.

Another example is $x^3 - 1$, which can be written $x^3 - 1 - 0$. We see that $x = 1$ is a solution, and we can find the other solutions using the polynomial division $(x^3 - 1) : (x - 1) = x^2 + x + 1$. The quadratic equation $x^2 + x + 1 = 0$ gives

$$x = \frac{-1 \pm \sqrt{1 - 4}}{2} = \frac{-1 \pm \sqrt{3}i}{2} = -\frac{1}{2} \pm \frac{\sqrt{3}}{2} i$$

The complex solutions of $x^3 = 1$ are therefore given by $z = 1$, $z = -1/2 + i\sqrt{3}/2$, and $z = -1/2 - i\sqrt{3}/2$, and they are shown in Figure A.1. Notice that if we write $z = x + iy$ for the complex roots, then the modulus $|z| = 1$. In fact, $z^3 = 1$ means that $|z^3| = |z|^3 = 1$, and since $|z|$ is a real number, $|z| = 1$ is the only solution of this equation. Moreover,

$$|z| = \sqrt{x^2 + y^2} = 1 \quad \Rightarrow \quad x^2 + y^2 = 1$$

It follows that the complex roots of $x^3 = 1$ must lie on the unit circle $x^2 + y^2 = 1$, shown in red in the figure.

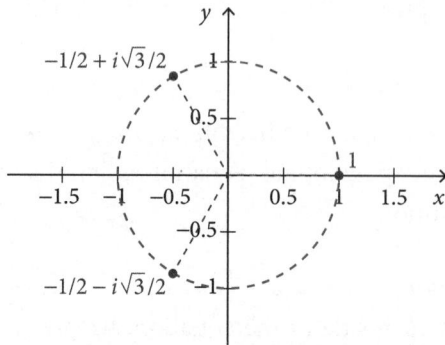

Figure A.1 The complex roots of the cubic polynomial equation $x^3 = 1$

Let us try a more complicated example, and consider the equation $x^5 = 1$. We see that $x = 1$ is a solution, and it is clearly the only real solution since $f(x) = x^5$ is an increasing function. We factor the equation as

$$x^5 - 1 = (x - 1)(x^4 + x^3 + x^2 + x + 1) = 0$$

using polynomial division. Since $x = 1$ is the only real solution, it not possible to find linear factors of $x^4 + x^3 + x^2 + x + 1$ with real coefficients. But there could perhaps be two quadratic factors with real coefficients, each giving two complex conjugate roots. Let us try to find a factorization on the form

$$x^4 + x^3 + x^2 + x + 1 = (x^2 + ax + b)(x^2 + cx + d)$$

Since

$$(x^2 + ax + b)(x^2 + cx + d) = \\ x^4 + (a + c)x^3 + (b + ac + d)x^2 + (ad + bc)x + bd$$

we must have $a + c = 1$, $b + ac + d = 1$, $ad + bc = 1$, and $bd = 1$. We try to put $b = 1$, and this gives $d = 1$, $a + c = 1$ and $ac = -1$. Solving the last two equations for a and c gives

$$c = 1 - a \quad \Rightarrow \quad a(1 - a) = -1 \quad \Rightarrow \quad a^2 - a - 1 = 0$$

We can solve this quadratic equation, which gives $a = (1 \pm \sqrt{5})/2$. We therefore find the following factorization of $x^5 - 1$:

$$x^5 - 1 = (x - 1)\left(x^2 + \frac{1 + \sqrt{5}}{2} x + 1\right)\left(x^2 + \frac{1 - \sqrt{5}}{2} x + 1\right)$$

Using the quadratic formula, we see that the two quadratic factors have no real roots since the discriminant $b^2 - 4ac$ is negative:

$$\left(\frac{1 \pm \sqrt{5}}{2}\right)^2 \cdot 1 \cdot 1 - \frac{6 \pm 2\sqrt{5}}{4} - \frac{16}{4} < 0$$

The first quadratic factor gives the two complex conjugate roots x_2 and x_3:

$$x = -\frac{1+\sqrt{5}}{2} \pm i\,\frac{\sqrt{10-2\sqrt{5}}}{2}$$

The second quadratic factor gives the two complex conjugate roots x_1 and x_4:

$$x = -\frac{1-\sqrt{5}}{2} \pm i\,\frac{\sqrt{10+2\sqrt{5}}}{2}$$

We conclude that the equation $x^5 = 1$ has one real root and two additional pairs of complex conjugate roots, in total five complex roots. As in the previous example, all five roots $z = x + iy$ have the modulus $|z| = \sqrt{x^2 + y^2} = 1$, since $|z|^5 = |z^5| = 1$. Therefore, all roots lie on the unit circle $x^2 + y^2 = 1$, and are shown in Figure A.2. Notice the beautiful, simple and symmetric nature of the figure. In fact, the five complex roots are the vertices of a regular pentagon.

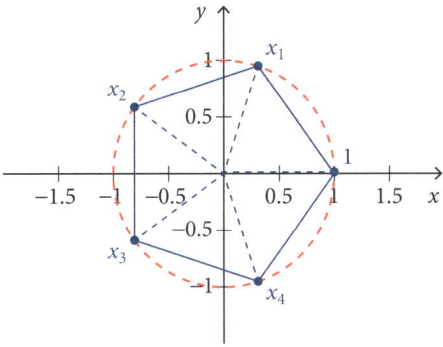

Figure A.2 The complex roots of the quintic polynomial equation $x^5 = 1$

It is no coincidence that the n'th order polynomial equations above all have n complex roots. In fact, we have the following theorem, sometimes called *the fundamental theorem of algebra*. The proof is too complicated to fit into this book.

Theorem A.4. Any polynomial equation $a_n x^n + a_{n-1} x^{n-1} + \ldots + a_1 x + a_0 = 0$ of degree $n \geq 1$ with real or complex coefficients $a_0, a_1, \ldots, a_n$ has complex roots. Moreover, there is a factorization

$$a_n x^n + a_{n-1} x^{n-1} + \ldots + a_1 x + a_0 = a_n (x - x_1)(x - x_2) \cdots (x - x_n)$$

such that $x_1, x_2, \ldots, x_n$ are complex numbers.

A.3 Polar coordinates and de Moivre's formula

Let $z = x + iy$ be a nonzero complex number. It corresponds to a point in the complex plane with coordinates (x, y). These coordinates are sometimes called the *Cartesian coordinates of the point*.

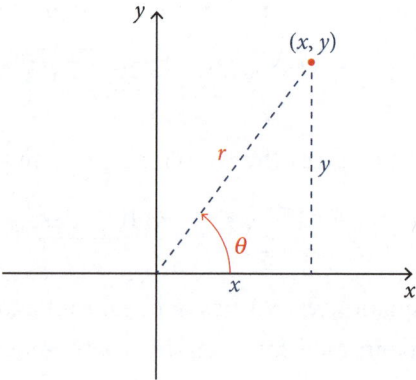

Figure A.3 Polar coordinates (r, θ) of the complex number $z = x + iy$

We can also describe the complex number $z = x + iy$ using the distance r from (x, y) to the origin $(0, 0)$ in the complex plan and the angle θ between the positive x-axis and the vector (x, y). The pair (r, θ) are called the *polar coordinates* of the complex number $z = x + iy$, and are shown in Figure A.3. The distance r is given by the modulus

$$r = |z| = \sqrt{x^2 + y^2}$$

of the complex number $z = x + iy$, and it is a positive number when $z \neq 0$. The angle θ is measured counter-clockwise starting from the positive x-axis, and can be both positive and negative. By convention, we define $(r, \theta) = (0, 0)$ to be the polar coordinates of $z = 0$.

For example, the point $(x, y) = (1, 1)$ has polar coordinates $(r, \theta) = (\sqrt{2}, 45°)$ and the point $(x, y) = (1, -1)$ has polar coordinates $(r, \theta) = (\sqrt{2}, -45°)$. Notice that while the distance $r = |z|$ is uniquely defined by z, the angle θ is only given up to an integer multiple of 360°, or one complete turn. For example, both $(\sqrt{2}, -45°)$ and $(\sqrt{2}, -45° + 360°) = (\sqrt{2}, 315°)$ are polar coordinates of the complex number $z = 1 - i$. The general formula for the angle of $z = 1 - i$ is $\theta = -45° + k \cdot 360°$ where $k = \ldots, -2, -1, 0, 1, 2, \ldots$ is any integer.

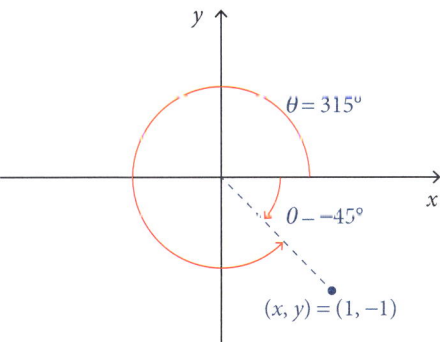

Next, we shall introduce some new functions that are useful for computing with polar coordinates. We refer back to Figure A.3 and consider the ratios x/r and y/r defined by a nonzero complex number $z = x + iy$ with modulus $r = |z| = \sqrt{x^2 + y^2}$ and angle θ. It is not difficult to see that the ratios only depend on the angle θ of the complex number. In fact, if $z_1 = x_1 + iy_1$ and $z_2 = x_2 + iy_2$ have the same angle, then (x_1, y_1) and (x_2, y_2) lie along the same straight line and form similar triangles. That is, $x_1/r_1 = x_2/r_2$ and $y_1/r_1 = y_2/r_2$.

We define the *trigonometric functions* $\sin(\theta) = y/r$ and $\cos(\theta) = x/r$. When the angle θ is given, we can compute numerical values for the trigonometric functions. For example, if $\theta = 45°$, then $x = y$ and $r = \sqrt{x^2 + x^2} = \sqrt{2x^2} = \sqrt{2} \cdot x$. Therefore

$$\sin(45°) = \frac{y}{r} = \frac{x}{\sqrt{2}x} = \frac{1}{\sqrt{2}} = \frac{\sqrt{2}}{2}, \quad \cos(45°) = \frac{x}{r} = \frac{x}{\sqrt{2}x} = \frac{1}{\sqrt{2}} = \frac{\sqrt{2}}{2}$$

This means that $\sin(45°) = \cos(45°) \approx 0.707$. The exact and approximate value of $\sin(\theta)$ and $\cos(\theta)$ are given in Table A.1 for some angles θ with $0° \leq \theta \leq 90°$. We can find approximate values of $\sin(\theta)$ and $\cos(\theta)$ for other angles using a computer or a calculator.

θ	$\sin(\theta)$	$\cos(\theta)$
0°	$0 = 0.000$	$1 = 1.000$
30°	$1/2 = 0.500$	$\sqrt{3}/2 \approx 0.866$
45°	$1/\sqrt{2} = \sqrt{2}/2 \approx 0.707$	$1/\sqrt{2} = \sqrt{2}/2 \approx 0.707$
60°	$\sqrt{3}/2 \approx 0.866$	$1/2 = 0.500$
90°	$1 = 1.000$	$0 = 0.000$

Table A.1 Some values of the trigonometric functions $\sin(\theta)$ and $\cos(\theta)$ for $0° \leq \theta \leq 90°$

A • Complex numbers and trigonometric functions

Let $z = x + iy$ be a complex number with polar coordinates (r, θ). Then we have that the Cartesian coordinates (x, y) are given by

$$x = r \cdot \cos \theta, \quad y = r \cdot \sin \theta$$

This follows from the definitions $\sin \theta = y/r$ and $\cos \theta = x/r$ when $z \neq 0$. If $z = 0$, then $r = 0$, and we see that the formulas above fit also in this case. Using polar coordinates, we can therefore write any complex number as

$$z = x + iy = r \cos \theta + ir \sin \theta = r(\cos \theta + i \sin \theta)$$

We shall see that this is a very useful way to write complex numbers, which makes many computations much easier. First of all, notice that $r \geq 0$ is the modulus $|z| = r$ of z, and that the modulus $|\cos \theta + i \sin \theta| = 1$. That is, $\cos \theta + i \sin \theta$ is a complex number on the unit circle $x^2 + y^2 = 1$ in the complex plane. In fact, it is the complex number on the unit circle with angle θ from the positive x-axis.

Lemma A.5. Let $z_1 = r_1(\cos \theta_1 + i \sin \theta_1)$ and $z_2 = r_2(\cos \theta_2 + i \sin \theta_2)$ be two complex numbers. Then $z_1 z_2 = r_1 r_2(\cos(\theta_1 + \theta_2) + i \sin(\theta_1 + \theta_2))$.

Proof. We multiply and get that

$$z_1 z_2 = r_1(\cos \theta_1 + i \sin \theta_1) r_2(\cos \theta_2 + i \sin \theta_2)$$
$$= r_1 r_2(\cos \theta_1 \cos \theta_2 - \sin \theta_1 \sin \theta_2 + i(\sin \theta_1 \cos \theta_2 + \cos \theta_1 \sin \theta_2))$$

Hence the result follows from the addition formulas for the trigonometric functions, which can be written

$$\cos(\theta_1 + \theta_2) = \cos \theta_1 \cos \theta_2 - \sin \theta_1 \sin \theta_2$$
$$\sin(\theta_1 + \theta_2) = \sin \theta_1 \cos \theta_2 + \cos \theta_1 \sin \theta_2$$

We shall prove these formulas in Proposition A.8 in the next section. □

Proposition A.6 (de Moivre's formula). Let $z = r(\cos \theta + i \sin \theta)$ be a complex number. Then we have that

$$z^n = r^n(\cos(n\theta) + i \sin(n\theta))$$

for any positive integer $n \geq 1$.

Proof. The case $n = 2$ follows directly from the lemma above. For $n > 2$, we can use the lemma repeatedly to show de Moivre's formula. □

As an example, let us find all the complex roots of $x^5 = 1$ using de Moivre's formula. Any complex root can be written $z = r(\cos\theta + i\sin\theta)$, and this implies that $z^5 = r^5(\cos(5\theta) + i\sin(5\theta))$. Since $z^5 = 1$ and the right hand side has polar coordinates $(r, \theta) = (1, 0° + k \cdot 360°)$, we find that $r^5 = 1$ and $5\theta = 0° + k \cdot 360°$. This gives $r = \sqrt[5]{1} = 1$ and $\theta = k \cdot 360°/5 = k \cdot 72°$. For $k = 0, 1, 2, 3, 4$, we find the solutions $x_k = \cos(k \cdot 72°) + i\sin(k \cdot 72°)$. These are exactly the solutions we found in the previous section. For example, we can compare $x_0 = 1$ and $x_1 = \cos(72°) + i\sin(72°)$ with $x_0 = 1$ and x_1 in Figure A.2. When $k \geq 5$, the roots start to repeat themselves, since $5 \times 72° = 360°$ is a whole turn. For example, $x_5 = x_0 = 1$ and $x_6 = x_1$. The same happens when $k < 0$.

Another interesting fact is that if we write $\omega = x_1 = \cos(72°) + i\sin(72°)$, then $\omega^k = x_k$ according to de Moivre's formula. This means that

$$x_1 = \omega, \; x_2 = \omega^2, \; x_3 = \omega^3, \; x_4 = \omega^4$$

We call ω a *primitive fifth root* of unity as it generates all the other roots. By the computations in the previous section, we have

$$\omega = \frac{\sqrt{5}-1}{2} + i\frac{\sqrt{10+2\sqrt{5}}}{2}$$

This means that $\cos(72°) = (\sqrt{5}-1)/2$ and $\sin(72°) = \sqrt{10+2\sqrt{5}}/2$.

A.4 Angles in radians

In the previous section, we measured angles in degrees. To study the trigonometric functions $\sin(\theta)$ and $\cos(\theta)$ in more detail, it is an advantage to measure the angle θ in the unit *radians* instead of degrees. Let us consider a nonzero complex number $z = x + iy$ with modulus $|z| = \sqrt{x^2 + y^2} = r$, corresponding to a point (x, y) on the circle $x^2 + y^2 = r^2$ of radius r in the complex plane. We shall explain how to express its polar coordinates on the form (r, θ) where θ is measured in radians.

The *arc of the circle* shown in blue in Figure A.4 is the part of the circle starting at the point $(r, 0)$ on the x-axis and ending at the point (x, y). We consider its length s, which is called an *arc length*. It is not difficult to compute s if we know the angle θ of $z = x + iy$. In fact, the circumference of the whole circle is given by the formula $2\pi r$, and this corresponds to an angle of $360°$. Therefore, s is given by $2\pi r \cdot \theta/360°$ when θ is measured in degrees. For instance, if $\theta = 60°$, then the arc length s is

$$s = 2\pi r \cdot \frac{60°}{360°} = \frac{1}{6} \cdot 2\pi r = \frac{1}{3}\pi r \approx 1.047r$$

In the last approximation, we used that $\pi \approx 3.14159$.

A • Complex numbers and trigonometric functions

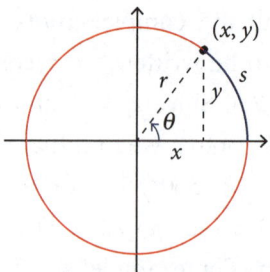

Figure A.4 The angle $\theta = s/r$ of the complex number $z = x + iy$ in radians

We define the angle θ of $z = x + iy$ measured in radians to be $\theta = s/r$. In the example above, we see that an angle of 60° is expressed as $\pi/3 \approx 1.047$ in radians. Some other examples are $90° = \pi/2$, $45° = \pi/4$, $30° = \pi/6$, and $72° = 2\pi/5$. In the rest of this appendix, angles will be expressed in radians.

A.5 Trigonometric functions

Let θ be an angle, measured in radians, and consider the complex number $z = x + iy$ in the complex plane with polar coordinates $(1, \theta)$. It corresponds to the point (x, y) on the unit circle $x^2 + y^2 = 1$ shown in Figure A.5. Notice that the arc length $s = \theta$, since $r = 1$ and θ is measured in radians.

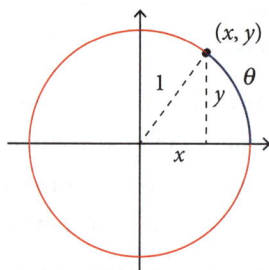

Figure A.5 The complex number $z = x + iy$ on the unit circle with angle θ

We have that $\cos \theta = x/1 = x$ and $\sin \theta = y/1 = y$, hence the point (x, y) can be written $(x, y) = (\cos \theta, \sin \theta)$. From this observation, we can write down a number of formulas for the trigonometric functions: For any (x, y) on the unit circle, we have that $-1 \leq x, y \leq 1$ and that $x^2 + y^2 = 1$. This means that

$$-1 \leq \cos \theta, \sin \theta \leq 1 \quad \text{and} \quad \sin^2 \theta + \cos^2 \theta = 1$$

for all θ. It is usual to write $\sin^2 \theta$ for $(\sin \theta)^2$ and $\cos^2 \theta$ for $(\cos \theta)^2$ as we have done in the formula above. From symmetries in Figure A.5 we get the following result:

Lemma A.7. Let θ be an angle measured in radians. Then we have:

a) $\cos(\theta + 2\pi) = \cos \theta$
b) $\cos(-\theta) = \cos \theta$
c) $\cos(\pi - \theta) = -\cos \theta$
d) $\sin(\theta + 2\pi) = \sin \theta$
e) $\sin(-\theta) = -\sin \theta$
f) $\sin(\pi - \theta) = \sin \theta$
g) $\cos(\pi/2 - \theta) = \sin \theta$
h) $\sin(\pi/2 - \theta) = \cos \theta$
i) $\cos 0 = 1$, $\sin 0 = 0$

Proof. The operation $\theta \mapsto \theta + 2\pi$ will not change the point (x, y), since $2\pi = 360°$ is a full rotation. The operations $\theta \mapsto -\theta$ and $\theta \mapsto \pi - \theta$ correspond to the reflections $(x, y) \mapsto (x, -y)$ and $(x, y) \mapsto (-x, y)$ through the x- and y-axis, and the operation $\theta \mapsto \pi/2 - \theta$ corresponds to the reflection $(x, y) \mapsto (y, x)$ through the line $y = x$. $\square$

Next, we consider the *addition formulas* for the trigonometric functions. They are a bit more complicated than the formulas above, and are given by

$$\cos(\phi + \theta) = \cos \phi \cos \theta - \sin \phi \sin \theta,$$
$$\sin(\phi + \theta) = \sin \phi \cos \theta + \cos \phi \sin \theta$$

We shall explain how to understand these formulas in geometric terms, and we will use this to prove them.

Let R be the transformation that rotates the entire complex plane by an angle θ counterclockwise around the origin. That is, $R(x, y)$ is the point (x', y') we obtain when we rotate the point (x, y) by an angle θ. We write $(x', y') = R(x, y)$, and show the rotation in the figure below.

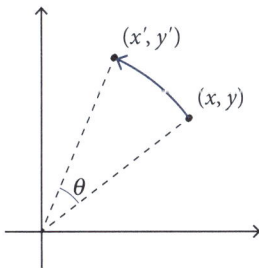

Figure A.6 Rotation of the complex plane by the angle θ

First, note that $R(1, 0) = (\cos \theta, \sin \theta)$, since the point $(1, 0)$ is rotated to the point with polar coordinates $(1, \theta)$. Since the point $(0, 1)$ has polar coordinates $(1, \pi/2)$, it is rotated to the point with polar coordinates $(1, \pi/2 + \theta)$.

A • Complex numbers and trigonometric functions

Moreover, it follows from Lemma A.7 that
$$\cos(\pi/2 + \theta) = -\cos(\pi - (\pi/2 + \theta)) = -\cos(\pi/2 - \theta) = -\sin\theta$$
$$\sin(\pi/2 + \theta) = \sin(\pi - (\pi/2 + \theta)) = \sin(\pi/2 - \theta) = \cos\theta$$

Therefore, we have that $R(0, 1) = (-\sin\theta, \cos\theta)$. For any point (x, y), we can think of (x, y) as a vector, and define the transformation T by the matrix multiplication
$$T(x, y) = \begin{pmatrix} \cos\theta & -\sin\theta \\ \sin\theta & \cos\theta \end{pmatrix} \cdot \begin{pmatrix} x \\ y \end{pmatrix}$$

Then $T(1, 0) = (\cos\theta, \sin\theta) = R(1, 0)$ and $T(0, 1) = (-\sin\theta, \cos\theta) = R(0, 1)$. This means that $R = T$, since
$$R(x, y) = R\left(x \cdot \begin{pmatrix} 1 \\ 0 \end{pmatrix} + y \cdot \begin{pmatrix} 0 \\ 1 \end{pmatrix}\right)$$
$$= x \cdot R(1, 0) + y \cdot R(0, 1) = x \cdot T(1, 0) + y \cdot T(0, 1)$$
$$= T\left(x \cdot \begin{pmatrix} 1 \\ 0 \end{pmatrix} + y \cdot \begin{pmatrix} 0 \\ 1 \end{pmatrix}\right) = T(x, y)$$

We have used that $R(\mathbf{u} + \mathbf{v}) = R(\mathbf{u}) + R(\mathbf{v})$ and $R(c\mathbf{v}) = cR(\mathbf{v})$, since sums and scalar multiples are preserved under rotation, and that $T(\mathbf{u} + \mathbf{v}) = T(\mathbf{u}) + T(\mathbf{v})$ and $T(c\mathbf{v}) = cT(\mathbf{v})$, since T is multiplication by a matrix. If we put all this together, we find that the rotation R of the complex plane by an angle θ is given by the formula
$$R(x, y) = \begin{pmatrix} \cos\theta & -\sin\theta \\ \sin\theta & \cos\theta \end{pmatrix} \cdot \begin{pmatrix} x \\ y \end{pmatrix}$$

The 2×2 matrix in this formula is called a *rotation matrix*.

Proposition A.8. Let ϕ and θ be angles measured in radians. Then we have:

a) $\cos(\phi + \theta) = \cos\phi\cos\theta - \sin\phi\sin\theta$

b) $\sin(\phi + \theta) = \sin\phi\cos\theta + \cos\phi\sin\theta$

In particular, we have that $\cos(2\theta) = \cos^2\theta - \sin^2\theta$ and $\sin(2\theta) = 2\sin\theta\cos\theta$.

Proof. Let us write $R(\theta)$ for the rotation by an angle θ, which is given by multiplication by the rotation matrix

$$\begin{pmatrix} \cos\theta & -\sin\theta \\ \sin\theta & \cos\theta \end{pmatrix}$$

discussed above. If ϕ is another angle, we must have $R(\phi)R(\theta) = R(\phi+\theta)$, since to rotate the complex plane first by the angle θ, and then by the angle ϕ means to rotate it by the angle $\phi + \theta$. On the other hand, matrix multiplication gives

$$\begin{pmatrix} \cos(\phi+\theta) & -\sin(\phi+\theta) \\ \sin(\phi+\theta) & \cos(\phi+\theta) \end{pmatrix} = \begin{pmatrix} \cos\phi & -\sin\phi \\ \sin\phi & \cos\phi \end{pmatrix} \cdot \begin{pmatrix} \cos\theta & -\sin\theta \\ \sin\theta & \cos\theta \end{pmatrix}$$

$$= \begin{pmatrix} \cos\phi\cos\theta - \sin\phi\sin\theta & -\sin\phi\cos\theta - \cos\phi\sin\theta \\ \sin\phi\cos\theta + \cos\phi\sin\theta & \cos\phi\cos\theta - \sin\phi\sin\theta \end{pmatrix}$$

This proves the addition formulas for the trigonometric functions. □

It is possible to define the power e^z when $z = x + iy$ is a complex number, and to show that these powers satisfy the usual algebraic power laws, such as

$$e^{z_1} \cdot e^{z_2} = e^{z_1+z_2}, \quad e^{z_1}/e^{z_2} = e^{z_1-z_2}, \quad \text{and} \quad (e^{z_1})^{z_2} = e^{z_1 \cdot z_2}$$

We shall skip the details, but this may be done using the Taylor series of the function $f(x) = e^x$, which is given by

$$e^x = 1 + x + \frac{1}{2}x^2 + \frac{1}{6}x^3 + \ldots + \frac{1}{n!}x^n + \ldots$$

This infinite power series also makes sense when we replace a real number x with a complex number $z = x + iy$. Fortunately, there is a simple formula that allows us to compute with complex exponents without using power series:

Proposition A.9 (Euler's formula). Let θ be an angle measured in radians. Then we have:

$$e^{i\theta} = \cos\theta + i\sin\theta$$

In particular, a complex number $z = x + iy$ with polar coordinates (r, θ) can be written in the form $z = re^{i\theta}$.

Let us show one example of how Euler's formula can be used: Let $z = x + iy$ be a complex number with polar coordinates (r, θ). Then $z = r\cos\theta + ir\sin\theta = re^{i\theta}$, and this gives

$$z^n = \left(re^{i\theta}\right)^n = r^n e^{in\theta} = r^n(\cos(n\theta) + i\sin(n\theta))$$

for all positive integers $n \geq 1$. This is exactly de Moivre's formula that we stated in Proposition A.6 earlier in this chapter.

A • Complex numbers and trigonometric functions

Problems

Problem A.1 Compute and write the answer in the form $z = a + bi$:

a) $2i - (1 + i)$
b) $(6 - i)(5 + 2i)$
c) $(\sqrt{3} - 2i)(2 + i\sqrt{3})$
d) $1/i$
e) $2/(1 - i)$
f) $(10 - 5i)/(3 - 4i)$
g) $(1 + i)^2$
h) $(1 + i)(1 - i)^{-1}$
i) $(1 + i)^3$

Problem A.2 Find all complex solutions of these equations:

a) $x^2 - 4x + 7 = 0$
b) $x^2 - 10x + 26 = 0$
c) $x^3 - 11x + 20 = 0$

Problem A.3 Find all complex solutions of the equation $x^6 = 1$.

Problem A.4 Find polar coordinates of the following complex numbers:

a) $2 - 2i$
b) $-2 - 2i$
c) $4i$
d) $\sqrt{3} - i$

Problem A.5 Find all complex solutions of these equations:

a) $x^3 = 2 - 2i$
b) $x^2 = i$
c) $x^3 = \dfrac{\sqrt{3} + i}{2}$

Problem A.6 Find all values of a such that the linear system has infinitely many solutions, and solve the system for these values of a:

$$6x - 4y = ax$$
$$5x - 2y = ay$$

CHAPTER B

Indefinite integrals

B.1 The indefinite integral

An *antiderivative* of a function $f(t)$ is a function $F(t)$ such that $F'(t) = f(t)$. For example, the function $f(t) = 2t$ has the antiderivative $F(t) = t^2$ since $(t^2)' = 2t$. Since the derivative of any constant is zero, it follows that $t^2 + C$ is also an antiderivative of $f(t) = 2t$ for any constant C.

> **Antiderivatives**
>
> If f is a continuous function defined on an interval I, then there exists an antiderivative $F(t)$ of $f(t)$. Moreover, all antiderivatives of $f(t)$ have the form $F(t) + C$ for a constant C.

We call $F(t) + C$ the general antiderivative of $f(t)$ in this situation. The general antiderivative is in fact an infinite family of functions, one for each value of C. We use the notation

$$\int f(t)\, dt = F(t) + C$$

for the general antiderivative, and call this an *indefinite integral*. The symbol $\int$ is called the integration symbol, and the symbol dt is a formalism that means that t is the integration variable. For example, we have that

$$\int 2t\, dt = t^2 + C$$

Note that the *integration constant* C appears in all indefinite integrals. It is an undetermined coefficient, and this is why the integral is called indefinite.

B.2 Computing indefinite integrals

We can compute many indefinite integrals using *integration rules*. We start with the simplest rules, given below. Since $\int f(t)\,dt = F(t) + C$ if and only if $F'(t) = f(t)$, it is easy to check that these integration rules hold by computing $F'(t)$ in each case.

> **Power rule**
> We have that
> $$\int t^n\,dt = \frac{1}{n+1}t^{n+1} + C \qquad \text{for } n \neq -1$$

The power rule can be used to integrate t^n when $n = 1, 2, \ldots$ is a positive integer. For example, in the case $n = 2$, we have that

$$\int t^2\,dt = \frac{1}{3}t^3 + C$$

But it can also be used to integrate t^n when n is zero, a negative integer with $n \neq -1$, or a rational number. For example, we have that

$$\int \frac{1}{t^2}\,dt = \int t^{-2}\,dt = \frac{1}{-1}t^{-1} + C = -\frac{1}{t} + C$$
$$\int \sqrt{t}\,dt = \int t^{1/2}\,dt = \frac{1}{3/2}t^{3/2} + C = \frac{2}{3}t\sqrt{t} + C$$

for $n = -2$ and $n = 1/2$. In general, it is often useful to rewrite a function as a power to integrate it. When $n = -1$, we have the following integration rule for $t^{-1} = 1/t$:

> We have that
> $$\int \frac{1}{t}\,dt = \ln|t| + C$$

Note that the function $1/t$ is defined for $t \neq 0$. An antiderivative should therefore also be defined for $t \neq 0$. For $t > 0$, we have that $\ln t$ is an antiderivative of $1/t$, since $(\ln t)' = 1/t$. For $t < 0$, the function $\ln(-t)$ is defined since $-t > 0$, and since

$$(\ln(-t))' = \frac{1}{(-t)} \cdot (-1) = \frac{1}{t}$$

the function $\ln(-t)$ is an antiderivative of $1/t$ for $t < 0$. For $t \neq 0$, it follows that $\ln|t|$ is an antiderivative of $1/t$, since

$$\ln|t| = \begin{cases} \ln(t), & t > 0 \\ \ln(-t), & t < 0 \end{cases}$$

B.2 Computing indefinite integrals

Integrals of linear combinations

For all expressions $u(t)$, $v(t)$ and all constants c, we have that

$$\int [u(t) + v(t)]\,dt = \int u(t)\,dt + \int v(t)\,dt$$

$$\int [u(t) - v(t)]\,dt = \int u(t)\,dt - \int v(t)\,dt$$

$$\int c \cdot u(t)\,dt = c \cdot \int u(t)\,dt$$

This means that we may integrate term by term, just as we differentiate term by term. For example, we have that

$$\int t^2 - 3t + 2\,dt = \int t^2\,dt - 3\int t\,dt + 2\int 1\,dt$$

$$= \frac{1}{3}t^3 - 3 \cdot \frac{1}{2}t^2 + 2 \cdot t + C$$

$$= 13t^3 - \frac{3}{2}t^2 + 2t + C$$

We have computed the integrals of t^2, t and $1 = t^0$ using the power rule.

Integrals of exponential functions

We have that

$$\int e^t\,dt = e^t + C$$

$$\int a^t\,dt = a^t \cdot \frac{1}{\ln(a)} + C \quad \text{for} \quad a > 0$$

Even though many indefinite integrals can be computed using the integration rules above, we must sometimes use more advanced integration techniques. In the next sections, we go through some of the most useful techniques.

B.3 Integration by parts

To differentiate a product, we use the product rule $(uv)' = u'v + uv'$. The product rule means that uv, which is an antiderivative of $(uv)'$ by definition, is an antiderivative of the right-hand side $u'v + uv'$, or that

$$\int u'v\,dt + \int uv'\,dt = uv + C$$

When we solve this equation for the first integral on the left-hand side, we obtain the following formula:

Integration by parts
For any expressions $u = u(t)$, $v = v(t)$, we have that

$$\int u'v\,dt = uv - \int uv'\,dt$$

We shall show how to use this formula to solve an indefinite integral of a product. Let us consider the following integral as an example:

$$\int t \cdot e^t\,dt$$

We let u' and v be the factors of the product in the integral. In this example, we can, for instance, let $u' = t$ and $v = e^t$. This would give $u = t^2/2$ and $v' = e^t$, since we integrate the first factor and differentiate the second factor to find u and v'. Therefore, we have

$$\int t \cdot e^t\,dt = uv - \int uv'\,dt = \frac{1}{2}t^2 e^t - \int \frac{1}{2}t^2 e^t\,dt$$

Note that we may choose $u = t^2/2 + C$ to be any antiderivative of t, and we choose the simplest one, corresponding to $C = 0$.

The method is called *integration by parts*, since we replace one integral with another. The idea is that the new integral, on the right-hand side, should be simpler to compute than the original integral. This is not the case in the example above. However, it is possible to switch the order of the factors in the integral and choose $u' = e^t$ and $v = t$, since

$$\int t \cdot e^t\,dt = \int e^t \cdot t\,dt$$

This would give $u = e^t$ and $v' = 1$, and therefore

$$\int te^t\,dt = te^t - \int 1 \cdot e^t\,dt = te^t - \int e^t\,dt = te^t - e^t + C$$

The method works well in this case, since the new integral is easier to solve.

Another example is the integral $\int \ln(t)\,dt$, which is important in itself. We may use integration by parts to solve it, since we can rewrite the integral as

$$\int \ln(t)\,dt = \int 1 \cdot \ln(t)\,dt$$

We let $u' = 1$ and $v = \ln(t)$, which gives $u = t$ and $v' = 1/t$, and therefore

$$\int \ln(t)\,dt = \int 1 \cdot \ln(t)\,dt = t\ln(t) - \int t \cdot \frac{1}{t}\,dt$$
$$= t\ln(t) - \int 1\,dt = t\ln(t) - t + C$$

The method works well since integrating 1 and differentiating $\ln(t)$ gives a simple integral that we can compute.

B.4 Integration by substitution

To integrate a composite function such as $f(t) = e^{2t-3}$, it is tempting to make a change of variables $u = 2t - 3$ to simplify e^{2t-3} to e^u. When we make this change of variables, we consider the function f as the composite function

$$f(t) = e^{2t-3} = e^u \quad \text{with } u = 2t - 3$$

with *kernel* or inner function $u = u(t) = 2t - 3$, and outer function e^u. Recall that to differentiate a composite function, we use the chain rule

$$\frac{df}{dt} = \frac{df}{du} \cdot \frac{du}{dt} \quad \text{or} \quad f'(t) = f'(u) \cdot u'(t)$$

In the example, this would give us $(e^{2t-3})' = e^u \cdot u' = e^{2t-3} \cdot 2 = 2e^{2t-3}$, since the derivative of e^u with respect to u is e^u. Note that by the chain rule, we multiply by the derivative $u' = u'(t)$ of the kernel when we differentiate a composite function.

When we use a substitution $u = u(t)$ in an integral, we should also take the derivative $u' = u'(t)$ of the kernel into account, and this is taken care of by the formalism

$$\boxed{du = u' \cdot dt} \quad \text{with } u' = u'(t)$$

For example, to compute $\int e^{2t-3}\,dt$, we let $u = 2t - 3$ and use $du = 2\,dt$ since $u' = 2$, which gives $dt = du/2$. The integral can then be computed by substitution:

$$\int e^{2t-3}\,dt = \int e^u \cdot \frac{du}{2} = \frac{1}{2}\int e^u\,du = \frac{1}{2}e^u + C = \frac{1}{2}e^{2t-3} + C$$

Notice that we use the equations $u = 2t - 3$ and $du = 2\,dt$ to write the integral as an integral in the new variable u, and this means that we *divide* by $u' = u'(t)$ in the integral.

> **Integration by substitution**
> When we use the substitution $u = u(t)$ to solve the integral $\int f(t)\,dt$, we use the equations $u = u(t)$ and $du = u' \cdot dt$ with $u' = u'(t)$ to rewrite the integral
> $$\int f(t)\,dt = \int g(u)\,du$$
> When using this method, we try to find a substitution $u = u(t)$ such that the integral $\int g(u)\,du$ in the new variable u is simpler to solve.

Let us try to use substitution to solve the integral $\int t \ln(t^2 + 1)\,dt$. In this case, we choose $u = t^2 + 1$, since this is the inner function in the last factor. The formalism $du = u'\,dt$ then gives $du = 2t\,dt$. We therefore obtain

$$\int t \ln(t^2 + 1)\,dt = \int t \ln(u) \frac{du}{2t} = \frac{1}{2}\int \ln(u)\,du = \frac{1}{2}(u \ln(u) - u) + C$$

We first replace $t^2 + 1$ with u in the logarithm, and then replace dt with du/u' using $du = u'\,dt$ and $u' = 2t$. It can be difficult to know from the start if the substitution will give an integral that is easier to solve, but it is the case here since all factors with t cancel. We use that $\int \ln(t)\,dt = t \ln(t) - t + C$ from the previous section to solve the integral $\int \ln(u)\,du$. It is usual to write the answer in terms of t, the original variable. Using $u = t^2 + 1$, we obtain

$$\int t \ln(t^2 + 1)\,dt = \frac{1}{2}(u \ln(u) - u) + C$$
$$= \frac{1}{2}(t^2 + 1)\ln(t^2 + 1) - \frac{1}{2}(t^2 + 1) + C$$

B.5 Integration of rational functions

A rational function is a function of the form $f(t) = p(t)/q(t)$, where $p(t), q(t)$ are polynomials in t. Examples of rational functions are

$$f(t) = \frac{t+1}{t^2 - 3t + 2}, \qquad g(t) = \frac{t+1}{t-7}$$

There are several techniques for integrating rational functions. We shall explain how to use polynomial division and partial fraction decompositions to simplify rational expressions and make them easier to integrate.

Polynomial division. A rational function can often be simplified by polynomial division (if the degree of the numerator $p(t)$ is equal to or greater than the degree of the denominator $q(t)$ in the rational expression). In the example $g(t)$ above, we can write

$$g(t) = \frac{t+1}{t-7} = \frac{t-7+8}{t-7} = \frac{t-7}{t-7} + \frac{8}{t-7} = 1 + \frac{8}{t-7}$$

We say that this polynomial division has quotient 1 and remainder 8. We can use this to integrate $g(t)$, since we have

$$\int \frac{t+1}{t-7}\,dt = \int \left(1 + \frac{8}{t-7}\right)dt = t + 8\ln|t-7| + C$$

To integrate $8/(t-7)$, we have used the substitution $u = t-7$ with $du = dt$.

More complicated polynomial divisions are often written in another form, similar to the way we write long division of integers. As an example, let us consider the rational expression

$$\frac{t^2 - 5}{t+3}$$

We can simplify this expression using polynomial division, which we write in the following way:

$$\begin{aligned}
(\ t^2 \quad\quad -5) : (t+3) &= t - 3 + \frac{4}{t+3} \\
\underline{-t^2 - 3t} & \\
-3t - 5 & \\
\underline{3t + 9} & \\
4 &
\end{aligned}$$

In general, to perform a polynomial division $p(t) : q(t)$, we divide the monomial in $p(t)$ of highest degree by the monomial in $q(t)$ of highest degree, which gives $t^2 : t = t$ in this case. This is the first term of the quotient. Next, we multiply this term with $q(t)$, and subtract the product from $p(t)$. In this case, this gives the result $(t^2 - 5) - t(t+3) = -3t - 5$. This is the remainder so far in the process. Finally, we repeat the process, with $p(t)$ replaced by the remainder so far, until we have obtained a remainder of smaller degree than $q(t)$. In this case, the next step is to divide $-3t$ by t, which gives -3, and then multiply this term back and subtract it from $-3t - 5$. This gives $-3t - 5 - (-3)(t+3) = 4$. Since this remainder has smaller degree than $q(t) = t + 3$, the remainder is 4, and the quotient is $t - 3$. Finally, we can compute the integral using the result of the polynomial division:

$$\int \frac{t^2 - 5}{t+3}\,dt = \int \left(t - 3 + \frac{4}{t+3}\right)dt = \frac{1}{2}t^2 - 3t + 4\ln|t+3| + C$$

Again, we use a substitution to solve the last integral. Integrals of this kind often occur, and we have the following result:

> **The case of linear denominator**
> For constants A, a, b with $a \neq 0$, we have that
> $$\int \frac{A}{at+b} \, dt = \frac{A}{a} \cdot \ln|at+b| + C$$

Integration by partial fraction decomposition. We must use additional methods to compute the integral of a rational expression when its denominator has degree higher than one. Sometimes it is possible to use substitution. For example, we find

$$\int \frac{2t+3}{t^2+3t+2} \, dt = \int \frac{2t+3}{u} \cdot \frac{du}{2t+3} = \int \frac{1}{u} \, du = \ln|u| + C$$
$$= \ln|t^2+3t+2| + C$$

using the substitution $u = t^2 + 3t + 2$ and $du = (2t+3)\,dt$. This substitution works well because $2t+3$ in the numerator cancels against $u' = 2t+3$ in the denominator. It would not work equally well in other cases, such as the example

$$\int \frac{3}{t^2+3t+2} \, dt$$

In cases like this, we simplify the integral using a *partial fraction decomposition* of the rational function: We factorize the denominator as $t^2 + 3t + 2 = (t+1)(t+2)$, and use this to find a decomposition

$$\frac{3}{t^2+3t+2} = \frac{A}{t+1} + \frac{B}{t+2}$$

for constants A and B. To find A and B in this decomposition, we multiply by the common denominator $(t+1)(t+2)$, and get

$$3 = A(t+2) + B(t+1)$$

The right-hand side equals $(A+B)t + (2A+B)$. Since the equation should hold for all values of t, we need the linear expression on the right-hand side to have the same coefficients as the one on the left. Hence $A + B = 0$ and $2A + B = 3$. This gives $B = -A$ from the first equation, and substitution into the second equation gives $A = 3$, and therefore $B = -3$. It follows that the partial fraction's decomposition is

$$\frac{3}{t^2+3t+2} = \frac{3}{t+1} - \frac{3}{t+2}$$

We know how to integrate each partial fraction, and we can therefore compute the integral as

$$\int \frac{3}{t^2 + 3t + 2} \, dt = \int \left(\frac{3}{t+1} - \frac{3}{t+2} \right) dt$$
$$= 3 \ln |t+1| - 3 \ln |t+2| + C$$

It is usual to rewrite this answer using the fact that $\ln(a) - \ln(b) = \ln(a/b)$:

$$\int \frac{3}{t^2 + 3t + 2} \, dt = 3 \ln |t+1| - 3 \ln |t+2| + C = 3 \ln \left| \frac{t+1}{t+2} \right| + C$$

If the denominator $q(t)$ has degree higher than two, the integral can be solved in a similar way using partial fractions if we are able to factorize $q(t)$. Sometimes this is difficult, such as in the case $q(t) = t^3 - 2t + 1$, and sometimes it is not possible using real numbers, such as in the case $q(t) = t^2 + 1$.

The case of irreducible quadratic factors in the denominator. A quadratic polynomial $at^2 + bt + c$ is called *irreducible* if it has no roots among the real numbers. In this case, the polynomial cannot be factorized in linear factors with real coefficients.

If the denominator of a rational function has irreducible quadratic factors, then we need other methods than partial fraction decompositions to compute its integral. For example, the integral

$$\int \frac{1}{t^2 + 1} \, dt = \arctan(t) + C$$

is given in terms of the inverse trigonometric function $\arctan(t)$. In general, when the denominator is an irreducible quadratic polynomial, we have the following formula:

The case of irreducible quadratic denominators
For constants A, a, b, c with $a \neq 0$ and $b^2 - 4ac < 0$, we have that

$$\int \frac{A}{at^2 + bt + c} \, dt =$$
$$\frac{2A}{\sqrt{4ac - b^2}} \cdot \arctan \left(\frac{2a}{\sqrt{4ac - b^2}} t + \frac{b}{\sqrt{4ac - b^2}} \right) + C$$

B • Indefinite integrals

For example, we have that $t^2 + 4t + 7 = (t+2)^2 + 3$ is an irreducible quadratic polynomial, since $t^2 + 4t + 7 = 0$ gives $(t+2)^2 = -3$, and this equation has no (real) solutions. Using the formula above, we find that

$$\int \frac{1}{t^2 + 4t + 7}\, dt = \frac{2}{\sqrt{12}} \arctan\left(\frac{2t+4}{\sqrt{12}}\right) + C$$

since $4ac - b^2 = 12$ in this case.

Problems

Problem B.1 Compute the indefinite integrals:

a) $\int (3t^2 - 12t)\, dt$
b) $\int (2e^t - t)\, dt$
c) $\int t\sqrt{t}\, dt$

d) $\int \frac{1}{t^3}\, dt$
e) $\int (t-1)^2\, dt$

Problem B.2 Compute the indefinite integral $\int \frac{t^3 - t^2 + 1}{t}\, dt$.

Problem B.3 Compute the indefinite integrals:

a) $\int t \ln(t)\, dt$
b) $\int t e^t\, dt$
c) $\int t^2 e^t\, dt$

d) $\int \frac{\ln(t)}{t^2}\, dt$
e) $\int \sqrt{t} \ln(t)\, dt$

Problem B.4 Use substitution to compute the indefinite integral
$$\int \frac{\ln(t)}{t}\, dt$$

Problem B.5 Compute the integral $\int e^{1-t}\, dt$.

Problem B.6 Compute the integral when a, b are constants with $a \neq 0$:
$$\int \frac{1}{at+b}\, dt$$

Problem B.7 Compute the indefinite integrals:

a) $\int 3t\sqrt{t^2+1}\, dt$
b) $\int \frac{t}{t^2-1}\, dt$

c) $\int 5t(t^2-1)^3\, dt$
d) $\int \frac{2t+3}{t^2+3t+2}\, dt$

Problem B.8 Compute the indefinite integrals:

a) $\int t e^{t^2}\, dt$
b) $\int t^3 e^{t^2}\, dt$
c) $\int e^{\sqrt{t}}\, dt$

d) $\int \sqrt{t}\, e^{\sqrt{t}}\, dt$
e) $\int \frac{2e^t}{e^t + e^{-t}}\, dt$

B • Indefinite integrals

Problem B.9 Use polynomial division to compute the integral:
$$\int \frac{t^2 - 3t + 7}{t - 4} \, dt$$

Problem B.10 Compute the indefinite integrals:

a) $\displaystyle\int \frac{t^2 - 3}{t + 4} \, dt$
b) $\displaystyle\int \frac{t + 1}{t^2 + 2t + 4} \, dt$

c) $\displaystyle\int \frac{t}{t^2 - 4} \, dt$
d) $\displaystyle\int \frac{3}{t(3 - t)} \, dt$